The Middle East in
World Politics

The Middle East in World Politics

A Study in Contemporary International Relations

TAREQ Y. ISMAEL

With Contributions
from

NASEER H. ARURI
P. EDWARD HALEY
NATALIE K. HEVENER
HARRY N. HOWARD

SYRACUSE UNIVERSITY PRESS 1974

327.56
I 83m

Library of Congress Cataloging in Publication Data

Ismael, Tareq Y.
  The Middle East in world politics.

  Bibliography: p.
  1. Near East—Foreign relations. I. Title.
DS62.8.I84   327.56   73-16637
ISBN 0-8156-0101-8
ISBN 0-8156-0102-6 (pbk.)

Manufactured in the United States of America

Contributors

TAREQ Y. ISMAEL, Associate Professor of Political Science, The University of Calgary, Calgary, Alberta, Canada, is the author of *Governments and Politics of the Contemporary Middle East* (Homewood, Ill.: Dorsey Press, 1970) and *The U.A.R. in Africa: Egypt's Policy Under Nasser* (Evanston, Ill.: Northwestern University Press, 1971), and co-editor of *Canada and the Third World* (Toronto: Macmillan, 1974), and was guest editor of *The Middle East Forum,* 1971–73.

NASEER H. ARURI, Professor of Political Science, Southeastern Massachusetts University, North Dartmouth, Massachusetts, is the editor of *The Palestinian Resistance to Israeli Occupation* (Wilmette, Ill.: Medina University Press International, 1970), and author of *Jordan: A Study in Political Development* (The Hague: Nijhoff's Beokhandel en Uitgevers mij., 1972).

P. EDWARD HALEY, Associate Professor of Political Science and International Relations, Claremont Men's College, Claremont, California, is the author of *Revolution and Intervention* (Cambridge, Mass.: MIT Press, 1970).

NATALIE K. HEVENER is Assistant Professor, Department of Government and International Studies, University of South Carolina, Columbia, South Carolina.

HARRY N. HOWARD, a retired U.S. Foreign Service Officer, is Adjunct Professor in the School of International Service, The American University, Washington, D.C. He is the author of *The Partition of Turkey* (Norman, Okla.: University of Oklahoma Press, 1931, 1966), *The Problem of the Turkish Straits* (Washington, D.C.: U.S. Government Printing Office, 1947), *The United Nations and the Problem of Greece* (Washington, D.C.: U.S. Government Printing Office, 1947), *The King-Crane Commission* (Beirut: Khayats, 1963), and other works.

32886

Preface

The October 1973 Arab-Israeli War again focussed world attention on the Middle East. Moreover, the war drew in big-power involvement more decisively than any of the past three Arab-Israeli conflicts in the last quarter century, threatening the delicate American-Soviet détente and in the words of President Nixon representing "the most difficult crisis we have had since the Cuban confrontation of 1962." While the war clearly identified America as Israel's patron and the Soviet Union as the Arab ally—facts long familiar in the international relations of the area—it also demonstrated how little control either big power has over its Middle East protégés.

The war, in fact, highlighted the importance of the Middle East in international affairs: the area is a focal point of international relations; it is an area that emanates international issues, not an area where they are merely played out. As a bridge between Asia, Africa, and Europe, as the oil-producing center of the world, as a battlefield of opposing nationalisms, as a major area of big-power competition, the Middle East plays a major role in the international system.

Yet, there is no area that is more misunderstood, particularly by the North American public, than the Middle East. North Americans view the Middle East with more myth and emotion than they do any other area of the world. They have little understanding of the forceful events occurring in the area, even as these events threaten to draw them into war. But they do have strong feelings about what is going on in the area. Thus, rather than being apathetic toward the Middle East, North Americans view the area with irrationality—a much more dangerous attitude insofar as foreign policies are concerned.

This book has been prepared for all thoughtful students of international affairs and Middle East studies who seek an objective analysis of the role of the Middle East in world affairs. Whether they be potential scholars in the field, government officials concerned with the Middle East, businessmen with interests in the area, or merely concerned observers who seek to know beyond the headlines, this book will be of interest to them. Because no person is totally free of biases—whether moral, social, or intellectual—the author has attempted to minimize the biases of any one individual, and thereby guarantee greater objectivity,

vii

by having certain chapters contributed by scholars with particular expertise in the areas they treat. The reader will thus benefit from the greater knowledge, objectivity, and diversity of style that is rendered by more than one head.

The first chapter provides an overview of the history of Middle East international relations, identifying the important developments that affect the area's contemporary international affairs. The next seven chapters deal with contemporary Middle Eastern relations to various centers of power in the international system. The emphasis in these chapters has been placed upon analysis rather than survey. Chapter Nine examines domestic influences on Middle East foreign policies to identify persistent domestic forces bearing on foreign relations and patterned foreign policy trends that establish an internal coherence within the region. Chapter Ten examines the most recent and dramatic development in Middle East international relations: the introduction of oil as a foreign-policy tool. And Chapter Eleven is a more specialized chapter addressed specifically to the student of international affairs and/or Middle East studies to introduce him to systems concepts to define the Middle East and establish its analytical basis.

I wish to thank the contributors, whose participation in this project was invaluable. I also wish to acknowledge my appreciation to The University of Calgary for providing research funds for this work to help defray some of the clerical expenses.

Baghdad, Iraq
Fall 1973   Tareq Y. Ismael

Contents

The Middle East in
World Politics

❋ 1 ❋

HARRY N. HOWARD

Historical Backgrounds

THE GREAT POWERS AND THE MIDDLE EAST

It has been well and repeatedly observed that the Middle East has been a center of world politics and attention—of international relations—for many centuries, thanks to its location at the intercontinental crossroads of Eurasia and Africa, to the fact that it is a center of land, sea, and now air communications, an area out from which important civilizing influences have radiated over large parts of the globe, and to the fact that the area has resources important to the world, especially oil. It has been argued that the Middle East never quite possessed the significance which former generations assigned to it and that, in any event, it no longer possesses any geographical significance in an age of missiles and instantaneous communication. It is our contention, to the contrary, that the significance of the area cannot be ignored in today's troubled world, more especially with the two superpowers, the United States and the Soviet Union, showing an intense interest in its development and destiny within the context of current world politics. This seemed well demonstrated during the fall of 1973, when the Arab-Israel, or Palestine, conflict erupted into open warfare once more.

What's past is prologue, if not always causative in character, and it may be useful, however briefly, to look backward a few centuries for a cursory glance at developments, particularly at the nodal points in the history of international relations concerning the Middle East. One need not indulge in a long disquisition relative to the rise and fall of great kingdoms and empires or the legacies of the past in Greece and Rome, Byzantium, the Arabs, or the Crusades, or even the rise, expansion and decline of the Ottoman Empire, although the reader would do well to bear them in mind as background, as he would the essential facts concerning the great cultural contributions of Judaism, Christianity, and Islam. For our purposes it would appear sufficient to begin with the eighteenth century and to proceed from that period to the present, for

1

rather obvious reasons. The eighteenth century was the era of the En-
lightenment, of the French Revolution, and the beginnings of the Napoleonic Empire, which, with its doctrines of liberty, equality, and frater-
nity (nationalism), had a profound impact on the Middle East. It was an
era of the rediscovery of Europe on the part of the Middle East and, in
a way, of the rediscovery of the Middle East on the part of Europe. It
was in this period, too, that, fundamentally, the so-called Eastern Question, the problem of the succession of the declining Ottoman Empire,
really began, with the Treaties of Karlowitz (1699) and Kuchuk Kainarji (1774) clearly marking the problem—hence our concentration on
the period since that time.

During the eighteenth and nineteenth centuries, and extending down
to the outbreak of World War I in 1914, the major powers interested in
the Middle East were France, Great Britain, the Habsburg Empire
(Austria-Hungary after 1867), Imperial Russia, and Imperial Germany.
As we shall see, even the United States of America developed commercial and cultural, if not enduring politico-strategic, interests, an oft-
neglected development reserved for separate treatment. France, even before it became a national entity in the modern sense of the term, had
long established commercial and cultural interests in the Middle East
(Lebanon and Syria) dating from the Crusades and, under Francis I,
signed a famous treaty of amity and commerce (1535) with Sultan Suleiman the Magnificent as an offset to the Holy Roman Empire of
Charles V. This treaty enshrined capitulatory or extraterritorial rights
and became a model for the rights of other states with developing interests in the Ottoman Empire. (These rights were conceded to Great Britain in 1579, Austria in 1615, the Netherlands in 1680, Sweden in
1737, Sicily in 1740, Denmark in 1746, Prussia in 1761, Spain in
1782, Russia in 1783, Sardinia in 1823, and the United States in 1830,
Belgium in 1838, the Hanseatic Cities in 1839, Portugal in 1843,
Greece in 1855, Brazil in 1858, and Bavaria in 1870.) For a relatively
brief period at the end of the eighteenth century, France may be considered the dominant external influence in the Middle East, through
North Africa, into Egypt and Syria, and even at Constantinople. In certain areas, especially Egypt and Syria, its influence remained a very
strong force, with commercial and cultural associations, on which political pretentions were based, predominant. France came into possession
of Algeria in 1830 and established protectorates in Tunisia (1881) and
Morocco (1904), and French *colons* came to dominant positions not
only in the commercial and economic life but in the polities of North
Africa. After World War I, moreover, France assumed the mandates in
Syria and Lebanon. As noted above, the legacy of the French Revolu-

tion, especially in the form of nationalism, was particularly strong; in the end, centering in Cairo and Alexandria, Beirut and Damascus, and Constantinople, as well as in the Balkan Peninsula, it inaugurated a force which was to strike at the edifice of the Ottoman Empire, shatter it to its foundations, and not only free Greece and the Balkan Slav states, but liberate the Arabs and Turks as well, at the end of World War I.

With the defeat of Napoleon (1799) after his ill-fated invasion of Egypt, Great Britain occupied a dominant position in the Ottoman Empire, and it maintained that position—Britain's moment in the Middle East—substantially until after World War II. Essentially, it has been observed with a certain justice, Great Britain was not really interested in the Middle East as such, but in the maintenance of British routes to India, the crown jewel of the British Empire. British policy sought preservation of the integrity of the Ottoman Empire, primarily against Imperial Russia. As such, like other powers, it sought to hold Russia at the Turkish Straits and along the Northern Tier of the Middle East. With the advent of Imperial Germany on the Middle Eastern stage, especially in the 1890s, maintenance of the Ottoman Empire as a policy was seriously questioned, and British policy centered on the maintenance of the approaches to the Straits and, after the opening of the Suez Canal (1869), purchase of shares in the Suez Canal Company (1875) and domination over Egypt. Like France, Great Britain was ready to strike bargains when World War I broke out in 1914. After the end of the war, Great Britain clearly dominated the Middle Eastern scene, with mandates in Palestine and Iraq, a protectorate over Egypt, a crown colony in Cyprus, and an assured position in the area of the Persian Gulf and the Arabian Peninsula.

Austria-Hungary was primarily interested in the Balkan region of the Ottoman Empire in the maintenance of its position in that strategic region and in the prevention of Russian domination. But it was also interested in the wider reaches of the Ottoman Empire as well. Imperial Germany, the senior partner in the Dual Alliance (1879) and Triple Alliance (1882), which came into being only in 1871, became especially interested in the Ottoman Empire with the advent of William II (1888–1918) to the throne. William II was concerned with both economic and political penetration of the empire, which he visited in 1897 (Constantinople and Jerusalem). The basic interest was illustrated in the well-known Baghdad Railway Agreement of 1903. The German company had obtained a concession for the Konia-Basra section in January 1902 and had sought Anglo-French cooperation in the financial arrangements. But, while the British government appeared well-disposed, the bankers were scared off by a press campaign, and both France and Great Britain ultimately rejected association in the project. Imperial Russia, which was not a party at all, was irreconcilably opposed to the entire project for rather obvious reasons. As the outbreak of World War I approached, Germany appeared to be moving toward a policy of double insurance in the Ottoman Empire, and bargains centering around the network of the Baghdad Railway were struck with Great Britain and France on the eve of the conflict in 1914. If the integrity of the Ottoman Empire were maintained, Germany might well dominate it, despite all the complicated problems involved in such an enterprise. If it were partitioned, the Baghdad enterprise might offer rich politico-economic rewards in the Middle East. The sending of the military mission of General Liman von Sanders (1913–14) to Constantinople offered another prospect for possible control and appeared as a direct threat to vital Russian interests at Constantinople and the Turkish Straits.

During the long history of the Ottoman Empire, Russo-Ottoman relations were often marked by war and hostility, and the fact that some thirteen conflicts had been fought since the seventeenth century left an enduring impress on the relationship. Leaving aside the Slavophile dream of the conquest of Constantinople (Tsargrad), which provided a certain motivation to Imperial Russian secular policy, the Russian Empire appears to have pursued two basic aims relative to the Ottoman Empire: (1) the achievement of a dominant position in the Ottoman Empire through close alliance which would establish a secure and unassailable Russian position or, failing that, the partition of the Ottoman Empire and the acquisition of the necessary strategic positions for the protection of Russian national and imperial interests; and (2) the attainment of a secure commercial and naval passage to and from the Black Sea and the Mediterranean Sea through the Turkish Straits, while barring that route to the naval forces of nonriparian powers, primarily Great Britain and France, but also Germany in the later years. The Treaty of Kuchuk Kainarji, July 10/21, 1774, brought Russia permanently to the Black Sea, which was no longer an Ottoman lake, and secured commercial passage. The Treaty of Unkiar Skelessi, July 8, 1833, which has an important bearing on Soviet policy relative to Turkey to this day, is one of the landmarks in Russian policy in the nineteenth century even though it endured for only six years, until 1839. Imperial Russia drove through the Balkans during the Russo-Ottoman conflict of 1877–78, and in the "secret agreements" of 1915 it sought, unsuccessfully, fulfilment of its ambitions relative to Constantinople and the Turkish Straits.

There was a very significant development of Russian commerce through the Straits, especially in the grain trade, which was particularly important in the Russian balance in international trade, during the nineteenth century. During the decade 1830–40, there was a very rapid growth and development in the economy of southern Russia, and the port of Odessa became particularly important in Russian export trade, remaining so to this day. By 1880, for example, it was estimated that some 50 percent of the total Russian export commerce went out of the Black Sea and the Turkish Straits and no less than 80 percent of the grain trade. When the Ottoman government closed the Straits for some six weeks (April–May 1912) during the Italo-Ottoman War, Russian merchants suffered the loss of millions of rubles, a situation which led Russian statesmen to seek solution of the Straits problem through control of the region of the Straits. The Russian Political Conference, composed of unofficial representatives at the Paris Peace Conference in 1919, estimated that, by 1914, 40 percent of the total Russian exports, 54 percent of the maritime exports, 74 percent of the cereals, 88 percent of the petroleum, 93 percent of the manganese, and 61 percent of the iron were exported via the Black Sea through the Straits to the outside world. It may be added that, at the close of the nineteenth and the opening of the twentieth century, the Russian government also gave evidence of its interest in the Suez Canal and the right of naval passage during the Russo-Japanese War (1904–1905).

WORLD WAR I AND ITS AFTERMATH

World War I opened up a new era in the Middle East. For one thing, Imperial Germany and Austria-Hungary went down in defeat in and were eliminated from the Middle East, while Imperial Russia underwent one of the world's great revolutions. The Ottoman Empire, which entered the war on October 28–29, 1914, on the basis of the German-Ottoman alliance of August 2, 1914, ultimately was partitioned along the lines sketched out in the secret inter-Allied agreements of 1915–17. Great Britain and France pressed their claims at the Paris Peace Conference in 1919, Jews set forth their claims to Palestine, and the Armenians and Kurds to independent states and the Arabs to independence and unity. President Woodrow Wilson sought to base a peaceful settlement in the Middle East on the foundations of self-determination, with a new mandate system under the League of Nations, oriented toward full independence. He despatched to the Middle East, during May–August 1919, the King-Crane Commission, which opposed a maximum Jewish National Home in Palestine and a French mandate in Syria, and proposed a British mandate in Mesopotamia and an Armenian mandate under the United States. There were also suggestions for an American mandate over a Constantinopolitan state in the area of the Turkish Straits, as well as one over the Turkish area on the Anatolian plateau. The King-Crane report was largely ignored, however, and, in the end, a British mandate was provided for Palestine, in which Great Britain had the impossible task, as seen in perspective, of facilitating the establishment of a Jewish homeland without infringing the rights of the overwhelming Arab population (ca. nine-tenths) in the country. Great Britain also was to have the mandate in Iraq, while France was assigned that in Syria and Lebanon. While the Arab world was thus divided, albeit under the mandate system of the League of Nations, under the great leadership of Mustafa Kemal Ataturk, Turkey emerged into nationhood and independence, following the tragic Greco-Turkish War.

The Allies had sought to impose the Treaty of Sèvres (August 10, 1920) on Turkey, an instrument which would not only have torn away vast territories from Turkish control, including the region of Izmir (Smyrna), which was to go to Greece, but would have subjected the area of Constantinople and the Straits—occupied since the war by British, French, and Italian forces—to their control and would have dominated even the Turkish homeland in Anatolia. The result was that peace did not come until the defeat of the Greek invaders and the signing of the Treaty of Lausanne on July 24, 1923, after more than four years of war. At the Lausanne Conference, Great Britain, France, and Soviet Russia played leading roles, to say nothing of Fascist Italy, and even the United States sent very active observers. The new arrangements brought the war to an end, and laid the foundations for peace in the Middle East during the interwar period down to the outbreak of World War II in 1939. At the conference and in the Treaty of Lausanne, the new Turkish Nationalist government renounced all rights and title to the territories detached from the now defunct Ottoman Empire, but it achieved its own complete political and even economic independence, free from the hated capitulatory regime and other controls. Turkey acquiesced in the establishment of an international Commission of the Straits, under the League of Nations, with guarantees of freedom of transit and navigation, since its security did not appear to be threatened thereby. Despite its own reservations, the Soviet Union ultimately signed the new convention on August 14, 1923, at Rome, but it never ratified the convention. The United States was not a signatory, although it negotiated an American-Turkish Treaty on August 6, 1923, which reserved American rights as to transit and navigation in the Straits under the Lausanne Convention. But that treaty was never approved or ratified, partly as a result of Armenian propaganda to the effect that the United States delegation had "sold out" the Armenian people for a mess of Middle Eastern oil. It was not until October 28, 1931, that a new treaty of establishment and sojourn was signed, and not until February 15, 1933, that ratifications were exchanged.

While the Lausanne Convention enshrined the principle of freedom of transit and navigation for commercial vessels in the Turkish Straits, it did not provide sufficiently for the security of the waterway. With the rise of Hitler in Germany, and the threat of trouble, the Turkish government, especially after 1932, sought revision of the Lausanne Convention to secure sovereignty over the region of the Straits, with the full right to arm the area. Having secured the support of the Soviet Union and Turkey's allies in the Balkan Entente (Greece, Romania, and Yugoslavia) and the reluctant acquiescence of Great Britain and France, Turkey submitted a formal note on the subject on April 10, 1936.

The result of the Turkish overture was the calling of the Montreux Conference, June 22–July 20, 1936, which elaborated a new convention of the Straits, under which Turkey, essentially, nationalized the Straits and brought the area under its sovereign control. The United States took no part at all in the conference and sent no official observers, since its sole expressed interest at the time lay exclusively in the maintenance of the principle of freedom of navigation and transit in the Straits for commerce, essentially as embodied in the American-Ottoman Treaty of May 7, 1830, and the statement of policy of May 5, 1871. However reluctantly, both Great Britain and France conceded the principle of Turkish sovereignty over the Straits. Despite the later strictures which the Soviet Union was to level at the new convention and the Turkish government relative to the Straits, the Soviet Union considered the Montreux Convention a great diplomatic victory, although the *desiderata* as to converting the Black Sea into a genuine Soviet *mare clausum* were not achieved, and remained for further consideration and demand during and immediately after World War II. The Soviet government, like the Tsarist government, claimed that the Black Sea differed from other seas, inasmuch as there was no exit at the other end, and on the closing day of the conference, Foreign Minister Maxim Litvinov both celebrated the Soviet victory and stated the limitations of the achievement, in the *Actes de la Conférence de Montreux:* "The Conference has recognized, although in an insufficient way, the special rights of the riparian states of the Black Sea in the Black Sea in connection with the passage of the Straits, as well as the special geographical situation of the Black Sea, in which the general conceptions of the absolute freedom of the seas could not be entirely applied." While freedom of commercial passage was recognized without limitation of time, with the exception of the warships of the Black Sea states (the Soviet Union, Romania, and Bulgaria), there were limitations on the navigation and transit of non-riparian warships and of their passage into the Black Sea.

Turkey pursued a very realistic and constructive foreign policy during the interwar era, a fact which partly explains the orderly processes by which it was able to achieve agreement on the Montreux Convention in substitution for that of Lausanne. By the Treaty of Ankara (October 30, 1930) between Greece and Turkey, following the settlement of the property claims of repatriated populations and other outstanding questions, Greece and Turkey recognized the territorial *status quo* and agreed to naval parity in the eastern Mediterranean Sea. On September 14, 1933, these two countries concluded a nonaggression agreement for ten years. On July 18, 1932, Turkey became a member of the League of Nations and helped to facilitate Soviet membership in 1934. During the period 1930–34, Greece and Turkey took the lead in the semiofficial Balkan Conferences (Albania, Bulgaria, Greece, Romania, Turkey, and Yugoslavia), which looked in the direction of cooperation among the Balkan states on broad political, social, and economic foundations. On February 9, 1934, under similar Greco-Turkish initiative, the Balkan Entente, composed of Greece, Romania, Turkey, and Yugoslavia, was formed to serve as a regional security arrangement in the area. This was followed, on July 9, 1937, by signature of the Pact of Sa'adabad among Afghanistan, Iran, Iraq, and Turkey—a consultative pact which, at the time, appeared to contribute to regional stability along the Northern Tier of the Middle East.

At the same time, Turkey continued to move in the direction of Great Britain and France as the war clouds darkened the European skies after 1936, while relations with the Soviet Union remained "correct" and those with Nazi Germany and Fascist Italy were tempered with much caution, despite strong economic and commercial underpinnings. In a highly realistic manner, Turkey reached agreement with France relative to Hatay (Alexandretta, Iskenderun), which became a republic (July 3, September 2, 1938) as a prelude to formal annexation in 1939. On May 12, 1939, Turkey concluded a mutual security agreement with Great Britain for mutual assistance in the event of aggression or war in the eastern Mediterranean. Despite close economic relations with Nazi Germany and much pressure, Turkey identified itself with the British bloc designed to contain possible German expansion into the Balkan area and the Middle East. When France reluctantly agreed to abandon Hatay to Turkey, Turkey and France concluded their nonaggression agreement on June 23, 1939. The Anglo-Franco-Turkish agreement ultimately developed into the mutual assistance treaty of October 19, 1939, some six weeks after the outbreak of World War II.

Meanwhile, there were basic developments in the Arab portions of the Middle East. Here Great Britain played the leading role among the Great Powers, as already observed, with mandates over Palestine and Iraq, and controls over Egypt and the Suez Canal, together with a preeminent position in the development of the oil resources in the Middle East. France continued its role in North Africa (Morocco, Algeria, and Tunisia), while Italy (since 1912) had established itself in Ethiopia during 1935–36. Among the Arab peoples, nevertheless, there was a national awakening which was already making itself felt. Saudi Arabia, for example, established itself in 1927 under the able leadership of King Ibn Saud and was duly recognized by Great Britain, which enjoyed a privileged position in the country. Soon it entered into treaties of friendship with Turkey (1929), Persia (1929), Iraq (1930, 1936), Transjordan (1933), Great Britain (1934), and Egypt (1937). Great Britain signed an agreement with Iraq on December 24, 1927, recognizing Iraqi independence, and promised to support its admission into the League of Nations in 1932. In return Iraq granted Great Britain three new air bases and agreed that British officers should train the Iraqi army. By 1930 Iraq was independent, although Great Britain had a primacy in the country and it entered the League of Nations in 1932. Soon it entered into its own arrangements with its neighbors (Persia, 1929, Nejd, 1930; and Saudi Arabia, 1936). Egypt also moved toward independence after a false start in 1922, when the British government agreed in principle, but reserved its rights especially in matters of defense, foreign policy, and finance. In a treaty of August 26, 1936, between Egypt and Great Britain, Great Britain agreed to withdraw its forces, with the exception of 10,000 men who were to be restricted to the Suez Canal Zone but could be reinforced in wartime. The British were to maintain a naval base at Alexandria for not more than eight years. Egypt was to have the right of unrestricted immigration into the Sudan and Egyptian troops were to return to the Sudan. The capitulatory regime was to be eliminated. Egypt was to be admitted to the League of Nations (1937), and a treaty of alliance was signed for a twenty-year period, after which the agreement was to be reexamined.

During the same period both Lebanon and Syria moved slowly and uncertainly toward independence from France, which had established firm control under the mandate. The French High Commissioner proclaimed Greater Lebanon a Republic under the mandate in 1926, and Syria, where there had been considerable resistance to French authority, in 1930. Finally, on September 9, 1936, a Franco-Syrian treaty was signed. Ratified on December 26, 1936, the mandate was to come to an end in three years and Syria was to be admitted to the League of Nations. The Jebel Druze, Alouite, and Alexandretta areas were to be included in the independent Syrian state, with special status, while Lebanon was to retain its individuality. A treaty between France and Lebanon was signed on November 13, 1936. Actually, however, the French government appeared to have little intention of granting genuine independence, and it was not until 1946, after World War II and the withdrawal of Anglo-French forces, that Lebanon and Syria really achieved independence. It was, moreover, noteworthy that a Pan-Arab Congress met at Bludan, Syria, on September 8, 1937, to deal with the problem of Palestine, and Syria became a center of Palestine insurgent activity during the Arab revolt of 1936—a harbinger for the future.

In Palestine the story was quite different, in view of the establishment of a Jewish National Home under the British mandate on what Palestinian Arabs, who constituted some 90 percent of the population, deemed to be their own land and country. While a separate mandate was set up in Transjordan in 1920, and ultimately it became an independent state (1946), this action did not settle the matter. Transjordan was organized as an autonomous state by Emir Abdullah (1923) and was recognized as "independent" in 1928, with Great Britain retaining military and some financial control. The Palestine mandate itself became unworkable in the 1930s because the British were unable to reconcile the conflicting claims of the two intense nationalisms involved— political Zionism and Arab nationalism. Serious uprisings occurred in 1921, 1925, 1929, and 1936. On July 8, 1937, a Royal Commission became convinced the Arabs and Jews could not get along together, and recommended partition of the mandate into a Jewish and an Arab state, with special status for the Jerusalem area. While the World Zionist Congress reluctantly accepted the plan with certain revisions, and the Permanent Mandates Commission of the League of Nations accepted the plan in principle (August 2, 23, 1937), the Arabs rejected it outright (September 8, 1937). Instead, the Pan-Arab Congress at Bludan demanded termination of the mandate and establishment of an independent Palestine in alliance with Great Britain, abandonment of the Jewish National Home, and cessation of Jewish immigration. The Jews were to have the status of a guaranteed minority within an Arab state. Difficulties in Palestine were so severe, however, that the Palestine Partition Commission concluded that the plan was unworkable, and it was abandoned in October 1938. A compromise also proved unacceptable when the British government considered it with Arab and Jewish representatives at the Palestine Conference in London, February–March 1939. The new plan was announced on May 17, 1939. It provided for limitation of immigration into Palestine of 75,000 Jews during the next five years. But it was rejected by both Jews and Arabs. When Great Britain entered the war, nevertheless, Zionist organizations the world over, not unnaturally, sided with Great Britain in the struggle against Nazi Germany. Any solution of the problem, however, now awaited the outcome of World War II.

THE IMPACT OF WORLD WAR II

World War II, even more than the great struggle of 1914–18, ushered in another era in the Middle East, which became a very significant center of military action during the war in view of its strategic location, its nexus of intercontinental communications, and the importance of its oil resources. Nazi Germany and Fascist Italy exerted heavy pressures on the area, and one of the most important campaigns of the war, heavily fraught with the destiny of the Middle East, was fought in North Africa. The United Kingdom, the Soviet Union, and the United States entered the arena. The Turks, Iranians, and the Arabs were all heavily involved in one way or another, and in the end, as many have pointed out, a sovereign Middle East was to emerge, whatever the weaknesses of the states of the area and their fragmentation, especially after 1956; the great powers, however reluctantly, had to deal with the peoples of the Middle East as free and independent.

As noted above, Turkey had been oriented toward the West ever since the Lausanne Conference of 1923 and more especially since the Montreux Conference of 1936, and it seemed clear on the eve of World War II what its basic position would be. The Turkish government was shocked, if not precisely surprised, when Italy took over Albania on April 7, 1939. It was highly disturbed by the Nazi-Soviet commercial and nonaggression agreements of August 18, 23, 1939, immediately prior to the outbreak of the war. When the war finally came, despite German pressures and thinly veiled Soviet threats, Turkey signed a mutual assistance treaty with Great Britain and France on October 19, 1939, which did not, however, obligate it to fight against the Soviet Union.

During World War II the Turkish Republic, as was natural in view of its strategic position at the intercontinental crossroads, was of great interest to the Axis Powers and the nations pitted against them, including the United States. A nonbelligerent ally of Great Britain and

France, based on the preliminary agreements of May–June 1939 and
the treaty of October 19, 1939, as the war moved down through the
Balkan area during 1940–41, there was much concern with the Turkish
attitude. This was especially the case after the entry of Fascist Italy into
the struggle in June 1940 and the attack on Greece on October 28,
1940, and the advance of German forces into Romania and then Bulgaria, with the ultimate Nazi aggression against Yugoslavia and Greece
on April 5–6, 1941. During January–February 1941, President Roosevelt sent Colonel William J. Donovan to this troubled region to stimulate resistance to the Nazis, and Turkey and the United States seemed in
basic agreement as to the general outlook toward the war. But Turkey
remained a nonbelligerent substantially until the end of the war, although American entry into the conflict on December 7, 1941, without
doubt, had a very positive influence in Ankara; the defense of Turkey
was declared vital to that of the United States under the Lend-Lease
Act, a principle which was extended to Iran in 1942 and to the Middle
East as a whole in 1944.

There was little difficulty concerning the problem of the Turkish
Straits during World War II, despite questions raised from time to time
relative to the passage of German war vessels. The region of the Straits
was dominated by the fact that German forces controlled the Balkan
area and were in occupation of Greece and the Greek Islands in the
Aegean and eastern Mediterranean seas. During the Hitler-Ribbentrop-
Molotov conversations of November 12–13, 1940, and the subsequent
diplomatic exchanges, the Soviet government (November 25, 1940)
made clear its desires as to revision of the Montreux Convention and
control of the Straits, with naval, military, and air bases in the area, and
delineated the center of gravity of Soviet interest and policy in the general direction of the Persian Gulf. It was also more than hinted that the
Soviet Union might join the Axis, into which Turkey might be pushed,
willingly or otherwise. There was considerable trouble about the problem of Lend-Lease supplies and Turkish shipment of chrome to Germany, much misunderstanding of the Turkish situation generally, and
great concern over the Turco-German agreement of June 18, 1941,
barely four days before the Nazi attack on the Soviet Union on June 22.
Shortly thereafter, however, Great Britain and the Soviet Union pledged
their fidelity to the Montreux Convention, announced that they had no
aggressive intentions or claims with regard to the Straits, and declared
that they were prepared not only scrupulously to observe the territorial
integrity of the Turkish Republic, but in the event of an attack by a European power, to render assistance.

While certain pressures were brought to bear relative to Turkish belligerency, particularly after the Moscow and Teheran Conferences (October–November 1943), at the Cairo Conference (December 1943), and during 1944, it now seems clear that, in the last analysis, neither the United States, nor the United Kingdom, nor even the Soviet Union actually desired Turkish entry into the "shooting war," or had any definite or concerted plans for Turkish action. On the other hand, the Turkish government, in the event of entering into actual hostilities, was anxious about sufficient supplies and equipment, and had no desire to undergo possible Nazi conquest or subsequent Soviet "liberation." Stalin showed little interest in the matter at Teheran in November 1943, although there had been some discussion of Turkish entry at the earlier Moscow meeting in October. At the Cairo Conference in December 1943, President Roosevelt was little interested and did not blame the Turkish leaders for not wanting to get caught "with their pants down," and General Marshall feared that supplies for Operation Overlord would be diverted to a secondary Balkan or Middle Eastern front and that the Turks would "burn up all our logistics." When President Roosevelt put the problem of Turkish entry to the Joint Chiefs of Staff in July 1944, General Marshall's reply was essentially in the negative. Turkey broke relations with Germany in August 1944 and formally declared war on February 23, 1945, some days after the conclusion of the Yalta Conference. On February 27, 1945, the Turkish government adhered to the Declaration by the United Nations.

It was natural that Turkey, at the intercontinental crossroads, should pursue a cautious, careful, and realistic policy during the war as, indeed, it did. The Turkish government remained, nevertheless, a faithful nonbelligerent ally of Great Britain under the alliance of October 1939, which was never formally invoked. Its position served well the interests both of Turkey and the Allies during the critical period of 1940–43. Turkey did not become involved in actual armed conflict largely because there were no concerted or integrated plans for Turkish operations, no Balkan campaign was carried out on a scale to involve Turkish forces, and no supplies were diverted by the Western powers for this purpose. Indeed, with the possible exceptions of the period when Italy entered the war in June 1940 and the winter of 1943–44, despite Churchill's position, the evidence would seem to indicate that the United Kingdom, the United States and the Soviet Union did not desire Turkey's entry into the conflict. The British Chiefs of Staff and the War Cabinet appeared very skeptical as to the advantage of active Turkish participation, compared with that already found in the Turkish position as a nonbelligerent ally with neutral status. The United States held firmly to the view that the knockout blow against Germany was to be delivered in the West and was opposed to diverting supplies to any secondary front. This is clear from the discussions at Quebec, Moscow, Teheran, and Cairo, where even Churchill was ready to settle for "strained neutrality" on Turkey's part. In spite of all the talk and propaganda to the contrary, the Soviet government and Marshal Stalin did not appear much interested in Turkey's active participation, as noted particularly at Teheran because of (1) the priority of Operation Overlord, which "must come first"; (2) the Soviet objection to Turkish or other non-Soviet forces in the Balkans; (3) the Soviet desire for concessions at the Straits and elsewhere in Turkey; (4) the Soviet opposition to Turkish representation at a postwar peace conference; and (5) the Soviet desire to "talk" and make propaganda out of Turkey's nonparticipation in the "shooting war." The Soviet position concerning Turkey during the era of Nazi-Soviet collaboration, when the Turkish government was given a transparent warning on October 31, 1939, because of its close association with Great Britain and France, throws Soviet policy relative to Turkey into very sharp relief, indeed. So also does Soviet policy in the period immediately following World War II.

Iran, like Turkey, was in a highly strategic position during World War II, and was subject to severe pressures, especially in 1941. On January 29, 1942, Great Brtain and the Soviet Union, which sent troops into Iran to prevent a possible Nazi coup and to hold Iran as a corridor for supplies to the USSR, agreed to respect the territorial integrity and the political independence and sovereignty of Iran. This policy was confirmed on December 1, 1943 at the Teheran Conference, when the United States, the United Kingdom, and the Soviet Union issued a declaration pledging both to assist Iran economically and to support its independence. Meanwhile, Soviet troops north of Teheran, British troops in the south, and American forces along the supply routes were to be withdrawn within six months after the end of the fighting. When Soviet troops, instead, remained in Azerbaijan, and the Soviet Union sought to set up a Kurdish republic, a major crisis developed in Soviet-Western relations and provided the newly established United Nations with one of its first great problems.

The Arab states were not called upon to make any major military contribution against Nazi Germany and Fascist Italy during the war, although they did occupy areas which were of vital interest. In any event, Arab attitudes relative to the world conflict were much colored by the Palestine problem and by the fact that Great Britain and France, whatever their positive qualities, had played an imperial role in the Arab world and had generated some hostility. The position of Lebanon and Syria was highly important. The French remained in Syria, of course, even after the fall of France in May–June 1940, and the Germans sought to use the position of Syria to achieve their objectives in the Middle East, especially as a corridor into Iraq. When revolt broke out in Iraq in April–May 1941, under Rashid Ali al-Gailani, the Jordanian Arab Legion, with British forces, played a very significant role in quickly suppressing it in what may have been one of the decisive, if brief, actions of the war. Rashid Ali al-Gailani and Haj Amin al-Hus-seini, the former Mufti of Jersualem, escaped into Iran and ultimately passed through Turkey to Rome and thence to Berlin, where they served, somewhat ineffectively, the Nazi propaganda apparatus through-out the war. But they had little influence on Nazi-Fascist policy and failed to secure their objective of a Nazi-Fascist declaration relative to Palestine or to Arab independence and unity, which the Führer con-sidered futile until Marshal Rommel and the Afrika Korps captured Al-exandria. The battle of El-Alamein (November 12, 1942) settled that and other matters. Meanwhile, confused fighting in Syria ended on July 12, 1941, with an armistice after British and Free French forces moved on Beirut and Damascus. British naval units landed troops in Lebanon, terminated the authority of the French Vichy regime over Syria and Le-banon, and cancelled German attempts to obtain control in this area. Possession of Syria and Iraq enabled the British to exert increased pres-sure upon Iran, whose government was persuaded to cooperate (August 28), after British and Soviet forces entered Iran. The Lebanese govern-ment proclaimed its independence on November 26, 1941, and the Free French proclaimed the independence of Syria on May 27, 1943, but de-manded a privileged position in Syria and Lebanon which largely nullified the proclamation. French troops remained in the area, and it was only under much Anglo-American pressure, and after more blood-shed, that independence was finally achieved, immediately after World War II, during 1945–46.

The Palestine question remained, with the highwater mark during the war, the so-called Biltmore Declaration of May 11, 1942, following a drive toward an independent Jewish state, under the leadership of David Ben-Gurion, chairman of the Executive of the World Zionist Or-ganization. Among other things, the Biltmore Declaration urged that the gates of Palestine be opened, that control over immigration into Pales-tine be vested in the Jewish Agency, and that Palestine be established as a Jewish Commonwealth integrated in the structure of the new demo-cratic world. In the wider context of the war, despite the Nazi holocaust in which some six million were said to have died and the pressures which were brought to bear, the Palestine question as such was largely shelved to await the day when it would be reopened in all its compli-

cated facets. Meanwhile, Zionist pressures were concentrated on the
United States which, it was thought, would be the determining influence.

Soviet policy relative to the Middle East underwent no significant
changes during the course of World War II or in the period immediately following, and the bases seemed firmly laid during the Hitler-Mol-
otov-Ribbentrop discussions of November 1940. On March 19, 1945,
the Soviet Union denounced the nonaggression agreement of December
17, 1925, and indicated that, as a price for a new arrangement along
the lines established in the new Soviet-satellite treaties in Eastern and
Southeastern Europe, Turkey would have to cede the Kars-Ardahan
area in Eastern Anatolia back to the USSR and sign an agreement relative to the Straits which would place the waterway substantially under
Soviet domination and control. The demands were repeated in June
1945 and were rejected by the Turkish government which, however, felt
itself under continuous Soviet pressure. The matter was taken up at the
Potsdam Conference in July–August 1945, when Stalin and Molotov
indicated that there was nothing new in the Soviet position and adverted
to the Russian-Ottoman treaties of 1798, 1805, and 1833. The discussions continued in the fall of 1945, with the United States and the
United Kingdom setting forth their position and the Soviet Union failing to achieve recognition of its demands. But it was not until August 7,
1946, that the Soviet Union made its formal demands on Turkey for the
elaboration of a new regime of the Straits, which would have placed
that waterway firmly under Soviet control. Once more the Soviet position was rejected, and ultimately the USSR recognized that the time was
not ripe for pressing matters.

It now became very clear, indeed, that Soviet ambitions in the Middle East had not altered, except in the direction of Soviet expansion
throughout the area. The demands upon Turkey were one thing. The
pressures upon Greece and upon Iran pointed in the same direction,
and the Soviet government still considered the area south of Baku and
Batum the center of Soviet interest and policy in the area. Soviet ambitions were pressed at all three points along the Northern Tier of the
Middle East. There were demands for a trusteeship over Libya and for
a commercial (naval) base in the Dodecanese Islands. One of the first
cases in the early history of the United Nations was that in connection
with Iran, when the United States took a firm position to bring about
the evacuation of Soviet forces from that beleaguered country.

With the end of World War II, and for obvious reasons, there was a
perceptible decline of the West and of Western influence in the Middle
East. One of the basic reasons for this development lay in the fact that,
after the war, neither Great Britain nor France was capable of sustain-

ing the imperial role, as in the past, although France continued to play it for a while in North Africa—Morocco, Algeria, and Tunisia—and Great Britain maintained its position in the outposts of empire in the Persian Gulf as well as in Egypt, along the Suez Canal, until 1956. The time of the older imperialism and colonialism, in any event, had passed after World War II, when the winds of change passed over Africa and Asia, and it is very doubtful that even the superpowers could have imposed their will on the peoples of the Middle East.

A second reason for the decline of the West lay in the emergent, and often strident, nationalism, especially among the Arab peoples, who came to resent and then to reject foreign tutelage in whatever form. Iran, Turkey, and Egypt, of course, had long-established identities, developed over the centuries, but this was not true of certain other parts of the Middle Eastern world, and it was only after World War II that Lebanon and Syria (1943–46), Jordan (1946), Libya (1951), the Sudan (1951), Morocco (1956), Tunisia (1956), Algeria (1962), and Kuwait (1963) really became independent. It may well be that the "sovereign" Middle East emerged only after the Suez conflict of 1956. One of the basic problems of the Western powers in the post–World War II Middle East was that of learning how to deal with the newly independent Arab communities, when they could no longer call the political tune as they had in the past. Arab "unity," of course, had long since been adovcated as an ideal, and on March 22, 1945, a few weeks before the United Nations Conference on International Organization at San Francisco, the League of Arab States was established, giving some institutional form, at least, to the sense of nationalism and unity among members of the League.

A third element in the distrust and decline of the West in the Middle East lay in the development of the Palestine problem and the emergence of the state of Israel (1948), for which the Western Powers, and especially the United States and the United Kingdom, were held primarily responsible, although the Soviet Union as well had supported the partition of Palestine and the establishment of Israel during 1947–48. The two superpowers which emerged after World War II with basic interests in the Middle East, and which came into competition and possible confrontation, were the United States and the Soviet Union, although neither was a newcomer to the area, as is sometimes assumed by those unacquainted with the Middle East and the history of the international relations of the area. Since these developments involved the United States so directly and so heavily, and so much dominated the area after World War II, it is, perhaps, best to treat them in subsequent chapters.

❀ 2 ❀

P. EDWARD HALEY

Britain and the Middle East

Contact has existed for millennia between the peoples of the regions that have come to be called Britain and the Middle East. During the last hundred of these thousands of years two developments altered decisively the pattern of Anglo-Arab relations from one of pilgrimmage and commerce to one of intervention and domination. The two developments were the steady acquisition by England of an empire in India and the first European sally out of Western Europe into Egypt. The conquests of Clive and his successors in India gave the British something to protect in Asia. The short-lived but ambitious campaigns of Napoleon in Egypt threatened to establish the French on an invasion route to India, passing through Persia. In response the British attempted to seize Constantinople and Egypt and, in the Persian Gulf, joined forces with the ruler of Muscat. The expeditions in the Mediterranean miscarried, but the Muscati agreement laid the foundations of more than a century of British primacy in the Persian Gulf.

From such hesitant, often calamitous, beginnings Britain achieved during the next century a position of unrivaled influence and power in the Middle East. On the eve of the Mudros Armistice in 1918 Britain dominated the Middle East. Cyprus, ruled by Britain since 1878, was annexed three months after the outbreak of the war. British armies occupied Egypt, already a British protectorate, and the Sudan, greater Syria, and Mesopotamia. All of the rulers of southern Arabia and the Persian Gulf, including Abdul Aziz Ibn Saud of the Nejd, had subordinated themselves to Britain.

In less than fifty years these proud conquests were undone and the ir-

The author wishes to express his gratitude to Professor Majid Khadduri of Johns Hopkins University and to Professor Richard S. Wheeler of Claremont Men's College. Their assistance significantly aided him in the preparation of this essay. He owes his original interest in the Middle East to the inspirational example of Dr. Fayez Sayegh.

18

resistible influence of the British Empire diminished and finally confined in a few sheikhdoms on the Persian Gulf and the councils of the
foreign oil companies. British governments after 1945 saw the initiative
in the Middle East pass from their hands into those of the Russians,
whom they despised and feared, and the Americans, whom they liked
but regarded as too unsophisticated and unreliable to succeed them. The
relations of Britain and the Middle East thus fall into three periods:
rise, luxuriant and fatal expansion, and decline.

This chapter seeks to provide an understanding of British policy, particularly from 1945 to the present; to explain the reasons behind Britain's downfall in the Middle East; and to ask if a role still exists for
Britain there. The first section gives an account of the rise and expansion of British power in the Middle East. Succeeding portions contain
an analysis of the economic and strategic motives of British policy in
Egypt, Palestine, Jordan, and Iraq. Britain's relations with Iran are examined briefly in connection with a discussion of oil in the Middle East.
The countries of the Persian Gulf and Southern Arabia are considered
in the course of an examination of Britain's possible future role in the
Middle East. Turkey and Cyprus are omitted for two reasons. World
War I and the revolution led by Mustafa Kemal tended to take Turkey
out of the Arab world. Cyprus, for its part, is tragically caught between
Turkey and Greece, and its international center of gravity now lies between these two nations, the United States, and Soviet Union, rather
than in the Middle East. The relations of Britain with Egypt, Palestine,
Jordan, and Iraq during the period of expansion, 1915–45, are ana-
lyzed in order to establish a basis of comparison to relations during the
period of decline from 1946 to the present. The two periods are then
examined for changes in diplomatic and economic relations between
Britain and the Arab states and for changes in Britain's uses of force
and influence in the region.

The origins of a number of developments fundamental to Britain's
decline in the Middle East are only indirectly related to Britain's presence in the region. The first and perhaps most striking of these developments is the qualitative change in the system of international politics
that occurred after World War II. It is more accurate perhaps, to date
the revolution in world politics from the Russian Revolution of 1917
and the defeat of Germany in 1918. After Versailles, nonetheless, an illusion persisted among European statesmen that the nineteenth-century
forms and patterns endured. French and British ministers attempted to
employ a limited, cabinet diplomacy in their dealings with totalitarian
governments. British statesmen acted as if all the major powers were
more or less equal, and British policy sought to balance France with

Germany as well as Germany with France. The abstention of the United States and the Soviet Union prolonged these illusions.

After 1945 no such illusions were possible. The old game was gone. The five or six more or less equal players had been replaced by two monopolists. This change alone might have been fatal to Britain's position in the Middle East. For decades, British governments had depended for success there on the conflicting antagonisms of their opponents. Austria opposed Russian expansion in the Balkans and at the Straits, France and Russia quarreled over the Levant, Turkey feared Russia and favored Germany, France sought revenge and security against Germany, Russia feared a two-front war against Japan and the Central Powers, and Germany too, before Schlieffen, struggled to avoid having to fight in the East and West. These enmities sometimes worked against British interests. More often, they allowed and even forced Britain to arrange affairs in the Middle East according to the exigencies of European diplomacy.

The success of British policy depended on the possibility, inherent in a contest of equals, of manipulating the shifting antagonisms in ways that would consume the power of all and leave little strength for disruption in the Middle East or anywhere else. Major war in the Middle East, though Britain would and did fight two such wars in twenty-five years, was a disaster for British policy. It meant that enough European power had not been consumed, that the Middle East was open for rearrangement and India, thereby, endangered. It follows that the luxuriant expansion of British influence into Palestine, Syria, and Mesopotamia after 1918 was a sign of weakness, not strength. That expansion could only have occurred after the destruction of the very international system that had guaranteed the success of British policy.

Three other developments hastened Britain's decline: the flowering of Arab nationalism, the weakening of imperial sentiment in Britain, and the destructiveness of two world wars in a quarter-century. The most fundamental of these developments was the growth of Arab nationalism. Throughout the long rise of British power in the Middle East, the Arab national movement spread. It remained, in Antonius' words in *The Arab Awakening:* "weak and impotent, but alive and growing, and borne slowly towards its destiny on the wings of a renascent literature." Without the extraordinary changes brought by two world wars, without the intrusion of British, French, American, and Soviet power, without the birth and expansion of Israel, Arab nationalism would still have altered beyond recognition the traditional politics and diplomacy of the Middle East.

The costs and sacrifices of World War II exhausted Britain physically, financially and, perhaps, spiritually as well. Massive and immediate American loans were needed to save the British economy. The transfer to the United States of responsibility for Iran, Greece, and Turkey was only the first of many similar decisions to dismantle the British Empire piece by piece. The surrender of responsibility in Palestine followed almost immediately. The drastic straitening of Britain's resources came at a moment in Britain's history when, despite Churchill's rhetoric, little enthusiasm could be stirred for the maintenance of the British Empire anywhere except, perhaps, in the Middle East, and particularly in Egypt. By 1956, even in the Middle East, the heavy artillery of British imperialism had become "wooden guns," [1] empty of the ammunition of capital and popular support, and deprived of the Indian army to carry and shoot them.

RISE OF BRITISH POWER

The rise of British power in the Middle East began in the nineteenth century and ended in 1914. The constant motive of British Middle Eastern policy, in 1833 as in 1956, was to protect the British Empire in Asia. All of Britain's actions in the Mediterranean and the Persian Gulf, save the brief love affair with Greece in the 1820s, were governed by this objective. Differences of opinion arose within British governments as to the best means to accomplish this objective, but a remarkable agreement may be traced throughout the entire century and a half. So strong was the belief in this objective that it endured long after Britain's Asian empire had vanished and inspired a last intervention at Suez that destroyed what remained of British influence among the Arabs. So general was the agreement among British statesmen that while Disraeli, a Conservative, bought the Khedive's shares in the Suez Canal, Gladstone, the Liberal, presided over the military occupation of Egypt.

In Palmerston's time, the focus of attention was the Dardanelles and the Bosphorus. Attempting to contain Russian expansion southward, British statesmen went so far as to impose on the tsar at Paris in 1856 a humiliating neutralization of the Black Sea, soon undone in London in 1871. The opening of the Suez Canal and Britain's occupation of Cyprus and Egypt reduced the importance of the Straits and emphasized the vital nature of the link between the Mediterranean and the Red Sea. As early as 1896 British leaders had serious reservations about defending the Straits against Russia. The next year Salisbury called support for a British defense of Constantinople "an antiquated standpoint." Ultimately, the Straits and Constaninople were abandoned altogether to Russia by the Constantinople Agreement of March–April 1915.

To protect Egypt and the Suez Canal became the new gathering point of British governmental opinion. Men as different as Salisbury, Granville, and Ramsay MacDonald accepted the crucial importance of the canal. Salisbury spoke of Egyptian neutrality, and defined it as "the maintenance of such a state of things that no great Power shall be more powerful there than England." Should the Ottoman Empire collapse or Egypt be divided, he instructed the British consul general, British interests required only that "the sea coast and communications remained under the dominant influence of England." [2] Granville claimed to seek completely free and uninterrupted transit through the canal, but wanted only free British transit, and was prepared to occupy Egypt until assured of attaining his goal.

Fifty years later, Ramsay MacDonald instructed the British High Commissioner in Egypt in equally unequivocal terms: "The communications of the British Empire in Egypt remain a vital British interest and [the] absolute certainty that the Suez Canal will remain open in peace as well as in war for the free passage of British ships is the foundation on which the entire defensive strategy of the British Empire rests." [3] This dominant view of Egypt and the canal as geopolitically vital was buttressed by the vast economic advantage of the canal to Britain.

The Middle Eastern policies of British governments throughout the nineteenth and for the first half of the twentieth century were shaped by strategic and economic considerations. India had to be protected, for, as the Committee of Imperial Defense observed, the British Empire was "naval, Indian, and colonial." The Middle East lay across the principal land and, later, water routes to India. The southern route to India was protected by Britain's possession of South Africa, a possession she fought a long, costly war to keep. Therefore, hostile powers must be kept from penetrating the Middle East, or, if they penetrated, their penetration must be rigorously controlled and made to work to British advantage.

Until the end of World War I the Middle East, apart from Egypt, the Sudan, South Arabia, and Persia, formed part of the Ottoman Empire. For decades, therefore, Britain held up the ailing "bear," in the tsar's words, preferring that the weak Turks should rule such vital areas and exclude all Europeans, particularly the Russians, French, and, later, the Germans. The Ottoman Empire fell apart slowly and required a century and a half to disappear. Turkey lost North Africa and the Balkans before World War I. Ottoman, German, and Austrian empires were lost forever with defeat in the Great War, and the Russian Empire was consumed as well despite its alliance with the victorious side. Still, a calamitous world war was required to destroy the Ottoman Empire. One must, therefore, recognize the success of British policy in maintaining the Ottoman buffer far past its expected demise and then in managing to play the principal role in its dismemberment, a role that every major European government coveted and that few survived to carry out.

To achieve this success British statesmen utilized war, threats of war, collective military and political intervention, unilateral military and political intervention, monetary subsidy, alliance, entente, conquest, protection, annexation, and spheres of influence. Examples of each for the period prior to 1918 would include the following: Palmerston utilized threats of war to undo the Russian gains achieved in the Treaty of Unkiar Skelessi. A threat of war was implicit in the Anglo-French encounter at Fashoda. Britain joined France and Turkey in war against Russia in 1854 and joined France and Russia against Turkey, Germany, and Austria in 1914. British protection was gradually extended to all of southern and eastern Arabia by 1915. The Sudan was conquered in 1898, Persia was divided with Russia in 1907, and Cyprus was annexed in 1914. Britain and France fashioned an entente in 1904 when each recognized the other's position in Egypt and Morocco, respectively. Britain made alliances with every power involved in the Middle East but Germany and Austria (counting Savoy as Italian). Monetary subsidies were regularly paid not only to rulers of the states along the Persian Gulf, but to the Saudi kings and to the rulers of the Ottoman Empire.

Throughout the century prior to 1918 Britain preferred collective to unilateral intervention. Palmerston's success against Russia was the essence of collective action, culminating in collective international military action against Muhammad Ali, a collective action not without its echoes today.* Collective action occurred again in the 1860s to protect the Christians of the Levant. Before occupying Egypt in 1882 the British government sought the approval and help of the other European powers concerned. Though collective action was preferred, British governments took unilateral action on a number of occasions when threat and risk seemed to demand it: in Egypt in 1882, in the Sudan in 1898, and in the Persian Gulf on several occasions in the nineteenth century.

---

* On August 24, 1970, the United States apparently tried to attract Russian support for a joint Russian-American police force in Sinai. An unidentified aide made the suggestion during a talk with editors and publishers in San Clemente. On August 31, President Nixon discounted the idea. See *Facts on File, 1970*, p. 622.

Expansion of British Influence

The motive of British policy remained constant during the period of expansion in the Middle East from 1919 to 1945. Before, during, and after World War I the overriding concern of successive British governments was to make of the Middle East a protective shield for and safe passageway to the empire in Asia, and in the process to extract whatever economic benefit possible. Oil became an increasingly important concern, but two facts must not be forgotten in this regard. First, Britain's strategic need for Middle Eastern oil was satisfied easily and early by the concessions in Iraq and Iran. Second, the dominant position of Middle Eastern oil in the world economy is a recent phenomenon. As late as 1938, the Middle East produced 15 million tons of crude oil, or 5.5 percent of the world's supply of 270 million tons. By comparison, in 1938 the United States produced 162 million tons, or 60 percent of the total.[4]

The Mandates and Preferential Treaties

The specifics of British policy changed radically during the period of expansion. The need for collective action disappeared with the Russian and German Empires. Freed from German and Russian opposition, the British pursued their objectives by means of bilateral military and political treaties with the new Arab states. A pattern soon marked Anglo-Arab relations. First came military occupation. Then, the period of disorder that followed and was in part stimulated by military occupation was seen to justify continued occupation. Finally, the British sought to achieve the benefits of occupation without its expense by concluding a preferential alliance that granted the British government the military access, troop transit, and martial control they demanded and relieved them of the cost and difficulty of administering the country directly. Alliances of this kind were concluded early with Iraq and Transjordan. There, as in all the Arab countries, the British sought to protect their empire to the east by a network of bilateral Anglo-Arab alliances that guaranteed them the widest possible rights of transit, storage, and communication and exclusive access to the local armed forces. The Arab rulers were to rule within the narrow limits left to them. Britain opposed any initiatives by the Arabs abroad and all political developments within Middle Eastern countries that might in any way reduce the substance of the British position. The British made this brutally apparent in Iraq from the start.

In the decade immediately after World War I ended, Britain completed a number of agreements with Iraq. All were unsatisfactory to Iraqi opinion because they denied genuine independence. Finally, a new treaty, signed in June 1930 and ratified the following year, replaced all previous treaties. It was to remain in force for twenty-five years. This treaty formed the basis for Anglo-Iraqi relations during World War II and until the creation of the Baghdad Pact in 1955. Iraqi nationalists bitterly opposed the continuation of British dominance, while the British refused to advance the moment of independence. Tension grew so great that one Iraqi prime minister, Abdul-Muhsin as-Sa'dun, committed suicide in November 1929 to escape being ground between nationalist demands and imperial power. The admission of Iraq to the League of Nations on October 3, 1932, eased but failed to resolve the dilemma that drove Abdul-Muhsin as-Sa'dun to suicide. Iraqi resentment of British imperialism continued to trouble Anglo-Iraqi relations long after all the old bonds had been severed.

The British succeeded in reconciling their interests with Iraqi sentiment just after they had failed to achieve an almost identical settlement with Egypt. The objective of both treaties was the same: to guarantee communications with the British Empire and Asia and at the same time to shift most of the burden of direct government from British to Iraqi and Egyptian shoulders. The treaty with Iraq established a military alliance and pledged the Iraqi king to provide "all facilities and assistance in his power including the use of railways, rivers, ports, aerodromes and means of communication." [5] The protection of "the essential communications of His Britannic Majesty" was declared of common interest. To this end, Iraq granted to Britain sites for air bases and authorized Britain to maintain armed forces in Iraq for twenty-five years. Britain alone would furnish all foreign military schooling, advisers, and armaments required by Iraq.

With Egypt, a preferential treaty was signed only after long, difficult negotiations over eighteen years marred by Egyptian terrorism and British military intervention. The difficulty lay in the importance of Egypt to the security of Britain's Asian empire. The British were willing as early as 1922 to make, in Field Marshal Allenby's words, "an Egypt enjoying the national prerogatives and the international position of a sovereign State." But the British government demanded absolute discretion over: (a) the security of the communications of the British Empire in Egypt; (b) the defense of Egypt against all foreign aggression or interference; (c) the protection of foreign interests in Egypt and the protection of minorities; (d) the Sudan. [6]

While Britain controlled these matters, whether by military force as in 1922 or by treaty as of 1936, Egypt enjoyed far less than full independence. A subsequent Foreign Office circular on Egypt, No. 2 Cd. 1617, was as blunt as Allenby had been:

> The welfare and integrity of Egypt are necessary to the peace and safety of the British Empire, which will therefore always maintain as an essential British interest the special relations between itself and Egypt long recognized by other Governments. These special relations are defined in the declaration recognizing Egypt as an independent sovereign State. His Majesty's Government have laid them down as matters in which the rights and interests of the British Empire are vitally involved, and will not admit them to be questioned or discussed by any other Power. In pursuance of this principle, they will regard as an unfriendly act any attempt at interference in the affairs of Egypt by another Power, and they will consider any aggression against the territory of Egypt as an act to be repelled with all the means at their command.

Though these arguments may have seemed reasonable and even generous to British statesmen, Egyptian leaders fought against them until Italy's invasion of Ethiopia and the deteriorating international situation of the late 1930s compelled them to seek an agreement with Britain.

The agreement finally reached in 1936 contained concessions by both sides. Britain agreed to terminate military occupation and to support Egypt's candidacy for membership in the League of Nations. Britain would help to end the capitulatory privileges of foreigners in Egypt. A military alliance was established between Britain and Egypt which obligated each to aid the other in case either became engaged in war. Ten thousand British troops would stay in Egypt to guard the Suez Canal until both parties agreed Egypt could protect the canal alone. In particular, Egypt was required to make available all possible facilities of transportation and communication. The Egyptian government undertook to construct additional roads, bridges, and railroad lines for the use of British forces and agreed to allow the British government to construct as many additional airfields as they desired. British forces could remain in Alexandria for eight years, the approximate period required to complete the improvements in railways and roads. After twenty years, the treaty could be opened for negotiation at the request of either party, and if agreement on revision could not be reached, the difference would be submitted to the League for decision. In addition to these advantages Prime Minister Mustafa Nahhas agreed in accompanying notes to accord diplomatic seniority to the British ambassador in Egypt and to place all foreign schooling, training, and equipping of the Egyptian armed forces exclusively in British hands. The military guarantees resembled those contained in the Anglo-Iraqi treaty of 1930.

The British found it nearly as easy to arrange affairs in Jordan as it was difficult in Iraq and Egypt. Feisal's brother Abdullah responded to the destruction of the Arab government in Syria in the summer of 1920 by moving north through Transjordan to attack the French. The British, who had made a small effort to administer Transjordan from Kerak and Amman, feared an incident with the French. Abdullah's move coincided with the conference of British Middle Eastern and colonial officials in Cairo. From Cairo, Churchill obtained cabinet approval of an intriguing plan to make Abdullah king of Transjordan.[7] In April 1923 the High Commissioner of Palestine, Sir Herbert Samuel, announced in Amman that Britain would recognize the independence of Transjordan under the rule of Abdullah if a constitutional regime were established and a preferential treaty concluded with Britain. Abdullah proclaimed the independence of Transjordan on May 25, 1923.

The establishment of constitutional government was not taken seriously by the British, but a preferential treaty was concluded on February 20, 1928. The treaty established a British Resident in Transjordan in charge of foreign affairs and acting on behalf of the High Commissioner for Transjordan. Britain delegated its authority in Transjordan to Abdullah with major qualifications. No foreign official could be appointed without British consent. No law could be made that would interfere with "the full discharge of the international responsibilities and obligations of His Britannic Majesty in respect of the territory of Trans-Jordan." Abdullah agreed to follow the advice of the British government in regard to foreign affairs and "the international and financial interests" of Britain in regard to Transjordan. Abdullah also agreed to submit for British approval the budget and all laws affecting currency, duties, the rights of foreigners, succession to the throne, money or land for the king, and sovereignty over land outside Transjordan. Abdullah pledged to carry out British recommendations about treatment of foreigners and protection of religious freedom. Britain could maintain armed forces in Jordan and raise and control local forces. Abdullah agreed to obtain Britain's consent before raising any armed forces of his own. Since the revenues of Transjordan could not pay the costs of administration, Britain pledged to pay the difference and to bear virtually all military costs. Abdullah promised to provide every facility for the communications, movement, and maintenance of British forces in Transjordan. No territory was to be placed in any way under the control of any foreign power, and the exploitation of all natural resources was subject to British supervision. Abdullah's despotic rule and the extraordinary extent of British prerogatives effectively closed Transjordan to the outside world.

With Palestine, no treaty, no self-government, no end to occupation or the misery and slaughter were possible from the beginning to the end of the mandate. Britain's presence in Palestine was founded on conquest from Turkey and approved by the League of Nations which recognized Palestine as a British mandate. Britain won French approval of the mandate in exchange for concessions to France in Europe and Syria. But what Britain could secure internationally in Paris and Geneva it could never gain locally in Palestine. Zionists supported a British mandate because in the mandatory agreement, as in the Balfour Declaration, Britain made itself responsible for creating conditions in Palestine that would, in the words of the mandate, "secure the establishment of the Jewish National Home . . . and the development of self-governing institutions, and also for safeguarding the civil and religious rights of all the inhabitants of Palestine, irrespective of race and religion." [8] The Arabs of Palestine boycotted every effort of the mandatory to foster a regime that offered less than complete self-government. Inherent in any other scheme, they believed, was the continuation of Jewish aggrandizement in Palestine. The Arabs wanted immediate self-government, while Arabs remained the majority, and they made plain their intention to limit if not destroy the dream of a Jewish National Home.

The public British position on Palestine after World War I was defined in four major policy statements: the Churchill memorandum of 1922, the White Paper of 1930, Ramsay MacDonald's letter to Chaim Weizmann the same year, and the White Paper of 1939.[9] In their official pronouncements the British government progressively narrowed the meaning of "Jewish National Home" which Lloyd George had left wide open.[10] At the peace conference, British statesmen ignored the glaring contradiction between "a National Home for the Jewish people" and the modifying clause "nothing shall be done which may prejudice the civil and religious rights of existing non-Jewish communities," as they ignored the contradiction between their promises to the French and to the Arabs. Major outbreaks of violence occurred between Arab and Jew in Palestine in 1920, 1921, 1927, 1928, and through the 1930s. After each outbreak the British government reduced their support of the Zionist cause.

In the Churchill memorandum of 1922, the creation of a Jewish Palestine was explicitly denied, and Jewish immigration was made subject to the "economic capacity of the country at the time to absorb new arrivals." In the White Paper of 1930, the British government took as the basis of the mandate the interpretation offered by the League Mandates Commission: that, as mandatory, their obligations to Arab and Jew in

Palestine were of equal weight, and that these dual obligations were not irreconcilable. The White Paper's emphasis on the rights of the Palestinian Arabs was unmistakable, particularly in the sections on transfers of land and Jewish immigration. The White Paper, together with the economic report of Sir John Hope Simpson released simultaneously, seemed to vitiate any hope of Jews becoming a majority in Palestine. Vociferous protests and violent demonstrations against the White Paper by Jews in Palestine and Europe led Prime Minister Ramsay MacDonald to issue an interpretive letter to Dr. Weizmann. The letter affirmed Britain's obligation "to facilitate Jewish immigration and to encourage close settlement by Jews on the land" and accepted the principle and practice of the Jewish Agency of exclusive employment of Jewish labor by Jewish organizations. MacDonald, after reversing the emphasis of the White Paper, insisted that British policy was to achieve a solution based "upon justice, both to the Jewish people and to the non-Jewish communities of Palestine." Rather than a soothing remedy, the letter became another irritant, for Arabs in Palestine reacted to the letter as Jews had reacted to the White Paper.

Beginning in 1936, large numbers of Arab Palestinians, with external Arab support, rose in rebellion against the British mandatory government and staged attacks on Jews and Jewish settlements. Probably more than 3,000 people—British, Arab, and Jew—were killed during the four years 1936–39. Like the inquiries into the disorders of 1929, the official inquiries into the Arab rebellion of the 1930s disclosed that a deep fear and hatred of Jewish settlement in Palestine and a nearly desperate desire for self-determination underlay violence by Arabs against Jews. The Peel Commission found, in part: "An irrepressible conflict has arisen between two national communities within the narrow bounds of one small country. About 1,000,000 Arabs are in strife, open or latent, with some 400,000 Jews. There is no common ground between them." The commission recommended in favor of partitioning Palestine into two states. A Palestine Partition Commission was then appointed, and they reported in 1938 in favor of partition, though the members were divided as to the best way to carry out the division, and the majority plan accorded a large and continuing role to the mandatory government. In November 1938, the British rejected partition on grounds that the committee's report had revealed "political, administrative, and financial difficulties" that made such a division impracticable. Instead of dividing Palestine, the British government conducted parallel negotiations in London in early 1939 with representatives of the Jewish Agency on one side and delegations from the Arab states and the Arabs in Palestine on the other.

Six months later, after the negotiations had failed to produce agreement, the British government released the final official statement of policy on Palestine before the outbreak of World War II. The White Paper of 1939, Cmd. 6019 of 1939, made public and "final" the proposal advanced by the British during the London negotiations. The government referred to the Churchill memorandum, but the policy adopted differed radically from that approved in 1922. In 1939, desperately in need of Arab support against Hitler's Germany, the British government rejected the concept of Jewish statehood and turned from the principle of allowing Jewish immigration within the limits of the economic absorptive capacity of Palestine. In particular the British asserted that the framers of the mandate and the Balfour Declaration "could not have intended that Palestine should be converted into a Jewish state against the will of the Arab population of the country." The British government gave as its objective in Palestine a single, unified state in which authority was shared by Arabs and Jews "in such a way as to insure that the essential interests of each community are safeguarded." Since relations between Arab and Jew would not permit this, "an evolutionary process," a "transitional period" would be required enroute to genuinely Palestinian statehood. At the end of ten years, it was hoped Britain would have participated in drafting the constitution of the new state and would have established bilateral treaty relations that would satisfy the commercial and strategic requirements of both countries. The treaty would also protect the Holy Places in Palestine and the status of the Arab and Jewish communities. In regard to immigration, the British government stated bluntly:

> It cannot be denied that fear of indefinite Jewish immigration is widespread amongst the Arab population and that this fear has made possible disturbances which have given a serious setback to economic progress, depleted the Palestine exchequer, rendered life and property insecure, and produced a bitterness between the Arab and Jewish population which is deplorable between citizens of the same country. If in these circumstances immigration is continued up to the economic absorptive capacity of the country, regardless of all other considerations, a fatal enmity between the two peoples will be perpetuated, and the situation in Palestine may become a permanent source of friction amongst all peoples in the Near and Middle East.

The flaw in this analysis was the assumption that time remained during which the "fatal enmity" between Arab and Jew might be forestalled. The British government pursued this phantom hope, as indeed it must have done in order to stay in Palestine and safeguard relations with the neighboring Arab governments. The White Paper of 1939 asserted that 75,000 Jews would be allowed into Palestine in five years, and then no more, "unless the Arabs of Palestine are prepared to acquiesce in it." A perverse and bloody fate, in decreeing the ghastly slaughter of Jews by Hitler's Germany, loosed a flood of refugees to Palestine that overwhelmed British and Arab hopes of limiting Jewish immigration. Long before that tragedy occurred, both communities in Palestine had rejected the White Paper of 1939. The Arabs condemned it as too Jewish; the Jews opposed it as too Arab.

Missing from the successive public statements of British policy on Palestine was any clear definition of the strategic value of the mandate. This may easily be deduced by examining the map, British conduct, and the political status of any Jewish commonwealth in Palestine. Geographically, Palestine was the gateway of the corridor to the Persian Gulf through Transjordan and Iraq. If the gate fell from British hands, the corridor became a vulnerable salient. Palestine also constituted a base covering the Suez Canal, and the British army attempted to develop a base there for this purpose in 1946 and 1947, down to the very moment when Britain renounced the mandate. Last, if, following the original British notion, a Jewish commonwealth emerged, it would have to depend on Britain for protection against the hostile Arabs.

All of these formulations presupposed the maintenance intact of British power, empire, and will. For twenty-five years Britain juggled the dreams and hopes of Arabs and Jews as well as her own strategic interests in the Middle East, each a flat contradiction of the other. British power and will kept all the balls aloft, and maintaining the empire justified the sacrifice required to perform the feat. In 1945, Britain seemed a juggler suddenly deprived of one arm. One after another, the balls crashed to earth. After the ten years mentioned in the White Paper of 1939, a major change occurred in Britain's relations with Palestine. But instead of signing a preferential treaty with a united state of Palestine, the British withdrew from a divided land and region that collapsed in war immediately on their departure and has been the scene ever since of constant political instability, massive warfare, and guerrilla campaigns of murder, piracy, and assassination.

Oil

For a half-century, from 1900 to 1951, the British enjoyed remarkable success in their efforts to control the sources and development of Middle Eastern oil. A desire to control the region's oil followed rather than initiated the intrusion of British power into the Middle East. Even if oil had never been discovered in Persia or Iraq or in Bahrein and Qatar, the general direction of British policy in the Middle East would have been the same. In the eyes of British statesmen, the protection of the British Empire required that so far as possible the governments and peoples of the Middle East be ordered to British advantage. This would have remained true if oil had never been struck. It is in this regard that Curzon's disclaimer of any involvement with oil interests makes sense. Curzon and his fellows in the cabinet based their attitude toward the Middle East on criteria independent of the presence or absence of oil. Oil was discovered, of course, first in Persia, then in Iraq, Bahrein, Qatar, Saudi Arabia, and Kuwait, in enormous quantities of prodigious monetary value. Profits on some investments ran 52 cents a barrel and much more.

The prospect of achieving naval self-sufficiency from Persian supplies alone explains the determination of Britain to exclude all other nations from sharing in the exploitation of Persian oil. British oil companies gained control in Persia, Iraq, and the Persian Gulf primarily because of the lack of any serious competition that enjoyed adequate governmental support. Only in Saudi Arabia did American companies exclude the British. Kuwaiti oil was shared by a British and American consortium. Britain's European competitors had been destroyed or radically transformed by world war and revolution. The United States protested British exclusive practices, but official American complaints became increasingly perfunctory as that country fell deeper into isolationism.

World War II

During the war Britain's enemies again attacked her position in the Middle East. Germany fomented an attempted coup in Iraq, while Italian and, later, German armies in North Africa threatened Egypt. The War Cabinet was determined "to defend Egypt against all comers with whatever resources could be spared from the decisive struggle at home." So great was the government's determination that even while the British Isles were threatened by imminent German invasion, nearly half the best available British tanks were sent around the Cape to Egypt.[11] For three years the Middle East remained the only theater where a major blow might be struck against Axis forces by the Western Allies.

According to one persuasive interpretation, that of George Kirk, the political objective of British Middle Eastern strategy during the war years was to continue to hold the allegiance of moderate Arab nationalism. This was accomplished with some difficulty in Egypt and Iraq while British forces occupied those countries. Palestine, Lebanon, and Syria presented a far more difficult problem because of the three-cornered nature of the situation: Arab-Zionist-British, and Arab-French-British. "It was evidently held that the Anglo-Arab *entente* was essential to the war effort and must therefore have precedence over the full satisfaction of Free French and Zionist claims. . . . The alternative was to alienate the moderate Arab nationalists and jeopardize the security of the Middle East, the pivot-theatre of the war from 1940 to 1943; whereas the alienation of the Free French and the Zionists could not affect the war effort, since they were in no position to withhold their cooperation." [12]

Nationalist struggles within the states of the Middle East and rivalry with the French created two kinds of problems for the British. The great costs of the war and the loss of India shortly after peace was won further sapped Britain's strength to withstand Arab nationalism. The many complications, dangers, and weaknesses fostered by these aspects of the situation in the Middle East, nonetheless, fail to explain the short duration of a major role for Britain in the area: only the thirteen years from 1945 to 1958 remained.

DECLINE OF BRITISH CONTROL

In 1945 as in 1918 Britain bestrode the Middle East, controlling Lebanon and Syria in addition to Egypt, Palestine, Jordan, and Iraq. British troops shared the occupation of Iran formally with the Soviet Union and informally with the United States. The motive of British policy remained unchanged: to preserve the Middle East as a shield and passageway of the Asian empire, and to safeguard the strategically vital Middle Eastern oil resources. The decline in British power, nonetheless, forced a striking change in the means chosen to reach this end. Before 1945, Britain controlled all of the lines of the foreign and defense policies of Palestine, Jordan, Iraq, Egypt, and the Gulf and south Arabian areas. Arab foreign and defense policy went through London, often originating there, and there connected with the rest of the world. After 1945, British policy lost its exclusively bilateral character.

Britain's weakness forced a dependence on a variety of multilateral approaches for the achievement of British objectives. The need to rely on the United States gave each diplomatic encounter at least three sides. The United States awoke only slowly to the collapse of European power in the Mediterranean basin and then accepted direct responsibility only in Greece, Turkey, and Iran, the countries closest to Europe or most directly threatened by the Soviet Union. Elsewhere in the Middle East, United States policy included three contradictory elements: the Americans desired to advance their economic interests, to leave political affairs to the British, and to oppose imperialism and colonialism. American policy tended, therefore, to eliminate British influence without replacing it and to aid Arab and Zionist nationalism without understanding those movements. The conflicts and vacuum that resulted from these actions opened the area to Soviet influence. Then, revolutionary governments came to power in Syria, Egypt, and Iraq that were unafraid of close ties with the Soviet Union.

While Stalin lived, the Soviet Union attempted to undermine the British presence and to acquire a share of the region's resources. Soviet support for the creation of Israel served the first objective, and the unsuccessful attempt to detach Azerbaijan from Iran served the second. When Stalin's successors turned to the Middle East, the Soviet Union remained an outsider without great influence, a position Russia had held since Palmerston's successes in the mid-nineteenth century. In 1955, however, the Middle Eastern countries faced a number of related problems that presented an opportunity to the Russians. If the Arab leaders made peace with Israel they could gain the respite they needed to carry out domestic reform and economic development, but making peace meant abandoning the cause of the Palestinian Arabs. Moreover, the Arab leaders could not accomplish domestic reforms without outside economic aid, but they feared that accepting the only aid available, from Britain and the United States, would prevent the realization of revolutionary changes. The Soviet Union, offering arms to fight the Israelis and rubles to build the Aswan dams of Arab socialism, seemed to offer a third choice, one free of these or any other dilemmas. Unhappily, the basic dilemmas remain. Only the identity and ideology of the principal external partner has changed.

American indifference and Soviet opposition were fatal to the British presence, given the straitened British economy, an anti-colonial Labor government, and the militant Arab nationalist movements. The British, nonetheless, attempted to overcome each of these barriers to the continuation of British primacy in the region. The thread running through an otherwise incomprehensible pattern of advance and retreat is the objective, first of the postwar Labor government and then of three Conservative governments, to use their dwindling power and influence to preserve the strongest position possible for Britain. Even so, it took the British ten years to find a way to retain military access to Egypt and

Iraq, by means of the Anglo-Egyptian Treaty of 1954 and the Baghdad Pact. These agreements lasted less than four years.

In October 1956, the British government chose to risk everything on one throw of the dice in a desperate try to recover prestige, authority, and primacy in the eastern Mediterranean. The failure of that last try mercifully ended the long misery of imperial decline in the Middle East. The check at Suez proved to be checkmate. Within two years of the ignominious defeat at Suez, Britain's once great sphere of control had shrunk to oil holdings and ties to the Persian Gulf Sheikhdoms and Oman and Aden. Then followed the independence of Aden, the stillbirth of an attempted federation along the Trucial Coast, and the decision to withdraw British forces from the Persian Gulf. Even before the departure of the last Britons, Iran began to present itself as the new guarantor of peace and order in the Persian Gulf.

The failure at Suez was the point of no return in the decline of Britain's power and influence in the Middle East. In order to understand that momentous failure and, above all, why the British chose to gamble everything on one halfhearted intervention, it is necessary first to examine briefly a number of earlier developments in Palestine, Egypt, Jordan, Iran, and Iraq.

New Treaties and a New British Role

Britain encountered few of the difficulties in maintaining the old relationship in Transjordan that frustrated similar attempts in Egypt and Iraq. The governments of Britain and Transjordan concluded two agreements during the first years after the war. The first, signed in 1946 just before the mandate ended, resembled closely the earlier preferential treaties that had defined Britain's role in the Middle East. This proved embarrassing when Iraq and Egypt rejected far more generous agreements. The British then concluded a second agreement with Jordan in 1948 essentially identical with the treaty rejected by Iraq.

The Anglo-Jordanian alliance of 1948 provided mutual assistance in case of war and specifically sanctioned the movement of British troops into Transjordan on request. Britain received permission to maintain air force units at Amman and Mafrak. The treaty created a joint defense board charged with formulating strategic plans and supervising training. Britain would pay for all facilities and construction required by its forces and would enjoy complete freedom to move military forces through Transjordan. The armed forces of Transjordan would be equipped with British arms and trained by the British government. King Abdullah continued to receive a large and essential subsidy from the British, and a former British officer, John B. Glubb, served as commander of the Arab Legion.

The Arab Legion fought well against the Israelis in 1948 and added much land west of the Jordan River to the king's domains. That gain proved short-lived, for in 1967 the Israelis seized all of the kingdom west of the Jordan. Another result of the first Arab-Israeli war proved both more enduring and more dangerous to the kingdom. During that first war, as a result of Jewish terrorism and a desire to escape the fighting, hundreds of thousands of Palestinian Arabs fled into Transjordan, leaving behind home and fortune. When peace came Israel refused to allow them to return. From that moment, Transjordan became a nation whose original inhabitants were outnumbered two-to-one by people forced to live in extreme poverty, who had suffered grievous loss, and who, as the years passed, grew more and more desperate and determined to gain revenge against Israel. King Abdullah was assassinated by a Palestinian in 1951. Two decades later, in the autumn of 1970, the government of King Hussein fought for its existence in a bloody civil war against Palestinian guerrillas. For its part, the Israeli government attempted to stop the infiltration and violence of the Arab refugees by launching large and ruthless raids into Jordan and Gaza. In addition to threatening the government of Jordan, the conflict between Arab and Jew threatened to involve Britain in war against Israel because of Britain's treaty obligation to defend Jordan.

Much of the turmoil in Arab countries grew directly out of the humiliation and trauma accompanying the creation of the state of Israel. When Britain withdrew from Palestine, the Arab armed forces failed to defeat and destroy the Jewish army. Arabs, and particularly the young officers, deeply resented the weakness and corruption revealed by the failures. They expressed their resentment and determination to change their nations by seizing control of one government after another. Within three years Syria and Egypt had passed under military rule. Iraq followed in 1958.

Realizing their weakness after the war, the British attempted to persuade the United States to share the burden of keeping Arab and Jew from making war in Palestine. As Churchill observed in the House of Commons on August 1, 1946, the British had to win American support or get out of Palestine. Anxiously, the British government tried to move the United States from "its position of private exhorter to a publicly responsible partner in Palestine affairs." [13]

Truman's was a vision of Palestine as a refuge for persecuted Jews and a place where "a great industrial system could be set up under the Jews, and the Arabs." The partition proposal, he said, "impressed me as the most practicable way to make progress in that direction." [14] The Joint Chiefs of Staff insisted and Truman agreed that no American troops could be employed either to keep the peace as a massive flow of Jewish refugees began or to implement partition against the wishes of the Arabs. Truman forced the American government into the invidious, if not unaccustomed, role of telling others what to do and refusing to accept the political and human consequences of the advice. In an uncharacteristic lapse of realism Truman placed his faith in the ability of the United Nations to achieve a peaceful solution. Over-all, the conduct of the American government toward the Palestine crisis showed American foreign policy at its worst. Truman declined to assume responsibility for the consequences of his exhortations, he refused to support the British as they tried to keep peace between Arab and Jew and achieve a solution acceptable to both, and he refused to step aside and keep quiet.

The U.S. State Department's Division of Near Eastern Affairs had warned Truman in September 1945 against allowing large Jewish immigration to Palestine: "No government," read the division's memorandum, "should advocate a policy of mass immigration unless it is prepared to assist in making available the necessary security forces, shipping, housing, unemployment guarantees." [15] Truman, like most high officials in England and the United States, supported the establishment of a Jewish state, and nothing could prevent him from securing the immediate admission into Palestine of 100,000 Jews—neither opposition from the State Department nor long-headed arguments from the British Prime Minister.

The British also attempted to open negotiations with the competing factions. Internally divided, the Zionists refused even to discuss the British proposals. The Arabs agreed to talk, but rejected all solutions that failed to make Palestine an Arab country with a maximum Jewish parliamentary representation of one-third the total. [16] This refusal by both sides finished British hopes for a peaceful, successful settlement that would not harm their relations with the other Arab nations. It also ended any hope of making Palestine British military headquarters in the Middle East, a project entertained after the offer in 1946 to evacuate all British troops from Egypt. In mid-February the Labor government announced its intention to turn to the United Nations. Relinquishing the issue to the UN was an admission of failure.

The General Assembly created a Special Committee on Palestine (UNSCOP) to deal with the problem. A majority of the committee offered three recommendations: (1) to end the British mandate; (2) to create two separate states, one Jewish and one Arab, in economic union in Palestine; and (3) to establish a UN trusteeship for the city of Jerusalem. On November 29, 1947, the General Assembly approved the principles advanced by UNSCOP and requested the Security Council to implement them. Four days later, on December 3, the British government announced it would evacuate Palestine and terminate the mandate on May 15, 1948. Fighting broke out immediately between Arab and Jew, and on May 15 war erupted between the Arab states and Israel. Neither side could gain a decisive victory, although the Israelis expanded beyond the partition lines on all fronts, north, south, and opposite Jerusalem. With the assistance of a UN mediator a series of armistice agreements were signed in the spring of 1949 replacing the sporadic truces of the previous summer and autumn. Britain, after the armistice, accorded Israel diplomatic recognition and resumed arms shipments to the Arab states.

The armistice agreements settled nothing. In an effort to concert their policies and to replace uncertainty and fear with security and calm, Bevin, Schuman, and Acheson issued in London a declaration on the Arab-Israeli conflict, May 25, 1950. The tripartite declaration expressed the opposition of Britain, France, and the United States to an arms race between the Arab states and Israel, while recognizing the need for arms adequate to preserve internal security and provide "legitimate self-defense." The three governments proclaimed their unalterable opposition to any threat or use of force between any states in the Middle East. If they found any of those states preparing to violate frontiers or armistice lines they would "immediately take action, both within and outside the United Nations, to prevent such violation." Of the declaration, Dean Acheson afterward observed: "Rarely has so large an undertaking been so unlucky in its timing or had so short-lived an effect." [17]

The new, multilateral pattern of British diplomacy emerged clearly during the British government's attempt to maintain its favored position in Iraq and Egypt and its dominant role in Middle Eastern affairs. Nationalists in Iraq and Egypt sought identical aims: total and immediate British withdrawal and severely limited rights of British military return. The Egyptians also sought sovereignty over the Sudan. In August 1951, the Egyptian government ended negotiations with the British and promised to abrogate the existing Anglo-Egyptian treaty before November. In a desperate effort to keep British power in Egypt, the Labor and then Conservative governments turned to the United States.[18] The British proposed to Truman and Acheson a form of multilateral Middle East military organization that included the United States. The proposal had been under active consideration in Washington since January 1951.

According to Acheson the American purpose was to make "more effective" Britain's ability to carry out her "primary responsibility" for the defense of the Middle East by coordinating American and British efforts under a general regional plan. On September 8, the two governments agreed on a Middle East Command, composed of a Supreme Allied Commander Middle East with headquarters in Cairo, and including Egyptian officers. The supreme commander would take his orders from a Middle East Chiefs of Staff Committee. Egypt would receive the British base at Suez, but it would be operated by the supreme commander.[19] Those British troops not assigned to the command would be immediately withdrawn. The number to remain would be settled by the commander with the agreement of the Egyptian government. After gaining admission to NATO later in September, Turkey joined Britain, France, and the United States in proposing the plan to the Egyptians.

On October 1, the last British personnel were withdrawn from the Anglo-Iranian Oil Company (AIOC) refinery at Abadan. Five days later Herbert Morrison, speaking for a Labor government about to be turned out of office, informed Nahhas he would make another offer on defense within four days. On October 8, fearing the fall of his own government (which in fact occurred three months later), Nahhas introduced two bills in Parliament abrogating the treaty of 1936 and the Sudan condominium agreement. On October 13, the four powers made their offer to establish a Middle East Command, and Nahhas rejected it without reading it. Two days later the Parliament abrogated the Anglo-Egyptian agreements. Acheson wryly observed: "Strange as it may seem nearly twenty years later we were innocent enough in 1950–51 to see promise in such a plan. . . . If ever there was a political stillbirth this was it."[20]

In Iraq, as in Egypt, the British tried to adapt the old treaty to nationalist sentiment and to preserve, so far as possible, the existing British political and military advantages. Although the Anglo-Iraqi agreement of 1932 continued in force, its term expired in 1956, and all attempts to renew it failed. Turkey's offer to Iraq to form a regional security pact seemed to offer the pro-Western Iraqi premier, Nuri es-Said, an opportunity to safeguard his country's relationship with Britain in a multilateral and, presumably, more acceptable form. Britain seems to have controlled the negotiations with, in President Eisenhower's words, the "support and encouragement" of the United States. Turkey and Iraq signed the agreement on February 24, 1955. Britain joined on April 5, Pakistan on September 23, and Iran on October 12. To the dismay of the British and Iraqis the United States refused to join.[21]

Nasser reacted immediately by unleashing a vitriolic propaganda barrage and by creating a southern alliance to offset the northern Baghdad Pact. Egypt based the southern security agreement on the proposition that an Arab security pact of 1950 no longer existed. In early March, Egypt, Syria, Saudi Arabia, and Yemen signed an agreement forbidding alliances with non-Arab states and providing for the creation of a unified military command and a common foreign policy. The rapid alignments and counter-alignments illustrate the antagonisms that formed the basis of the international politics of the Middle East in 1955. Saudi Arabia joined Egypt in order to defeat any scheme likely to strengthen a Hashemite monarch. Part of Nuri's attraction to the northern pact lay in a chance to assert Iraqi leadership in the Fertile Crescent. Syria opposed the plan for exactly the reasons Nuri supported it. Britain coauthored the alliance in order to prolong its presence in the region. The British could stay in the Middle East only if the "good Arabs"—Nuri's Iraq, for example—received protection and gained the leadership of Arab opinion. To this end, whatever raised Nuri seemed to lower Nasser. The United States joined Britain in inspiring the pact for its value in organizing the Arab countries against the intrusion of Soviet influence in the Arab world.

Acting in accord with Article 1 of the Baghdad Pact, Britain and Iraq then replaced their old security pact with a new one, signed on April 4, 1955. The new treaty gave Iraq sovereignty over the air bases at Shu'ayba and Habbaniyah. Britain retained the right to land and service aircraft at the bases, to fly over the country, to station British troops in Iraq to train members of the Iraqi forces and to service aircraft, and to own the facilities needed for aircraft operations. Britain also pledged to defend Iraq in case of attack or threat of attack. The new agreement expressed the reduction in Britain's direct role in Iraqi affairs caused by nationalist sentiment and British weakness and loss of empire. Gone were the provisions requiring Iraq to cooperate in "the permanent maintenance and protection in all circumstances of the essential communications of His Britannic Majesty." The old treaty left it to Britain to determine the number of British troops to be stationed in Iraq. The new agreement required the withdrawal of all British forces from Iraq and authorized the presence in peacetime of training and service troops only. Iraq's withdrawal from the Baghdad Pact caused the special agreement to lapse.

Following the overthrow of the Egyptian monarchy in 1952, the Conservative government resumed the search for agreement on defense, evacuation, and the Sudan. The British continued to carry out their pledge to allow the Sudanese to decide their own future. Instead of opposing this policy, the new Egyptian government began to try to outbid the British in hopes of winning unification with the Sudan through the gratitude and the electoral efforts of the Sudanese National Unity Party, a coalition of five pro-Egyptian parties.[22] At last, on February 12, 1953, Egypt and Britain agreed on Sudanese self-government. Elections were held in late 1953, and in August 1955, the Sudanese government requested the withdrawal of Egyptian and British troops within three months, in accordance with Article 11 of the Anglo-Egyptian agreement. This action started the final transition to independence. All foreign troops were withdrawn, and the Sudan became independent on January 1, 1956. The Egyptian government's indirect course to unity with the Sudan had failed, but their plan to oust Britain from the Nile Valley won its first success in the Anglo-Egyptian agreement of February 12, 1953.

The British government rejected the denunciation of the Anglo-Egyptian treaty of 1936. In the fall of 1952, however, the British undertook an official review of Middle East strategy. The result was a decision in principle to move military headquarters in the Middle East to Cyprus. The island lacked a natural harbor, and the British declined to construct a port capable of handling great warships and transports. As Eden observed: "The cost of building one would have been very high. We did not do so and were to pay dearly for that omission." [23]

Eden gave three reasons for Britain's change of attitude about the importance of the Suez base. First, Turkey had joined NATO, and her accession strengthened Western capabilities for regional defense. Second, "financial considerations" made necessary the reduction of British forces deployed in the Middle East in peacetime. Third, the destructiveness of nuclear weapons made liabilities of great bases garrisoned by large numbers of troops on the outbreak of hostilities. In regard to the military importance of the base, Eden observed: "The Suez Canal remained of supreme importance, the base was yearly less so. . . . It did not seem likely that in this nuclear age we should ever need a base on the past scale. Smaller bases, redeployment and dispersal would serve our purpose better." [24] This new outlook on defense made agreement with Egypt much easier. The negotiations began to turn more and more on how hard a bargain the two sides could drive. As happens so often in politics, an important dispute was conducted in terms different from the real conflict. Control of the Suez Canal was the issue. An agreement allowing easy British entry into the Canal Zone would affect decisively the political conditions in Egypt that would decide whether the canal was managed to Britain's advantage or detriment. This connection of military and political questions explains the difficulty of agreeing about a military base the British thought obsolete.

The British sought a general settlement that would include (1) a phased withdrawal of British troops; (2) maintenance of a military base in the Canal Zone available immediately to Britain and her allies in case of war; (3) an Anglo-Egyptian organization for the air defense of Egypt; (4) Egyptian participation in a Middle East defense organization; (5) military and economic assistance for Egypt from Britain and the United States. Churchill and Eden personally sought American support for these objectives early in 1953. Eden gained Eisenhower's approval of these goals and a qualified promise that American and British military and diplomatic representatives could jointly approach the Egyptian government. Eisenhower's qualification wrecked the joint approach. The president required an Egyptian invitation before he would allow the United States to join the negotiations in Cairo. Only a foolish or mad Egyptian government would voluntarily consent to American participation on Britain's side. The Egyptians rejected an American role, and the United States refused to use its economic, military, or political influence to gain admission as Britain's partner. While the British searched for leverage against the Egyptians, the United States not only declined to support them actively but sold arms to Egypt.

The British government ought to have begun to perceive a pattern to American policy in the Middle East. The pattern was set during the Palestine crisis, renewed during the abortive joint approach to Egypt, repeated over the Baghdad Pact, and confirmed without mercy in the Suez crisis. The United States offered British governments advice, conciliatory speeches, and no material support in maintaining British power in the Middle East. Again and again Zionism and Arab nationalism exercised a veto over American support for Britain. The fear of being branded "neo-colonialist" and of the propaganda advantage this would offer the Soviet Union paralyzed the government in Washington and fostered there a vehement and growing Anglophobia.

The Anglo-Egyptian negotiations over the Suez base hold general as well as specific significance. All over the Middle East postwar British governments encountered the same choices they faced in excruciating clarity in Egypt. If the British refused to compromise, the local governments would attack British soldiers and subjects and perhaps invite Russian help. Unilateral evacuation stripped away any hope of maintaining an important future role. The third course was to attempt to discover the most persuasive and internationally defensible position from which to negotiate.

The British chose the last course in Egypt, Jordan, and Iraq. They achieved agreement with Egypt on October 19, 1954. The agreement required the withdrawal of all British forces by June 1956. Britain terminated the treaty of 1936. If Turkey or any member of the Arab League were subjected to armed attack, British forces could return to the Suez base, and the Egyptian government would provide all necessary facilities for the operation of the base. Egypt would maintain parts of the Suez base for immediate British use. Egypt and Britain would consult in case of the threat of attack on Turkey or the members of the Arab League. The two governments recognized the Suez Canal as a waterway of international importance and expressed their "determination" to uphold the Constantinople Convention of 1888, which required unimpeded transit for all commercial vessels in peace or war. Egypt nonetheless continued to bar vessels belonging to or bound for Israel, although some "neutral" ships going to Israel were allowed to use the canal. The British air force was granted facilities for overflight and servicing. Unless both governments agreed to extend the treaty, it would terminate seven years after signature.

The stability gained with such difficulty lasted only a few months, for the British then tried to use the Baghdad Pact to create a pro-British bloc in the Middle East. Potential Arab members were at least Iraq, Syria, Lebanon, Jordan, and Egypt. The British hoped the Russian threat would provide the cement and that the multilateral framework would make the scheme respectable. One can understand why the British expected Jordan to join, and even Lebanon. Jordan came close to joining in December 1955, despite riots and sharp resistance. How they hoped to win Egyptian and Syrian cooperation remains a mystery. Eden himself spoke to Nasser four days before the signature of the Turco-Iraqi agreement. Then, in Cairo, at the British embassy, he learned from Nasser of the impossibility of Egyptian membership. Instead of comprehension of Arab hopes for unity and self-reliance the visit taught him that Nasser was one of those for whom "it is never the right time." [25] Eden chose to risk the improvement in Anglo-Egyptian relations that had followed the conclusion of the treaty just four months earlier. He chose to risk the stability gained in protracted negotiations marked by violence over eight years for a chimerical alliance dependent on one unpopular authoritarian, Nuri, an alliance offensive to Israel and repugnant or dangerous to every Arab government. Seldom have British statesmen attempted an initiative more unfortunate in conception or harmful in consequence.

The northern pact could hardly have been launched at a less propitious moment. A week before Turkey and Iraq signed, Ben-Gurion returned as Israeli defense minister. Four days after the signature, Israel struck ferociously against an Egyptian military camp in Gaza. Nasser immediately asked the United States for arms. Confident he could not pay, the State Department offered cash terms only. Nasser dropped the request, turned to the Soviet Union, and in September announced the purchase of arms from Czechoslovakia valued at between $90 million and $200 million. In these ways, Anglo-Iraqi relations and the effort to create, in Eden's words, "a sort of Middle East NATO arrangement" with a joint headquarters in Cyprus, became entangled in the events leading to the Suez crisis. Nasser's overtures to the Soviet Union alarmed the British and American governments. By March 1956, Eden had identified Nasser as the arch-enemy: "Our general policy in the Middle East was founded on the need to protect British interests in Iraq and the Persian Gulf. The main threat to these interests was the growing influence of Nasser with his anti-Western ideology and collusion with Soviet Russia, especially in arms supply." [26]

Oil

Since 1945 two developments have altered the production, transportation, and marketing of Middle Eastern oil. They are the self-assertion of countries possessing oil and the vast growth in production and importance of Middle Eastern oil. Both developments have affected Britain, the international oil companies, and every nation possessing or hoping to possess an industrialized economy. The countries possessing oil asserted themselves by demanding and sometimes taking greater benefits and control away from the oil companies. This development really began with the dispute over the nationalization in 1951 of the Anglo-Iranian Oil Company. An interim episode occurred in 1961 when Iraq with Law 80 effectively cancelled the Iraq Petroleum Company's rights of exploration in all its areas and in the newly discovered, rich field in North Rumaila. The Iraqi government completed the nationalization of all IPC holdings on June 1, 1972. The dispute over the North Rumaila oil deprived Iraq of revenue from the new field, and in 1968 the Iraqis announced the field would be exploited by the Iraqi National Oil Company.[27] The latest phase in this development opened in January 1971, when the countries possessing oil demanded and later received more money for and more control of it. The countries, joined together in an exporters' consortium—the Organization of Petroleum Exporting Countries, which includes the North African countries and Venezuela— threaten serious retaliation if the oil companies refuse to meet their requirements. The importance of Iranian oil to Great Britain suggests the need to consider at some length the Anglo-Iranian crisis of 1951–54.

Dean Acheson observed, in commenting on the crisis, "in simpler times and places armed intervention, known as 'gunboat diplomacy,' would have resolved this problem in favor of the stronger power." [28] The British declined to practice gunboat diplomacy in dealing with Mohammed Mossadegh. Instead, they froze Iran's sterling accounts, achieved an effective boycott of Iranian oil, and threatened Iran by moving troops to Cyprus and warships to the Persian Gulf. Force was not used because the Labor government was reluctant but, above all, because the United States was unwilling to support British military intervention. Moreover, the ideological split in world politics had destroyed the context necessary for successful punitive expeditions. In 1907 and again in World War II, Britain and Russia had divided Persia between themselves. Neither the convenience of imperial spheres of interest nor the threat of Germany unleashed existed to justify punishing Iran for nationalizing a major British holding. The British had to get their results without the overt use of force.

When the American government's patience with Mosadegh ran out and when the economic misfortunes of nationalization and economic sanctions had undermined him, Mosadegh was overthrown and a settlement obtained. An international consortium was created in late 1954 to produce and market Iranian oil. The terms of the agreement granted Iran more revenue than the agreement of 1933, but not more than the Iranian government might have won by accepting any of a number of offers made during the previous four years. The new members of the consortium were American companies who paid AIOC $214 million in order to join. This arrangement (with additional revenue rights equivalent to another $280 million) satisfied Anglo-Iranian's demand for compensation. The shares of the consortium were divided as follows: Anglo-Dutch—54 percent (British Petroleum, 40 percent, Royal Dutch–Shell, 14 percent); American—40 percent (each received 8 percent: Standard of New Jersey, Standard of California, Socony-Vacuum, Texas Oil, Gulf Oil); and French—6 percent (Compagnie Francaise des Petroles).

The British government first sought Middle Eastern oil in order to acquire an independent source of fuel for the royal navy. As late as 1938, Britain still received 57 percent of her oil from the Western Hemisphere and 22 percent from the Middle East. After thirty years, these figures became strikingly reversed. In 1968, Britain imported approximately 80.2 million metric tons of crude oil. Of this, some 65 million tons came from the four principal Middle Eastern suppliers and Libya. [29] The Middle East also supplies 95 percent of Japan's oil, and about three-quarters of the oil used in Western Europe. The United States imported 15 percent of its consumption from the Eastern Hemisphere in 1972. The Eastern Hemisphere's share of imports may well rise to 35 percent of total consumption by 1980. Since 1945, Middle Eastern oil has grown enormously important to the survival of the economies of Western Europe and Japan. Moreover, three-fifths of the world's proven oil reserves are held by Middle Eastern countries.[30]

Despite political difficulty and military withdrawal, Britain has managed to retain a large share of the marketing, production, and transportation of Middle Eastern oil. Unlike most European countries, therefore, Britain profits from the act of meeting her own requirements for petroleum. In 1968, the principal crude oil exporting countries in the Middle East were Iran (141.9 million metric tons), Saudi Arabia (141.5), Kuwait (122), Iraq (73.9), Abu Dhabi (24.1), Kuwait Neutral Zone (22.3), Qatar (16.2), and Muscat and Oman (12). British companies own all or much of the oil operations in every one of these countries except Saudi Arabia (American) and the Neutral Zone (Anglo-American)* The dependence of Britain on Middle Eastern oil and the extent of British ownership of oil operations makes all the more remarkable the decision of the Labor and Conservative governments to withdraw from the Persian Gulf.

The success of oil development in the Middle East is a story of fabulous wealth, with an increasing share of the total income going to the exporting countries, although little of the money actually benefits most of the inhabitants of those countries. Although the countries' share of income from oil operations averages 65 percent, the governments of these countries argue that income from actual production and sale of crude oil represents only a small portion of the actual revenue made possible by their oil. European governments, for example, receive substantial income from high gasoline taxes, and the Organization of Petroleum Exporting Countries contended in January 1971 that their members received only $1 of every $14 paid for petroleum products by the average automobile owner in Western Europe. Part of the explanation for this sense of grievance lies in the wealth the oil companies have obtained from the sale of oil and from investments made possible by oil revenues. The original AIOC was capitalized at £2,000,000 in 1910. In 1968, its heir, Iranian Oil Participants, guaranteed the Iranian govern-

---

* The breakdown is: Iranian Oil Participants (British Petroleum 40 percent, Royal Dutch–Shell 14 percent); Iraq Petroleum Company (British Petroleum 23.75 percent, Royal Dutch–Shell 23.75 percent); Kuwait (British Petroleum 50 percent with offshore drilling 100 percent Royal Dutch–Shell); Abu Dhabi (same as Iraq Petroleum Company); Qatar (same as Iraq Petroleum Company with offshore drilling 100 percent Royal Dutch–Shell); and Muscat and Oman (Royal Dutch–Shell 85 percent).

ment $1,000 million annually, regardless of the amount of crude oil sold. It has been extremely difficult for uncertain, nationalist governments in the Middle East to resist exploiting the widespread hostility in their countries toward Western oil companies. No recent developments suggest it will be easier to resist in the future. Moreover, the Arab-Israeli dispute continues to deepen the difficulties inherent in oil operations in the Middle East by intensifying anti-Western sentiments either in countries that possess oil or in those whose territory run the pipelines vital to its cheap transport.

Suez

The skeleton of events that took place in the summer and autumn of 1956 has become part of the mental furniture of those born before World War II: the Egyptian opening to the Soviet Union, the American cancellation of funds for the High Dam at Aswan, the nationalization of the Suez Canal Company a week later, invasion by Britain, France, and Israel at the height of the Hungarian crisis in Europe, and the ignominious failure and withdrawal of the invaders as a result of American opposition. One is reluctant to add anything to the growing literature already published. The official archives are still closed, and sure documentary proof of many points is doubtful because of the conspiratorial way the British, French, and Israelis conducted their negotiations over intervention.

Among the various kinds of influences that affected British policy during the Suez crisis, four stand out. First, the crisis coincided with the grave personal illness of the highest statesmen in London and Washington. During the worst days of October and November 1956 Dulles and Eden were seriously ill. Eisenhower had only recently recovered from a serious heart attack. In early November Dulles entered the hospital for a cancer operation. The disease killed him within three years. Eden's account of his own illness is chilling. Second, domestic pressures in Britain, Israel, and Egypt strongly influenced the politics adopted by their leaders. Much is made by British and French commentators of the impact of the Republican desire to win the elections of 1956 on the actions of Dulles and Eisenhower. It would seem that Anglo-French fears of the possible effects of the campaign on American policy counted for much more than the effects themselves. Nothing in my research suggested that Eisenhower and Dulles would have acted differently in an off-year. Expectations in London and Paris of a more sympathetic response arose from a misunderstanding of Dulles' view of the conflict between his need to preserve the loyalty of European allies and his hope to gain the cooperation of Arab nationalists.

The Suez crisis was far more directly and decisively shaped by domestic politics in Britain, France, and Israel than by electoral politics in the United States. To the French government, the overthrow of Nasser promised to end the war in Algeria. The future of Algeria was a question tied intimately to the future of France and the survival of the Fourth Republic. The domestic importance of the Algerian war was so great that the inability of a string of regimes to end the war satisfactorily brought civil strife to France and caused the overthrow of the Fourth Republic.

In Israel, the decisive domestic events occurred more than a year before the crisis. In February 1955, David Ben-Gurion returned from the wilderness and became defense minister in the cabinet of Moshe Sharrett. The differences between the two men can best be summarized, perhaps, by noting that as premier Sharrett retained the foreign minister's post for himself, and Ben-Gurion as premier kept the defense portfolio. Ben-Gurion's return foreshadowed greater Israeli militancy. On February 28, ten days after Ben-Gurion entered office, the Israeli army struck ferociously against an Egyptian army camp in Gaza, killing thirty-eight. Kenneth Love has argued persuasively that this raid started a cycle of action and reaction that culminated in the tripartite invasion of Sinai twenty months later. How an outside power might have broken the tightening spiral of terror, distrust, and reprisal is difficult to imagine.

Britain's prime concern during this period was to persuade as many Arab nations as possible to join the Baghdad Pact. The opposition of the "southern" Arab states, led by Nasser, and a desire to avoid stirring the hostility of the Palestinians, prevented even Jordan from joining. The Conservative government in Britain found themselves in an unenviable position. They were under pressure from within their own party to do something about the alarming and humiliating collapse of the empire. They sensed public impatience at the constant abuse and hatred and bloodshed involved in letting go. But nothing seemed to work. Palestine was gone, there was fighting in Cyprus, the last British troops were leaving Suez, no one would join a British-centered security pact in the Middle East. The Conservative and Labor Parties knew that most Britons wanted strong action and would not quibble about means, provided they were successful.[31]

The question remains: Why did Eden choose to risk everything to overthrow Nasser, even when he knew he did not have strong American support? The British leaders decided to invade Egypt because they believed that Britain could have a future role in the Middle East only if

Nasser were defeated. What they meant was not that, however. If Nasser won over Suez all British influence would not disappear from the Middle East. Only the century-old British role as arbiter of Middle Eastern affairs would disappear. It was this role that Eden and his colleagues sought to retain. They had been trying since 1945 to adjust the form of their relations with the Arab countries in order to preserve the substance. The substance was control of the Suez Canal, Persian oil, Jordan, and Iraq. They wanted to keep the old imperial framework, but the empire was gone. A British Commonwealth of Asian and African nations remained, and retention of leadership in the Middle East would secure leadership in the Commonwealth. Like all imperial powers, Britain feared the domino effect of every defeat. Eden saw the dispute over the Suez Canal primarily in terms of the future (and the past) of the empire and the Commonwealth.

There were also serious commercial and strategic considerations involved. As Eden observed:

> We estimated that the United Kingdom had reserves of oil which would last for six weeks, and that the other countries of Western Europe owned comparatively smaller stocks. The continuing supply of fuel, which was a vital source of power to the economy of Britain, was now subject to Colonel Nasser's whim. . . . More than half of Britain's annual imports of oil came through the Canal. At any time the Egyptians might decide to interfere with its passage. They might also prompt their allies to cut the pipelines. We had to gauge the implications of bringing oil from the Persian Gulf by the long haul around the Cape of Good Hope.[32]

These questions were not decisive in persuading the British government to send troops into Egypt. The canal question could probably have been settled in such a way as to meet the British desire to "insulate" the operation of the canal from "the politics of any one country." Indeed, the six principles adopted by the Security Council seemed to go far toward meeting these kinds of requirements.[33] A settlement of the Suez Canal dispute alone would not have satisifed the British. There always remained the larger imperial question, and Eden and his colleagues were determined to settle that question on their terms. They wanted Nasser out, and nothing else would do.

Two events in March 1956 started Eden toward a collision with Nasser. On March 1, King Hussein summarily dismissed Glubb Pasha, a British officer commanding the Jordanian army.[34] Then, riots erupted when the foreign minister, Selwyn Lloyd, visited Bahrein on his way to a conference in Karachi. Eden attributed both of these events to Nasser and responded with severity. The British at this time joined the United States and Iraq in an attempt to overthrow the pro-Egyptian government of Syria. Eden also caused Archishop Makarios to be deported from Cyprus to the Seychelles on March 9. He acted against Jordan by calling home the remaining British officers in the Jordanian army, explaining: "Our general policy in the Middle East was founded on the need to protect British interests in Iraq and the Persian Gulf. . . . Britain's national interest was to maintain the independence of Jordan which was an outpost of Iraq. It was not to our advantage to drive King Hussein to extreme courses. . . . The right solution, at some later date, might be for the two countries to come together, but the time was not ripe for that."

Two points remain for discussion before attempting to assess the consequences of Britain's failure at Suez. They are, first, the genesis of the tripartite alliance against Egypt, and, second, the reasons why the invasion failed to accomplish its aim. Kenneth Love has shown persuasively what common sense has long suggested about the three-power invasion of Egypt. France had become Israel's chief source of war material. The two were natural partners for any action against Nasser's Egypt. Apparently, the French made the first formal proposal to Israel for joint action against Nasser. The French also acted in liaison between Israel and Britain, persuading each to accept the other. Both European powers intended from the moment of nationalization to coerce Nasser, and they initiated joint military planning on August 3. Israeli participation provided a convenient pretext: to separate the belligerents and protect the Suez Canal. Anti-Israel sentiment was so strong in Arab countries and British interests were so extensive there that any overt cooperation with Israel would be most harmful to Britain's position. Israel's "sudden" invasion of Sinai would provide the basis for an intervention designed to overthrow Nasser and, at the same time, would disguise Anglo-Israeli cooperation. Eden was drawn to the coalition, and the cabinet approved as one after another opportunity for intervention slipped away.[35]

The French broached the full plan for collusion to Eden at Chequers on October 14. Eden flew to Paris with Lloyd on October 16, met with Mollet and Pineau, and agreed to join France and Israel in attacking Egypt. The three agreed that Israel would strike into Sinai. Britain and France would then order both sides to retire from the Suez Canal, though the closest Israeli forces would be a small detachment of paratroops on the east side of the Mitla Pass. When Nasser rejected the joint ultimatum British bombers would destroy the Egyptian air force. A bombardment of Egypt ("aero-psychological warfare") came next, and then invasion. British and French troops would seize the Suez Canal and "turn right" into Cairo. After overthrowing Nasser and establishing a more pliable regime in his place, the Europeans would withdraw. The three partners signed an agreement at Sèvres on October 24. The next day the British cabinet approved in principle the Anglo-French military action.

General André Beaufre, the French combat commander, mercilessly revealed the military shortcomings of the plan in his book, *Suez*. The plan was haltingly conceived, by committees and politicians. It lacked the sudden driving ruthlessness needed to overthrow a foreign government by force. It carried too much political cargo. As Beaufre demonstrated, a landing at Alexandria and an advance on Cairo was the surest way to finish Nasser. Nothing else made military sense. Unhappily, from the French general's point of view, Eden desired complete political safety *and* military effectiveness. They did not go together. The unsuitable Anglo-French plan gave the Americans the opportunity to defeat the invasion by denying Britain financial, diplomatic, and material support.

The consequences of the Anglo-French-Israeli invasion were exactly the opposite of Eden's intentions. He had intended, first, to preserve Britain's position in the Middle East. As a result of the invasion, Britain soon found her role restricted to the tiny sheikhdoms of South Arabia and the Persian Gulf. Eden went to war to overthrow Nasser, keep the canal open, and protect Europe's oil supplies. As a result of the war, Nasser gained in strength and stature, the canal was closed, and the oil supplies disrupted. From the British government's point of view, Eden had committed the worst of all diplomatic blunders. His policy fell between two stools.* It contained neither enough force to overthrow

* Eden succeeded Churchill as prime minister on April 6, 1955. Churchill, who desired to hold every possible strong point of empire, thus escaped the extreme developments in Anglo-Egyptian relations that followed Czechoslovakia's sale of arms on September 27, 1955, and the United States cancellation of the financing of the High Dam at Aswan project on July 19, 1956. Eden is, therefore, the crucial figure on the British side. My view of this complex and gifted man may be stated briefly. Before and after World War II, Eden's successes came from his skills as a diplomat. His were the perfect tactics to Churchill's strategy. Force and cunning lay with Churchill; Eden knew how to reap the advantages these qualities sowed. On his own as prime minister, Eden remained a diplomat. Finally in power late in life when illness sapped his strength, he could not find the force and cunning needed to make his own diplomacy succeed. When Bourgès-Manoury called Nasser another Hitler, he struck the rawest nerve of every British statesman in power before the war. None of them, least of all Eden, haunted by the memory of those dreadful years before 1939 when he was foreign secretary, could have resisted the analogy, so patently wrong to outsiders. The Suez intervention called for qualities foreign to the diplomat, particularly the resolution and insensitivity required to undertake a sudden, violent invasion and to

Nasser nor enough guile to isolate and befriend him. Either approach promised to remake the Middle East according to Eden's pattern. In failing, Eden caused greater harm than the choice of either singly would have done.

BRITAIN'S FUTURE IN THE MIDDLE EAST

The Anglo-French defeat at Suez and the overthrow of the monarchy in Iraq had consequences both immediate and distant. The immediate result was to compel Britain to limit its deployment of military forces in the Middle East to southern Arabia and the Persian Gulf. Britain's other major base in the region, in Kenya, was evacuated in 1964. The distant result was to expose what remained of the British role in the Middle East to intensified attacks from the forces of Arab nationalism at a time when domestic opposition to a continued British role "east of Suez" was rising and the British economy was in serious trouble. These three developments found specific expression in civil war in Yemen and Aden colony, stimulated by Egyptian intervention in both places, in the intention announced by the Labor Party during the election campaign of 1964 to withdraw from Aden and Singapore, and in Britain's chronic balance of payments deficits and lagging economic strength.[36]

The coincidence of these developments eventually made impossible the retention of any British forces on the ground in the Middle East.[37] For eight years after Suez, nonetheless, Britain's Conservative governments avoided withdrawal and kept large numbers of troops abroad in spite of Britain's ailing economy. In fact, the ten years from 1956 to 1966 were a time of intense and costly British diplomatic and military interventions, not only in southern Arabia and the Persian Gulf, but in East Africa and Southeast Asia as well. For four years, some 50,000 British troops blocked and defeated Sukarno's "confrontation" of Malaysia. British forces intervened in Kenya and Tanganyika in 1964 to quell mutinies in the local armed forces, and began an airlift of petroleum products to Zambia. At the request of the ruler of Kuwait, some 7,000 British troops occupied that country for five months in 1961 at a time when it seemed possible that the Iraqi dictator General Abdul Karim Kassim might attack Kuwait. British troops were soon replaced by a token Arab force, an outcome which satisfied the hopes of all but the Iraqi government: of Egypt and Saudi Arabia to see Iraq defeated,

overthrow a foreign government. Those qualities were not Eden's and never had been, neither in 1938 nor in 1956. The title of Eden's memoirs, *Full Circle,* has an ironic meaning he would not like.

and of Kuwait and Britain to see protected the tiny sheikhdom's sovereignty, vast oil reserves, and sterling investments in London.

The outcome in southern Arabia and the Persian Gulf came neither tidily nor soon and deserves more extensive discussion. Britain's diplomatic and military responsibilities in these continguous areas rested on the British government's assumption in the nineteenth and early twentieth centuries of responsibility for the foreign affairs and defense of Kuwait, the sheikhdoms of the southern Gulf Coast, and of Oman and Aden. These obligations fell first on the British government in India, who controlled British policy in the gulf and along the Arabian coast. The success of the Indian government in ending the slave trade and piracy, in imposing a degree of internal peace, and in excluding foreign political influence from these areas advanced British commerce and protected Indian security. In a strict legal sense, Britain was sovereign only in Aden, a British colony from 1837, although in practice Britain exercised extensive influence in the internal affairs of her wards. Protection was extended to the sheikhs who controlled the hinterland above Aden as a means of guaranteeing the colony's security against indigenous and foreign attack.

After the independence of India in 1947 the British government in London inherited all these responsibilities. In the mid-1950s, pursuing a pattern often to be repeated as the British empire disintegrated, the British government decided to create a federation in southern Arabia by linking the sheikhdoms above Aden colony. Aden colony would then join the federation, and Britain would eventually grant the new unit independence and retain its base in what would be Aden state. On paper the idea is irresistible. It promises the retention of the base, the creation of a quasi-viable economic unit, and the dilution of the influence of Aden colony's radical nationalists. In practice it proved impossible. Six of the sheikhs agreed to federation in 1959. More joined later, and Aden colony was then pushed into the federation, which was given the name of the Federation of South Arabia. Both Arab sides were unhappy. The sheikhs disliked merging with the people of Aden, whom they scorned as urban dwellers and feared as radical nationalists. Most of those who were politically active in Aden colony regarded the sheikhs as reactionary and pawns of the British and the federation as a means of perpetuating British political and military control of the area. At this stage the British intended to maintain control of the base at Aden indefinitely. The constitution of the federation, for example, permitted Aden to secede after six years, but the path to independence was closed: Aden out of the federation could only regain its status as a British possession.

A number of events combined to defeat this plan. The overthrow of the monarchy in Yemen in 1962 started a civil war there. Egypt intervened in Yemen and through Yemen gave aid to nationalists in Aden who needed little prompting to raise rebellion against the British and their federation. Terrorism began in Aden in 1963 with a grenade attack on the British High Commisioner, who survived thanks to the efforts of an aide who was killed by the explosion. Guerrilla warfare began upcountry in Radfan in 1964, and the British army intervened in force and destroyed the guerrillas. Thereafter, the British army fought the urban terrorism of two nationalist factions, who also began to fight one another ferociously as British withdrawal drew closer. In October 1964, the Labor government of Harold Wilson took office pledged to withdrawal east of Suez. The same year the British government announced the new federation would become independent by the end of 1968. Two years later, as terrorism intensified, the British government announced that they would not attempt to maintain British troops or a military base in Aden after independence in 1968.

The announcement in 1966 of total withdrawal from Aden is full of implications, and the defense message that year itself represents an important change in postwar British foreign policy.* The announcement revealed Britain's inability and the Labor government's unwillingness to maintain a foreign base against widespread and violent opposition. The decision to quit Aden was another step away from the maintenance of worldwide overseas deployments and toward a decision to concentrate Britain's political and military resources in Western Europe, a decision that was to come just two years later. Even the Labor government yielded grudgingly to Britain's weakness. British forces in the Persian Gulf were to be strengthened by a small increase, the government declared: "We shall give up the base at Aden and disengage ourselves until we have reached the hard core of our obligations to the States in the Persian Gulf." The British actually withdrew from Aden on Novem-

---

* In the 1966 defense statement, the British government announced major reductions in the defense budget and placed a three-year ceiling on defense expenditures. In this way, they hoped to be able to cut the 1969–70 defense budget by £400 million or 16 percent. Britain would maintain major forces outside Europe, subject to three limitations: (1) Britain would undertake no major war operations except with allies; (2) no military assistance would be given to any country unless Britain received all facilities necessary to make the assistance effective in good time; and (3) "there will be no attempt to maintain defense facilities in an independent country against its wishes." The Conservative government had always based its description of British defense policy on Britain's three alliances. In this first important Labor message on defense the SEATO alliance was not mentioned by name, and CENTO was mentioned on the same level as a treaty with Libya and "responsibilities" in Cyprus.

ber 29, 1967. The National Liberation Front, one of the competing factions, defeated the sheikhs and its opponent, the Front for the Liberation of South Yemen, and established the People's Republic of Yemen
after the British withdrawal. Meanwhile, the "hard core" proved extremely soft. On January 16, 1968, two months after devaluing the
pound, Prime Minister Wilson announced the decision to withdraw all
British forces from east of Suez by the end of 1971.

The decision of January 1968 had little effect in the Sultanate of
Oman. An exchange of letters in 1955 between the British government
and the former sultan now defines Britain's obligations there. In the letters, the British agreed to train and equip the sultan's forces in exchange for landing rights on the island of Masirah off Oman's southern
coast. The present sultan, Qabus, took power in July 1970 in a palace
coup. He ousted his father, a man bound to the past, in order to enable
the country to deal more effectively with its backwardness and the en-
demic rebellion in Dhofar, led by the Popular Front for the Liberation
of the Occupied Arab Gulf. Plainly, Britain maintains a commitment to
Oman and gives it force by sending small numbers of men and arms to
that country. The risk of a larger British involvement, nonetheless,
seems slight, for it would require both a major shift in policy and a
stronger British economy. Neither seems likely in the immediate future.

In the Persian Gulf, the message of January 1968 deprived the
sheikhdoms of the director of their external policy and defense. The
message also gave warning to the principal local powers, Iran, Iraq, and
Saudi Arabia, and to the major powers, the Soviet Union and the
United States, that the time would soon come for a rearrangement of influence and power in the gulf. The immediate solution of the British
was a familiar one: the trucial sheikhdoms would form a federation that
would create an entity large enough to have some hopes of survival and
economic progress.

The sheikhs and the British began negotiations in 1968 with all nine
of the small gulf states, including Bahrein and Qatar. On December 2,
1971, after nearly four years and the departure of Bahrein and Qatar,
the Union of Arab Amirates was born as an independent state, the
132nd member of the United Nations and the 18th member of the Arab
League. The union is actually a confederation of the seven small enti-
ties. Its highest body is the federal supreme council composed of the
seven rulers. A vote of five of the seven, including the assent of the rulers of oil-rich Abu Dhabi and Dubai (whose incomes are respectively
about 340 and fifty times greater than the combined incomes of all the
other five), is required to enact laws. The constitution permits the
wealthiest rulers to repeat their terms as president and vice-president. A
prime minister and council have executive authority. Most of these

posts are held by members of the ruling families and their allies. The constitution also established a legislature composed of forty members appointed by the rulers for terms of two years. It may discuss and approve the budget and legislation submitted by the ministers.

The provisions for the union's defense show signs of Britain's concern to protect its oil interests in the sheikhdoms and the flow of investments to London. Britain and the union replaced the old treaties of protection with an agreement to consult in case of need. The Trucial Oman Scouts became the Union Defense Force. The new Defense Force is led by two dozen British officers and a hundred British noncommissioned officers. It is a mercenary force, 1,700 strong, subject in practice to the control of the rulers of Abu Dhabi and Dubai, who comprise most of the federal government and all of the Higher Defense Council.

This new desert flower is delicate as well as exotic. It can survive only in a temperate domestic and foreign climate, marked by the absence of radical internal attack and the presence of considerable international equilibrium. Such a climate exists now thanks to the conflicting antagonisms and interests of the principal local and major powers. The union is particularly vulnerable to a sudden advance by Saudi Arabia or Iran or both, perhaps in the wake of real or imagined rebellion. The Iranians demonstrated their ability to make this kind of move when they seized the islands of Abu Musa and Greater and Lesser Tumbs on November 30, 1971, just before Britain terminated its protection of the sheikhdoms. The strength of Iran's army will increase dramatically in the next decade, for on July 24, 1971, as Britain left the gulf, Britain and the United States pledged to extend a billion dollars of military aid to Iran, to include missile-equipped frigates, helicopters, and eight hundred tanks. The Iranian armed forces are four times the size of the Saudi and twice as large as those of Iraq. The gross national product of Iran is twice as large as that of any other Arab state, and only Egypt possesses a larger population.[38] At the same time Iran's margin of strength over its neighbors on the gulf discourages any overt military action on their part, during a crisis that same margin of superiority may tempt Iranian leaders into following the pattern of sudden armed intervention, along the lines of the recent Indian and Israeli military successes. Monarchies are not necessarily conservative when it comes to using military force. The potential for hostility between Arab and Persian and uncertainty about the reactions of the Russians and Americans, impose restraint on all sides, as does the desire to avoid damaging and interrupting oil production. But these are rational restraints, and the gossamer strands of reason seldom confine either wars or governments. It is perhaps safe to conclude only that her decisions since 1961 to shrink the armed forces and remove them from the

Middle East will deny Britain a significant role of her own in the settlement of any important disputes in the Gulf in the future.

The years since Suez and the Iraqi revolution have been active and costly for Britain in the Middle East. The changes in British policy forced by domestic opposition and economic difficulty showed most obviously there, at the margin of British strength. In 1961, an informed British observer could declare that British forces were in Aden "to defend the British protected states of the Persian Gulf and the Aden Protectorates, both those that have oil and those that have not, against subversion from within or aggression from their independent neighbors." [39] Scarcely seven years later, a British prime minister announced the withdrawal of all British forces from the Far East and the Persian Gulf, arguing in part: "There is no military strength, whether for Britain or for our alliances except on the basis of economic strength. . . . We therefore intend to make to the alliances of which we are members a contribution related to our economic capability while recognizing that our security lies fundamentally in Europe and must be based on the North Atlantic Alliance. . . . It is not only at home that . . . we have been living beyond our means."

The Conservative government of Edward Heath, elected in June 1970 with the firmest intentions "to enable Britain to resume, within her resources, a proper share of responsibility for the preservation of peace and stability in the world," have managed no change in the gulf and contribute a battalion and a few destroyers to the five-power defense of Malaysia and Singapore.[40]

At the United Nations Britain now leans toward the Arab side, particularly in regard to debates and resolutions about the conflict with Israel. The rule seems to be for Britain to be more partial to the Arabs than is the United States and somewhat less partial than France. In Big Four discussions on the Middle East Britain has played a cooperative if invisible role. British initiatives have also come reluctantly and sometimes not at all. In September 1970, for example, during the civil war in Jordan between King Hussein and the Palestinians, Britain apparently declined an American proposal for joint intervention to save Hussein's government. In contrast, on September 17, President Richard Nixon told a group of newspaper editors: "The United States is prepared to intervene directly in the Jordanian civil war should Syria and Iraq enter the conflict and tip the military balance against the government forces loyal to King Hussein." Three days later Syrian tanks entered Jordan, and on September 21 the Department of Defense in Washington disclosed that 20,000 American troops had been alerted for movement to the Middle East.

Only twelve years before Britain had matched the American landings in Lebanon with a British intervention in Jordan. Now the British resorted to an unarmed diplomacy. On September 17, the British government requested Jordan and the Palestinian commandos to safeguard the lives of British citizens. On the day Syrian tanks entered Jordan Britain asked for a statement by the Big Four opposing foreign intervention, and on September 21 the Foreign Office, through the Soviet ambassador in London, requested the Soviet Union to persuade Syria to withdraw from Jordan.

Economic necessity seems to have been more important than strategic thought in causing the British government to abandon a major role in the Middle East. One observer, F. S. Northedge, concluded in an article in *International Affairs,* January 1970, that the British found it extremely difficult and painful to accept the idea that Britain had ceased to be a world power, and that this "psychological inertia" led to "a most characteristic behavior pattern of Britain since the Second World War: the tendency to be driven towards decisions and policies not because they are the most desirable, or least undesirable, options currently available, but because other options have ceased to be available."

To the extent that strategy informed the decisions to withdraw, three arguments carried most of the weight. First, the presence of British troops aggravates the domestic troubles of the very regimes Britain most wishes to spare such troubles. Second, Britain alone cannot stop any major invasion in Asia or the Middle East. Last, there is no use for military force in protecting British (and implicitly Western) oil interests in the Middle East. The presence and military action of large numbers of British troops in 1956 and 1967 utterly failed to prevent the interruption of oil supplies to Europe.

These arguments give the logic of withdrawal. They offer little help to those who ask how to make peace in the eastern Mediterranean, or how to combine diplomacy and military force in such a way as to assure adequate oil supplies and stable currencies for the industrially advanced nations as their dependency on Middle Eastern oil grows. But that is appropriate, for Britain by herself can offer little help in solving these problems. If the Western European nations ever fashion joint foreign and defense policies, the British may find a use for their experience and knowledge of the Middle East, helping a greater Europe to protect its oil and impart a modicum of order and stability to its relations with the governments of the Middle East. Meanwhile, there is only "the decay of that colossal wreck," Britain in the Middle East.

❀ 3 ❀

NASEER H. ARURI
and NATALIE K. HEVENER

France and the Middle East

THE OTTOMAN EMPIRE

The Ottoman Empire reached the zenith of its power under Suleiman the Magnificent (1520–66). He conquered Belgrade, the gateway to Central Europe, in 1521, and during the following year he entered Rhodes and established hegemony in Persia, Arabia, and the Balkans. In their contest with the Hapsburgs for world supremacy, the Ottomans were able to enlist the support of France, particularly after the latter's defeat in 1525 by the Hapsburgs. The French-Ottoman alliance became an integral part of the European state system and a factor in the balance of power.

The treaty of 1535 concluded by Suleiman the Magnificent and Francis I formalized this alliance against the Hapsburgs and remained for three centuries as the basis of French-Ottoman collaboration. George Lenczowski stated in the opening pages of *The Middle East in World Affairs* that "a strong Ottoman Empire was a conscious aim of France and the maintenance of its integrity became an axiom of French foreign policy a long time before England gave thought to Turkish questions." Agreements modeled on the first Treaty of Capitulations (1535) were signed between France and the Ottoman Empire at various intervals. Such agreements provided the countries with extraterritorial jurisdiction over their nationals residing in each other's countries. The agreements also provided for exemptions from customs duties and other taxes.

Ottoman power began to dwindle in the latter part of the seventeenth century. The Hapsburgs entered into an alliance with Poland and Venice in 1684 and defeated the Ottomans in the Battle of Vienna, which ended with the Treaty of Karlowitz. This treaty was a turning point in the history of the Ottoman Empire. Henceforth, the Ottoman sultan became preoccupied with the survival of the empire and the maintenance of its territorial integrity. The major European powers—including Russia, Austria, Britain, and France—embarked upon a series of diplomatic and military moves designed to fill the vacuum created by the erosion of Ottoman power but to prevent the complete disintegration of the empire and disruption of the balance of power. British and French interests in the Mediterranean placed them against Russia, which was aiming to secure an outlet to the warm waters of the Mediterranean and assert itself as the protector of Orthodox Christianity in the Ottoman realm.

Throughout the nineteenth century, Britain and France cooperated against Russian imperialism. They helped the Ottomans against Russia in the Crimean War (1854–56). This war was caused by a local dispute for control of the Holy Places in Palestine between French-supported Catholics and Russian-supported Orthodox Christians. France and Lebanon, after Russia's defeat, began to consolidate her economic, cultural, and strategic interests in the Middle East. Having acquired the status of Special Guardian of the Maronite Catholic Ottomans by a 1649 decree, France, in the aftermath of the Crimean War, was able to push forward her claim as the champion of Catholicism in the Levant. In Mount Lebanon, where power had passed to the Maronite Shihabis in 1756, France emerged as the most influential of the Western powers. Her influence was challenged by the British who supported a rival sect, the Druze. Exploitation of local animosities by the big powers gave rise then, as it does now, to communal warfare and ethnic conflicts.

Between 1841 and 1860, France and Britain attempted to divide Mount Lebanon into Druze and Christian districts. They forced the Ottoman sultan in 1841 to set up a local council organized along sectarian lines. The council was a short-lived experiment in sectarian politics. A Druze uprising against the French-supported Maronites in 1860 precipitated French intervention. Although the Ottoman government was able to restore order, the French refused to evacuate the region, but after a nine-month occupation were forced by Britain to withdraw. With help from the big powers, Lebanon's Christian region was separated from Syria in 1864 and declared an autonomous *sanjaq* (district) ruled by a Christian governor. This arrangement was a compromise alternative to French demands that Lebanon be set up as a French protectorate.

Despite France's inability to rule Lebanon directly, French interest flourished under this arrangement and French predominance in Lebanon was recognized by the Vatican and reflected in the Berlin Treaty (1878) which permitted the Catholic authorities in Lebanon to conduct their affairs with local officials through French diplomatic representatives. The Jesuits revived their order, suspended by the Pope since

1773, and founded the Université de St. Joseph in 1875 along with an important Catholic printing press. By 1914, nearly half the school children attended French Catholic institutions. The Roman Catholic Church was becoming an instrument of French foreign policy, compensating for the failure of French merchants (French East India Company) to open up parts of the Levant for trade with France.

EGYPT IN THE NINETEENTH CENTURY

Britain vied with France for power in the east Mediterranean in order to protect her trade route to India. When Napoleon conquered Egypt in 1798 and sought to threaten this route, England joined the Ottomans and defeated his fleet at Abouqir off the Egyptian coast. He abandoned his troops and returned to France in 1800 but soon afterward Egypt was occupied by Muhammad Ali, an Albanian soldier, who was recognized by the Ottoman sultan as the viceroy of Egypt in 1805. Muhammad Ali, who sought to expand his power in Syria and Palestine (1831–40) at the expense of the Ottomans, relied upon French help. Britain, which backed the sultan, occupied Aden to outflank France and Muhammad Ali and expelled the latter from Syria in 1840.

Although French colonial ambitions were frustrated by Britain, French cultural and commercial activities flourished throughout the Ottoman Empire. Napoleon, who hoped to encourage commercial interests in the Ottoman realm, was accompanied during the Egyptian campaign by French experts in the fields of medicine, engineering, history, agriculture, and linguistics; their mission was to transform Egypt into a modern society and make it profitable to France. But the task of modernizing Egyptian society fell on the shoulders of Muhammad Ali, whose admiration for Western technology and military organization led him to invite a French military mission and a host of French technicians in 1810. These technicians were active in all areas relating to economic, military, and technological development. A school of medicine was founded at Abuzabel and became an important center for the translation into Arabic and Turkish of works on medicine and science in European languages. French technicians helped Egypt establish steel foundries, a ship-building plant, and factories for sugar refining, glass, armament, woolen products, and cotton. Muhammad Ali sent 339 students to France and Britain for technical and humanistic training between 1813 and 1848. His program of modernization alarmed the Ottoman sultan and Britain, which remained concerned about her trade routes. In 1840, the Ottoman sultan and most of the big European powers except France defeated Muhammad Ali and put an end to his modernization efforts. These efforts were reversed during the rule of Ali's successors, Abbas and Said. Said, who ruled between 1854 and 1863, gave Ferdinand de Lesseps, a former French consul-general and engineer, the concession to construct the Suez Canal, which was opened in 1869. It seemed that the Suez Canal would be important as a spearhead of French influence in Egypt, but with the purchase of Egypt's interest by Britain in 1875, the latter emerged as the dominant European power in Egypt. Britain subsequently invaded and occupied Egypt (1882) and it was not until 1954 that this occupation was ended completely. While Britain insisted that her occupation was temporary, France did not cease to remind her of this for twenty years.

Anglo-French rivalry, however, was transformed into an alliance to check the rising influence of Germany. The traditional rivals met in July 1898 in southern Sudan as they were striving for control of Africa. The British threatened to drive France out, but a compromise solution was reached. Both powers realized that the continuation of hostilities would work to Germany's advantage. France agreed in 1904 to refrain from reminding Britain of her "temporary occupation" of Egypt, and Britain agreed to recognize a French sphere of influence in Morocco. France had already occupied Algeria (1830) and Tunisia (1883).

The Anglo-French Entente of 1904 ended French colonial ambitions in Egypt, but it recognized French cultural influence there such as the right to maintain schools and to nominate the Director-General of the Egyptian Antiquities. By the end of the nineteenth century French political influence was felt in Lebanon, Tunisia, Algeria, and Morocco. Her commercial and cultural influence, however, was felt throughout the Ottoman Empire. The Ottoman Bank was reestablished in 1863 with a majority of French and British capital. It issued banknotes and set up branches in all the principal cities of the empire. A program of public works and communications was initiated with French help in the Empire in the 1860s, and in 1868, the French obtained a concession for the construction of a railroad between Salonika and Constantinople. In the same year a program of secular education was launched with French encouragement. This secular education encouraged generations of Egyptians, Syrians and Turks to challenge the pan-Islamic ideas which flourished in the second half of the nineteenth century.

Morroe Berger wrote in *Bureaucracy and Society in Egypt* that the Egyptian public bureaucracy resembles the French more than the British despite the fact that British political influence was greater. The early phase of Egyptian nationalist thought assumed a Western liberal orientation as a result of French influence. Rifa'a Rafi al-Tahtawi (1801–73), one of the first and most important Egyptian intellectuals to attempt to reconcile Islam with European rationalist thought, was associated with the school of medicine at Abuzabel, which had been established by Muhammad Ali under French guidance. Tahtawi, whose early education was religious, traveled to France to study European civilization. Upon his return to Egypt, he promoted a program of translations, particularly in political theory and science.

Arab nationalism in Syria and Lebanon at the close of the nineteenth century also assumed a pro-French orientation.

WORLD WAR I

The First World War completed the subordination of the Arab people to Western political control. The Entente powers—Britain, France, and Russia—began to divide the Ottoman Empire into zones of influence in March 1915. It was clear that France was interested in Syria, including Palestine and Cilicia. The Sykes-Picot Agreement, which was drawn up secretly by Britain and France in May 1916, designed an area from Damascus to Mosul for direct French control. Britain was to control an area from Kirkuk in Iraq to Gaza in Palestine. It must be pointed out that Britain had entered into negotiations with Sharif Hussein of Mecca with the object of enlisting Arab support in the war against Turkey. Sir Henry McMahon, the British High Commissioner in Egypt, began a correspondence with Sharif Hussein on July 14, 1915, which continued until January 1916. Hussein promised to declare war on Turkey, and McMahon pledged England to support the independence of the Arabs in the large area bounded, in the north by the 37th parallel, in the east by the Iranian border down to the Persian Gulf and in the south by the Arab Gulf States. The coastal belt of Syria, lying to the west of the districts of Damascus, Homs, Hama, and Aleppo, were excluded on the grounds that they were largely Christian. According to the Sykes-Picot Agreement, the zone between the French and British territories was to form the independent Arab state promised by McMahon on behalf of the British government. But contrary to the promise, this zone was to be divided into spheres of influence for Britain and France. The French government agreed "after great difficulties" that the towns of Damascus, Homs, Aleppo, and Hama be included in the Arab dominions to be administered by the Arabs under French influence.

It was obvious that Britain had made conflicting promises to France and to the Arabs. Not until December 1917 did the Arabs discover the facts of Sykes-Picot as a result of publication of the secret agreement by the newly proclaimed Bolshevik government in Russia.

In May 1919 President Woodrow Wilson appointed a commission composed of Henry King and Charles Crane to make an assessment of the desires of the population in the Middle East. The King-Crane Commission reported on August 28 that the Arabs opposed French rule and Zionist colonization. France had refused to participate in the commission and vigorously invoked the provisions of Sykes-Picot at the Paris Peace Conference in 1919. France regarded all northern Syria within her jurisdiction, while Britain seemed interested in making minor revisions of the Sykes-Picot Agreement in order to guarantee her interest in the region and fulfill some of her promises to the Arabs. Britain argued that the Anglo-French joint declaration of November 8, 1918, which promised to encourage and assist in the establishment of indigenous governments in Syria and Mesopotamia, was to supersede the Sykes-Picot Agreement. Actually, Britain was now convinced that a friendly Arab state replacing the Ottoman Empire would serve as a bulwark of defense for her life-line to India. Moreover, Britain feared French ambitions in the Middle East.

In the end, however, and in spite of the recommendations of the King-Crane Commission, Britain acquiesced to France's demands and removed her troops from Syria and Cilicia, thus acceding to French control of these areas. The Arabs claimed them on the basis of the McMahon pledges to Sharif Hussein.

A general Syrian congress declared Syria independent in March 1920 and offered Faisal, Hussein's son, the Syrian crown. On April 24, 1920, at the San Remo Conference, France was assigned a mandate for Syria and Britain a mandate for Iraq and Palestine. Mosul was transferred from the French to the British zone of influence after Britain promised France a share in the Mosul oil deposits.

Faisal's assumption of the Syrian throne appeared to the French to be contrary to the decisions of the San Remo Conference and the Sykes-Picot Agreement. In the meantime the British had abandoned their Arab wartime allies. They sent Faisal to France to plead his case personally to the Council. But the realities of the military situation in Syria favored the French. General Gouraud, who had been appointed high commissioner and commander-in-chief of the French army replacing British troops in Syria, sent Faisal an ultimatum on July 19, 1920. He demanded that Faisal recognize the French mandate in Syria and allow French forces to replace his own troops. Although Faisal acceded to France's demands, General Gouraud engaged Faisal's forces in the bat-

tle of Maisaloun and conquered Damascus on July 25. He claimed that
Faisal's reply had come after the time prescribed by the ultimatum.

THE MANDATES

The Act of Mandates signed under the auspices of the League of Nations on July 24, 1922, established France in the Levant as a Middle
Eastern power. They were all class A mandates designed to enable the
supposedly minor population of the area to develop a political sophistication and to arrive one day at self-government.

Politically, the French administration applied the old maxim of divide and rule. In an attempt to keep the population disunited, the man-
dated area was divided into five distinct regions—Lebanon, Damascus,
Jebel Druze, Latakia, and Aleppo. Lebanon was expanded to its present
borders in response to Maronite demands. This meant the addition of
Beirut, Tripoli, Tyre, and Sidon, all predominatly Muslim cities.
Greater Lebanon was proclaimed a state on August 20, 1920, and the
state of Syria was proclaimed on December 5, 1924. In both states
France authorized elections of constituent assemblies which drafted constitutions. They were modeled on the French pattern—a chamber of
deputies would elect a president for a five-year term, who would then
appoint a prime minister and cabinet. The system, however, remained
subservient to the French high commissioner who often suspended the
constitution, dissolved the national assembly, manipulated elections, and
suppressed opposition.

By the time World War II broke out, it was clear that both the
French and British mandates had failed to institute the principle of
self-government. Whenever the local governments in Syria and Lebanon
asserted an independent role in political affairs, the high commissioner
stepped in. Nor did the French permit the area under its control to develop an independent economy. Railroads, banks, and public utilities
were controlled by France.

Independence was proclaimed during the Second World War. The
Vichy regime was defeated in Syria by the British in 1941. The government of General de Gaulle reached an agreement with Syria and Lebanon which would lead to their independence on September 28, 1941.
But France remained unwilling to transfer the functions of government
to the new republics until 1946. De Gaulle insisted on a preferential arrangement which would give France exclusive military rights, supervision of foreign affairs, and linkage of the local currency with the franc.

Nationalist resistance between 1941 and 1946 was dealt with ruthlessly by the French. Damascus was subjected to French air and artillery bombardment on May 29, 1945. Finally, Britain intervened with a virtual ultimatum to the French to cease fire. France complied and on July 7, 1945, gave her consent to Syrian and Lebanese independence. In the following year, United Nations arrangements for French withdrawal were completed thus ending a tutelage which had lasted for twenty-five years.

Expelled from Syria and Lebanon, France turned to meet organized opposition in her colonies in Indochina and North Africa. "The overthrow of the Fourth Republic and the emergence of de Gaulle gave the appearance of a complete break with the past which enabled France to develop new relationships with her former possessions, in a way which has been completely denied to Britain," according to Ann Williams, in *Britain and France in the Middle East and North Africa*. Henceforth, France which declined as a colonial power, embarked on a policy of decolonization which earned her respect among the people of the Middle East and other parts of the Third World.

FRENCH POLICY SINCE 1945

Abiding French Interests

Since 1945 French policy toward the Middle East has undergone essential changes which are the direct result of the dissolution of French colonialism. The basic national interests which France pursued in the area from the original establishment of the colonies remain unchanged: economic interests in oil and trade; military interests in the strategic protection of the Mediterranean border and access to the oil; and political interests in the maintenance of France as a major power in the world, in part by retaining a capability to influence the actions of the Middle Eastern nations. Formerly, France depended upon her position in the colonies to provide the base of action for advancing her varied interests. Once political control was no longer possible, persuasion rather than domination provided the only means for implementing French policy.

Before De Gaulle

A major influence on every nation's policy in the Middle East is the Arab-Israeli conflict. During the Fourth Republic, France constructed its Middle East policy on the basis of the Tripartite Declaration (1950), according to which it pledged itself, along with Britain and the United States, to protect the independence and the "territorial integrity" of Israel. Both France and Israel were united in a common hatred of Arab nationalism. To France, Egypt was the principal source of aid for the Algerian nationalists. To Israel, Nasser was the idol of the Arab masses who sought to restore the rights of the Palestinians. Moreover, there was a natural affinity between "socialists" in France and in Israel who were in command of the affairs of state in the two countries. Together with the right-wing French Radicals who vowed to keep Algeria French, they helped bring about a French-Israeli entente. France became the crucial source of Israel's armaments which included the Mystere aircraft. At first arms were delivered secretly in violation of the Tripartite Declaration, but after the Czech arms deal with Egypt in 1955, France began to supply Israel openly with its most modern aircraft. Israel's first jet-engine plant was set up near Lydda in 1954 under a license from France. This plant began to manufacture Fouga Magister jet trainers and attack aircraft in 1958. In addition, France supplied Israel with exports and matériel from its nuclear complex at Pierrelatte under a 1957 secret agreement, and assisted in the construction of Israel's 24-megawatt nuclear reactor at Dimona. The Israeli author Michel Bar Zohar described the French mood during the early phase of the Algerian war by saying that France was extremely anxious to have someone who would fight against Nasser.[1] And in 1956 Britain joined Israel and France in an invasion of Egypt. France and Israel were not merely allies; they were now co-belligerents.

De Gaulle's Policy in World Perspective

The Suez crisis was soon followed by renewed hostilities in Algeria. The collapse of French control there coincided with (and was in fact responsible for) the 1958 return to power of Charles de Gaulle and the advent of the French Fifth Republic. De Gaulle's policy toward the Middle East was derived from his over-all plan for the future of France in the world. This plan arose from his general aversion to bipolarism which he believed was corresponding less and less to the real situation. Hence, French diplomacy aimed at the development of a third force with sufficient strength and independence to influence significantly the behavior of the big powers. This third force requires a minimum degree of conformity. It makes few demands of its members; it is not monolithic; it does not call for modification or alterations in domestic policies. The states involved make only a general policy commitment to promote the aims of the force.

Leadership of the force would afford France an independent posture enabling her to play an active and constructive global role. De Gaulle asserted that "France is sure of serving the balance, the peace, and progress of the world." [2] Moreover, this independent posture was designed to restore freedom to French decision-makers and enhance French international prestige. By following an independent policy, France hoped to redress the imbalance of dissuasion and help create conditions in which recourse to the use of force is minimized. Realizing the currents of world evolution and the postwar developments in the international environment, de Gaulle proceeded to develop the means of accomplishing France's mission, i.e., a French-led third force.

He relied primarily on diplomacy, new and old, refining and then abandoning sophistication, but always making his message clear. He moved in several directions at this level, developing a policy to attain his objective. First, he stressed the responsibility of the big powers, including France in this group, for settling international issues. Secondly, he made use of the United Nations, limited by the restriction that French consent must be a prerequisite for peace-keeping operations. This participation in international organization was an extension of the first point into an already structured setting. Thirdly, de Gaulle sought a nonaligned position, breaking free of the United States and Britain without allying himself on the side of the Soviet Union or China. De Gaulle himself affirmed this position at the Kremlin in stating: "I am not displeased to have the U.S.S.R. as a counterweight to American hegemony, and I am no more displeased to have the United States as a counterweight to Soviet hegemony." [3] Fourthly, he appealed to potential participants to consider their position and to realign themselves with France in the third force. He emphasized that the force requires a presence on all five continents to insure the possibility of mediation and to present alternatives to domination by the United States, the USSR, or China. To implement this aspect of the policy, de Gaulle capitalized on nationalist sentiments in both Latin America and Canada. In Asia he embarked on developing relations with key nations such as India and Japan which are potentially in the Chinese sphere of influence, and he sought to recover French influence in embattled Southeast Asia. He exchanged visits with leaders of Eastern Europe and complimented Romania on her independent policy. In Africa, he sustained the French position through affirmation of cultural ties with former colonies; in the Middle East, he restored French prestige almost overnight.

De Gaulle's Policy Before the June War

De Gaulle began remolding French policy in the area almost as soon as he took office. He astutely removed the Algerian hurdle, in accordance with a policy of decolonization, thus ending France's personal quarrel with Nasser. The Socialist Party of Guy Mollet, which allied itself with Ben-Gurion's party, was now out of office. And the French Radicals along with Israeli supporters of the Organization de l'Armée Secrète conspiracy against de Gaulle were now held suspect by the Fifth Republic. In the meantime French enterprises had suffered tremendous losses in the Middle East because of the Suez war and the Algerian situation. It was against this background that de Gaulle's government began to reassess its policy in the Middle East. It rediscovered the Arab world where it once possessed cultural influence and hoped to recover that influence and to participate in the exploitation of the region's natural resources. Diplomatic relations were reestablished with the United Arab Republic following the Evians accord which ended the Algerian conflict in 1962.

As for Israel, France still remained the main supplier of modern armaments. Between 1961 and 1964, Israel secretly purchased from France seventy-two Mirage 3-C warplanes. Israeli technicians forwarded suggestions for improvement of the Mirage S jetplanes, and Israeli pilots helped demonstrate these jets before purchase by South Africa, Australia, and Switzerland. Moreover, according to the *Christian Science Monitor,* January 1, 1970, the French arms manufacturer, Marcel Dassault, supplied Israel with twenty-five surface-to-surface missiles (MD 660) capable of carrying warheads of 1,000–1,200 pounds, with a range of 280 miles. When Ben-Gurion paid a state visit to France in 1961, de Gaulle told him that he considered Israel a friendly and allied nation. Arabs and Israelis alike respected France's new look at the Middle East. The influential foreign editor of *Le Monde,* André Fontaine, said in an interview with the British Broadcasting Corporation in 1966 that de Gaulle was popular in the Arab states and Israel and alluded to the approval of both Tel Aviv and Cairo of de Gaulle's reelection in the 1967 French presidential elections.

De Gaulle and the June War

As long as de Gaulle was able to keep French policy in a middle position and remain nonaligned in the Middle East, he could conceivably pursue a course of action that would maximize his objectives without risking his security. This reasoning was behind his actions during the crisis of May and June of 1967. France remained publicly silent in regard to the crisis until May 24, when Israel's foreign minister, Abba Eban, met with de Gaulle while en route to London and Washington. Naturally, Eban was seeking to determine the extent of backing his country could expect from the Western powers. Specifically, he wanted to know whether these powers intended to carry out a 1957 commitment to insure free navigation in the Gulf of Aqaba for Israeli ships, the *New York Times* reported on May 26, 1967. In return for this commitment, Israel had agreed to evacuate Egyptian territories captured during the Sinai campaign in 1956.

The response of France was motivated by a desire for noninvolvement. Conscious of this situation, de Gaulle attempted to dissuade the two parties from starting hostilities. At the conclusion of the talks with Eban, the French government issued a statement through George Gorse, the information minister. In this statement Gorse was critical of the withdrawal of the United Nations Emergency Force (UNEF) from Sinai, Gaza, and Sharm el-Sheikh; but he hastened to add that the Egyptian request and U Thant's approval were perfectly legal. He noted that it might have been wiser politically to consult with the big powers before taking such action. Similarly, the statement, carried in the *New York Times* on May 25, 1967, endorsed the principle of free navigation in the Gulf of Aqaba, noting that such free passage exists between the Aegean and the Black Sea. The *New York Times,* May 26, reported unofficially that while in Paris, Abba Eban received the impression that whereas France supported free shipping through the Straits of Tiran, it nevertheless took notice of Egypt's legal position that the acceptance of UNEF did not insure freedom of navigation for Israel. As a further illustration of its neutrality, France refrained from joining Britain and the United States in challenging the validity of the Aqaba blockade. It should be noted that several maritime nations expressed similar reservations about the United States efforts to challenge the blockade. Among them were Italy, Germany, Sweden, Japan, Portugal, Netherlands, Turkey, India, Finland, and Australia, according to *Le Monde,* June 4–5, 1967.

France no longer based its policy on the Tripartite Declaration as did Britain and the United States. In fact, France considered the Tripartite Declaration unrealistic and irrelevant, since it did not take into account the fact that Russia had become a power in the Middle East shortly after the declaration was signed, and since the withdrawal of UNEF and the blockade of Aqaba did not, in France's view, threaten the territorial integrity of Israel, let alone its destruction.

For these reasons the tripartite agreement did not afford a remedy; rather a Four Power conference was seen by France as corresponding more to the "real situation" than did the tripartite agreement. Moreover, since France's concern was to shift the confrontation from the military to the diplomatic plane, and to avoid a possible test of the 1957 commitment, the proposed conference was seen as the most rational course. The Soviet Union, having already blamed the United States for the crisis, was reluctant to participate in a top-level conference. It rejected the French proposal on May 30.

France, hoping to play a constructive role, took the position that agreement by the big powers was essential to positive action in the Security Council. And on June 2, de Gaulle issued a warning to both belligerents that any party initiating hostilities would have neither the approval nor the support of France. He also stated, as reported by *Le Monde* on June 3, that France would not involve itself directly on either side. "France is not pledged in any way, or in any respect, to any of the states concerned. On her own initiative, she considers that each of these states has the right to live. But she deems that the worst would be the opening of hostilities. Consequently, the state that would be the first— wherever it might be—to take up arms will not have either the approval and even less her support."

When all diplomatic efforts failed to prevent the outbreak of hostilities, and Israel struck on June 5, the French position continued to favor big power coordination in order to exert pressure on the belligerents. France reaffirmed its neutrality by suspending arms delivery to both sides in the crisis area, and urged others to do the same. The French ambassador to the United Nations, Roger Seydoux, called for a ceasefire and withdrawal to the previous positions. He spoke of French traditional ties to the region which France could preserve only by taking an objective view. He assured Israel of French sympathy with her concern about the right to exist, and expressed his government's understanding of Arab feelings about independence and dignity. Couve de Murville, the foreign minister, restated this position, saying that it would be unthinkable to alter twenty-five years of strong ties with the Jewish state or to compromise the cultural ties with the Arabs.

If France had upheld the 1957 agreement, it would have risked being involved militarily on Israel's side. The crucial issues of war and peace in the Middle East were seen as being more than the question of navigation in the Gulf of Aqaba; hence the need for the Four Power agreement on the broad issues which complicate peace. This frame of reference guided the French position; France hoped not only for a role in the big power councils, but possibly for a mediating role between Arabs and Israelis. France, alone among the big powers, was able, initially at least, to keep the confidence of the two antagonists.

France proceeded in a second attempt to win Soviet approval for the proposed big power agreement. The United States, which had accepted the idea prior to the June War, felt no compelling need for the big power conference, since the outcome of that war had created a status-quo not unfavorable to her interest. And so France oriented its policy at the United Nations toward giving greater emphasis to the responsibility of the Security Council for peace-making between Israel and the Arab states. Because the United States and the Soviet Union were divided on the basic issue, the Security Council, however, failed to yield any results. The *New York Times* reported on June 15 that the Soviet Union introduced a resolution to condemn the Israeli attack as the "grossest violation of the United Nations Charter and the generally recognized principles of international law." France abstained from voting, taking the position that the road to peace was not through condemnation but negotiation. And again, France abstained in regard to a second paragraph of the resolution which demanded the withdrawal of Israeli troops "immediately and unconditionally" behind the 1949 armistice lines. This was in agreement with the French view that long-range peace-making in the Middle East requires a discussion of *all* the issues involved. Withdrawal alone was not seen as the essential element of a settlement. Moreover, France, which had already criticized the withdrawal of UNEF, could not support a move calling for Israeli withdrawal behind the armistice lines, since the armistice had been superseded, though not legally, by UNEF.

The failure of the Security Council to reach an agreement on a Middle Eastern settlement on June 14 focused world attention on the General Assembly. The Soviet Union successfully requested a special session of the General Assembly, hoping to compensate for its failure in the Security Council.

While en route to New York to introduce the Soviet resolution at the General Assembly, Alexei Kosygin stopped in Paris on June 16 to solicit French support. De Gaulle stressed to him that French policy was one of "deliberate objectivity." Later, Couve de Murville assured the National Assembly that despite the meeting with Kosygin, the French position remained unchanged. This attitude was seen once again at the General Assembly, where France abstained from voting on the Soviet resolution. The failure of both organs of the United Nations served to demonstrate that durable peace requires the agreement of the big powers.

In the beginning of July, France took two steps which constituted a bid for Soviet cooperation and for a broad four power meeting. Premier Georges Pompidou traveled to the Soviet Union on July 3 to convince Soviet leaders of the need to work for the rights of all in a Middle East settlement. Specifically he sought Soviet recognition of the principle of free navigation in the Straits of Tiran and the Suez Canal. The joint communiqué, however, gave no indication that the Russians agreed. It called for withdrawal of troops from the Middle East and expressed agreement by the two nations to direct their efforts toward helping to create conditions for the preservation of peace in the Middle East. In the meantime, the French delegation at the United Nations supported a resolution introduced by Yugoslavia on behalf of the nonaligned nations. This resolution called on Israel to withdraw its troops immediately from all the occupied Arab territories. French support of this resolution stemmed from the paragraph which called for a subsequent Security Council action to settle the outstanding issues in the longstanding dispute. France had abstained on previous Soviet resolutions calling for withdrawal due to the absence of such provision. But again the powers were divided, with France and the Soviet Union supporting the Yugoslav resolution and Britain and the United States favoring a rival Latin American resolution which linked the withdrawal of Israel from the occupied Arab lands with the end of all states of belligerency. Both resolutions failed to win the necessary two-thirds vote for adoption.

The failure of the United Nations to break the impasse in the Middle East was but one more indication of the impossibility of a solution while the big powers had not themselves reached an agreement on the kind of settlement which they would jointly enforce. De Gaulle made use of every opportunity to express the view that only an effective concert of big powers could be useful under existing circumstances. He expressed concern, however, that the international environment was not ripe for such action, and that the Vietnam war had shattered the short-lived détente between the United States and the Soviet Union, making the possibility of a settlement in the Middle East remote.

A summary of the exact French position on the substantive aspects of the Middle East dispute is necessary for a meaningful evaluation of French capacities for peace. To the Arabs, France has repeatedly expressed disapproval of the threat to destroy Israel, stressing that each state in the area has the right to live and see its security guaranteed. The *New York Times,* June 22, 1967, reported that de Gaulle stated that his country "considers it just that each state concerned—notably Israel—be able to live. Consequently, France disapproved the threat to destroy Israel brandished by her neighbors and reserved our position as to the mortgage placed on that state in the case of navigation in the Gulf of Aqaba." This position was reaffirmed by de Gaulle in a letter to Ben-Gurion dated December 30, 1967, in which he said: "from the outset, my country and I myself did not spare our sympathy towards this construction of a nation (Israel), and you cannot doubt that, if necessary, we would have been opposed to its being annihilated, as guaranteed by our official conversations of former times and by the fact that in them I had publicly called Israel a 'friendly and allied state.' " [4]

But France condemned the opening of hostilities by Israel and refused to recognize any territorial changes based on military acquisition in violation of the United Nations Charter. She favored a settlement based on the evacuation of territories seized by force and the end of all belligerency coupled with recognition of each of the states involved by all the other states. Implying that certain frontier adjustments would be made, de Gaulle said in his November 27 news conference that after these first steps, the United Nations could assist in laying down "exactly the frontiers, conditions for life and security of both sides, the fate of the refugees and minorities and the details of free navigation for all in the Gulf of Aqaba and the Suez Canal." [5] According to the French position, Jerusalem must have an international status, contrary to Jordan's view that the Arab sector of Jerusalem belongs to Jordan. Contrary to Israel's policy of seeking a settlement through direct negotiations with the Arab states, France conceived of an international solution.

De Gaulle's first major statement in May calling for a meeting of the Big Four was interpreted as a request for Security Council action in the hope that the permanent members would be able to find a peaceful solution to the problem. This hope was behind de Gaulle's statement of June 3, warning both sides that France would not approve or support a resort to force. And this position remained once the hostilities had begun. In the French view the United Nations provides an effective organ for action only in the presence of big power consensus, and de Gaulle's policy was constantly aimed at improving the conditions in which agreement could be reached. When the Big Four talks finally got under way, shortly after Richard Nixon became president of the United States, the French government saw these talks as a vindication if its position. The minister of foreign affairs said on April 13, 1969: "The government welcomes with satisfaction the fact that the permanent members of the Security Council have met today in New York to seek a suitable means for starting the Middle East crisis on the path of a peaceful settlement. Convinced of the necessity of four-power action to prevent it even before the conflict began in June 1967, it had, on last January 15, again taken an initiative in this direction to try to bring to an end a situation which is deteriorating more and more each day." [6]

France took the same position among the big powers as she did among the parties in the crisis area: a position of nonalignment. A reflection of the positive moves taken in this direction was Couve de Murville's statement on August 31, carried in *Le Monde* on October 26, urging restoration of normal diplomatic relations between the Middle Eastern states and the big powers, that is, between the Arab countries and Britain and the United States on the one hand, and between Israel and the socialist-bloc nations on the other. The support of the British Resolution 242 adopted by the Security Council on November 22, 1967, which incorporated major points from both sides,* is an additional indication that the French view fell centrally between that of the United States and that of the Soviet Union. This independent stance is, of course, a continuation of the policy which de Gaulle began long ago. It earned France the confidence of all concerned in the region, Israel and the Arab republican regimes as well as the conservative monarchies. De Gaulle did not want to risk the loss of any country which might support his hopes for a third force. During a July visit to London, King Hussein was told by British Prime Minister Harold Wilson that direct negotiations with Israel would afford a solution to the crisis. De Gaulle, on the other hand, who viewed such advice as unrealistic, evoked an enthusiastic response by Hussein. The *Times* (London), July 5, 1967, reported that on emerging from his talks with de Gaulle, the king declared: "General de Gaulle has always had the goodness to be my friend and a friend of the Arab people. He has always courageously taken a stand for justice."

Israeli leaders, as would be expected, were critical of French policy on "moral" grounds, but as Moshe Dayan, the defense minister, recognized, the French position was neutral. Dayan also agreed with de Gaulle that the Middle East crisis would not be solved without the assent of the Soviet Union. The weekly overseas edition of the *Jerusalem Post,* December 18, 1967, said that Levi Eshkol, former premier of Israel, called de Gaulle a friend but suggested that he might be friendlier if he ended the embargo on the sale of fifty Mirage aircraft ordered by Israel prior to the war.

---

* The Security Council Resolution adopted November 22, 1967, emphasized the inadmissability of the acquisition of territory by force and the need to withdraw Israeli forces from territories occupied in the recent conflict. This is in line with Soviet and Arab demands. It further affirmed the necessity of terminating all claims or states of belligerency, of respecting the territorial integrity and political independence of all states, and of guaranteeing freedom of navigation in international waters. This is in line with United States and Israeli demands.

The United States and Britain were condemned by the Arabs as pro-Israel, and the Soviet Union was condemned by Israel as pro-Arab; but even though French inaction during the June War evoked some hostility on both sides, France alone among the big powers maintained its normal ties—diplomatic and otherwise—in the area. Surely, French policy was received more favorably by the Arabs than by Israel. But this was not due to any partiality toward the former. It was the change from previous hostility to neutrality which pleased the Arabs, and from co-belligerency to neutrality which disappointed Israel. In most Western capitals, where there exists a sense of guilt for past treatment of the Jews and a tendency to view the Jews as more "like us," the press was generally critical of what seemed to be a pro-Arab policy.

De Gaulle's Impact on the Arab World

In the Arab world, de Gaulle won wide praise from the revolutionary leaders and the traitional monarchs. Shortly after the war, Houari Boumediene, Algeria's president, addressed a message of appreciation for the "remarkable position" of neutrality which the French government had taken. De Gaulle then expressed satisfaction that French policy was understood. King Hussein expressed profound gratitude "for the sympathy and understanding" which de Gaulle had shown him during a difficult period. After an agreement was reached to widen economic relations and technical and cultural cooperation, the *Times* (London), July 5, said that Syria's foreign minister declared in Paris: "We came to express our people's appreciation of the independent political line followed by General de Gaulle."

France, which, since the Suez crisis in 1956 had lost all her cultural influence in Syria and Egypt, restored this influence overnight. According to the agreement concluded on December 15, reported in the *Jerusalem Post* on December 18, Syria agreed to "open her doors wide to French language and culture." In return, France pledged technical aid in the industrial and agricultural fields. After de Gaulle expressed his views on the Middle East at his sixteenth press conference on November 27, the *New York Times* reported on November 30, 1967, that Dr. Mohammed Zayyat, Egypt's official spokesman, said the general's remarks "show our people that there are people of principle and of courage in the West."

Libya's then prime minister, Abdul-Hamid Bakush, who visited Paris in April 1968, said, according to the *New York Times* on April 21: "France is more than ever the friend of the Arabs, especially at this moment when their territory is being invaded." Also during the same month, Saudi Arabia and Tunisia expressed approval of the French president's policy. De Gaulle's toast at a dinner honoring the Iraqi president, General Abdul Rahman Arif, on February 7, 1968, is especially illustrative of the new tie:

> It can be said that the circumstances which contradicted the counsels of sentiment and of good sense have changed profoundly. . . . For the Arab and the French peoples, who once again in history are beckoned toward renouncement by numerous sophisms and temptations, hegemonies could not be accepted; nor certainly, could it be accepted that these people and those who, everywhere, resemble them in this respect should forbid themselves to maintain on the outside the relations that are useful to them. But through respect for themselves and through awareness of what is owed to the *world balance,* they reject any enfeoffment, be it ideological, political, economic, or military. Hence, between them, there is an elemental solidarity that they have the best reasons to practice and to organize.[7]

And again, the French-Iraqi communiqué issued at the close of Arif's visit to France expressed the connection between French arms and independence from the superpowers: "General de Gaulle and General Arif also examined the problem raised in the military field and agreed that, above all, it is a matter for Iraq to affirm its *independence* and contribute to the maintenance of peace." [8] Moreover, the French inclination toward rapprochement with the Arab world was designed to keep a channel open between the Arabs and the West at a time when Arab disillusionment with the West had reached high proportions.

Finally, a French presence in the Arab world is in agreement with de Gaulle's policy of appealing to the Third World. France's independent political line which had previously been recognized in Cambodia, Latin America, and Eastern Europe has become more evident in view of recent French policy in the Middle East. In general, this policy has significantly increased opportunities for trade, cultural agreements, aid, and oil agreements between France and the Arab countries.

Economic and Political Effects of De Gaulle's Policy

The implications of de Gaulle's policy were even more far reaching than the immediate diplomatic response indicated. The general attitude of approval was translated into specific results in the various Arab nations. French economic, political, and cultural interests in the Middle East which survived the collapse of colonialism were greatly furthered by the policy initiated by de Gaulle.

The initial drive for raw materials (particularly fuel), markets, and investment opportunities, augmented by political status and strategic motivation, which led France to a colonization policy, persists today. Formerly France had dominated her territories with activity directed at maximizing the returns to French private business and government. Some of this activity indirectly provided benefits to the colonies. Most significant were the explorations which uncovered oil and natural gas; other important side effects were roads, ports, urbanization—general concomitants of colonial economic policy. Today, rather than controlling these nations, France's advanced economic position allows her to exercise leverage over her former colonies, in many instances justifying claims of neocolonialist activity.

We can best discuss the interdependent political and economic interests of France in the Middle East and her leverage there by artificially dividing the subject according to four topics: oil, currency, trade, and aid.

Oil

French economic interest in the area is rooted in the fuel supplies which are essential to her continued prosperity. The Arab world provides 90 percent of French oil needs, according to the *Middle East Economic Digest,* April 17, 1970. Algeria, which has the greatest economic involvement with France, was the hardest for France to lose, in part because of the economic loss it represented. French companies have been responsible for 70 percent of the oil production of Algeria. The two major companies are Elf-Erap, which is state controlled, and Compagnie Francaise des Petroles (CFP), 35 percent of which is government controlled. At present Algeria is providing about 30 percent of the fuel needs of France, so that France relies heavily on maintaining good relations with Sonatrach, the Algerian state-owned organization for oil. Sonatrach is responsible for 30 percent of the oil production of Algeria.

In 1962, through certain provisions of the Evian agreements, which ended the Algerian War of Independence, France attempted to insure that French companies would continue to maintain the major position in fuel exploitation. The Algerian government consented to an equal division of the profits based on the realized price rather than fixed tax-reference price. This question of tax-reference price is quite important in the context of the weakening of the Middle East oil oligopoly which has been able to fix and maintain high prices. Now, with crude oil outrunning refinery facilities, the competition can drive the prices down as all compete to unload their crude oil. CFP, having obtained crude oil from new areas, including Iraq, is selling crude oil at discounted prices, below that of the posted price which would ordinarily be used for tax purposes. Thus, CFP may increase revenue by increasing total sales, although the separate Middle Eastern nations lose because the price of the oil has fallen (and for many this means fallen revenue as well).

In 1965 a new French-Algerian arrangement provided for a tax-reference posted price to safeguard oil revenues. France agreed to provide Algeria with two hundred million francs a year for five years (160 million francs in twenty-year low-interest loans and 40 million francs in direct loans, according to the *Middle East Economic Digest,* March 5, 1971); the money was to be devoted to exploration for new sources of oil. The 1965 agreement provided for a revision after December 31, 1968, and a general revision in 1970. Accordingly the Algerian government notified the French companies in January 1969 that the reference prices set by the agreement of July 29, 1965, had to be considered provisional as of January 1, 1969. Moreover, the companies were advised in March to post prices in line with the international market ($2.61–$2.66 per barrel).[9] Negotiations on the revision of the reference prices were officially opened on November 24, 1969. The Algerian government requested a new price of $2.85 per barrel. France on the other hand conceded a rise from $2.08 to $2.16, which would be increased by increments to $2.31 in 1975. After fifty-two days of negotiations over a period of fifteen months the parties failed to arrive at a compromise. The French government suspended the negotiations on February 4, 1971, thus causing Algeria to nationalize the gas fields and pipelines and to take over a 51 percent share of the French oil-producing companies on February 24. The Algerian government pledged to indemnify the French companies for the nationalized portion of their interests and to continue supplying France with Algerian oil at market prices. The French government protested the move and showed its influence on the Algerian economy through a boycott * which pushed Sonatrach into an agreement which raised the amount of compensation substantially above the original offer but not as high as the French demand. However,

---

* The boycott, which involved cessation of purchases of Algerian wine and other Algerian products, expanded to further hostile economic measures: pressure against Algerian products exported elsewhere; pressure against aid to the country; threats against purchasers of the disputed oil; and withdrawal by the oil companies of their technical advisors in Algeria.

France still plays the major role in fuel exploration and extraction; she knows her interests are best served through compromise with the Algerian government, and by July, the head of the Foreign Relations Committee of the French National Assembly was satisfied that France and Algeria had restored their common bond. The *New York Times,* February 26, 1971, reported that Michel Debré, the defense minister who deplored the nationalization measures, insisted that Mediterranean solidarity be held paramount; otherwise, "insecurity and foreign powers will prevail." The French premier, Jacques Chaban-Delmas, expressed the view before the French National Assembly that cooperation between France and Algeria will continue as long as it is of common interest and "in that case only." He told the National Assembly on April 20, 1971, that "our ties with Algeria are too ancient, too numerous, too important . . . to be ended." However, it can be said that relations between the two countries have ceased to be privileged.

The nationalization presented France with a moral dilemma. On the one hand the French government did not question the sovereign right of Algeria to nationalize, an attitude which conforms with France's liberal attitude toward her former colonies. President Pompidou himself often spoke of Africanization of capital and personnel. But when Algeria did just that, France's attitude revealed a mercantilist tendency.

The oil dispute between France and Algeria persuaded the latter to diversify its trading partners. Companies from Britain, Belgium, Italy, and the United States are now involved in building gas liquefaction plants, textile mills, and pipelines in Algeria.

The problems France encountered in transforming her economic role in Algeria from domination to cooperation were fundamentally similar to those she encountered in Tunisia. The severity of the problems were reduced, however, by (1) the absence of vital French economic concerns; (2) the relatively smaller size of the resources and investment involved; and (3) the consequent relative simplification of the termination of colonialism.

In Tunisia the small homogeneous population, the strong single-party political system, and the acceptance of Bourguiba's leadership have provided an environment conducive to investment and development. The relative success of the Tunisian economic and political system has facilitated continued French cultural, political, and economic involvement. The modest size and importance of Tunisian activity tends to remove economic issues from the political arena, thereby simplifying their solution. In addition, the absence of revolutionary ideology from Tunisian ruling interest groups facilitates accord with France. During the recent oil dispute between France and Algeria, Tunisia did not ally herself openly with her Arab neighbor, despite the fact that she had direct interests by virtue of an oil pipeline through her terrain. Tunisian reaction was to "regret" the quarrel and hope for its rapid settlement. France has guaranteed investment in Tunisia and recently has bound herself to collaborate on World Bank investment projects in Tunisia. She has also won concessions to explore for oil in the south of the country.

France has regained a place of significance outside North Africa as well amid other Middle Eastern states by her enlightened policy towards the Arab-Israeli conflict. The French policy of nonalignment, rejecting Soviet or American hegemony, makes her an attractive partner in trade and development. In addition, France is frequently willing to make up in economic terms what she lacks in military and political power.

The French oil concern, Erap, has discovered large oil sources in Iraq and has been successfully marketing crude Iraqi oil. In 1968 Libya permitted French oil interests in the country, ending the Anglo-American monopoly there. Libya now provides 17 percent of French oil needs. Kuwait has sent negotiators to France to discuss a joint project to exploit her natural gas reserves. And Saudi Arabia has invited French engineers to explore for oil on its coast of the Red Sea. These inroads can be of great importance to France if she learns from the Algerian experience that exploitation may in the long run prove to be a losing game. Her influence on the economy of other Middle Eastern states is limited; such a situation encourages fair dealing.

Currency

French economic activity in the area is greatly facilitated by the existence in North Africa of the franc zone. This tie enables France to extend certain monetary policies into her former colonies by regulating convertibility and influencing their internal money supplies. The French Central Bank looms large in all monetary decisions, indirectly affecting trade and loans. Trading within the zone is easier for members than trade with "outsiders" (even when the "outsiders" are geographical neighbors), and trade with France is particularly attractive as a result of ease of payments and convertibility.

As in other areas, French influence in currency matters appears to be decreasing but still significant. Shortly after independence, Algeria created her own central bank with special ties to the French banking system. A year later, to stop the outflow of capital resources, the treasury extended to franc zone countries the same rigid currency controls established earlier for foreign money. In an attempt to answer criticism on these grounds, the French government asked all French oil firms operating in Algeria to deposit 70 percent of sales revenues in that nation.

France is aware of the monetary problems of other Middle Eastern nations and has attempted to ease trade and development through long-term loans and acceptance of "soft" currencies. In September 1970, a Franco-Arab Bank was officially inaugurated; the Credit Lyonnais, an outstanding French banking establishment, holds 40 percent of its 100-million franc capital. Seventeen Arab banks have participated in this establishment.

Trade

By a policy of combining trade and aid, France pursues a position of strength with regard to developing nations badly in need of capital, equipment, and foreign exchange. The countries of the Middle East, however, have not failed to observe the trend toward diversification of trade and aid partners and to the extent that they can turn elsewhere, French influence can be offset. Diversification has weakened the French position in her former colonies while strengthening her role in nations formerly tied to other major powers.

France continues to be the most important trading partner of each of her former North African colonies. In addition to fuel, France imports wine from Algeria and Tunisia. Her trade with these nations, however, is characterized by a payments deficit on their part, keeping her in a dominant position. In the first nine months of 1970, France took 55 percent of Algeria's exports. The implications for French influence are obvious. French goods are attractive to the North African nations; they import f3,550 million worth of French products each year, and the trend has been toward increasing purchases, as shown by Table 1.

In 1970 France agreed to help Tunisia to make up the payments def-

TABLE 1

	Imports (in 10 million francs)			Exports		
	1967	1968	1969	1967	1968	1969
Algeria	262	275.1	307.4	199.6	232.6	235.6
Morocco	105	93.2	105	93.3	83.3	94

SOURCE: *Europa Year Book,* 1971

icit between the two nations. A favorite French policy is to provide aid in the form of credit; this procedure results in increased purchases of French products and a resultant rise in future business through parts replacements and service.

France has reestablished diplomatic relations with Morocco following a break over the Ben Barka affair. The first order of business following the resumption of relations was discussion of increasing trade and French offers of credit. In April 1970 France agreed to make available to Morocco f22 million to be used to help cover the payments deficit and to provide credit for capital equipment purchases if made in France.

France has openly recognized the desire on the part of developing nations to diversify their trading partners. She has gracefully accepted such moves by Algeria. Pompidou has seen such action as a necessary part of the de Gaulle strategy for building a Third World force.

The principle of diversification is in practice throughout the Middle East, and although France has lost some influence she has gained in Arab areas not traditionally within her realm of association. Much of the new French economic activity in the Middle East is the result of severing her military alliance with Israel and the decline of Anglo-American influence after the Six-Day War. French exports to the republican Arab states more than trebled between 1964 and 1970, as seen in the *Middle East Economic Digest,* August 1, 1969. France is now the Middle East's second biggest supplier. If we exclude the Maghreb, France ranks seventh. Its exports include military supplies, electrical and mechanical goods, iron, steel, chemicals, textiles, agricultural products, and automobiles. Iraq purchased f170 million worth of armored cars in 1968 and signed a technical cooperation and cultural agreement with France. The contract for the Suez-Mediterranean pipeline was awarded by Egypt to a consortium of eleven firms, seven of which are French. France advanced one-fourth of the cost ($175 million) to Egypt as a loan. French trade with Egypt increased from $38 million in 1965 to $54.6 million in 1968 and since then has doubled. French commercial involvement in the Arabian Peninsula, which was negligible, showed a significant increase in 1968. French exports which amounted to f259 million in 1968 jumped to f665 million in 1969. In the Persian Gulf states, French exports more than trebled (f89 million in 1968 rose to f298.6 million in 1969). Sales to Israel slumped during the same period (f354 million in 1969 against f489 million in 1968), according to the *Middle East Economic Digest,* December 18, 1970.

A Franco-Arab Chamber of Commerce was established in December 1970 to boost cooperation in trade, industry, and technology. It aims to double trade with the twenty Arab member states in five years. More than thirteen hundred French enterprises and an equal number of Arab firms have joined the chamber. The Franco-Arab Bank and the chamber of commerce seem to fit in well with France's Mediterranean policy.

An important instrument of French trade policy is the European Economic Community (EEC). France has worked within the community to achieve special status for her former colonies; such a policy serves the short-term economic interests of the North African states by guaranteeing them good prices for their primary priducts and reduced competition from other developing states. It may, however, be less satisfactory in the long run since it serves to keep these nations dependent on primary-product trade and leaves them in a fixed subservient economic position with regard to full members of the European community. In addition, community associate status pits the developing nations against each other and discourages organization among themselves; most would prefer an immediate economic advantage to possible long-term results.

France benefits from the arrangement by securing markets for her own goods and increased control over the activities of the associate states. They are hopeful of improving their positions and someday gaining full membership status. Such a change in position can only come through strong French sponsorship. France has also tried to use her EEC membership to influence other Arab states. In 1967 she held out on approval of a new Israeli associate agreement until arrangements with the UAR and Lebanon had been discussed.

A further French trade innovation in the Arab Middle East is military equipment. De Gaulle signaled a new attitude toward arms sales when on June 3, 1967, he placed a general embargo on arms shipments to the Middle East. This embargo has been maintained with various restrictions until the present. The sale of Mirage jets to Libya is the most spectacular, but other arms deals are being discussed and several have been carried out in Lebanon, Iraq, Saudi-Arabia, and Kuwait.

Aid

France enjoys the role of leadership and the concept of a French community of nations. In equatorial Africa the concept has received greater formal recognition, but even in North Africa the strong remnants of French culture, education, and society have their economic and political implications. France would like to see these countries develop and is gradually becoming aware of the unpleasant fact that such development, as in the case of Algeria, will mean increased independence from France.

France has an impressive assistance program with regard to her former colonies. The French national interest is clear in such programs: credit, as mentioned, frequently tied to French purchases and special concentration on French related activity. Technical assistance in part comes from the French program allowing professionals to fulfill their military obligation by service in the former colonies. This policy has provided a pool of architects, lawyers, doctors, administrators, and teachers—all of whom are extremely valuable to developing nations.

Algeria and France are engaged in a joint project to build a gas liquefaction plant in Skikda. (One-third of Algeria's natural gas is imported by France.) France is assisting in the building of a phosphate fertilizer plant at Annaba, and with the Soviet Union is helping to con-

TABLE 2
French Aid in Millions of Dollars
% = % of total aid

	1968		1969	
Algeria	222.7	13%	215.3	12.4%
Morocco & Tunisia	35.4	2.1%	45.6	2.6%

SOURCE: *Europa Year Book,* 1970

struct the El Hadgar steel complex. Both France and the Soviet Union are subsidizing Algeria's wine crop. By April 15, 1971, French cultural and technical assistants serving in Algeria numbered 7,846, and more than 600,000 Algerian immigrants were employed in France, according to *France,* May 1971, published by the French Embassy.

France agreed in 1969 to substantially increase aid to Tunisia and to extend cooperation into a large number of new areas. The following year, after Tunisia was hit by floods, France offered to compensate for damage done to several projects and directly aided devastated areas.

The aid arrangement with Morocco has been discussed; typically it requires purchases in France. Morocco and Tunisia together receive about 2.5 percent of France's aid allotment, as shown in Table 2. Algeria, for obvious reasons, is a major recipient of French aid.

France has done an adequate job of salvaging her influence following the disastrous colonial policy of opposing independence. Under de Gaulle France made strides to strengthen French elements in the society and reap the economic benefits of cultural attachments. If France can continue to support development and not oppose diversification of trade, aid, and investment partners, she may well maintain and expand her economic influence, revitalize her cultural ties, and forge new political bonds throughout the Middle East.

Since De Gaulle

After de Gaulle's resignation in April 1969, the *New York Times,* May 21, 1969, reported that Allain Poher, the interim president, implied that he did not fully agree with his predecessor's Middle East policy. But President Georges Pompidou, upon election, announced that French foreign policy would not deviate substantially from the master's plan. His actions since taking office substantiate the verity of this commitment.

First, he has maintained the Gaullist aversion to big power hegemony and has adeptly moved between the Soviet Union and the United States, showing friendship for each but stopping short of bilateral bonds. His foreign minister, Maurice Schumann, in his address to the United Nations General Assembly on September 18, 1970, stated that the United Nations is founded on an "equilibrium of responsibilities." This equilibrium would be upset if the big powers relinquish their responsibilities or if some of them assume the responsibilities of others. Thus, he said: "Hegemony, exclusive or shared, is the surest way of preventing the United Nations from breathing." Based on this belief, Schumann concluded the following:

> 1. Dialogue and rapprochement of the major powers is desirable; "when in one of the most troubled regions of the world (the Middle East) the movement toward peace receives the new stimulus of the dialogue happily reestablished between Moscow and Washington, naturally we should rejoice about it." He referred to Pompidou's recent visits to the United States and the Soviet Union.
>
> 2. The international community must not have guardians. Hence, "no one except the country itself may decide the destiny of a nation." The presence of Soviet and American fleets in the Mediterranean is disturbing to France, a "bordering" country.
>
> 3. The permanent members of the Security Council who are not superpowers have a special duty in the preservation of the "equilibrium of responsibilities." Action by the big *four* (not two) provides a safeguard against tutelage and guardianship.[10]

In keeping with this view France supports strong United Nations action, through the Security Council, on the continuing Lebanese-Israeli hostilities. She has herself proposed or supported all the Security Council resolutions since the 1968 Beirut airport attack, which denounce Israeli intervention in Lebanon, holding that Lebanon is not responsible for uncontrollable acts of the guerrillas. In February 1972, France cosponsored Security Council Resolution 313 which demanded that Israel halt military action against Lebanon and withdraw its forces. Jacques Kosciusko-Morizet, French representative to the United Nations at the time, stressed that events should be judged in the context of a continuing Middle East crisis; but he criticized (1) Israel's refusal to cooperate with United Nations observation and peaceful settlement efforts, and (2) Israeli reprisals which are out of proportion to alleged provocations.[11]

France elucidated her attitude toward the American role in the crisis in a speech by the French representative to the General Assembly. He criticized the American initiative for a Mideast settlement, commonly known as the Rogers' plan, which called for a cease-fire with standstill arrangements and a resumption of talks under the auspices of Gunnar Jarring. Alleged violations of the cease-fire agreement and the termination of the talks by Israel contributed to the failure of the Rogers' plan. This failure was attributed by France to the fact that the Big Four were not involved in guaranteeing the cease-fire: "the destiny of peace is not determined by one or two while the member states of the United Nations are reduced to playing the role of spectators. . . . If one wishes to construct something solid, one must begin with a wider base."[12]

In his speech to the 26th session of the United Nations General Assembly (September 28, 1971), the French minister of foreign affairs saw America's uncritical support of Israel as the main obstacle to the implementation of Security Council Resolution 242. He seemed willing to modify a well-established French position. He said that without unanimous determination by the permanent members of the Security Council, "either the Assembly takes the floor or the international community is doomed to silence."

President Pompidou was more open in his criticism of the United States position on the Middle East. In an address honoring Leonid Brezhnev of the USSR, in Paris on October 25, 1971, Pompidou said: "In order to seek a solution we have, we and you, within the framework of consultations between the four permanent members of the Security Council, observed that our ideas were close, and on important points, identical. But I regret that the action of the *others* has singularly slowed down end that the mission of Ambassador Jarring has reached an impasse."[13]

Brezhnev made it clear that the French government, like the USSR, calls for Israeli withdrawal from all occupied Arab territories.

Pompidou continues to refer to France as an ally of the United States but has expressed a clear desire to fulfill the alliance "outside of any organization of the NATO type." French cooperation with the Soviet Union, begun under de Gaulle, has been continued by Pompidou. However, he has not felt bound to either side, explaining that French overtures to the Soviet Union do "not prevent us from passing judgment on one or another act of Soviet diplomacy or action, exactly as our alliance and our deep friendship with the United States did not prevent us from passing judgment on some aspect of American diplomacy or action we did not approve." [14] And France was very critical of the unilateral U.S. action in support of Israel during the October 1973 war, objecting to the exclusion of Europe from any discussion of policy, even with regard to the military alert.

Secondly, as an extension of this attack on bipolarism, Pompidou has continued French efforts to calm down the Arab-Israeli hostilities. The arms embargo initiated in June 1967 has continued in various forms. In October 1967, the embargo was limited to those belligerents that had a common border with Israel. As Schumann pointed out: "Surely, Israel, because it was our major customer, suffered eminently the consequences of the measure adopted, just as it was the first to benefit from the easing of restrictions, (in Oct., 1967) . . . that enabled Israel to acquire material of a defensive nature, for example, patrol ships or radar for surveillance." [15]

But in December 1968, Israeli commandos raided the Beirut International Airport, destroying approximately one-half of Lebanon's commercial airfleet (ownership of which was shared by a number of nations). De Gaulle, particularly angered at the use of French Alouette helicopters for the raid, reapplied a total embargo to the belligerents but relaxed the restrictions on Lebanon.

At his first presidential news conference on July 10, 1969, Pompidou dispelled all speculation that he might prove friendlier to Israel and lift entirely or return to a selective embargo. He held that all arms shipments to the belligerents from any source should be halted. He has also insisted that a just settlement to the problem will only result from a coordinated effort by the major powers, an effort which is further thwarted by the adoption of client nations in the crisis area.

Pompidou reaffirmed de Gaulle's policy in his July 2, 1970, press conference: "There is no French plan for a settlement nor must there be a Soviet plan for a settlement. It is necessary—since they alone can do this—that the four powers present a common plan for a settlement, for only a common plan may be accepted by both sides and any plan submitted by one nation alone is automatically suspect to one of the contending parties." [16]

Thirdly, Pompidou believes that, in the long run, the development of a third force is the most promising alternative to big power hegemony. He has continued to appeal to a wide variety of nations, particularly those in the throes of development, to steer the middle course which de Gaulle so strongly recommended. Schumann, in his speech to the General Assembly, September 18, 1970, on the mission of a reconciled Europe in the world, said: "It is right that from the shores of the Mediterranean to Latin America people turn to this Europe and place in it their hopes. For it is known that, fortified by its own originality, it will be certainly not a threat but an attraction for the independence of others." [17] One of the most controversial moves in the Middle East, the sale of jets to Libya, reported in the *Christian Science Monitor* on January 23, 1970, was in part designed with this objective in mind.

Pompidou saw very quickly that by courting the new Libyan government, France might widen her field of influence and possibly remove this nation from cold war pressures. With French aid, Libya might convert to and maintain a policy of nonalignment. The Libyan government itself reportedly hoped that its successful appeal to France would be an example to other nations wishing to avoid falling victim to the bipolar blocs. Schumann, in explaining the French sale of jets to Libya, cited the strict conditions of "nonreexport from Libya and nonutilization from foreign airports" as insuring that the spirit of the French embargo would not be violated. In addition, it was estimated that the Libyan pilots would require at least four years of training to enable them to handle the new Mirages, and France staggered the deliveries over a four-year period (1971–74) to insure that the contract provisions would not be violated. However, in April 1973, following the assassination raid by Israelis against Palestinians in Beirut, there was unsupported speculation that some or all of the sixty Mirage jets already delivered to Libya had been transferred to Egypt. The French government issued a categorical denial that such transfer had taken place. The *New York Times,* January 28, 1970, reported that French Premier Chaban-Delmas said that the arms deal with Libya was the result of hard competition among arms suppliers in which Libya preferred France because it is a Mediterranean country and because it pursues a policy of decolonization. He emphasized the advantage to French security in having good relations on the southern side of the Mediterranean. It is interesting to note at this juncture that President Boumediene of Algeria, like Pompidou and Chaban-Delmas, often speaks of the need to rid the Mediterra-

nean of all foreign powers. The French government views a French
presence in the Mediterranean as essential to the stability of the region.
The minister of foreign affairs told the National Assembly on June 9,
1971, that without a French presence, there would be a void in the
whole region which would inevitably attract the forces of one side or
the other.

And fourthly, Pompidou has not shown signs of deviating significantly from the attachment to nationalism which General de Gaulle so
openly proclaimed. His fervent nationalism has two main effects on
French foreign policy. One is the tendency to evaluate foreign-policy alternatives in terms of their short-range immediate effects on French national interests. He does not shy away from national interest justifica-
tions for policy decisions. His nationalism also makes him sensitive and
sympathetic to the nationalism of the states with which he is working.
He does not expect them to make compromises and sacrifices which he
himself would view as unrealistic. His own nationalism and his awareness of others' nationalism are both revealed in a statement he made on
French policy in the Middle East. He reaffirmed de Gaulle's belief that
France "owes it to herself" to defend her "moral and material interests"
in the Mediterranean by reestablishing good relations with the Arabs,
securing guaranteed borders for Israel, and providing for the rights of
the Palestinian populations.[18] This consideration of national interest was
vindicated during the 1973 Arab oil embargo when France, unlike some
of her neighbors, received more favorable treatment as a result of her
detachment from U.S. support of Israel and her improved relations with
the Arabs.

The Middle East is of course one of the most difficult areas in which
to pursue successfully a foreign policy which favors nationalism. The
reason for this problem is simple: such a policy is not a guide to
decision-making in the Arab-Israeli conflict, especially since the June
War.

France has by no means altered her basic objective of maintaining
good relations with both sides in the dispute. She has consistently reaffirmed her commitment to the state of Israel. Chaban-Delmas tried to
make this consistency clear by stating: "France's policy vis-à-vis Israel
has not varied. France affirmed—and this was long ago—that she specifically guaranteed Israel's right to existence, that is, its independence,
security, and the exercise of its full sovereign rights. None of this has
been changed." [19]

Franco-Israeli relations were damaged by French overtures to the
Arabs, but strong ties remain. Israel strained its relations with France

by its successful secret maneuver to secure five gunboats from the harbor at Cherbourg, focusing world attention on an embarrassed and deceived Pompidou. But the mildness of Pompidou's reaction indicated the French desire to minimize contention with Israel. In December 1972, the French ambassador to Israel called on Abba Eban to try to improve French-Israeli relations. He emphasized that by supporting Israel in the European Economic Community negotiations and making little public comment on most of Israel's activities in the occupied territories, Pompidou had earned warmer Israeli response. However, this overture seemed in vain when in January 1973 Golda Meir decided to appear at the Socialist International—in connection with her position as vice-president of the organization—on the same platform with François Mitterand, Pompidou's arch-rival in the national elections. Both Israeli and French newspapers noted that this action would no doubt strain relations between the two countries, particularly following the Pompidou victory in April 1973. Yet, despite the difficulties, France and Israel remain friendly, if cautious, in their relations.

Although France has defended the right of Israel to maintain a nation in its 1949 borders, she has also recognized validity in the claims of the Palestinians. De Gaulle, though late in embracing the principle of self-determination, held firmly to it when speaking of Quebec, Biafra, and Vietnam. Pompidou's reaction to the Palestinians has been guarded but clearly sympathetic. Kosciusko-Morizet said to the General Assembly on October 30, 1970: "There must be a just settlement, especially for those whom we can no longer call just Palestinian refugees . . . who have the right to dignity and the *freedom to choose their own fate.*" [20] The same was reiterated by Ambassador Louis De Guiringaud in an address to the Security Council on June 13, 1973: "After the war of June 1967 the problem [of the Palestinians] acquired new dimensions. Beyond its humanitarian aspects, for which UNRWA is responsible, its political aspect has appeared and developed in recent years to such a degree that no settlement could or henceforth should overlook the problems of the Palestinian people." [21]

Since the 1967 war French spokesmen at the United Nations have insisted on the withdrawal of Israeli forces from occupied territories. They have voted with the majority of the Security Council in censuring Israel for its "reprisals" against Arab countries for Palestinian activities in occupied lands. In 1967, while voicing concern over the violence on both sides, the French representative made a distinction between the acts of the occupied and the occupier. Referring to France's own occupation in World War II, he expressed sympathy for the Palestinians and held that Israel could expect such acts of resistance to subside only after withdrawal from the occupied territories through implementation of the United Nations resolution of November 22, 1967.

French officials often emphasize the advantage Israel may derive from a settlement. Pompidou stated in July 1970: "There must be peace in the Middle East. . . . Otherwise, yes, the balance of forces will constantly deteriorate and, in particular, whatever we do, it will constantly deteriorate to the detriment of Israel." [22]

In a speech on October 30, 1970, Kosciusko-Morizet asked: "How can Israel, who owes the founding of her state to this UN, reject a security which the superiority of arms, always transitory, cannot alone insure. . . . The desire for absolute security would lead Israel to an unlimited expansion and thus to an endless war; the same desire would lead the Arabs to seek the destruction of Israel." And, as if to emphasize French neutrality, he concluded: "We believe that today the current crisis—and in this it can be beneficial—offers Israel the unique opportunity of making her legitimacy recognized by her neighbors, offers the Arabs the unique opportunity of freeing their occupied territories, and offers the Palestinians the unique opportunity of affirming their rights to existence and justice." [23]

Today the French position with respect to the Arab-Israeli conflict may be summarized as follows: First, the continued occupation by Israel of sizable territories belonging to sovereign Arab states constitutes a violation of the principle of the inadmissability of the acquisition of territory by force. Second, "the two essential elements in Resolution 242 (1967) are inseparable: No withdrawal without commitments for peace, but no commitments for peace without withdrawal." Third, Israel's negative reply to Ambassador Jarring's *aide-mémoire* of February 8, 1971, requesting a commitment to the principles of Resolution 242 including withdrawal from occupied Arab territories, constitutes a real obstacle to "the beginning of a process leading to peace." [24] Fourth, self-determination for the Palestinian people is essential to a peaceful settlement. Fifth, a settlement requires the setting up of demilitarized zones and the stationing of a UN force which could not be withdrawn without the unamimous approval of the Security Council.

CONCLUSION

Thus France has moved from a powerful colonizing power through a series of bitter defeats into a new phase of international prominence. Charles de Gaulle, so instrumental in the securing of the "overseas territories" in the 1940s, became a champion of "decolonization" in the 1960s. By astute political observation and calculated diplomatic moves, he formulated a contemporary foreign policy which aimed at reducing United States or Soviet hegemony, creating a third force with French leadership, and rebuilding French spirit and international stature. Although in several instances he failed to achieve his policy objectives, the present status of France in the Middle East would, on balance, appear to be a success. De Gaulle's plan, for the most part continued by Pompidou, called for a restoration of a significant French political, cultural, and economic presence in the Arab countries while maintaining solid ties with Israel. The former is gradually being realized; the latter is mainly endangered by Israeli interpretation of French activities according to the rubric "those not for us are against us."

French national interests have been substantially furthered in the Middle East, but de Gaulle's hopes that France would be instrumental in finding a solution to the Arab-Israeli conflict have remained unfulfilled. Consistent French support for UN action through the Security Council, continued reaffirmation of the November 22, 1967, resolution, and maintenance of the embargo on arms which was to set an example to arms suppliers have all failed to move the parties toward a settlement. Perhaps as much as any situation, the impotence of the Gaullist strategy in this international dispute reflects the basic validity of de Gaulle's attack on bipolarism and Soviet-American hegemony. In the final analysis, a Middle East settlement, if and when it comes, will be little influenced by France.

❋ 4 ❋

TAREQ Y. ISMAEL

The Soviet Union and the Middle East

The role of the Soviet Union in the Middle East has been of interest to political scientists, historians, strategists, and policy-makers since the Revolution of 1917, when the West's concern over traditional Tsarist interests in the area was compounded by a fear of bolshevism. Although Soviet involvement in the area was minimal prior to World War II, it has steadily increased since the war, encroaching ever more effectively upon Western interests there. Thus, from the onset of the Cold War, the Middle East has been a virtual battleground of Soviet-American competition, escalating the area's local conflicts into potential triggers of nuclear holocaust. What are Soviet objectives in the Middle East? Although opinion is by no means undivided on many questions, the subject has been well worked over. Yet the issues are so critical to world peace, Soviet-American ideologies so completely polarized, and the rhetoric so charged that it is difficult to view the subject critically and unemotionally. We hope to accomplish this here.

The purpose of this chapter on the Soviet presence in the Middle East is to examine recent developments in the light of earlier trends and to analyze the significance of these events in terms of their impact upon this critical region of the developing world. The 1917–45 period of Soviet–Middle Eastern relations will not be examined, as the author feels that, in the absence of new documentary sources, little is to be gained from another discussion of the diplomatic history of this era. The years from the end of World War II to 1967 are examined chiefly in terms of the trends they reveal and for the information they can impart on Soviet views and objectives.

THE POSTWAR SETTING, 1945–55

In observing the growth of Soviet influence in the Middle East, we may find it helpful to understand that three sets of factors have influenced the development of the foreign policies of the major powers in their relations with the Third World and, indeed, with each other. The foreign activities of a state are shaped in the context of domestic politics. Thus, in periods when the USSR was involved in domestic crises—as in 1917–21, 1936–39, and 1953–56—its involvement in foreign affairs and the strength of its initiatives outside its boundaries have diminished. Second, the foreign policies of a state and its rivals are not independent of each other but, rather, interact to create a resultant situation neither may have intended. Finally, in relations with the Third World, the countries which are the objects of foreign policy initiatives are not simply malleable puppets, to be changed and directed at will, but have a range of choice which makes their receptivity an important variable. The interaction of these factors sets, and not any one alone, determines the effect and direction of the foreign policy of either East or West.

In particular, a coincidence of factors culminating in the 1945–55 period interacted to introduce the Soviet Union as a potential power in the Middle East. The nationalist movements seeking independence in the area gathered strength during the war, while the colonial powers were weakened. At the same time, reaction against Western imperialism and the political and moral bankruptcy of the regimes in power, together with growing support for social reform, contributed to the growth of pro-Soviet and pro-Communist sympathies. The Communist Parties of Egypt, Syria, Iraq, and Iran (which were both small and illegal) gained strength, particularly among the intelligentsia. The Soviet Union, isolated from direct contact with the Arab world prior to the war, was able to establish diplomatic relations with most of the Arab countries as a product of the Soviet alliance with Britain and the United States. Thus, the Soviet Union was in a favorable position to establish friendly relations with the governments and peoples of the Middle East, while the influence of the Western states, with respect to preventing such a trend, was weakened.

Following the war, however, Soviet relations with Middle Eastern governments hardly flourished. A long-smouldering dispute with Turkey over the Turkish Straits and the east Anatolian border areas came to the surface in early 1945, threatening to seeth into open hostilities. It was abated, although not resolved, in 1947 with President Truman's enunciation of the Truman Doctrine. Iran's common border with the USSR, like that of Turkey's, gave the Soviets special interest in the po-

litical, military, and economic affairs of the country. Unlike the dispute
with Turkey, however, the Soviet Union attempted overt intervention in
Iran to resolve outstanding issues—including the questions of oil concessions and commercial and strategic relationships—in Iranian–Soviet
relations. Soviet troops had occupied Iran during the war to guarantee
its value as a source of oil and as a transit route between the Allies and
the USSR. According to the Tripartite Treaty of 1942, the troops were
to withdraw within six months after the termination of the war. Not
only did the troops remain, but they aided the secession of two provinces, Azerbaijan and Mahabad, to form autonomous republics under
Soviet tutelage. Iran protested to the United Nations, but to no significant avail. The Iranian premier, Qauvam es-Saltaneh, through bilateral
negotiations with Moscow, secured the withdrawal of Soviet troops
from Iran on May 9, 1946, but at the expense of far-reaching concessions to Moscow on oil exploitation, the status of Azerbaijan, and Communist participation in the Iranian government. The agreement was
short-lived, however, for with Soviet troops removed, the government
was able to crush the Azerbaijan rebellion, suppress the Tudeh (Iranian
Communist) Party, and refuse ratification of the Irano-Soviet oil agreement. Thus, the Soviet Union's policies in Turkey and Iran only
achieved the alienation of large segments of Turkish and Iranian society, not to mention the distrust of their governments. The subsequent
participation of Turkey and Iran in Western alliance systems designed
to forestall Soviet aggression is hardly surprising.

   While practical considerations of security motivated Soviet policies in
Turkey and Iran, ideological conceptions shaped Soviet relations
throughout the remainder of the area. National liberation movements, it
was believed, could never succeed without Communist leadership. The
newly independent countries, rather than serving as a contradiction to
this tenet, were considered doomed to movement within the orbit of imperialists. The possibility of a neutral camp was not considered either
among states or in terms of national liberation movements within a
state. The Wafdist and (after July 1952) the revolutionary government
of Egypt were exposed to severe criticism. The various Syrian regimes,
from 1947 to 1954, did not escape Soviet attacks, both ideological and
political. As Walter Lacqueur noted, in *The Soviet Union and the Middle East,* "the Iraqi governments up to July, 1958, . . . were considered
beyond redemption." Surprisingly enough, the feudal monarchies in
Saudi Arabia and Jordan (except during King Abdullah's reign), as well
as the Zionist movement (previously under consistent attack) and Israel,
escaped the Soviet campaign during most of this period.

   The Soviet government reversed its long-standing opposition to Zionism to support the creation of Israel in the United Nations. This shift in policy was at least partially motivated by the Russian desire to see Britain expelled from Palestine. The Soviet Union followed through with the sale of arms and aircraft to Israel (through the agency of Czechoslovakia) in 1948 and with an affirmative vote for Israel's admission to the United Nations in March 1949. It appears that this was intended to prevent the establishment of an exclusive Western influence in the Jewish state, and thus to further the removal of Britain from the eastern Mediterranean.

Although the governments of the Middle East were usually under attack by the USSR, the national liberation movements gained Soviet support; however, this was generally qualified by suspicion of bourgeois nationalism where the Communist Party did not play a leading role. The primary interest of the Soviet Union seemed aimed less at the creation of friendly relations than at the use of anticolonial movements to weaken Western powers.

INTRODUCTION OF SOVIET INFLUENCE

Although events of the postwar decade revealed a continuing Soviet interest in the Middle East, the Russians were faced with Western resistance and with a lack of rapport with the leaders of the independent countries of the area. However, Western influence, especially that of France and Britain, was rapidly diminishing, and a series of developments created a fertile environment for the growth of Soviet influence in the 1953–55 period.

First, due to its perception of "Russian expansionism," the USA had initiated the formation of a series of organizations and alliances designed to contain the Soviet Union within its formal boundaries. After the Truman Doctrine was enunciated in 1948 and massive aid granted to Greece and Turkey, this policy was prosecuted with the formation of NATO in 1949 and the creation of its military forces in 1950; a series of bilateral American treaties with Turkey, Iran, and Pakistan, for coordination of defense policy in the Middle East; the abortive attempt to form a Middle East Defense Organization; and the Baghdad Pact, formed in February 1955. This organization of the area into alliances was vigorously opposed by Egypt and precipitated the deterioration of American-Egyptian relations. Egyptian policy thus came to coincide with Soviet policy, which, not unnaturally, opposed the creation of military alliances on its southern boundaries. "It has been said," wrote Pierre Heim, in *Eurafrica-Tribune du Tiers-Monde* (Brussels),

March–April 1970, "that the Baghdad Pact brought the USSR back into the East. That is true."

In addition, the changes in Soviet policy subsequent to Stalin's death * resulted in a more flexible approach in the Middle East. Some Arab regimes were reappraised as constituting progressive forces, and a national-front policy was adopted. This ideological shift was paralleled by a moderating trend in the Soviet Union's diplomatic and political stance. The Kremlin was now willing, as Walter Lacqueur stated in *The Struggle for the Middle East,* "to cooperate with kings and sheiks as well as ultra-revolutionaries. The fact that some of these leaders were militantly anti-communist was no obstacle." [1] Egypt's President Nasser signified the Soviet approach while opening a Soviet-funded spinning mill at Damietta. "In spite of the clouds that have, at times, loomed over our relations, the economic agreement [of January 1958] was never affected. At no time did the Soviet Union utter one single word threatening to boycott us economically and on no occasion did the Soviets reproachfully remind us of the economic aid they extended to us or the loans they provided for our industrialization schemes." [2]

Some Arab countries, it should be noted, were more receptive to Soviet overtures. While Turkey and Iran were border states with a history of Russian threats of domination, the Arab world had never had this kind of experience with the Soviet Union. Moreover, the Arab world linked "the United States and the West with the evils of the past and the present and [placed] on them the burden of reform." [3] And although the Arabs overlooked Soviet support for the founding of Israel, they condemned Britain and the United States for their large-scale economic and political support of the Zionist state.

There was also suspicion among the Arabs that the West did not wish to further (but perhaps wished to retard) their development; and that American denials of certain kinds and quantities of arms to Arab states, together with the involvement of Middle Eastern countries in American defense alliances, was to allow Israel not merely to survive, but to extend her borders. *Al-Ahram,* a semiofficial organ of the Egyptian government, reflected this view and commented on March 9, 1955, in an editorial that "America has chosen Israel and will never arm the

---

* Stalin's death was followed by a more lenient policy almost everywhere. During 1955, Soviet policy tended to be more conciliatory in character in Europe—Austria, Yugoslavia, and Finland—and in the United Nations. This movement was later to lead to the development of the line of "peaceful coexistence"; in 1954 the elements of the policy were there even though the enunciation of it was still to come. It should also be noted that this policy was the subject, and the product, of the contest for power in the Kremlin subsequent to Stalin's death.

Arab states because Israel doesn't want that." Nasser, identifying the Baghdad Pact as a manifestation of the West's policy toward Israel geared to contain Nasser's leadership of the pan-Arab struggle, noted in the same issue of *Al-Ahram:* "As long as Egypt is the shield of Arabism in its fight with Zionism, complete victory for the Western policies requires, first of all, the isolation of Egypt from her Arab sisters."

The formation of the Baghdad Pact coincided with a major Israeli raid on the Gaza Strip—the product of long-simmering tensions on the cease-fire line which had produced a series of raids and retaliations. This attack lent new urgency to Egyptian demands for arms, but these were still denied by the United States and its allies. In the autumn of 1955, Egypt was able to conclude an agreement with the Soviet Union for the purchase of arms from Czechoslovakia with Egyptian cotton. As Cremeans described the basis of this transaction in *The Arabs and the World:* "Convinced as he has been of the reality of the Israeli military threat and of the existence of a considerable body of opinion in the Western governments that his downfall would be in the interest of the West, Nasser found irresistible the Soviet offer to supply him with arms at reasonable prices and in generous quantities in exchange for cotton which he had in good supply, no questions being asked about the ability of his armed forces to absorb them." [4]

Some of the causal relationships underlying the events which followed are unclear to this day, but in May 1956, Nasser's government recognized the People's Republic of China—at that time still on closest terms with the Soviet Union. Although recognition had previously been extended by America's ally, Britain, Egypt was the first Arab state to take this step. At this point, the American line, as enunciated by Secretary of State John Foster Dulles, was that Egypt was anti-Western and not to be trusted. In July 1956, the United States withdrew its offer of $56 million for the financing of the first stage of the High Dam at Aswan, and the contingent loans from the World Bank and Great Britain—totaling $214 million— were also withdrawn. In reaction, Nasser nationalized the International Maritime Suez Canal Company. The resultant crisis was capped by the Israeli invasion of the Sinai on October 29, 1956, followed by British and French attacks on the Canal Zone in early November. The Soviet Union (which until the Bandung Conference of 1955 had maintained friendly relations with Israel) utilized the occasion to demonstrate its solidarity with the Arab cause, but it was the supportive actions of the United States that made the United Nations cease-fire agreements and peacekeeping operation successful. Whatever good will the United States might have generated over the Suez crisis was dissi-

pated by the enunciation of the Eisenhower Doctrine in January 1957.
While the Arabs were willing to believe that the Soviet Union was their
ally because of their common Western enemies, they were unwilling to
accept the assertion of the United States that the Soviet Union, as an
enemy of the West, was thereby an enemy of the Arab people.

DEVELOPMENT OF THE SOVIET POSITION, 1956–67

The record of the extension of Soviet influence into the Middle East
over the decade following the Suez crisis certainly seems to justify the
judgment of one scholar, O. M. Slomansky, in the spring 1970 issue of
Orbis, that "Soviet gains have more often than not resulted from Western blunders or from the West's inability to resolve conflicting interests
and commitments in the area."

Soviet economic and cultural relations with some Arab countries
gathered momentum in the second half of the fifties. Soviet-Syrian ties,
for example, were strong enough by 1957 to stir domestic and international fears concerning what then seemed to be a steady and fast drive
to make Syria the first Arab satellite of the Soviet Union. Later, despite
the fact that the formation of the Egyptian-Syrian Union in 1958 was at
least partially motivated by a desire to prevent communism from
achieving ascendancy in Syria, the United States took a negative attitude
toward the new United Arab Republic. This was followed by an intervention in Lebanon by U.S. Marines during civil strife precipitated by
the Lebanese president's insistence on renewing his tenure in office; although peace was restored, the government was ultimately replaced with
one more favorable to Nasser despite the intervention. This action, together with the landing of British troops in Jordan, followed the coup
by General Abdul Karim Kassim in Iraq. The West gained little from
what appeared to be an attempt to salvage their position—a position
gained from the corrupt Iraqi monarchy. When the Yemeni monarchy
fell in 1962, the United States, which had recognized the republican regime earlier, shifted sides and supported the Imam and Saudi Arabia
against the revolutionary government of Abdullah Sallal, which was
supported by the Egyptians. In each of these cases the West appeared to
be utilizing the well-known and feared instruments of imperialism to
support reactionary regimes against the people. And in 1964, the
United States completed its alienation from the Arab world by stopping
the "important program of food sales to the U.A.R. . . . this made
President Nasser more dependent on the Soviet Union and offered the

Russians opportunities for a more dominant role than had been possible in the past." [5]

Parallel to the growth of Soviet influence in the Arab Middle East, another Soviet initiative with its neighbors in the south was being shaped. Soviet-Iranian relations, although representing at various times the nearest Russian approach to presence in the Middle East, were never characterized by the same degree of hostility which was apparent in Soviet-Turkish relations. The dispute of 1946 about Soviet troops placements, the Azerbaijan dispute, the fall of the government of Mohammed Mossadegh, and the suppression of the Tudeh Party in 1953–54—all proved to be merely temporary setbacks for Soviet policy with respect to Iran. In the post-Stalin era, the Soviet Union adopted a new foreign policy based on "peaceful-coexistence" with countries of different political, social, and economic systems. Indeed, the new policy was broad enough to accommodate differences with no less than the United States itself. Consequently the Soviet government proved flexible enough to accept the proposition that it would achieve its major aims and protect its vital interests in Iran without obtaining a position of dominance and, thus, without taking the risks necessary to obtain that position.

This new development dovetailed with the U.S.-supported Iranian domestic policy which aimed at widening its base of support by seeking rapport with Russia in an attempt to appease the local anti-Western forces. Consequently, in 1956, Shah Mohammed Reza Pahlevi visited Moscow and came away with a three-year commercial agreement which resulted, the following year, in the Soviet Union providing the market for 27 percent of Iran's exports.

The rapprochement appeared in danger when Iran rejected a Soviet nonaggression treaty proposal and accepted a bilateral defense treaty with the United States in 1959, but this crisis was brought to an end in August 1960. The Soviet Union laid aside its concerns when, in 1962, Iran decided not to permit the stationing of nuclear missiles on its territory. In succeeding years, a number of economic and technical agreements were signed, culminating in the arms agreements concluded in 1967–68, and marked by a steel mill constructed at Isfahan and the trans-Iranian gasline.

The strain in Soviet-Turkish relations began to relax in 1961, when Ismet Inonu became prime minister of Turkey. A temporary setback occurred when the conservative and pro-Western Justice Party came to power in 1965, but in December 1966, Kosygin paid a visit to Ankara, and relations once again began to improve. The Soviet shift in policy with regard to Cyprus, together with Premier Suleyman Demirel's visit to Moscow in 1967, "eliminated the last traces of hostility from Soviet-Turkish relations." [6] Trade relations between Turkey and the USSR, supplemented by Turkish trade with several Eastern European countries, helped to further promote the rapprochement.

While the Soviet Union was implementing a good neighbor policy with respect to Turkey and Iran, the United States was removing its Jupiter missile bases from Turkey in 1962 and informing the Turkish government "that it could not count on automatic American support if by its actions (with regard to Cyprus) it provoked Moscow to intervene." [7] Moreover, while the Soviet Union was acting as if the Turkish Communists did not exist and condoning the suppression of the Tudeh Party in Iran while at the same time building trade bridges with both Turkey and Iran, the United States cut back economic aid to Turkey in 1968, to be totally ended in 1972, and the United States aid mission to Teheran was cancelled in 1967.

The Soviet foreign policy-makers built their policy toward the less-developed countries (LDC's) in accordance with their conviction that economic aid as well as economic relations with these countries would certainly promote gradual elimination of Western predominance and at the same time widen the opportunity for more Soviet influence. For this reason, trade with the LDC's grew six-fold from 1955 to 1966 in comparison with total Soviet trade, which only increased about two and one-half times. The proportion of LDC trade to the total increased in both exports (from 4.0 to 13.0 percent) and imports (from 6.0 to 11.0 percent). Trade with the nations of the Middle East amounted in 1966 to about one-third (exports) and one-fourth (imports) of total Soviet-LDC trade. More than half of this trade was with Egypt. [8]

1967—A Turning Point?

The status of Soviet influence in the Middle East as of May 1967 and the effect of the June 1967 Arab-Israeli war upon Soviet involvement in the area are matters much disputed among observers. Most would agree with the proposition that the proximity of the Soviet Union to the area causes a natural desire to bring it within the USSR's sphere of influence. Some conclude that the twenty-year rivalry (since the Truman Doctrine in 1947) between the United States and the Soviet Union demonstrated that the Russians were able to force a way into the Arab world and secure for themselves a solid presence in spite of, if not with the help of, American efforts and policies. John S. Badeau, in *The*

American Approach to the Arab World, thus concludes that by 1967 the Russians "had made deep inroads into American relations with the Arabs and could use their position in the Middle East as a warning and a counter to American-Communist confrontation elsewhere, as in Southeast Asia." [9] On the other hand, Leo Mates, in the April 1970 issue of *Foreign Affairs,* has used the 1967 war as a demonstration of the proposition that "the individual major powers proved to be unable to impress their less powerful friends and influence their policies even when serious efforts were made either individually or in concert with others." Uri Ra'anan, in the May 1969 issue of *Midstream,* notes a serious weakness in the Soviet position when he states: "In a period of three to four years, the Brezhnev regime had saddled its 'doctrine of irreversibility' with a 'credibility gap' of vast proportions. In some four or five 'revolutionary democracies,' the leftist regime has been overthrown, while two others have lost a war and considerable stretches of territory, without Soviet protection proving to be of the slightest value in either of these contingencies."

We are thus confronted with two opposing views of the Soviet position in the Middle East: one portrays the period from 1945 as an unbroken succession of Western retreat and Russian advances; the other maintains that Soviet strength was exaggerated. In favor of the latter view, one might point out that the Soviet record, while spectacular, was not matched by a corresponding development of secure day-to-day relations, nor was the West excluded from much of the Middle East. Recently, Geoffrey Kemp has stressed "the relative weakness of Soviet military power in this area, especially in the period 1945–1967. The Soviet Union has had no overt defense treaty with any of the countries in the Middle East since 1945. Balanced against this, the United States has had bilateral defense treaties with Turkey, Iran, Pakistan, and military-base agreements with Morocco, Libya, and Saudi Arabia." [10] This is not to say that the Soviet Union did not make significant gains during this period, nor is it to imply that the West has maintained its position; it is to point out that Western observers, wary of Soviet encroachment, may tend to look for signs of Russian advances while taking for granted the areas of continuing Western strength. Furthermore, it does not appear that the Soviet-Western contest in the Middle East is a zero-sum game in which one side's losses are the other's gain.

The attribution to the Soviet Union of precise (and invariably accurate) calculations in its foreign policy has also been exaggerated, and has lost favor with a number of scholars since 1967. The June War is viewed by some writers as a result of the loss of Soviet control over the Arab states, and as a consequence of a poor understanding on the part of the Soviet Union of the meaning attributed by the Arabs to certain of their statements. In fact, it appears as if the USSR had failed to appreciate the determination of the Arabs to defend their interests, as they defined them. In short, the USSR's claim that "the Soviet stand is a dependable guarantee of the Arab countries' security" [11] proved to be quite untrue and represented a serious miscalculation.

Even if the Soviet Union was not in such complete command of the situation prior to 1967 as is sometimes assumed, it might be thought that the war dealt the final blow to waning American interest or that Soviet influence in the area increased markedly, thus making June 1967 a genuine turning point in the history of Soviet involvement in the Middle East. These possibilities must be carefully examined.

By 1967 the United States had alienated about half of the Arab governments and much of Arab public opinion through its affronts to President Nasser and other Arab nationalists. This situation was aggravated by the anti-Nasser tone of American public opinion and the belief that Nasser's prestige in the Middle East constituted a barrier to the policies of at least some American decision-makers. The June War did much to confirm the Arab opinion that the United States was wholly committed to Israel, and thus to further alienate the Arabs from America. The United Arab Republic and several other Arab countries severed relations with the United States (several had broken off relations previously). Many believed the United States had given military support to the Israeli attack on Egypt.

In contrast, by 1967 the Soviet Union had created much good will throughout the Middle East through its diplomatic and political support for Arab nationalism and Palestinian rights and through its "no strings attached" aid programs. The June War presented the first real test of the USSR's commitment to the Arab cause. The Soviets "became the champions of the Arab cause at the United Nations. . . . At the same time they moved swiftly to begin re-equipping the shattered Egyptian army, proffered arms to Jordan, and cultivated high-level contacts with Algeria, Syria, and the U.A.R. They also established a naval presence at the mouth of the Suez Canal as a gesture of support to the U.A.R." [12]

Thus, while the United States has lost much of its stature in the Arab world, the Soviet Union's influence has advanced greatly. From a Cold War perspective, it appears that the Soviet Union has encircled Iran and Turkey and has extended its power throughout the Middle East. What has happened since 1967?

DOMINATION OR ENTANGLEMENT

Considering the question posed in the title of this section, Bernard Lewis sketched out the extreme forms of the two views of the consequences of the June War of 1967 in an article in *Foreign Affairs,* July 1969:

> According to one view, the Russians have during the last two years achieved an immense success—the fulfillment of the centuries-old dream of the Tsars. They have won great political influence in the Arab lands—dominant in some, powerful in others, threatening even in those countries that are still more or less in the Western camp. Russia is now an established Mediterranean power, with friendly ports on the eastern and southern shores, and is reaching across the land bridges to Asia and Africa.
>
> A diametrically opposite view is expressed in the saying that the Middle East is Russia's Vietnam. According to this interpretation, Russia was unwittingly sucked in on the losing side, with a perilous and endless commitment, in an undertaking of great risk, high cost, and dubious results.

A writer who follows the first view, Ciro Zoppo, looks at Soviet involvement in the Mediterranean this way, in an article in the spring 1970 issue of *Orbis:* "The Soviet squadron represents a permanent Soviet presence in the Mediterranean and a firm commitment to the Arabs. . . . Soviet ships roaming the Mediterranean also expand the confrontation of the superpowers beyond Europe and bring into question the military boundary between the Soviet and American spheres of influence." On the other hand, another article, by Donald W. Mitchell in the same number of the same journal, asserts: "Without doubt the Soviet move into the Mediterranean represents the assumption of considerable risk. . . . The Soviets may find that their course bares them to commitments, risks and responsibilities with no ideological payoff."

Lewis attempts to resolve this question by cataloguing gains and losses for the Soviet Union, and J. C. Hurewitz, in *Soviet-American Rivalry in the Middle East,* after describing the advances made by the Soviet Union, concedes that the Russians have incurred serious risks at considerable expense to themselves. From the lack of consensus among observers of the Middle East as to the actual gains made by the Soviet Union since 1967, we must conclude that the June War, while certainly significant, marked no cataclysmic turning point. The Soviet Union made substantial gains at that time due to its support of the Arabs, and the United States lost a good deal of support due to its partisanship of

Israel. However, the majority of Arab states have not been involved directly in the struggle against Israel, and they still retain a detached view of the Soviet Union. It should also be remembered that the Arabs lost the 1967 war and that the Soviet Union was unable to prevent that defeat. Even John C. Campbell revised his estimate of the stark disaster awaiting the West from an expansion of Soviet influence until, after a decade had passed, he could say:

> This stark contrast suggests a succession of Soviet advances and Western retreats equivalent to a decisive change in the balance of military and political power in the region. Such was not the case. What happened was that the Soviet Union had become a Middle East power whereas before it had been virtually excluded. . . .
>
> It was inevitable that the Soviet Union, as one of the superpowers, should have asserted itself in a strategically important area bordering on its own frontiers. . . . This transformation of the area into one of active competition did not spell Soviet domination, but it proved that the old system of Western domination was ended and would not be replaced by an American substitute, even in the guise of alliances and economic cooperation.[13]

Before proceeding to describe events since 1967, we must, therefore, accept the position of Bernard Lewis, when he says that the situation in the Arab lands and the attitude of their peoples and even governments are more complex and less one-sided than might appear.

The Soviet Union has continued its policy of improving relations with Turkey and Iran, as well as Afghanistan and Pakistan to the east. It should be noted that this rapprochement has been made possible, at least in part, by the Soviet recognition that good relations were possible despite the membership of Turkey in NATO and the membership of Iran and Turkey in CENTO. Walter Laqueur's opinion, given in an article in *Foreign Affairs,* January 1969, that "since 1965 a determined Soviet effort has been made to neutralize Turkey and Iran," should perhaps be modified to read: since 1965 the Soviet Union has attempted to improve relations with Turkey and Iran to its own benefit by acting toward them as though they were neutral and ignoring their continuing, if weakened, commitment to the West. The Soviet contribution to the Iranian economic plan is of particular significance, even though the USSR is still only seventh on the list of Iranian trading partners. Developments in the Northern Tier are likely to follow a pattern of slow easing of tension and development of better relations, but, while it is possible that the area will be neutralized, it is unlikely that it will fall into the Soviet sphere of influence.

These developments in the Northern Tier may affect Soviet relations with the Arab states, either adversely or favorably, through the current dispute over the fate of the Persian Gulf. Once again we find a division of opinion about the prospects and dangers facing this area—the source of much of the world's oil. On the one hand, a popular view has it that Russia may establish a presence in the Persian Gulf and shut off the oil supply to Western Europe. Others see the primary danger resulting from the Soviet assumption of Britain's former position as arbiter of the region's quarrels. Both views reflect, in Robert R. Sullivan's opinion, in the spring 1970 issue of *Orbis,* that the Soviet Union is being presented with an opportunity by the "development of a dangerously unstable bipolar (Iran *vs.* Saudi Arabia) international subsystem in the Persian Gulf."

On the other hand, an analysis of the benefits for the Soviet Union from involvement in the area, together with the Soviet capacity to act, shows that much of this danger is ephemeral. The direct advantages to the Soviet Union—military and economic—are not worthwhile, while the indirect advantages—denial to the West of a locus for a military buildup, the communications facilities of the area, and oil—work out to be of considerable risk with uncertain benefits. The basic point is that nothing in the area, except the oil, is important enough to start a war about, and in time of war it would not matter who was in nominal control of the Persian Gulf. The strong probability is that in peace the oil will flow to Western Europe and in war it will not, no matter whether the Soviets or the Arabs control it. The Soviet Union does seek influence in the area, but it is not likely to take any precipitous actions with regard to it.

The Kingdom of Saudi Arabia, while not intentionally exacerbating relations with the Soviet Union, has demonstrated no willingness to forego either its military or its economic relationship with the West. Similarly, Kuwait, concerned with its own wealth and security, has shown no enthusiasm for departing from its established policy of neutrality on both the Soviet-American and Arab conservative-revolutionary axes. In the remainder of the Arabian peninsula, only Yemen and South Yemen have been of interest to the Soviet Union, and its record there has been cautiously anti-imperialist. After supporting the Imam Yahya against the British for years, the Soviets shifted, in line with UAR policy, to support for the regime of Sallal against that of Imam Badr, but its participation was indirect, by way of Egypt, and there was no attempt to force a confrontation. More recently, the USSR has tried to develop friendly relations with both Yemen and South Yemen, but has avoided involvement in local disputes.

In the core region of the Arab world, Soviet progress since 1967 has been mixed. On the one hand, as Harry N. Howard notes:

> It not only exploited its support of the Arab states in their contest with Israel, but increased its influence through both military and economic assistance. By the end of 1968 it was estimated that the Soviet Union had given the United Arab Republic at least $1 billion in military and $250 million in economic assistance, while Syria and Iraq had received some $1,500 million, Algeria, $500 million, and Iran sought a $900 million credit. The Republic of Turkey received a $250 million credit in 1968 in technical and economic assistance.[14]

Thus, the extensive Soviet economic and military aid to the UAR (the most influential Arab country in the Middle East) certainly cannot be underestimated. Reequipping an army of a state which was in complete defeat, together with dispatching quite a number of training missions (mainly to Egypt), carried the Soviets into the heart of the military establishment which is the basis of political power in many Arab countries. In return, "The Soviet Mediterranean fleet was given storage and repair facilities, or the equivalent of naval base rights, at Alexandria and Port Sa'id; and Soviet pilots were allowed to fly Soviet-made planes with Egyptian markings on Soviet missions in the Mediterranean, representing the equivalent in Egypt of air-base rights." [15] The respected journal *International Conciliation,* September 1970, traced some developments of early 1970:

> In January 1970, after a thirty-six hour occupation by Israeli troops of the Red Sea island of Shadwan, which protects the Egyptian naval base at Safaga, President Nasser flew secretly to Moscow and asked the Soviet Union for more advanced weapons, including MIG-23 fighter-bombers and anti-aircraft equipment. In March, the Soviet Union began installing SAM-3 ground-to-air missiles around Alexandria, Cairo, the Aswan Dam, and Helwan. By July the Russians were reported to have built up an elaborate air defense system for most of Egypt.

It was even reported in the same journal, although disputed, that Soviet pilots were flying missions over Israeli-occupied territory. The Soviet Union also established a powerful naval presence in the Mediterranean. In the opinion of some this was an indication of great Soviet influence. At the least, a repetition of the 1958 landings in Lebanon and Jordan is no longer possible for the West, even if such an act is not yet possible for the Soviet Union.

Soviet relations with Jordan, unfriendly up to June 1967, improved somewhat after the war. The Soviet Union apparently offered to supply arms to Jordan to replace the losses sustained in the conflict, and it renewed the offer in 1968, according to Aryeh Yodfat, in the March–April 1969 issue of *Mizan*. Jordan rejected the offer, but King Hussein visited Moscow in October 1967. Despite Israeli and Palestinian pressure on Jordan's military strength, the Jordanian army is still equipped with American-made matériel. The Jordanians take the view that the Soviet Union is a friend of the Arabs and as such should be treated cordially unless it attempts to interfere in the internal affairs of Jordan. The Soviet Union for its part views Jordan in a more favorable light than formerly. A real, although limited, extension of relations seems to be occurring.

The Soviet Union participated in Syrian economic development by financing half the cost of a dam on the Euphrates in 1966; the dam was initiated in 1968. After the June War, Syria received about $300 million worth of military aid, according to Yodfat's article, and about 700–1,000 Soviet military advisers were resident in Syria.

CONCLUSION

Soviet influence is one of the most obvious facts in the politics of the Middle East today. Actually, it is not mere Soviet influence that is being felt in the area, but a very real presence at all levels. We may conclude, then, that Soviet policy certainly has been successful in establishing the USSR as a power in the Middle East. Far from bringing the area into its sphere of influence, however, or even neutralizing it, the Soviet Union became involved in the politics of the Middle East. This was the case despite the fact that even in the pro-Soviet Arab countries the local Communist Parties were systematically pulverized by the USSR-supported governing elites. Indeed, the Soviet Union's foreign policy in the area was flexible enough (or expedient enough, as some would like to call it) to seek presence in the Middle East not only through the above-mentioned elites who were militantly against the local Communist Parties but also at the expense of the latter.

In other words, the Soviet Union's influence in the area derived initially not from ideological alignments, military alliances, or economic exigencies, but from its position in international relations vis-à-vis the United States. And so long as Israel has the solid support of American aid and diplomacy, the Arabs will continue to seek Soviet support as a counter-balance. Also, so long as the confrontation with Israel persists,

Egypt and Syria in particular are dependent upon Soviet military aid. To what extent the Arabs will cooperate with the Soviet Union to ensure its support is problematic. The USSR's success in the area has hinged on two factors: first, its noninterference in the internal affairs of the states in the area (to the sacrifice of local Communist Parties and ideological commitment); and second, within the Arab community, at least, the lack of a perception of threat from the Soviet Union.

With some $4–5 billion invested in military aid alone, buttressed by massive economic aid, it does not seem that the Soviet Union could long be content to be merely a foil to American policy in the area. The risks of this role are indeed high, for the place of the Middle East in the contest between the powers has never been clearly defined, and it is therefore likely to remain one of the main danger zones in world politics in years to come. Will the Soviet Union make demands in the area for some type of return on its investments and for more tangible reasons to take such risks? If so, the Soviet Union may be on a merry-go-round, for interference in the internal affairs of the area's states would certainly be resented and could brand the Soviet Union as a threat to national integrity, causing these states to seek allies to counterbalance Soviet policy. There is some indication that this indeed may be the case. The Soviet-Egyptian and Soviet-Iraqi Treaties of May 27, 1971, and April 9, 1972, respectively, formalized Soviet relations with these countries in the military, cultural, economic, and technological spheres, in effect consolidating the Soviet position in both nations. There was speculation in the *Christian Science Monitor,* April 12, 1972, that a similar treaty with Syria will follow. The Soviet-Iraqi treaty was attacked in some Arab newspapers and by the Libyan government as a revival of imperialism in the tradition of the Baghdad Pact. On April 13, 1972, Libya announced it was withdrawing its ambassador from Iraq and requested that Iraq recall its ambassador from Libya. In addition, Soviet acceptance of the Rogers' Peace Plan and UN Resolution 242 of November 1967 and its participation in the Four Power talks seeking an imposed settlement of the Middle East issue has alienated the Palestine Liberation Movement, who now call the Soviet Union a "social imperialist" and opt for Chinese rather than Soviet ideological direction. In becoming an established power in the Middle East, the Soviet Union has become committed to the status quo and has lost its revolutionary image.

What types of bonds with the Middle East may the USSR be seeking? Economic ties, long considered by Western observers as subservient to political objectives, are rapidly developing, and, according to the *Middle East Economic Digest* (London), August 28, 1970, are "sufficiently valuable to provide a motivation for the Soviet Union's foreign policy as well as being a result and manifestation of it." The report continues by pointing out the three primary areas of Soviet interest and influence —trade, aid, and oil. By 1969, the Soviet Union was the fifth largest supplier to the Middle East, with its exports to the area valued at $337.9 million. The Soviet Union is in fact increasing its exports to the region faster than any of the other leading industrialized nations; in 1969 they reached nearly five times their 1959 value.

While the UAR accounts for the largest volume of Soviet trade in the Middle East, this trade is by no means restricted to a few favorite nations. In 1959, markets in the UAR, with a value of 79.2 million rubles, represented almost half the total value of Soviet markets in the area. By 1969, however, although the value of the UAR market had increased to 214.4 million rubles, it now represented only about 30 percent of the total Soviet market in the area. In the same period, the value of Soviet markets in Iran, Iraq, Turkey, Algeria, and Syria increased from about 30 percent in 1959 (46.5 million rubles) to approximately 50 percent in 1969 (362.3 million rubles), thus illustrating both the growth and diversification of Soviet markets in the area.

The distribution of trade is closely associated to the distribution of aid, for Soviet aid is granted primarily in the form of bilateral credits. The *MEED* report notes that "although the aid is very often tied to specific projects and almost invariably to Soviet goods, the limitations have to be set against the considerable advantages of the barter arrangements which are often made to clear the credit. For several Middle East countries such deals provide an invaluable outlet for the produce of their manufacturing ventures."

Soviet interest in Middle East oil, according to the *MEED* report, is based on indications that domestic consumption is beginning to outpace production. Trade agreements that include oil have already been concluded with Algeria, Iraq, Syria, and Iran. The report concludes that "the new importance of oil is now the chief economic factor behind Soviet policy in the Middle East."

In conclusion, we should point out that, despite their gains in the area and despite the decline of Western power, the Russians do not appear to be as happy about the Middle East situation as one might expect. The Soviet Union took the lead in initiating the Four Power talks at the United Nations and have not rejected the Rogers' plan for a negotiated settlement. This would seem to indicate that, as a power in the area, the Soviet Union is now as concerned as is the West with establishing stability in the area and with defining the boundaries of power to minimize friction.

Despite impressive gains at the expense of the West, Soviet involvement in the Middle East since the June War has rested on an uncomfortable dilemma. On the one hand, much Soviet influence in the Arab world has depended on her willingness to fill Arab demands for arms to be actively deployed in the liberation of Israeli-occupied territories. On the other hand, the USSR does not want to provoke a confrontation with the U.S., which would be the inevitable result of any forcible Arab attempt to attain their objective. Recent developments in Soviet policy toward Egypt, Iraq, and Syria have brought this dilemma into clear focus. There are strong indications that recent Soviet policy has tried to resolve this dilemma by placing priority on stabilizing the Middle East. It is undertaking measures at the same time to mollify Arab militancy without losing the basis of its support in the region.

Immediately after the June War, the Soviet task was clear-cut: to rebuild the shattered Arab forces. At this time of general weakness, there was no tendency on the part of the Egyptians to distinguish between defensive and offensive weaponry; thus the sincerity of Moscow's support was not suspect. As late as 1970, Egyptian aspirations remained limited to the prevention of deep penetration raids by Israeli aircraft. These were curtailed by the installation of SAM-2 and SAM-3 shields around Cairo and Alexandria. Egypt's growing self-defense capability was matched by a corresponding desire for offensively oriented weapons— MIG-23's and Tatest Soviet tanks. The Russians released only a small number of new aircraft to direct Egyptian control, the rest being operated by Soviet technical and military personnel. Soviet qualifications and limitations on the offensive strength of the Egyptian armed forces caused Sadat to lose much credibility in 1971, his uneventful but highly touted "year of decision." This precipitated the eviction of Soviet advisors *en masse* in July 1972. Although the consequences of this action were a definite setback for Moscow, the basis of Egyptian relations remained intact.

Even prior to its Egyptian setback, the Soviet Union had taken steps to soothe Arab militancy. After excoriating attacks by Kaddafi and Numeiry in 1971, the Soviet Union has sought to diversify the scope of its involvement. This too seems motivated by a two-fold desire to consolidate her influence without appearing to forsake the Arabs in the struggle against Israel. The main direction of this reorientation has been to Syria and Iraq. The USSR placed much more emphasis in developing a relationship based more on economic and technical interaction and cooperation than substantial quantities of military assistance.

Syria's President Assad requested, in addition to Soviet military and technical aid, more advanced military hardware for the Syrian armed forces. This the Soviets accepted, but only on the condition that they be operated by Russian troops, and not under the direct command of the Syrian armed forces. Assad refused this condition. Soviet emphasis on technical aid coupled with military restraint was received more favorably in Iraq. In particular, the Iraqis were anxious to have the Russians complete a dam across the Euphrates in Syria.

Immediately following its expulsion from Egypt the Soviet Union signed two important treaties with Egypt and Iraq that further indicate its concern with restraining Arab military zeal. The documents place heavy emphasis on economic and technical cooperation, as opposed to new military equipment. They lay repeated emphasis on the duty of the Soviet Union to protect the Arab cause at all costs, as reported in the *New York Times,* July 24, 1972.

In the same connection, the protocols state that it is a duty of the Soviet Union to defend the Arabs from "imperialist aggression." The spirit of the agreements, as expressed by the Soviet ambassador to Egypt in *Rose-al-Yusuf,* November 8, 1971, is:

> The only way to eliminate the consequences of the aggression are for you to be strong. Those who kept silent in the past have now resumed talking about the possibility of a peaceful settlement. Their voices have risen. Why? Because you have *become* strong [emphasis added]. As your strength has increased [peaceful] voices have risen more and more, and your opportunity to free your land becomes closer and closer. . . . This requires strengthening of relations with the Soviet Union and the socialist states, inasmuch as this is part of the strengthening of Egypt and the Arab states.

It is highly noteworthy that in all these instances, the Soviet Union has inculcated the appearance of a one-sided commitment to the Arab cause. Meanwhile, the content of that commitment has been severely conditioned by the Soviet aim of stabilizing the region in order to consolidate the influence she has thus far managed to obtain on the basis of her military commitment. The Arab states have become as strong as the over-all stability of the Middle East permits. This was sharply demonstrated in the October 1973 Arab-Israeli War when Israel was unable to repeat its spectacular success of 1967, and in fact, appeared on the defensive throughout most of the action. Soviet military equipment, especially the SAM-6 missiles the Russians contributed to build an elaborate air defense system for Egypt, and the military training programs they sponsored in Egypt and Syria, were the critical factors affecting the military balance in the Arab-Israeli conflict. Just as significant was the Soviet Union's continued staunch support for the Arabs in the face of complete American support for Israel.

The October 1973 War in fact consolidated the Soviet Union's military commitment to the Arabs. It's confrontation with the United States, particularly over the implementation of the cease-fire, raised Soviet popularity to new heights in the Arab world, at all levels. With the American role in the Arab world bankrupted by its total commitment to Israel during the war, the future should witness greater Soviet-Arab cooperation in the political and economic realms.

❊ 5 ❊

HARRY N. HOWARD

The United States and the Middle East

BASIC INTERESTS AND POLICIES

The United States has enduring interests in the Middle East, and, as one of the great world powers, it is confronted with a wide range of issues and problems in that highly troubled region. These include the seemingly unyielding conflict between Israel and the neighboring Arab states and the Palestinians over Palestine, the long-standing Greco-Turkish controversy relative to Cyprus, the tension between Iran and the Arab states of the Persian Gulf area, and the inter-Arab rivalries concerning position, influence, and ideologies, to say nothing of the problems which arise as a result of the expansion of Soviet influence in the eastern Mediterranean and the Middle East. With the exception of Europe and South Vietnam, in recent years, no part of the world has been of greater concern to American policy-makers since World War II, when the United States emerged as one of the superpowers.

The United States is interested in the Middle East as an intercontinental crossroads between Eurasia and Africa—as a highway to and from the Mediterranean area and South Asia. It is interested in the maintenance of land, sea, and air routes and the communications facilities of the area. It is also much concerned with the orderly and equitable access to the vast oil resources in the Middle East and North Africa, with some 380 billion barrels of proved reserves, or about 70 percent of the free world's supply of oil. These resources are of vital importance to the economies of American allies in Western Europe and the Far East. As the energy crisis deepened in the United States in the 1970s, Middle Eastern oil became of increasing concern. But the United States is also basically concerned with the peace, security, welfare, and orderly development of all the peoples of the Middle East. Without that concern, and without some understanding of the history, culture, and aspirations of the peoples of the region, it may well be questioned that the United States can achieve whatever short- or long-range objectives it may have in the Middle East.

The American people have had an association with the Middle East for some two hundred years, especially in the commerical-economic and missionary-educational-philanthropic enterprises. Enduring American politico-strategic interests, however, date only from World War II, when President Franklin D. Roosevelt in 1941 declared the defense of Turkey and the Middle East vital to the defense of the United States. Enduring military commitments came only after World War II, in response to the threat of possible Soviet domination of the Middle East, where the USSR, too, has long-term and wideranging interests. These Soviet, or Russian, interests have centered along the Northern Tier of the Middle East—Greece, Turkey, and Iran—in the urge to the open sea, especially since the eighteenth century, and have broadened and deepened in the Arab world since 1955. As President Richard M. Nixon observed in February 1970, "the United States would view any effort by the Soviet Union to seek predominance in the Middle East as a matter of grave concern."

The United States has given much assistance throughout the Middle East, but it has military commitments only to Greece and Turkey under NATO (February 15, 1952), on the southern flank of NATO, and to Turkey and Iran under the bilateral arrangements of March 5, 1959. While there have been many policy statements regarding the Arab-Israeli conflict, the only formal commitments, as the Senate Foreign Relations Committee observed in April 1969, are those embodied in the United Nations Charter. The various presidential statements relative to the peace, security, and orderly development in the area of the Arab-Israel conflict rest, essentially, on the Anglo-Franco-American Tripartite Declaration of May 25, 1950. Much of American attention today, of course, is centered on Palestine, the primary national interest in which lies in seeking a just, peaceful, and viable solution, in the reduction and containment of Soviet influence, and in the avoidance of escalation into a possible confrontation with the Soviet Union.

FOUNDATIONS OF AMERICAN INTEREST AND POLICY

The Middle East and its problems have been with us since the beginnings of recorded history, and there is every reason to assume that they will be with us in the years which lie ahead. Today the area is important in contemporary world politics essentially because of its strategic location at the intercontinental crossroads and of its petroleum resources. The problem of the Turkish Straits dates from the Trojan Wars (1194–84 B.C.) and that of a possible canal at Suez from the fifth century B.C. Even oil was not unknown in the ancient era, although it did not have its modern significance. While much has been written in years past of the "Eastern Question" and conflicts among the European great powers relative to the succession in the declining Ottoman Empire, it is rather seldom noted in the standard histories that the United States and the American people developed an abiding concern with the Middle East, especially in the nineteenth century.

As early as 1767, it appears, American merchantmen plied an uncertain, if profitable, trade in the Middle East, and Smyrna figs appeared on the Boston market as early as 1785. The Continental Congress sought diplomatic recognition of the Sublime Porte in 1774. In 1792, during the administration of President George Washington, a treaty which recognized the independence of Morocco was signed with the Sultan of Morocco. The United States fought a naval conflict with the Barbary States along the North African coast of the Mediterranean Sea during 1801–1805, and United States Marines still sing not merely of the "Halls of Montezuma" but of the "shores of Tripoli." By 1816, the United States maintained a naval squadron in the Mediterranean—a predecessor, as it were, of the United States Sixth Fleet. In 1826, Secretary of State Henry Clay attempted to develop a group of young American officials who would be proficient in the use of Eastern languages and decided to put "a midshipman or some other youth" under the care of the American consuls in Tunis, Tripoli, Algiers, and Tangier, to study Turkish, Arabic, and other languages.

The first religious mission was established by the American Board of Commissioners for Foreign Missions in 1820, and missionaries began going to the Middle East to take their gospel back to its birthplace. While they did not convert many Muslims or Jews, and finally worked more among the "nominal Christians" in Istanbul, Beirut, Damascus, and Jerusalem, they inaugurated the work which culminated in the establishment of Robert College (1863), the Istanbul Women's College (1871), the American University of Beirut (Syrian Protestant College, 1866), and the American University of Cairo (1919), to say nothing of other institutions. It would be difficult to measure the beneficent influences which radiated from these institutions in the Middle East, whatever their current problems. The legacy, the interest, and the work have remained.

Commodore William Bainbridge took the first American warship into Constantinople—bearing tribute—on November 9, 1800, and an American consul, although not recognized, was named at Smyrna in

1802. An American trading house was established in Smyrna in 1811. But it was not until May 7, 1830 (ratified in 1831) that the first American-Ottoman Treaty of Amity and Commerce was signed. The treaty stressed freedom for American commerce, most-favored nation treatment, the maintenance of capitulatory rights, and freedom of commercial passage through the Turkish Straits. A new treaty was signed in 1862, and in 1871 the United States enunciated the principle that the Sublime Porte had no legal right to close the straits, even to American warships, while the Ottoman Empire was at peace, and refused to recognize the right *de jure* to do so, although it made no special issue of the principle. Meanwhile, it signed treaties of friendship and commerce with the Sultan of Musqat (1833, ratified 1835) and the Shah of Persia (1856, ratified 1857).

While the commercial-economic interests in the Middle East remained largely aspirational until World War II, and there were few politico-strategic interests, still, it was two Americans, Henry Eckford and Foster Rhodes, well-known shipbuilders, who practically rebuilt the Ottoman fleet in the early 1830s, after the disaster of Navarino (1827). Moreover, a group of former Union and Confederate officers, anxious to refurbish both their military reputations and their fortunes, supervised the modernization of the Egyptian armed forces, carried out extensive engineering surveys, prepared detailed maps, and projected a dam at Aswan during the years 1870–83. In a way these almost forgotten episodes constitute the first American naval and military assistance programs in the Middle East, anticipating the official assistance programs after World War II, when the Middle East had moved from the far-off periphery more toward an active center of American interest and concern.

Although there was little political interest, there was concern at times as to Russian imperial moves toward the Turkish Straits, some involvement in the Armenian problem, especially after 1890, and interest in the struggles of the Greeks and the Balkan Slavs against the Ottoman Empire. These were all duly recorded in the diplomatic correspondence of the day; they make interesting reading, but they called for no action on the part of the United States. The United States showed no overriding concern with the Middle East during World War I, did not declare war on the Ottoman Empire as an ally of Germany and Austria-Hungary, although it did break relations, and had no troops in the area. But it was interested in the peace and security of the region. In his Fourteen Points Address of January 8, 1918, President Woodrow Wilson called for Turkish sovereignty in the Anatolian homelands, "unmolested opportunity of autonomous development" for other nationalities then under Ottoman rule, and permanent opening of the straits "as a free passage to the ships of commerce of all nations under international guarantees."

At the Paris Peace Conference, President Wilson sought to develop a viable program for peace in the Middle East. In that interest, he not only fostered the mandate system, but sent the King-Crane Commission to investigate conditions in the Middle East and to report and recommend concerning peace. The commission recommended a general American mandate, including mandates over the region of the straits and Armenia. In the end, however, none of this program, which was highly critical of the French claims in Syria and opposed to the extreme Zionist position on Palestine, worked out. The United States took no formal part in the negotiation of the abortive Treaty of Sèvres in 1920, rejected any responsibility in the Middle East, and sent only talkative observers to the Lausanne Conference of November 1922–July 1923.

During the interwar period, the United States was concerned with the rights and properties of American citizens, freedom of opportunity for American business under the principle of the "open door," maintenance of the capitulatory regime, the missionary-education-philanthropic enterprise, and archaeological research. While there was an interest in freedom of the Turkish Straits—even for Soviet Russia—the United States refused participation in the International Commission of the Straits under the League of Nations, and it did not ratify the American-Turkish Treaty of August 6, 1923. It took no part at all in the Montreux Conference (1936) for revision of the Lausanne Straits Convention, since its only interest lay in the maintenance of the principle of freedom of commercial passage through the Turkish Straits, a matter of some regret ten years later. While the U.S. Congress approved a resolution in 1922 relative to a Jewish "homeland" in Palestine and endorsed the British mandate, the primary interest even in this matter largely lay in the rights and properties of American citizens, as reiterated in 1938.

THE IMPACT OF WORLD WAR II

The enduring American politico-strategic interest in the Middle East, ultimately involving military commitments, dates from World War II. The period immediately prior to American entry into the war witnessed an increasing concern with the expansion of the conflict in the Middle East. During January–February 1941, President Franklin D. Roosevelt sent an emissary to this troubled region to stimulate resistance to Nazi

Germany. The Turkish government, under President Ismet Inonu, shared something of the American view concerning the war and pursued a cautious policy as a nonbelligerent ally of the United Kingdom and France (October 19, 1939), with neutral status. President Roosevelt stated the basic principle, in extending lend-lease assistance to Turkey on December 3, 1941, just four days prior to the Japanese attack on Pearl Harbor, when he declared the defense of Turkey "vital to the defense of the United States." The principle was extended to Iran on March 10, 1942, and on March 6, 1944, President Roosevelt declared that the United States had "a vital interest in the Middle East," the peace and security of which were "of significance to the world as a whole." [1] Nevertheless, and despite the large deployment of American troops to protect supply lines to the Soviet Union in Iran and of American troops in the later stages of the North African campaign in 1943, it was quite evident that the Middle East was of secondary interest to the United States as a military theater as compared with Western Europe, where Operation Overlord was to be the major operation against Germany. It was agreed specifically at Casablanca in January 1943 that the British government would "play the cards" in the Middle East. [2]

Granted the significance of the Middle East as vital to the defense of the United States, it is nevertheless clear from the conferences at Quebec, Moscow, Teheran, and Cairo in 1943 that the United States, with its concentration on Operation Overlord, did not favor the entry of Turkey into the shooting war. It is also doubtful that the United Kingdom or the Soviet Union did so either, whatever the propaganda and the pressures to the contrary at very critical moments during the conflict. When the question of possible Turkish entry was raised on July 19, 1944, the American Chiefs of Staff, in response to a question put by President Roosevelt, declared themselves formally in favor but also stated that the United States was not "commmmitted to military, naval, or air support of any campaign in the Balkans." There were no concerted plans for a campaign in that area, and neither troops nor supplies were to be diverted from Operation Overlord. [3]

POSTWAR RIVALRIES

President Harry S Truman was confronted with Middle Eastern problems from the very outset of his administration, primarily because of the continuing threat along the Northern Tier of Greece, Turkey, and Iran, and also because of the Palestine problem, the dangerous implications of which were already becoming evident. The Soviet Union had set forth its position concerning the Middle East during November 1940. As a price for possible entry into the Axis, with which it was then closely associated under the agreement of August 23, 1939, the USSR had demanded a new regime of the Turkish Straits, with bases in the area, and had declared that the center of gravity of Soviet policy and interest lay in the area south of Baku and Batum, in the general direction of the Persian Gulf.

That position did not change with the end of World War II. Soviet ambitions were pressed at all three points along the Northern Tier, and there were Soviet demands both for a trusteeship over Libya and for a commercial (naval) base in the Dodecanese Islands. The Soviet demands relative to the Turkish Straits were pressed during 1945–46, and on August 15, 1946, President Truman advised the Turkish government that the United States would support it—as did the United Kingdom—in opposing Soviet demands which would have converted Turkey into a Soviet satellite.[4] One of the first cases in the early history of the United Nations was in connection with Iran, when the United States, along with the United Kingdom, took a very firm position to bring about the withdrawal of Soviet troops from that country, where the USSR sought to detach both Azerbaijan and Kurdistan and to subvert the entire country to its will. As President Truman had declared in his Army Day Address of April 6, 1946, the Middle East was "an area of great economic and strategic importance, the nations of which" were "not strong enough individually or collectively to withstand powerful aggression." It was easy to see how this region could "become an area of intense rivalry between outside powers, and how such rivalry might suddenly erupt into conflict." No country, he thought, had interests in the Middle East which could not be reconciled with those of other nations through the United Nations.

The threat to Greece, which took the form of internal subversion and guerrilla action along the northern frontiers, was met within the United Nations and through American and British economic and military advisory assistance, training, and equipment. The presence of the United States Sixth Fleet in the Mediterranean no doubt also exercised a salutary, restraining influence in this instance, on both Greece and Turkey. The Greek problem called forth the Truman Doctrine on March 12, 1947, in one of the most far-reaching pronouncements of American foreign policy in the immediate postwar period. President Truman declared that the United States was prepared to assist both Greece and Turkey to preserve their independence. If Greece fell under the control of an armed minority, he said, the effect upon Turkey "would be immediate and serious," and "confusion and disorder might well spread throughout the Middle East." Moreover, if the United States, the only country capable at the time of rendering assistance, failed to aid Greece and Turkey, the effect would "be far-reaching to the West as to the East." Mr. Truman believed that "it must be the policy of the United States to support free peoples who are resisting attempted subjugation by armed minorities or by outside pressures." He felt that they must be assisted to "work out their own destinies in their own way," and that assistance should be primarily through economic and financial aid. Congress was asked to provide authority for initial assistance in the amount of $400 million.[5]

No political or military commitments were involved in the agreements with Greece (June 20, 1947) and Turkey (July 12, 1947) for the administration of the assistance. These came only when Greece and Turkey, on their own volition and in defense of their own national interests, entered the North Atlantic Treaty Organization on February 18, 1952. As applies to Greece and Turkey, the NATO commitments of the United States were extended to cover the territories of these two countries and, therefore, to the eastern Mediterranean. Within the NATO framework, an attack upon either Greece or Turkey was to be considered an attack upon all members. It was agreed that if such an attack occurred, each party would come to the assistance of the victim of aggression, individually or in concert, by taking such action as it deemed necessary.

The United States was, of course, much involved in the developments which led to the partition of Palestine under the United Nations resolution of November 29, 1947, and the subsequent establishment of the state of Israel in 1948. But it is well to recall that its concern with the problem, almost until the end of World War II, lay in the protection of American citizens and property in that troubled area. As late as October 30, 1942, on the twenty-fifth anniversary of the Balfour Declaration, despite the pressures which were brought to bear, Secretary of State Cordell Hull considered that the United States should have a wider objective than the refuge which many Jews had sought in Palestine. He did not endorse the Biltmore Declaration of May 11, 1942, which called for establishment of a "Jewish Commonwealth," but wanted "a world in which Jews, like every other race, are free to abide in peace and honor." [6]

Reluctantly, the United States participated in the Anglo-American Committee of Inquiry concerning Palestine during 1946, which recommended the issuance of 100,000 certificates for entry into Palestine, but did not recommend the establishment of either a Jewish or an Arab state. As the committee viewed the problem, Palestine ultimately should become a state which guarded the rights and interests of Muslims, Jews, and Christians alike.

After approval of the resolution of November 29, 1947, President Truman was determined to avoid the use of American troops in implementing it, and he attempted to backtrack into temporary trusteeship during March–April 1948, particularly when he saw intense continuation of the conflict over Palestine. Secretary of State Dean Acheson, it is interesting to observe, did not share President Truman's views as to Palestine, which could not absorb the displaced European Jews "without creating a grave political problem." Moreover, to transform Palestine into a Jewish state "capable of receiving a million or more immigrants would vastly exacerbate the political problem and imperil not only American but all Western interests in the Near East." In urging an American official policy, Mr. Acheson believed that American Zionists obscured "the totality of American interests" in the Middle East.[7]

The establishment of Eretz Israel on May 15, 1948, with American recognition following within nine minutes, and the ensuing conflict intensified the Arab-Israeli problem, and there were grave fears as to the future. In response to this complicated series of problems and their potentialities for trouble, France, the United Kingdom, and the United States, in the Tripartite Declaration of May 25, 1950, in the interest of avoiding an arms race in the area, recognized that both Israel and the Arab states needed to maintain their armed forces at a certain level to assure both internal security and legitimate self-defense and to permit them to play a role in regional defense. Moreover, the three powers declared "their deep interest in and their desire to promote the establishment and maintenance of peace and stability in the area and their unalterable opposition to the use of force or threat of force between any of the states of that area. The three Governments, should they find that any of these states was preparing to violate frontiers or armistice lines, would, consistent with their obligations as members of the United Nations, immediately take action, both within and outside the United Nations, to prevent such violation."[8]

The Tripartite Declaration was violated in 1954 by a secret Franco-Israeli arms arrangement, and probably became invalid for both France and the United Kingdom after the Suez conflict in 1956. But it remained as a fundamental guideline of American policy in the area of the Arab-Israeli conflict. It should be observed that the declaration was not a commitment directly either to Israel or to the Arab states, but a statement of policy relative to peace, security, and orderly development in the area, and was so considered at the time by both Israel and the Arab states. Certainly it embodied no direct commitment as to the use of American forces.

THE EISENHOWER ADMINISTRATION

President Dwight D. Eisenhower brought no fundamental change in American policy in the Middle East, although his administration pursued a more balanced policy in the Arab-Israeli conflict and it was much concerned with the problem of regional security in the Middle East, as the Truman administration had been. After an official visit to the Middle East during May 1953, Secretary of State John Foster Dulles observed that the peoples of that area were deeply concerned about independence and better standards of living. The United States, he thought, should allay the deep resentment against it which resulted from the creation of the state of Israel. The United States should seek to reduce tensions in the Middle East. Mr. Dulles was now convinced that the establishment of a regional security arrangement in the area was a matter for the future, not an immediate possibility. When the attempt to establish a Middle East Command, or Middle East Defense Organization (1951–52), with American, British, Turkish, and Arab and Israeli participation, failed, Dulles concentrated on the Northern Tier of Turkey, Iran, and Iraq, and ultimately his policy led to the elaboration of the Baghdad (CENTO) Pact in 1955, which also included Pakistan and the United Kingdom.[9] While the United States did not adhere to the Baghdad Pact, it helped to initiate the arrangement, and it participated both in committee meetings and in meetings of the ministerial council. Moreover, on March 5, 1959, the United States entered into bilateral arrangements with Turkey, Iran, and Pakistan, as members of CENTO, which stated that, in the event of aggression, the United States, in accordance with the U.S. Constitution, would "take such appropriate action, including the use of armed forces," as might be "mutually agreed upon" and as was "envisaged" in the Eisenhower, or American, Doctrine of March 5, 1957, in order to assist the government concerned at its request. The NATO obligations to Greece and Turkey and these bilateral arrangements constitute the only formal agreements which stipulate specifically the possible commitments of American forces in the Middle East. There are no others.

The United States was, of course, much concerned with the developments which led to the Suez conflict during October–November 1956, and especially with the problem of transit and navigation in the Suez

Canal, after the Egyptian nationalization of the canal company, although that problem had been substantially settled, in principle, by October 13, 1956. At the onset of the conflict, however, Secretary of State Dulles indicated that the United States, which did not intend to "shoot its way" through the Suez Canal, sought only a peaceful solution to this complicated problem. It roundly condemned the Israeli-Anglo-French attack on Egypt, and sought the evacuation by Israel of territories occupied both in the Sinai Peninsula and the Gaza Strip. It based its position on the principle that aggression should not be rewarded and threatened the imposition of sanctions to force withdrawal. Claims to the contrary notwithstanding, as to the well-known *aide-mémoire* of February 11, 1957, which Dulles handed to Ambassador Eban, the United States made no commitment relative to passage of the Straits of Tiran or of the Gulf of Aqaba as a price for Israeli withdrawals from Egyptian territory. Dulles indicated that the United States considered that the Gulf of Aqaba comprehended international waters and that no nation had the right to "prevent free and innocent passage in the gulf and through the Straits [of Tiran] giving acces thereto." But he stated only that the United States, "on behalf of vessels of United States registry," was "prepared to exercise the right of free and innocent passage and to join with others to secure general recognition of this right." Following Israel's withdrawal, the United States was ready publicly to "use its influence, in concert with other United Nations members, to the end that . . . these other measures will be implemented."

Following the Suez conflict, President Eisenhower enunciated the Eisenhower Doctrine, somewhat modeled on the Truman Doctrine of 1947, relative to the Middle East. As finally approved in the Joint Congressional Resolution of March 9, 1957, designed to "promote peace and stability in the Middle East," the president was authorized to cooperate with and assist any nation or group of nations in the general area of the Middle East desiring such assistance in the development of economic strength dedicated to the maintenance of national independence; undertake military assistance programs with such nations; and use some $200 million for implementing the provisions of the Mutual Security Act of 1954. It was duly noted that the United States regarded "as vital to the national interest and world peace the preservation of the independence and integrity of the nations of the Middle East." If the president so determined, the United States was prepared to use its armed forces to assist any nation or group of nations "requesting assistance against armed aggression from any country controlled by international communism," consonant with its treaty obligations and with the Constitution. Ambassador James P. Richards was sent to the Middle East in the in-

terest of securing adherence to this policy, but, with the exception of
Lebanon, Greece, Turkey, and Iran, there were no direct endorsements
of the policy embodied in the Eisenhower Doctrine.[10]

A spate of troubles involving Egypt, Jordan, and Syria and a possible
Soviet threat to Turkey, accused of designs against Syria, called forth
concentrated American attention in 1957. By August 1957 the Syrian
situation had gotten out of hand; the Syrian government charged the
United States with an attempt to overthrow it, and the respective ambassadors were withdrawn. In turn, there were American fears that
Syria might fall under the control of "international communism." Deputy Under-Secretary of State Loy W. Henderson was sent to the Middle
East August 22–September 4, 1957, to confer with officials concerning
the alleged danger. But it was difficult to obtain frank discussion,
though Ambassador Henderson reported concern lest Syria become a
victim of "international communism" and, perhaps, become a base for
further "threatening the independence and integrity of the region." At
the same time Syria accused the Turkish government of preparing an attack and brought the charge, with full Soviet support, to the attention of
the United Nations General Assembly.

But it was the Lebanese crisis in 1958 which called for action. On
July 15, 1958, following an appeal by President Camille Chamoun, the
United States began landing some 15,000 American troops in Lebanon;
the troops remained there until October. While it is altogether probable
that the troops were actually sent in response to the Iraqi revolt of July
14, which overthrew the Hashemite dynasty, and as a demonstration in
force that the United States was prepared to act against a possible Soviet-
UAR threat to subvert the Lebanese government, the presence of the
troops assisted that country in choosing a successor to President Chamoun in accordance with its own constitutional processes. At the same
time, the presence of the U.S. Sixth Fleet in the Mediterranean also appears to have been helpful both in this instance and in that of the troubled situation in Jordan in 1957 and 1958. It would also appear, despite restrictions on the United Nations Observation Group in Lebanon
(UNOGIL) and the fact that it was unable to find evidence of "massive
intervention" on the part of the United Arab Republic, that UNOGIL
rendered a very useful service in moral influence and in contributing to
the establishment of conditions which helped to distinguish the predom-
inantly domestic crises from the external complications.

During the difficulties in Jordan, in the same general period, the establishment of a symbolic United Nations presence had a salutary psychological impact. While the UN presence remained in Jordan for some

years, United states forces left Lebanon on October 25 and British forces were withdrawn from Jordan on November 2, 1958.

THE KENNEDY AND JOHNSON ADMINISTRATIONS

Neither the Kennedy nor the Johnson administrations made any basic changes in the publicly stated American policy or commitments in the Middle East, though there were much pressure and propaganda at times to bring about a special security arrangement between the United States and Israel. Secretary of State Dulles resisted this pressure during 1959, for example, as did President John F. Kennedy during 1961–63, when there were various official statements expressing American concern with the peace and security as a whole. On October 25, 1962, President Kennedy assured Prince Faisal of American support "for the maintenance of Saudi Arabia's integrity." [11] On March 8, 1963, Secretary of State Dean Rusk reiterated the American concern with the independence of the Arab states and observed that the United States was very much interested "in the independence of our friends in Jordan and Arabia" and would "be very much alert to any threats against them." [12] On April 3, 1963, President Kennedy spoke of his hope that the "military balance" would continue. It had not changed, he remarked on May 8, and, in words reminiscent of the Tripartite Declaration of May 25, 1950, he emphasized: "We strongly oppose the use of force or the threat of force in the Near East, and we also seek to limit the spread of communism in the Middle East which would, of course, destroy the independence of the people. This Government has been and remains strongly opposed to the use of force in the Near East. In the event of aggression or preparation, whether direct or indirect, we would support appropriate action on our part to prevent or to put a stop to such aggression, which, of course, has been the policy which the United States has followed for some time." [13]

President Lyndon B. Johnson sounded much the same note in February 1964, during the visit of Prime Minister Levi Eshkol of Israel, declaring American support "for the territorial integrity and political independence of all countries in the Near East" and firm opposition "to aggression and the use of force or the threat of force against any country." He repeated these principles when Israel's President Shazar visited Washington on August 2, 1966.[14] Whatever the shortcomings in implementation, this was the policy set forth prior to, during, and after the conflict of June 1967. Mr. Johnson reiterated the established policy on

May 23 and June 19, 1967, and its essence was embodied in the UN Security Council Resolution of November 22, 1967. But there was no commitment of American military, naval, or air forces, despite Egyptian claims of Anglo-American collusion with Israel in the "preemptive strike" against the United Arab Republic. These were statements of policy and not commitments "to take particular actions in particular circumstances." Whatever else may be said of the statements, or of American predispositions, the United States sought to use its influence for a peaceful solution, and it was felt that the use of American armed forces could have serious consequences for international peace extending even beyond the Middle East.[15]

While there was much loose talk during the 1968 presidential campaign—as in 1972—as to commitments to Israel as an "ally," and though ultimately, on December 28, 1968, it was agreed to send some fifty F-4 Phantom jet military aircraft to Israel to maintain the "military balance" in Israel's favor, American policy, officially and publicly, remained as it had been expressed over the years. The United States, it was said, desired to limit the Middle East arms race, and it was committed to the peace, security, and stability of all states in the area. In the area of the Arab-Israeli conflict, whatever the basic American concern, there are no formal commitments like those to Greece, Turkey, and Iran, along the Northern Tier of the Middle East. As the Senate Foreign Relations Committee reported in April 1969, the source of the widely held view that the United States "is committed to the defense of Israel even though we have no security treaty with that country" is "in fact nothing more than a long series of executive policy declarations." Not one of these declarations is based on a treaty ratified by the U.S. Senate. "The only treaty commitment the United States has in the Middle East is as a signatory to the United Nations Charter, under which the United States is obligated to support and help implement any action which the United Nations may take." It was not the committee's position, however, that the United States should not come to Israel's support in the event of aggression, but, "should so significant an obligation be incurred, it ought to be the result of a treaty or other appropriate legislative instrumentality." [16]

THE NIXON ADMINISTRATION

The problem of peace in the Middle East remained a matter of primary concern to the great powers, and especially to the United States, the Soviet Union, the United Kingdom, and France, all of which had important interests in the area. At the very outset of his administration, in January 1969, President Richard M. Nixon considered the Middle East "very explosive" and a "powder keg" which needed to be defused, and he indicated his intention to take initiatives in new directions with new leadership.[17] He proposed to attack the problems along several fronts, with continued all-out support of Ambassador Gunnar V. Jarring's United Nations mission, bilateral and four-power discussions with France, the United Kingdom, and the USSR, talks with Israel and the Arab states, and consideration of long-range economic development in the Middle East. In the event of an agreed settlement, he proposed, as did Secretary of State Dulles on August 26, 1955, the possibility of a major-power guarantee. The president took his position evidently in the light of the basic American interest in the containment of the conflict, which could otherwise very well involve "a confrontation between the nuclear powers, which we want to avoid."

Hopes for a formal settlement appeared to rest on the possibility of a concerted program, based on the Security Council Resolution of November 22, 1967, elaborated by the United States, the USSR, the United Kingdom, and France, which called for the withdrawal of Israeli forces from occupied Arab territories and termination of all claims or states of belligerency and respect for and acknowledgment of the "sovereignty, territorial integrity, and political independence of every state in the area and their right to live in peace within secure an recognized boundaries free from threats or acts of force." The resolution affirmed the principle of freedom of navigation through international waterways, called for a just solution of the Arab refugee problem, and noted the necessity of guarantees for the "territorial inviolability and political independence of every state in the area, including the establishment of demilitarized zones."[18] A number of four-power meetings were held in New York during 1969, to say nothing of bilateral American-Soviet discussions. While there was general accord as to the desire for peace, there were basic differences over the form of the discussions, the nature of the final settlement, Egyptian obligations as to the Straits of Tiran, the negotation of "secure and recognized" frontiers, and the Arab refugee problem.

The United States presented proposals on October 28, 1969, to which the Soviet response was negative, and on December 9, Secretary of State William Rogers set forth the American position publicly, observing that there was "no area of the world today that is more important, because it could easily again be the source of another conflagration."[19] Continuation of the Arab-Israeli conflict would be "extremely dangerous," and Mr. Rogers felt that the parties alone could not achieve a political settlement. The American position was based on recognition of a number of factors: that (1) while nations not directly involved could not make peace for those which were, they could be helpful; (2) a durable peace must meet the legitimate concerns of both sides; (3) the only framework for a negotiated settlement was one in accordance with the entire text of the UN Security Council Resolution of November 22, 1967; and (4) a protracted period of "no war, no peace," recurrent violence, and a spreading chaos would not serve the interests of any nation, in or out of the Middle East.

While there had been a measure of understanding with the USSR, there were also substantial differences. Rogers noted the Arab view that Israel would not withdraw from occupied territories and the Israeli belief that the Arab states were not ready "to live in peace with Israel." Essentially, American policy was "to encourage the Arabs to accept a permanent peace based on a binding agreement and to urge the Israelis to withdraw from occupied territory when their territorial integrity was assured as envisaged by the Security Council Resolution." The United States supported all elements of the 1967 resolution, including the withdrawal of Israeli forces, and favored a "lasting peace" which required security for both Israel and the Arab states. The United States could not "accept unilateral actions by any party to decide the final status" of Jerusalem, which should be unified, with open access to all faiths and nationalities, with roles for both Israel and Jordan in the civic, economic, and religious life of Jerusalem. Rogers expressed an awareness of the new dimensions of the Arab refugee problem, of the new consciousness among Palestinians and of the frustrations which were involved. New formulae had been discussed with the UAR, involving a binding commitment by Israel and Egypt with each other, detailed provisions relating to security safeguards, and withdrawal of Israeli forces from Egyptian territory.

The Rogers statement appeared as an uncertain groping toward a more balanced American policy. It was well received in the United Kingdom and Western Europe, but was denounced in the USSR, and considered as a divisive and diversionary tactic in the Arab world, while, as the *New York Times* reported on December 13 and 15, 1969, the Israeli government openly accused the United States of "moralizing" and roundly condemned the Rogers statement.

Meanwhile, the Egyptian government had renounced the 1967 cease-fire on March 29, 1969, and the Israeli government escalated the conflict in January 1970 with deep bombing raids inside Egyptian territory. This move prompted Soviet Premier Alexei Kosygin, on January 31,

1970, to warn the United States, "in all frankness," that if Israel continued on this course, the USSR would be "forced to see to it that the Arab states have means at their disposal, with the help of which a due rebuff to the arrogant aggressor could be made." President Nixon rejected the Soviet view, indicated that he was using all his influence to continue the cease-fire, and observed that the United States favored limitation of arms shipments to the Middle East, and had always opposed steps which might draw the major powers into the conflict. As he had indicated on January 25, the United States was carefully watching the balance in the area and would not "hesitate to provide arms to friendly states" as the need arose, as the *New York Times* reported the Kosygin-Nixon exchange on February 5 and 26, 1970.

President Nixon repeated the American position in his Report to the Congress of February 18, 1970, and he called attention to the activity of the USSR in the Mediterranean and the Middle East, noting that the United States "would view any effort by the Soviet Union to seek predominance in the Middle East as a matter of grave concern." While the United States had pressed efforts to restore the cease-fire and had urged agreement on limitation of arms shipments, it would "maintain careful watch on the balance of military forces" and "provide arms to friendly states as the need arises." But balance was all too often interpreted in the terms of Israeli military superiority, especially in the air, and on March 21 and 23, 1970, President Nixon and Secretary of State Rogers announced their decision as to further shipment of arms to Israel, along with a $100 million short-term credit to that country. The president broadly defined the American goal in the Middle East in terms of cease-fire—to get Israel and the Arab states to reappraise their positions, to urge all concerned to cooperate with Ambassador Jarring, and to engage the other major suppliers to the Middle East in early arms limitation talks.

But the essence of the problem in the Middle East lay in the implementation of policy—in the policy of the deed more than in the policy of words, declarations, and statements, however eloquent and significant the latter might be at times. Meanwhile, the scale of the conflict intensified and extended, especially after January 1970, and included all fronts, from the Suez Canal to Jordan, Syria, and Lebanon, and involved increasing Soviet support to Egypt and increasing Israeli demands for further American military and economic assistance. While there were some signs of reluctance on the part of American policymakers, whose estimates of broad American interests in the Middle East, to say nothing of Israel's military requirements, did not neces-

sarily coincide with those of the Israeli government, there appeared little question as to the direction and focus of American policy.*

As the situation in the Middle East grew more threatening during the
spring of 1970, the United States became much more directly involved
in efforts to bring about the renewal of the cease-fire, based on the Security Council Resolution of November 22, 1967. President Nasser declared on May 1, 1970, that Arab-American relations were approaching a "crucial moment" and that any American move to insure
"military superiority for Israel" would damage American interests in
the Middle East "for decades and maybe hundreds of years to come." If
the United States wanted peace, it would have to order "Israel to withdraw from Arab territory" or, if that proved impossible, to refrain from
giving Israel further assistance "as long as it occupies our Arab territory." Mr. Nasser indicated that the USSR was assisting Egypt, not to
"launch aggression" but to "liberate our occupied lands."

Following Nasser's address, namely on June 19, 1970, Secretary of
State Rogers urged Egypt, as well as upon Israel and Jordan, that the
most effective way to achieve a settlement would be for the parties
under Ambassador Jarring to begin working out the detailed steps necessary to implement the resolution of 1967. Mr. Rogers proposed that
Israel, Jordan, and Egypt subscribe to restoration of the cease-fire at
least for a limited period and agree to designate representatives for discussions with Ambassador Jarring for the purpose of achieving agreement on a just and lasting peace, and he evidently pledged American
support to Israel to maintain "the military balance." The American position was set forth publicly on June 25. After a visit to the USSR,
President Nasser accepted the proposal on July 23, and Jordan followed
on July 26, while Israel reluctantly accepted on August 4, and a ninety-
day cease-fire entered into effect on August 7.[20]

Meanwhile, there was silly talk in high places in the United States of
"expelling" the Soviet Union from the Middle East, and President
Nixon reiterated that, when the balance of power shifted where Israel
was weaker, there would be war and, therefore it was in the American

---

* James B. Reston wisely observed in the *New York Times* on March 8, 1970:
"In the short run these Phantom Jets have power, but in the long run, power in
the hands of two and one half million Israelis is an illusion against seventy million Arabs backed by the military power and expansionist determination of the
Soviet Union." A conservative estimate of "capital imports" by Israel during
1950–67 put assistance at some $9.267 billion, according to Oded Remba, "The
Dilemmas of Israel's Economy," *Midstream* 15, 2 (February 1969): 50–62, some
$3 billion since 1969. Recent estimates have put U.S. official assistance at $1.174
billion prior to that year.

interest "to maintain the balance of power." He added that the Arabs had to recognize Israel's right to exist, and Israel had to withdraw to defensible borders—sentiments which were repeated in a more reasonable statement on July 21, reported in the *New York Times* the next day.

Talks were initiated with Ambassador Jarring on August 25, but Israel broke them off after one procedural session, on the charge that Egypt had violated the cease-fire by establishing new SAM-3 sites in the Suez Canal Zone. The talks were not renewed, and there was much concern lest the conflict be resumed in November. Much against the wishes of the United States, Egypt and its associates brought the situation in the Middle East into the plenary session of the UN General Assembly and, on November 4, 1970, by a vote of 57-16-39, a resolution was approved (Resolution 2628 [XXV]), which called for another three-month extension of the cease-fire and for unconditional renewal of the discussions under Ambassador Jarring.

But while the cease-fire was extended, there was much delay in the discussions, which were resumed only in January 1971. Israel insisted on direct negotiations leading to a binding agreement, and was very reluctant to give up any of the occupied territories in accordance with the 1967 resolution. On the other hand, the Arab states insisted on complete withdrawal from the occupied territories, although both sides appeared to desire to maintain the cease-fire. The United States appeared for a while to give unalloyed support to Israel and the USSR to Egypt, although neither wanted any escalation of the conflict. As the discussions continued briefly, Israel, Egypt, and Jordan all sent communications to Ambassador Jarring outlining their positions, which embodied no essential changes.

Essentially the talks broke down again when, on February 8, 1971, Ambassador Jarring asked Israel to give a commitment as to withdrawal from occupied territories.[21] Once more there were serious questions as to the cease-fire beyond February 5, 1971, and as to any change in the positions of the contending parties. The cease-fire was extended for one month, until March 5, 1971, with the prospect that some "progress" might take place within that period. None was achieved, however, with the result that, although the cease-fire was not formally "renewed," in principle it remained informally in effect, since neither Israel nor Egypt evidently wanted to reopen the kind of fighting which had prevailed up to August 7, 1970.

Meanwhile, the United States became directly involved in the situation in the Middle East when the turmoil in Jordan reached crisis stage in September–October 1970, with renewed fighting between fedayeen elements and Jordanian government forces. As the United States government, rightly or wrongly, saw the issue, the crisis occurred when the Jordanian government decided to reestablish full control of Amman in the face of serious fedayeen inroads. On September 18, a Syrian tank force, camouflaged as Palestinians, crossed into Jordan, took up positions, and was promptly attacked. The United States warned the Soviet Union "of the serious consequences which could arise if Syria did not withdraw." It dispatched the Sixth Fleet into the neighboring area and alerted airborne troops, while Israel began "precautionary military deployments." With a Syrian withdrawal, "the danger of a serious international confrontation dimmed."

Arab foreign ministers now sought to mediate the situation in Jordan, and on September 22 a cease-fire was announced; a further agreement between the fedayeen and the Jordanian government was concluded on October 13, although there was sporadic fighting through the rest of 1971. Meanwhile, the United States considered the deterioration of the situation in Jordan as "the gravest threat to world peace since the Administration came into office." With the Soviet Union "so deeply involved in the military operations in the UAR, and with firm United States support of the survival of Israel, the risk of great-power confrontation would have been real indeed." The Nixon administration felt that it had "no responsible choice but to prevent events from running away with the ability to control them." The United States, therefore, took a firm stand against Syrian intervention, and acted to stabilize, "but not to threaten, to discourage irresponsibility without accelerating the moment of crisis."

With the formal end of the cease-fire, the United States sought continuance of peace discussions, and in that interest, Secretary of State Rogers visited the Middle East May 4–8, 1971, when he had discussions in Egypt, Israel, and Jordan. While there were some indications of "cautious optimism" and of clarifications of the issues involved, there were hardly any signs at all of concrete progress toward the opening of the Suez Canal, withdrawal of Israeli forces from occupied Arab territories, or of formal settlement, largely because Egypt insisted on steps toward total withdrawal and Israel refused to take such steps. Assistant Secretary of State Joseph J. Sisco visited Israel again July 28–August 6, 1971, in the interest of steps toward settlement, and engaged in "in-depth discussion, exploratory in nature," during which he neither expected nor achieved "decisive breakthroughs," although he thought that a practical basis for future progress on an interim Suez Canal agreement could be achieved. Moreover, he still considered an interim Suez Canal agreement the best way to assure that relative quiet would continue. The Department of State *Bulletin* for September 6, 1971, said that the United States would maintain its own effort to achieve an interim agreement because "it would constitute a practical test of peace that in time could help move matters toward an over-all settlement in accordance with the November 1967 Resolution of the UN Security Council."

Secretary of State Rogers sounded much the same note in his statement of October 4, 1971, when he presented a six-point program centering on an interim Egyptian-Israeli agreement, in which more details were spelled out in the public position of the United States.[22] Having taken two major steps toward peaceful adjustment in the Security Council Resolution of November 22, 1967, and of the cease-fire of August 7, 1970, which had now endured for almost fifteen months, in Mr. Rogers' view it was now necessary to take a third major step in the elaboration of an interim Suez Canal agreement. An interim agreement would be merely a step toward "complete and full implementation of Resolution 242 within a reasonable period of time and not an end in itself." A cease-fire, in the interest of all, would entail agreement as to the "zone of withdrawal," raise the question of "an Egyptian presence" east of the Suez Canal, and present issues as to the "nature of supervisory arrangements" and "the use of the Suez Canal." The United States, he observed, had long held that the canal should be open to passage "for all nations without discrimination." Since the parties had asked the United States, it would continue its "determined effort to assist them in arriving at an interim agreement. The effort was imperative, in the Rogers view, because there was no more realistic and hopeful alternative to pursue. Both Arabs and Israelis, however, were skeptical concerning this approach.

Whether the effort would succeed was, of course, another matter. Much would depend on the political realities in the Middle East and upon those in the United States. Would the United States, fairly and squarely, face up to the complex problems of Arab and Palestinian nationalism in their impact on Israel, its policies and actions, especially in the occupied Arab territories? Would it face up to the problems in American domestic politics, especially when a presidential or Congressional election approached? As noted at the outset, American policy appeared to be groping, however uncertainly, toward a greater degree of balance in the Middle East. "Balance" all too often seemed a transparent euphemism for the maintenance of Israeli military superiority. In any event it became clear by 1972 that more military and economic assistance had been given to Israel during the Nixon administration than in those of all his predecessors since 1948. There was much solid ground for basic criticism of American policy in the Middle East, however, both in the United States and abroad on the ground of bias, prejudice, and partisanship and of failure to measure up in the problems of the Arab refugees, Jerusalem, and generally to serve American interests in the peace, security, and more orderly development in the area. Granted the desire for peace, there was much skepticism during 1972–73 that practical steps would be taken toward a viable, formal settlement of the problems involved in the Arab-Israeli conflict. American policy objectives during this period continued to look toward a comprehensive and final settlement of the Arab-Israeli conflict, not a return to the armistice regimes which had been established in 1949, within the framework of Security Council Resolution 242 of November 22, 1967, and it sought avoidance of great power confrontation and the continuation of the cease-fire. It sought an interim agreement between Israel and Egypt and reopening of the Suez Canal. But there were few indications that these objectives were about to be achieved. While the Egyptian government dismissed some 15,000 to 20,000 military and civilian technicians from the USSR in July 1972, President Sadat indicated on a number of occasions that there had been little response from the United States and Israel. He also indicated that the only way to recover lost dignity and lost territories was through force. In October 1973 a fourth round in the Arab-Israel conflict erupted, more bloody than any since 1948.

OTHER FACETS OF AMERICAN POLICY AND INTEREST

But there were other facets of American policy and interest in the Middle East, even if formal commitments were limited to Greece, Turkey, and Iran. Although the Sixth Fleet has been maintained in the Mediterranean since 1946, and there are an Air Force training mission in Saudi Arabia, naval units in the Persian Gulf, and military personnel in Turkey under NATO and other arrangements, the United States, as already observed, has no military commitments other than these. In view of the statements of President Nixon and Secretary of State Rogers, additional formal commitments appear unlikely. While there has been an evident weakening of NATO ties, there would appear to be little question of the usefulness of the alliance, whether in Europe or along the southeastern flank, involving Greece and Turkey. Granted a weakening of the southeastern flank because of developments both in Greece and in Turkey, and the inability of the United States to take sides in the Greco-Turkish controversy relative to Cyprus, NATO was reaffirmed following the Soviet invasion of Czechoslovakia in August 1968. On November 15–16, 1968, the NATO Council observed that "the new uncertainties resulting from Soviet actions" extended to the Mediterranean. Moreover, as Dana Adams Schmidt wrote in the *New York Times,* January 18, 1971, the council warned that "clearly any Soviet intervention directly or indirectly affecting the situation in Europe or the Mediterranean would create an international crisis with grave consequences." It may well be that advances in military technology may render the alliance obsolete. While final answers can never be given to questions of this type, there is every indication that political and military leaders do not think so.

Although the NATO commitments to Greece and Turkey are direct and clear, some questions have been raised as to the nature of the American involvement with CENTO—the former Baghdad Pact—in the origins of which the United States played a primary role in the 1950s. There are questions as to viable defense arrangements with Iran in view of its geographical location. Although there is no direct commitment of American forces, as in the instance of NATO, the possibility of their use is foreseen. Whatever CENTO's defects as a regional security arrangement, much has been accomplished in the technical and economic fields, and there would appear to be sound psychological and political reasons for keeping it in being. This seems all the more true after the events of 1967 and the enhancement of the Soviet position in the Middle East in the years which have followed.

There seemed little question, as the year 1973 moved on, of enduring American interest in the Middle East, highlighted by the energy crisis and the factor of Middle Eastern oil, whatever the skepticism as to American policies, which often seemed in conflict with basic American interests. In any event American interests were both long-term and wide-ranging in character. How they would be adjusted with those of other powers was another matter.

❊ 6 ❊

TAREQ Y. ISMAEL

The People's Republic of China and the Middle East

We are hardly accustomed to considering the People's Republic of China as a factor in Middle East international relations. But now China sits in the highest international forum where the fate of the Middle East has been a volatile issue for the last twenty-five years. China's new Security Council seat, coupled with its status as a world power in diametric opposition to the two primary extra-systemic Middle East actors— the United States and the Soviet Union—thrusts upon China a significant role in the debates that have weighed the Middle East's fate and have challenged the capacity of the United Nations for the last quarter century. The roles of all the other participants in the recurring Security Council debates on Middle East questions are well defined. The United States, the Soviet Union, France, and England have Middle East positions patterned by their global, regional, bilateral, and intranational commitments. Unlike any other permanent Security Council member, however, China has neither such commitments to constrain it nor vested interests in the area nor a history of involvement in the Middle East. But long before taking its seat in the Security Council in Nuvember 1971, China was keenly interested in the Middle East and was pursuing a policy in the area. These facts take on significance in light of China's new role in international affairs. Whereas China's presence is unlikely to break—and may compound—the deadlock that has made the Security Council virtually ineffective in dealing with questions on the Middle East, China can use its position to increase its influence in the Middle East. Perhaps more than any other area in the world, the Middle East offers a role in search of a hero. Is China interested in this role? What is the nature of its interest in the Middle East? What policy has it been cultivating in the area?

138

CHINA'S INITIATIVE

China's contacts with the Middle East were initiated at the Afro-Asian Conference convened at Bandung, Indonesia, in April 1955. Prior to that, China had no diplomatic representation in Africa or the Middle East. The independent Arab states refused to recognize the Communist government in Peking, recognizing instead the Chiang Kai-shek regime in Taiwan. Israel was the only state in the area that recognized the Peking government, but China did not reciprocate.

By 1954, however, China appeared interested in establishing some contact with the Middle East and made a tentative step in that direction toward Israel. On July 30, 1965, *Devar Hoshavua* (Tel Aviv) reported that while David Hakohen was Israeli ambassador to Burma in 1954, China expressed an "interest in creating commercial and diplomatic ties with us." A conversation with Chou En-lai in Burma in June 1954, reported Hakohen, was followed by an official invitation for a visit of an Israeli delegation. A six-member commission consisting of David Hakohen and his wife, Brakha Chabas, Dr. D. Levin, director of the Asia Department in the Israeli Foreign Office, M. De-Shalit, a senior official in the foreign ministry, Mosheh Bezerano, an industrialist and commercial attaché in Moscow, and Yosef Zarkin, director of the Export Department, was authorized "to discuss all questions referring to the two friendly nations," and left for a one-month tour of Canton, Peking, Tientsin, and Sian in February 1955. The delegation met with Chinese Deputy Minister of Commerce Lee-Jin-Min, who expressed China's interest in buying fertilizers, chemicals, drugs, artificial teeth, industrial diamonds, tires, and spare parts from Israel; a memorandum was signed. "We love Israel," Deputy Foreign Minister Chang Han-Fu told David Hakohen. However, no diplomatic exchange occurred. Preparations for the Bandung Conference were already under way, and China, not surprisingly, switched its focus from Israel to the Arab world.

The Bandung Conference offered China the opportunity to establish contacts with the Afro-Asian world. Israel was excluded from the meetings, but it appeared that Gamal Abdel Nasser would be there as spokesman for nationalist elements in both Africa and the Middle East. David Ben-Gurion, then Israeli premier, recognized Israel's disadvantage in seeking relations with China, commenting years later in *Devar Hoshavua,* August 6, 1965:

> The Chinese have no grounds for hating Israel, but they have cause for seeking Arab friendship because they are boycotted by

the UN, by America and by some European countries. We were one of the first countries to recognize China, but it has not recognized us. Because we have no value for China while the hundred million Arabs have great value for her, as have the hundred million Indonesians who have left the UN and the hundred million Pakistanis. If she deliberates with whom to make friends, with Israel or with the Arabs, with Pakistan or Indonesia, she makes the second choice. That is where her interests lie. This is our situation in the world.

It was indeed Nasser that the Chinese decided to court. On April 16, 1955, *Al-Ahram* reported that when Nasser and Nehru arrived at Rangoon Airport in Burma en route to Bandung, Chou En-lai met them at the airport. Within five minutes of the meeting, reported the *New York Times,* on April 16, 1955, Chou En-lai invited Nasser to visit China, but Nasser "was non-committal." Chou broached the possibility of substantially increasing China's purchases of Egyptian cotton, and both agreed to continue discussions at Bandung, according to the *New York Times,* April 22, 1955. At Bandung, Chou En-lai and Nasser not only discussed the prospects of increasing China's purchases of Egyptian cotton, but Chou En-lai also declared Chinese support of and sympathy for the people of Algeria, Morocco, and Tunisia in their struggle for self-determination and independence—primary issues that Nasser wanted to win support for at Bandung. John K. Cooley, in an article in the winter 1972 edition of *Journal of Palestine Studies,* wrote that Chou also promised Nasser to intercede with the Soviets to obtain Soviet arms for Egypt.

In April 1955, Major Salah Salem, Minister of National Guidance, reported Cooley, hinted that Egypt might extend recognition to China to increase cotton sales in view of the threatened program of subsidized U.S. cotton exports. *Rose El-Youssief* (Cairo), May 21, 1956, stated that Dr. Abdul Munim Al-Qasioni, Minister of Economics, declared: "Economic relations between Egypt and China were a prelude to political recognition." The *New York Times,* April 22, said that Nehru urged Nasser to extend recognition to China, and, according to *Al-Ahram,* May 1, 1955: "Nehru was very successful in establishing cordial and friendly relations between President Nasser, the leader of the most powerful state on the African Continent, and Chou En-lai, the head of the largest and most powerful state on the Asian continent. Thus, the struggle against imperialism, and the expulsion of the imperialists from both continents, became closely associated with the relations and friendship between the Egyptian and Chinese leaders. Both played their roles with great success at Bandung. And each was friendly to the other."

Nasser, however, refrained from extending formal recognition until May 1956. It was finally extended in retaliation for the Israeli arms deal. *Al-Jumhoriyah* (Cairo), May 17, 1956, described Egypt's withholding of recognition to Communist China as a diplomatic courtesy to the West and declared in an editorial: "Probably Egypt's recognition of the People's Democratic Republic of China was a powerful blow to the West. . . . That is actually what it was meant to be." Two months later, Syria also recognized China.

This cordial beginning was buttressed by China's firm support for Egypt during the Suez Crisis. On November 4, 1956, Chou En-lai declared: "China firmly demands that the British and French governments immediately put an end to their aggression against Egypt, that armed provocations against the Arab countries be halted, and that there should be no further delay in carrying out peaceful negotiations on the questions of the Suez Canal." [1] Two days later, *Al-Ahram* reported on November 8, the Egyptian ambassador to Peking announced that a quarter of a million Chinese volunteered to fight with the Egyptians on Egyptian soil. Egypt declined this offer, but did accept China's gift of U.S. $5 million.

Following the Suez Crisis China supported the Egyptian proposal for an "Afro-Asian People's Solidarity Conference" to be held in Cairo. Organized at the nongovernmental level, the conference was attended by 577 delegates representing forty-six Communist and non-Communist Asian and African countries. Its purpose, as explained by an official Egyptian publication, was to "mobilize the nationalist forces in the Afro-Asian countries to fight imperialism in all its forms throughout the world." [2] The conference provided China with the opportunity to make friendly contacts at the party level. The Cairo conference established a permanent Afro-Asian Solidarity Council with its secretariat in Cairo. According to the agreements for its establishment, Anwar as-Sadat, president of the Egyptian National Assembly, became president, with a Russian and an Indian as vice-presidents, and Yusief as-Sibai, one of the original free officers, as general secretary. Of the other ten secretaries, there was to be one each from the USSR and China. Thus, China had a permanent channel through which to maintain contacts and funnel propaganda to Afro-Asian nationalist movements.

Other Chinese activity at this time included exhibitions at trade fairs in Morocco and Tunisia and the opening of a New China News Agency office in Cairo in early 1958. China also recognized the Sudan upon the latter's independence in 1956, but the Sudan failed to respond until after the military coup in October of 1958.

Throughout this early period the Chinese were acting largely as a force supplementary to the activities of the Soviet Union. In 1959, however, a difference of opinion arose between the two Communist states over the proper approach to the Algerian question. On September 16, 1959, President Charles de Gaulle offered terms of self-determination to Algeria, which were rejected by the Algerian Communist Party but supported by the French Communist Party. The Algerian Provisional Government (GPRA) proposed cautious terms for the initiation of negotiations. Delegations from both Algerian groups attended the celebrations in Peking marking the tenth anniversary of Communist rule. On October 17, 1959, the Chinese announced their opposition to the de Gaulle proposals. Khrushchev shortly thereafter announced his approval of the de Gaulle offer. The Chinese, alone of the world Communist Parties, opposed the Soviet position, going so far as to offer planes and volunteers to the GPRA. Tension mounted for some time thereafter, as Khrushchev was maintaining a pacific stand in view of the approaching summit meeting in Paris. The issue quieted in light of the failure of the Paris summit and the subsequently increasing militancy in the Soviet position.

The dispute stemmed from differing assessments on the part of the two powers of the efficacy of the approaches of peaceful coexistence and revolutionary action. The Chinese placed more emphasis upon armed struggle, while the USSR had relied upon peaceful competition in its dealings with the West. These differences arose from the national positions and historical experiences of the two states. The Russians fear the escalation of wars of liberation into general war, while the Chinese feel that armed struggle is necessary to weld the kind of Communist-dominated united front upon which a successful revolution must, in their estimation, be based. In part, the Chinese position rests upon the idea that through armed struggle the strength of imperialist powers may be sufficiently reduced to prevent them from launching a world war. Also, their doctrinal assertion that the imperialist camp is a camp of war, while the socialist bloc is the camp of peace, leads to the conclusion that a war against imperialism is, in fact, a blow for peace.

Chinese contact with the Middle East, begun in 1955, was primarily a ramification of China's desire to broaden relations with the new states of Asia and the Middle East. By 1959, however, the level of Chinese involvement had risen substantially and China was establishing itself as an influential factor in Afro-Asian affairs. From 1959, competition between the USSR and China was becoming a dominant factor in the relations of the two states to the Afro-Asian nations. This growth in competition between the two greatest Communist states coincided with the rapid dissolution of colonial empires in Africa. As W. A. C. Adie noted: "The third period, from 1959 on, is marked by increasingly open struggle in Tropical as well as North Africa and in the Communist International front organizations, which operate in Africa, between orthodox, or Soviet-oriented Communism and what Khrushchev has denounced as 'Mao Tse-tungism.' " [3]

Richard Lowenthal, in a chapter on China in *Africa and the Communist World,* edited by Zibigniew Brzezinsky, also saw this competition building from 1959 on and identifies it with the different concepts of "national democracy" held by the Chinese and the Russians. The Russians expect that the first stage in the development of a revolution will be a revolution of the national bourgeoisie. After the success of such a revolution, the Communist Party may overthrow the nationalist leaders and assume power on its own. The Chinese experience in the 1920s, however, convinced them that the use of this tactic was disastrous in their circumstances, and that the Communist Party must lead the revolution, although in cooperation with a broad united front organization including workers, peasants, national bourgeoisie, and petty bourgeoisie. [4]

The first phase of disagreement between Russians and Chinese was not essentially harmful to the Communist cause in Afro-Asia. That the two powers supported different countries or different groups had little effect upon their positions, and appeared to perform some of the functions of a division of labor. The effect was to render their efforts more complementary than competitive, although they may have been uncomfortable playing this role. From 1961 on, however, the issue was carried more to the organizations of the Afro-Asian states disrupting the workings of these organizations. There was a tendency for the Russians to rely upon the World Peace Council while the Chinese worked through the Afro-Asian machinery. However, at the time when the Maoist phases of Chinese foreign policy began, after the signing of the nuclear test-ban treaty, the Russians defeated the Chinese in the Afro-Asian executive committee meeting in Nicosia, Cyprus. The Chinese regarded the test-ban as a "betrayal" and as trafficking with imperialists; the fact that they were then developing their own nuclear capacities, and felt that the agreement was directed against them, contributed to the Chinese bitterness. As the Afro-Asians rejected the militant Chinese view, the Russians were able to gain their support. This divergence on tactics, growing into an organizational competition, marked the beginning of the real Sino-Soviet split. At that point, the question ceased to be one of tactics, of emphasis or priorities, and became one of strategy and of doctrine.

The extent of Sino-Soviet competition came to light in the course of the preparation (and subsequent cancellation) of the "Second Bandung" —the second Afro-Asian Conference scheduled for November 5, 1965, at Algiers. Occurring in the shadow of Sino-Soviet dispute, Communist China and the USSR each sought UAR support against the other. For the Soviet Union, Egyptian support was necessary in order to get its candidature for the conference accepted. Communist China sought the UAR's support to keep the Soviet Union out of the conference. Nicolas Lang, in the periodical *Est et Ouest* (Paris), November 16–30, 1965, reported that Chou En-lai visited Egypt on four occasions in an attempt to secure Egypt's cooperation against the Soviet Union. The first occasion was in April 1965. In June, he visited Nasser on his way to and returning from Tanzania. Chou En-lai failed to enlist Nasser's support against the Soviet Union, and at the conclusion of the third visit, relations between the UAR and China were strained. The final visit was occasioned by the fall of Ben Bella. Serious and extensive negotiations took place during Chou En-lai's twelve-day visit. The results were that Nasser agreed to maintain neutrality in the Sino-Soviet dispute and to support China on certain other issues of importance to it. In return, China agreed to coordinate its policy in the Arab world with Egypt, to recognize the UAR's role as spokesman for the neutral nations, and to support the UAR on other issues of importance to it. In September 1965, Nasser went to the USSR. During this visit, the Soviet Union not only agreed to step up work on the High Dam at Aswan but also to participate to the amount of 350 million rubles in the construction of a sawmill and prospecting and substructure operations. In return, Nasser supported the USSR's candidature at the Algiers conference.

The "Second Bandung" was subsequently cancelled, and a decade of Afro-Asian conference diplomacy ended. That decade had seen China greatly expand its contacts throughout Afro-Asia, but it had also witnessed the consolidation of Soviet ties in the Middle East. With American interests in the area well entrenched on one side of the political spectrum and the Soviet Union on the other, there appeared little room for a Chinese role in the Middle East. But China's strong interest in the area persisted, as testified to by the fact that during the cultural revolution of 1966, 1967, and 1968, the number of Chinese top-level diplomatic posts abroad dropped from forty to one. That one was Cairo, as noted by the *Christian Science Monitor,* July 18–20, 1970. The Chinese ambassador to Egypt, Huang Hua, was a man with impressive credentials and a close friend of Chou En-lai.

China, of course, could not match the massive aid poured into the Middle East by both the United States and the Soviet Union, and therefore could not effectively compete for influence at the governmental level. At the same time, however, China was not committed to the maintenance of a status quo, as were both the United States and the Soviet Union. Prior to June 1967, there appeared no serious challenge to the status quo, and American and Soviet spheres of influence seemed to have attained an equilibrium. The June War, however, introduced a new element into Middle East politics. Out of the agony and frustration of defeat and Israeli occupation there arose a viable and popular Palestinian guerrilla movement. This movement posed a threat to both established American and Soviet interests in the area and threatened the delicate equilibrium of the status quo. At the same time, people's wars of liberation broke out on the Arabian Peninsula. China's commitment to armed struggle made it the natural ally of these movements. Thus, there was a role in Middle East politics that neither the United States nor the Soviet Union could fill. In the following pages we shall examine the new Chinese role in the area.

THE PALESTINE ISSUE

The Palestine issue has loomed in the forefront of Middle East politics since the partition of 1948, but by the mid-fifties the rights of the Palestinians to return to their homeland appeared a moot point in international affairs. Israel ignored all United Nations resolutions endorsing this, and the Arab regimes recognized their inability to effect a return. The issue, however, remained at the very heart of Arab nationalist sentiment, and no Arab leader could ignore it. Nor did the Soviet Union, whose increasing support to nationalist Arab governments from 1955 had by the mid-sixties won it a role in Middle East politics comparable in scale to the American role there. For Arab governments, however, problems of political stability, modernization, and national sovereignty took precedence over the Palestine question. For the Soviet Union, Palestine was an issue, not a cause. The Russian aim was to win friends and influence in the area, and Russian support, like American support at the other side of the political spectrum, was utilized to buttress recipient regimes against external and internal threats to their power. Thus, by the mid-sixties no one took the Palestine issue very seriously, aside from its sentimental and emotional impact. The existence of Israel was a fact; the Palestinians, ensconced in refugee camps, appeared relatively pacific; and each Arab regime had its own problems to reckon with.

Following the Bandung Conference, China vociferously supported "the Arabs in their struggle against imperialism and Zionism," but did not take any particular note of the Palestine issue. However, the *Yearbook for the Palestine Question for the Year 1964* (Beirut) noted that "Chinese support on the Palestine question went beyond . . . [this] to clearly indicate the *legitimate* rights of the Palestinians to return to their usurped land." Indeed, in 1964 China initiated aid to al-Fateh (then a little-known underground Palestinian organization), and China's attention to the Palestine issue became a prominent feature of its Middle East policy. On March 27, 1964, the *Peking Review* reported that a rally was held in Peking to demonstrate Chinese "support for the Palestinian people's struggle to regain their legitimate rights and return to their homes!" This position was officialized in the joint communiqué reported in the *Peking Review,* May 22, 1964, of Chairman Liu Shao-chi of China and Sudanese President Abboud during the latter's visit to China that month.

When the Second Arab Summit Conference of September 1964 endorsed the establishment of a Palestine Liberation Organization (PLO), no one took it very seriously—neither the Arab regimes nor the Soviet Union, neither Israel nor the United States. Its purpose, as envisaged by most observers, was to satisfy popular Arab sentiment, not to confront Israel.

In the *Peking Review,* September 18, 1964, China hailed the creation of the Palestine Liberation Organization as an advancement of the Palestinian struggle "to new heights." But even more than moral support, which the PLO received from many corners, China gave concrete material aid, which the Palestinians discovered was in short supply, even from their founders. Ahmad Shuqairy, president of the PLO, relates in his memoirs that he went to the Chinese embassy in Cairo for the first time in February 1965 to express his desire to visit Peking. Within four days of this request, the Chinese ambassador went personally to PLO headquarters to notify Shuqairy that "Comrad Chou En-lai welcomes your arrival at your earliest convenience with a delegation of your choice. This invitation is extended to you both personally and in your capacity as President of the Palestine Liberation Organization." [5]

Highest diplomatic honors were apparently afforded the Palestinian delegation. "As if we were a sovereign, independent state," wrote Shuqairy, the Chinese ambassador and his aides were at the airport to bid the delegation farewell on its departure for Peking on March 15, 1965. Upon arrival in Peking, Shuqairy's delegation found awaiting them "a splendid reception" with a crowd that numbered "in the thousands." The full diplomatic corp resident in Peking had been gathered in a reception line, and the delegation was met by Marshal Shin-Yi, China's foreign minister and deputy vice-chairman of the State Council.

In his meeting with Chou En-lai, Shuqairy reports that the premier listened to him "very intently" for a full two hours. The dialogue that followed is well worth repeating verbatim as reported by Shuqairy:

Chou: Exactly what do you want from us?

Shuqairy: In addition to political support we want military aid.

Chou: And what do you want explicitly?

Shuqairy: We need small and medium arms. We also need to send a mission of our officers to train on guerrilla warfare. You have a wealth of experience on this subject.

Chou: You know we are always ready to support any liberation movement in the world as much as we can. Our responsibilities toward our people are great; we're not rich. But we feel we have a responsibility toward the liberation movements in the world in support of the oppressed nations to fight American imperialism. We will not delay in helping you as much as we can.

Shuqairy: Our demands are not great. I leave up to you the amount of aid that you can give us.

Chou: We're not like everybody else who offers aid and expects payment with interest. This is political payoff. This is not our method.

Shuqairy: We don't want planes or tanks. We need the arms that are appropriate for guerrilla warfare.

Chou: And where do you want the arms to arrive? Have you agreed with any of the Arab governments? Have you talked with President Nasser on the subject?

Shuqairy: Really, I did not discuss the subject with anybody, but I believe Cairo will not object to that. We would like the arms to be shipped to the port of Alexandria.

Chou: We're ready to do this, and we can send you the arms free. We'll ship them on our ships directly to Alexandria. We don't trust other ships for the American fleet is closely watching. Announce what you want. We're not afraid of the Americans, but we do fear the Americans for you.

Shuqairy: I can't find the appropriate words to express my great gratitude. As long as your ships are going to Alexandria, is it possible for us to send our officers on it too, to begin their training with you?

Chou: Of course that's possible. It's better if you keep in close touch with our embassy in Cairo to make all necessary arrangements for the arms and the officers.

Shuqairy: I'll never forget this favor. . . .

Chou: This is our duty. There is no reason to thank us. You want to fight for your land. We can't abandon you, and we can't abandon the Afro-Asian nations. . . . Did the Russians give you anything?

Shuqairy: Nothing received till now from Moscow.

Chou: What aid have you requested from Moscow?

Shuqairy: We have asked for military and cultural aid, but nothing has been received till now.

Chou: I know you are a close friend of the Soviet leaders.

Shuqairy: The friendship is still there, but the aid isn't.

Chou: But from us, friendship and aid. I would like to emphasize that we will be very delighted if the Russians offer you any aid. We do not want our friendship to be at the expense of your friendship with Moscow. If they offer you any aid we will be very happy. What concerns us is that you win your independence and freedom.

Shuqairy: This is the revolutionary spirit.

Chou: Continue your efforts with the Soviet Union, although I think you'll get nothing from them. No political or cultural aid. Moscow recognized Israel and has economic relations with her. In addition, the Soviet Union agreed with America to the partition of Palestine and the creation of Israel.

Shuqairy: That is true. The Arab world remembers this stand. . . . Would you allow us to open an office in Peking?

Chou: Tomorrow morning. We will give you the office space, recognize the PLO, and will give your office diplomatic immunity. We will treat them like any other friendly embassy. . . . We are with you, and we are ready to do whatever we can.[6]

On the eve of the June War, May 15, 1967, a rally for the support of the Palestinian movement was sponsored by the Permanent Afro-Asian Writers' Organization and the Afro-Asian Journalists' Organization. The PLO representative in Peking, Rashid Jarbou, affirmed the strength of Chinese support, stating: "And from Peking the Arab nation of Palestine finds complete moral and material support for the liberation of its homeland. On this occasion I would like to greet and thank the government and the nation of the Chinese People's Republic and its great leader, Mao Tse-tung, for its positive support of the Palestinian people's struggle." [7]

Why did China alone give such significance to the Palestine liberation movement? The movement certainly did not appear credible in 1965–66. However, in addition to China's strong commitment to support people's wars of liberation, there were few avenues open for Chinese influence in the Middle East. Perhaps, too, China saw the potential of such a movement. After all, had not Chairman Mao and his embattled comrades marched over 6,000 miles against incredible odds to ultimate victory? Had not the Chinese alone recognized and supported the Algerian liberation movement when the rest of the world considered it capricious? Whatever the reasons, the Peking government must have felt vindicated when, in the aftermath of the June War, the Palestine resistance movement arose as a viable force in Middle East politics that posed a significant threat to the status quo. Thoroughly opposed to American policy in the area, and disappointed with Soviet policy, the Palestine resistance movement drew heavily upon Chinese support. (John Cooley, one of the most seasoned of Middle East correspondents, reported in the *Christian Science Monitor,* August 1970, that "Communist China and Arab governments, which in turn receive arms from East Europe, have been main suppliers of arms" to the resistance movement. Of the eleven principal guerrilla groups, the following five have made public their gratitude for Chinese aid: al-Fateh, Palestine Liberation Organization, Popular Front for the Liberation of Palestine, Popular Democratic Front for the Liberation of Palestine, and the Popular Organization for the Liberation of Palestine.) Radical groups patterned themselves on the Chinese ideological style, and the thoughts of Chairman Mao, if not quoted, were certainly paraphrased. One need only examine the publications and speeches of the spokesmen of the Popular Front for the Liberation of Palestine, the Popular Democratic Front for the Liberation of Palestine, and the left-wing of al-Fateh to see the strength of Chinese influence. While this did not make China a political power in the Middle East, from 1967 onward it was certainly an ideological ally to a growing radical movement in Middle East politics. Following China's admission to the United Nations, *Free Palestine* (London), December 1971–January 1972, noted that *Voice of Fateh* announced on October 29, 1971: "The Palestine Resistance welcomes China's recovery of its lawful rights at the UN, since China is the state closest to the Resistance in its attitude to liberation in strategy and practice."

This examination of China and the Middle East began with the query of whether China is interested in "a role in search of a hero." Affirming this interest, on December 8, 1971, Deputy Chinese Foreign Minister and Chairman of China's delegation to the United Nations Chiao Kuan-hau, in a speech on the Middle East question before a plenary session of the General Assembly, attacked both the United States and the Soviet Union as "colluding with each other" in the Middle East. With America supporting Israel and the Soviet Union supporting several Arab governments, China made the issue triangular by placing her full support behind the Palestinian people. In his speech, Kuan-hau affirmed for the world that "the Chinese Government and people always stand on the side of the Palestinian and other Arab peoples who are subjected to aggression, firmly support their just struggles and give them assistance within the limits of our capability." He rejected an imposed settlement of the Middle East situation—as proposed in the four-power talks of the United States, the Soviet Union, France, and England—demanding instead that "the destiny of the Palestinian and other Arab peoples must be decided by themselves; their affairs must be handled by themselves. We oppose all conspiratorial activities of aggression, subversion, control, and interference carried out by any superpower against the Arab countries and peoples." [8]

THE DHOFARI REVOLUTION

On June 9, 1965, an armed struggle was initiated in Dhofar—the western province of the Sultanate of Muscat and Oman on the coast of the Arabian Gulf—by the Dhofar Liberation Front. The front, according to *Al-Tali'ah* (Kuwait), July 17, 1968, was formed in 1964 by a coalition of the Dhofari branch of the Arab Nationalist Movement and the Dhofar Benevolence Society (a Dhofari separatist organization), and was primarily a nationalist movement dedicated to the liquidation of the autocratic and repressive Sultanate of Muscat and Oman. Without sources of outside material support, the movement remained small and relatively ineffective in the first years following its initiation. But for the sultan's heavy-handed tactics against the Dhofari population in dealing with the rebellion, it appears that it could have been contained. By 1968, however, the sultan had effectively alienated the entire Dhofari population; the rebels found immediate moral support from the new, radical regime of South Yemen, and through South Yemen, they began obtaining material support from China. Contingents of rebels were received in Peking for political and guerrilla training, the *Times* (London), reported on August 3, 1970, and they returned to Dhofar with ideological as well as technical assistance. Radicalization of the movement became quickly evident. At its second congress at Himrin in 1968, the Dhofar Liberation Front became the Popular Front for the Liberation of the Occupied Arab Gulf, reflecting a strong anti-imperialist position and the expansion of scope to a people's war of liberation for the entire Arab Gulf. *Al-Thawri* (Aden), June 8, 1971, noted that scientific socialism was adopted as a revolutionary theory, and a People's Army of Liberation was formed.

The Popular Front for the Liberation of the Occupied Arab Gulf has received little support from the Arab world. In an interview with *Al-Tali'ah,* July 17, 1968, a front spokesman stated: "The Front has had official contacts with the League of Arab States and Arab capitals, to explain the question of the revolution in Dhofar. Effective help was requested by the Front in favor of the revolution, but most replies have been negative." The *New York Times,* July 12, 1970, reported that primary support for the movement comes from the People's Democratic Republic of Southern Yemen and from China. Yemen supports the Dhofari movement for both ideological and geopolitical reasons and has acted as intermediary between the Dhofari movement and the Chinese. China supplies the guerrillas through Southern Yemen, trains guerrillas in Peking, and has military advisers with the guerrillas in Dhofar, according to the *Times* (London), August 3, 1970.

The Popular Front for the Liberation of the Occupied Arab Gulf controls most of the interior of Dhofar and several cities—Dalkut, Râkhyut, and Sadah. China has provided the primary source of the revolution's supplies and, more significantly, the basis of its ideology. Aside from China's ideological commitment to support the people's war of liberation, there are high stakes in this oil-rich area where the rapid introduction of wealth is already causing instability in the Arab Gulf's tradition-bound societies.

IN THE 1970s

China's staunch support to the Palestine and Arab Gulf liberation movements was the most sensational aspect of its Middle East policy by the end of the sixties. While this won for China ideological influence over radical movements throughout the area, the strong ideological orientation of its Middle East policy constrained China in the diplomatic arena. By 1970, China had relations with only the nationalist regimes of the Middle East—Egypt, the Sudan, Syria, Iraq, and North and South Yemen. And only in South Yemen did China effectively compete with the Soviet Union for influence. Furthermore, it did not have relations with any non-Arab Middle East government. In contrast, Soviet relations with Turkey and Iran steadily improved throughout the late sixties in spite of their close ties with the United States.

By 1972, however, it was evident that China's Middle East policy was undergoing fundamental changes. Dictation of policy by ideology appeared considerably lessened, if not altogether dropped, as China established relations with such incompatible regimes as Kuwait, Bahrein, Qatar, Lebanon, Iran, and Turkey—countries previously classified as the "running dogs of imperialism." Following Kuwait's recognition of China in March 1971, John K. Cooley reported in the *Christian Science Monitor* on April 9 that Peking newspapers and broadcasts beamed to the Middle East praised Kuwait, despite its monarchial regime, as a country using its oil riches "to support the struggle against imperialism and Zionism." Similarly, following Iran's recognition in August 1971, Chou En-lai publicly praised the shah as a "leader striving for uplift of oppressed masses," and China officially praised Iran's nationalistic oil policy as a "just struggle to safeguard its national independence and sovereignty and to protect its natural resources," as Cooley wrote in the *Christian Science Monitor* on September 23. Thus, only Jordan, Saudi Arabia and Israel remained without relations with China, but it was reported in the *New York Times,* October 17, 1971, that China and Israel were holding secret talks.

The success of China's new approach became evident in the General Assembly vote on China's admission to the United Nations. Countries previously considered staunch supporters of American efforts to keep Nationalist China in the United Nations voted for its expulsion. Only Saudi Arabia of the Middle East states voted with the United States, while Bahrein, Jordan, and Lebanon abstained.

Most observers saw China's drive to expand relations as a considerable moderation of Chinese policy. Other events—most notably China's support of Pakistan during the Bengali rebellion—corroborated the view that China was following a more pragmatic foreign policy based on national interest rather than ideology. Pragmatism became evident in Chinese policy in the Middle East, too, when China supported President Djafar el-Numeiry of the Sudan in his extermination of Sudanese Communists in the aftermath of an abortive coup in July 1971. The Soviet Union, on the other hand, supported the coup, which was led by alleged Communist Party members and sympathizers. The coup was aborted through the concerted action of Libya and Egypt, and Numeiry returned to power to wield his wrath against the Sudanese Communist Party and the Soviet Union. China's position in the Sudan subsequently improved at the expense of Moscow.

An even greater indication of China's new orientation was provided on the occasion of the visit of the Chinese minister of foreign affairs to Iran in June 1973. With the blessing of the United States and a massive arms arsenal provided by America, Iran in 1973 undertook to be the guardian of the Arab Gulf, with the announced intention of insuring stability in the area and guaranteeing the flow of oil to Western markets. According to *Al-Muhrer* (Beirut), June 16, 1973, the Chinese Foreign Minister not only expressed his country's support for Iran's policy in the Gulf, but also expressed China's support of Iran's acquisition of American armaments, describing them as "necessary, important, and understandable."

Most states in the area hoped that normal relations with Peking, together with this new pragmatism and the possibility of a détente with the West (raised by President Nixon's visit to Peking) would result in a lessening of Peking's support to the Palestinian and Arab Gulf liberation movements. But in his speech during the debate on the Middle East question at the plenary meeting of the United Nations General Assembly in December 1971, Chiao Kuan-hau, chairman of the Chinese delegation, strongly affirmed China's support for the liberation movements. Can ideology and national interest be reconciled in China's Middle East policy? Can China seek expanding trade relations and accommodation on issues of importance to it in the United Nations with governments while it actively supports guerrilla movements who seek to overthrow these governments? What are the principles and objectives of China's policy in the Middle East, and how are they being implemented?

PRINCIPLES AND OBJECTIVES OF CHINESE POLICY

The principles of Chinese foreign policy are based on an ideology that theorizes a world order achieved through revolutionary struggle by oppressed peoples against exploitation. All policy statements are coached in a revolutionary rhetoric that belies the motivation of national interest. The two are not independent, however, for the pursuit of national interests is conducted in a world perceived through an ideological framework. Without conducting a lengthy discussion of Chinese ideology, we can simply assume that, as with any state, national survival is the immediate goal of both internal and external policy, and maximization of power is the long-term goal; ideology imposes a view of the world that identifies threats to survival and defines the concept of power. The principles of foreign policy are a reflection of the ideology, while the objectives are a function of geopolitical, strategic, and economic motivations mediated by ideology.

In terms of principles, the Middle East is viewed as one of the potential revolutionary rural areas of the world struggling against imperialism. The theme of the anti-imperialist struggle is a prominent aspect of Chinese policy in the Middle East. Interstate relations with Middle Eastern nations were formulated on the Bandung principles. During his visit to Cairo in 1964, Chou En-lai elaborated five principles of China's relations with Arab countries. These principles were formalized in the joint communiqué of Chinese and Yemeni heads of state issued June 15, 1964, and carried in the *Peking Review,* June 19, 1964: (1) China supports the Arab peoples in their struggle to oppose imperialism and old and new colonialism and to win and safeguard national independence; (2) China supports the pursuance of a policy of peace, neutrality, and nonalignment by the governments of Arab countries; (3) China supports the desire of the Arab peoples to achieve solidarity and unity in the manner of their own choice; (4) China supports the Arab countries in their efforts to settle their disputes through peaceful consultation; and (5) China holds that the sovereignty of the Arab countries should be respected by all other countries and that encroachment and interference from any quarter should be opposed.

When Chou En-lai set forth these principles the Middle East was an area of interest to China but of no vital strategic or economic concern. To the Middle Eastern states, too, China appeared a remote state peripheral to their problems and policies. We may recall that from their assumption of power in 1949 until the Bandung Conference of 1955, the Chinese People's Republic showed little interest in Afro-Asian affairs and no interest in the Middle East. From Bandung until 1959 their policy was one of cooperation with the Soviet Union and development of ties of friendship and cooperation with Afro-Asian states. From 1959 until 1961 they were involved in a number of tactical disagreements with the Soviet Union which created tension between the two states and led them to compete for influence in Afro-Asia. Throughout this period, the activities of the USSR and China were complementary in their effects, though competitive in nature. From 1961 until 1963 the dispute became involved in competition for the dominance of various organizations of the Afro-Asian and nonaligned countries. From 1963 onward, it is impossible to separate Chinese policy in Afro-Asia from the ideological dispute within the Communist world.

Competition with the Soviet Union is the singular most significant factor of China's active Middle East policy. The first priority of Chinese foreign policy, according to Lin Piao, in the *Peking Review,* September 3, 1965, is the struggle against imperialism and revisionism. China's interest in the Middle East relates directly to this principle. The Soviet attitude toward the West relaxed in 1958–59, to the consternation of China. The Chinese viewed coexistence—the new Soviet approach to East-West relations—as an imminent threat to the progress of world communism and, more particularly, to the advancement of Chinese interests in Asia. Well-entrenched Western interests in Asia in effect circumscribed Chinese relations in their vital sphere, and to acquiesce to Western dominance in the area appeared as much a danger to the security of China as an ideological capitulation to capitalism. China's expanded role in Afro-Asia was designed not only to counterpose Western influence but also to undermine the Soviet policy of coexistence and return it to active opposition to the West. Thus, while the Middle East is not at the center of Chinese policy, the issues at stake bear heavily upon the defense of Chinese vital interests.

Prior to 1967, China's ability to influence events in the Middle East was severely restricted due to its peripheral connections with the area and its inability to compete with the massive amounts of American and Soviet aid. The thrust of its policy was propaganda aimed at exposing American plots and Soviet machinations. Governments of the area responded with suspicion to Chinese incitement to armed struggle. China's support of Arab issues, while appreciated by Arab governments, could hardly counterpose their ties with either the United States or the Soviet Union. The only area outside both American and Soviet spheres of influence was the Palestine liberation movement, and from 1964 China intensified its activities within this movement with aid, propaganda, and technical assistance. If not a brilliant calculation, it proved to be a timely gesture, for the Palestine liberation movement exploded—to the consternation of both the United States and the Soviet Union—to become after 1967 the rallying point of nationalists throughout the Middle East. The liberation movements saw a sellout of their interests in the Egyptian and Soviet acceptance of the Rogers' peace Plan, and accepted the Chinese viewpoint, expressed in *Bina As-Sin* (Peking), October 10, 1968, that "the Soviet revisionists betrayed the Arab peoples in last year's war. . . . After the Glassboro talks, Soviet revisionists and American imperialism intensified their collusion and together they planned a major conspiracy to force the Arab countries to accept a humiliating surrender. . . . The Soviet revisionists concocted a 'resolution' for 'Political settlement' of the Middle East issue . . . in conjunction with American imperialism. . . . Simultaneously, they sought to impose their own political, military and economic domination on the Arab countries under slogans of 'solidarity and assistance.' "

Echoing this view, an al-Fateh central committee spokesman stated in *Klassekampen* (Oslo), no. 9, 1970: "Today the Soviet Union has total control of Nasir. . . . We call the Soviet policy social imperialism. . . . The Soviet 'peaceful coexistence' means increased cooperation with U.S. imperialism and is intended to bring to an end all flaming revolutionary movements." In the Arab Gulf, too, China gained considerable ideological influence over the Popular Front for the Liberation of the Occupied Arab Gulf. Indicating concern over the advancement of Chinese influence in the ideological sphere, according to the *New York Times,* January 1, 1972, the Soviet Union has attempted to repair its revolutionary image by offering both the Palestine and Gulf movements more aid.

China's immediate aim in the Middle East is to counter Soviet regional strategy in the area, to involve the United States in volatile complications there, and to create a generally revolutionary atmosphere, the *Frankfurter Allgemeine Zeitung für Deutschland* stated on September 24, 1970. The slightest conflict between the Soviet Union and the United States in the Middle East, even a state of affairs that compel the two to keep forces stationed in readiness, helps to both weaken the strategic position of the one in the Far East and delay the advance of the other. When bogged down with crises in the Middle East, their attack and encirclement potential of China is lessened as China moves nearer to its over-all strategic turning point of achieving a nuclear stalemate by manufacturing intercontinental ballistic missiles of its own. But the potential of Chinese strategy in the Middle East is limited by the fragmented nature of the revolutionary movement and by American and Soviet ability to bring pressure to bear on Arab governments to limit the freedom of guerrilla groups and withhold support from them. Soviet ability to exert influence in this area was evidenced by its pressure on the Syrian government in September 1970 to withhold military support from the guerrillas while they were being routed in Jordan. In addition, continued Chinese aid to guerrilla movements is dependent upon the goodwill of Arab governments through which arms shipments must be supplied. The only government where Chinese influence competes with Soviet influence is in South Yemen.

While the Soviet Union has been consolidating its position with Arab governments through treaties with Egypt and Iraq in 1971 and 1972, China has been cultivating the seeds of suspicion of Soviet motives in the area. National sovereignty is still a volatile issue in the Middle East, and dependence on Moscow is an issue of growing concern in an area conscious of nationalism. Just as the Soviet Union entered the Middle East on a tide of frustration with Western domination, it does not seem farfetched to hypothesize that Middle Easterners will be seeking leverage against Soviet influence, if not alternatives to it. China's expanded relations with governments in the Middle East gives it greater communication with governments and political leaders throughout the area. Its new role in international affairs and its power position vis-à-vis the United States and the Soviet Union makes its position on Middle East issues of vital concern. While Chinese influence is unlikely to replace Soviet or American influence in the Middle East, both Soviet and American positions are complicated by the need now to take China into account. Just as the Soviet Union and the United States were approaching a negotiating position on Middle East issues, China pledged its opposition to imposed settlements in the area, declining a French invitation to participate in the four-power talks, as *Al-Ahram* reported on November 22, 1971.

Even while seeking expanded relations in the Middle East, however, China confirmed its continuing support to liberation movements in the area and its opposition to Israel in spite of a number of Israeli gestures to establish a dialogue. China even rejected an Israeli government cablegram congratulating it on its admission to the UN. But China will not be insensitive to the positions of the Arab states. This was communicated to Egypt's Foreign Minister Mahmud Riyadh by China's delegation to the UN, reported by *Al-Nahar* (Beirut), December 2, 1971. The Chinese put forward three points of their position: (1) China will concentrate first on supporting the Palestinians in their struggle for recovery of their country and, second, on aiding the Arab states in ending Israeli occupation of their territory; (2) China will continue to reject Security Council Resolution 242 of November 22, 1967; and (3) China will watch the "attitude of progressive Arab states" and support their decisions.

It is easy to conjecture from China's interest in the Middle East a desire for the area's oil. But while Chinese strategy may indeed seek to hamper supplies to the West, present information indicates that China is now self-sufficient in oil, its production having reached 100 million barrels a year and its estimated recoverable reserves being the twelfth largest in the world, according to the *Middle East Economic Digest,* October 30, 1970. China's economic relations with the Middle East, however, have become increasingly important over the last decade. For example, in 1962, the UAR received the largest volume of Chinese exports in the area, a little over £6,000,000 in value. By 1969, Kuwait had taken the lead, with imports from China exceeding £1,000,000. In the same period, the volume of trade with Iraq, the Sudan, and Syria almost tripled.

China's trade with the Middle East has been relatively independent of political considerations. Table 1 demonstrates the nature of increased Chinese trade with the area even with countries to which China has been politically hostile.

China's expanded diplomatic relations in the Middle East are likely to be a prelude to greater economic interaction and may have been a significant motive for increasing its representation in the area. Trade figures for 1969–70, given in Table 2, indicate that China's trade with some states in the area fluctuated slightly but these were more than offset

TABLE 1
Chinese Exports to the Middle East (£000)

	1962	1963	1964	1965	1966	1967	1968	1969	% Change 68–69
Bahrein	—	225	369	509	1,044	1,385	2,130	3,327	+ 56.2
Iran *	1	—	—	592	4,453	1,481	722	683 ‡	− 5.4
Iraq	3,305	4,478	5,188	6,043	7,576	6,368	7,132	8,275	+ 16.0
Israel	—	—	3	—	1	—	94	8	− 91.5
Jordan	n.a.	715	784	1,317	1,999	1,432	1,912	2,030 ‡	+ 6.2
Kuwait	792	1,031	2,095	4,358	5,438	6,763	9,712	10,408	+ 7.2
Lebanon	534	961	1,298	1,753	2,774	2,894	2,468	3,911	+ 58.5
Saudi Arabia †	27	5	8	35	n.a.	n.a.	7	n.a.	n.a.
South Yemen	23	30	393	660	505	677	1,127	1,943	+ 72.4
The Sudan	1,361	1,523	2,340	2,342	4,540	6,202	7,168	5,833	− 18.6
Syria	1,338	1,072	1,920	2,062	4,797	4,918	4,346	7,087	+ 63.1
Turkey	—	—	—	—	—	52	101	83	− 17.8
UAR	6,446	7,107	6,371	9,552	14,398	8,311	8,506	5,363	− 36.7
Total	17,644	20,550	26,261	35,922	59,378	52,390	56,518	62,111	+ 9.9

SOURCE: *Middle East Economic Digest*, October 30, 1970, p. 1,262.

* Iranian year beginning in year stated.
† Hijri year beginning in year stated, except in the case of 1968, where the figure refers to the Gregorian year.
‡ estimate.
n.a. = not available.

TABLE 2

Chinese Trade with the Middle East 1969–70 (£1,000)

	Imports		Exports	
	1969	1970	1969	1970
Abu Dhabi	n.a.	n.a.	87	76 *
Bahrein	—	3	1,800	3,600
Dubai	n.a.	n.a.	2,635	2,758 *
Egypt	6,019 †	7,593 ‡	7,092 †	6,463 ‡
Iran §	222 ¶	754 ¶	689 ¶	177 ¶
Iraq	1,600	1,230	6,080	7,010
Israel	1	7	8	8
Jordan	185	1,736	2,042	1,746
Kuwait	n.a.	n.a.	10,408	8,424
Lebanon	107	20	33,700	28,300
Qatar	n.a.	n.a.	511	578
Saudi Arabia	n.a.	n.a.	n.a.	n.a.
South Yemen	12	20	1,900	2,100
The Sudan	5,300	5,200	29,200	45,300
Syria	3,932	5,509	7,087	3,574
Turkey	33	367	83	41
Yemen	n.a.	n.a.	1,943	2,758

SOURCE: *Middle East Economic Digest,* October 30, 1970, p. 1,301.
* 12 months ending March 1971.
† 12 months ending June 1969.
‡ 12 months ending June 1970.
§ not including oil.
¶ 12 months ending 20 March.
n.a. = not available.

by the substantial increase of trade with the Sudan (where economic advantage was indeed dependent upon political factors and was achieved at the expense of the Soviet Union.)

CONCLUSION

President Nixon's 1972 odyssey to Peking marked more than a rapprochement in relations between the United States and the People's Republic of China. It also coincided with the change in China's foreign-policy orientation. After twenty years in the relative isolation of the revolutionary cocoon, Peking is asserting itself as a major force in world politics, including the Middle East. From a Western perspective, this is often regarded as a disturbing prospect, given the Chinese propensity to support revolutionary, anti-traditional groups throughout the world, motivated by an impeccably activist Marxist-Leninist ideology. This view, however, appears to be a myth: numerous incongruities already exist between Chinese national self-interest and its ostensibly disinterested world view, as a result of the Chinese emergence.

Most Western attention and experience of Chinese foreign policy in action has focused on the Indian subcontinent, where the duality of Peking's interests and ideology are most evident. It was long thought remarkable, for instance, that China consistently sided with Pakistan in the Indo-Pakistani feud—this despite the virulent anti-Communist character of both the Ayub and Yahya Khan regimes. The middle-class socialism of Ali Bhutto is of an even milder form than that of the Indian Congress Party. Indeed, this inconsistency has led to questioning the sincerity of Peking's "progressive socialist" ideological line when in conflict with national interest. Such suspicions were not allayed by Chinese indifference to the Bangladesh liberation movement, and was certainly intensified after Peking's indifference to the fate of Maoist elements in Sri Lanka, suppressed by Mrs. Bandaranaike.

These contortions have been rationalized on the basis of the proximity of China to the subcontinent: distaste of having a powerful neighbor to the south as well as the north was the security consideration that naturally outweighed considerations of class struggle. Core values such as national security naturally evince a greater reaction when irritated than any long-range conceptions embodied in the visionary national anthem, "East is Red."

If this rationale is correct, one could expect the emergent Chinese attitude toward areas further afield to follow a more consistent ideological line. While this may be true, it is so only in a relative sense. Events in the Middle East in particular indicate it will become less and less so during the seventies. These general trends in the Middle East earmark the nascent stage of a Chinese big power role.

After the eviction of most of the Soviet advisors from the UAR, there followed a marked increase in Chinese solicitation of established regimes in the area. This extended even to the establishment of friendly links with the Kuwaitis, not well known for their revolutionary ardor; this action was taken, of course, because of the funds that Kuwait has paid as tribute to the Palestinian cause.

The purity of Chinese support for the revolutionary groups itself, however, is not unalloyed. The late sixties and early seventies have witnessed the abatement of Chinese support of the movement for the liberation of the Arab Gulf, operating against the most reactionary forces in the Middle East and perhaps anywhere. And in June 1973 China supported Iran's policy in the Gulf—a policy which aimed at the sup-

pression of liberation movements in the area. Chinese stock in the Palestinian cause has apparently risen; nevertheless, arms shipments to the
Palestinians, reduced since the sixties, now have strings attached: continued receipt is contingent on their not being distributed to the most
active revolutionary groups, including Black September.

The most decisive single example of Chinese flexibility occurred in
the Sudan. It can hardly have been a fear of insecure boundaries that
led to Peking's support of the Numeiry regime in the wake of the abortive coup of 1971. When the Sudanese government narrowly defeated
an allegedly Communist coup attempt of mid-July, 1971 the Chinese
sent a message congratulating General Djafar Numeiry, although he was
conducting an anti-Communist witch-hunt in the Sudan.

These trends have not yet hardened into a full-fledged big power outlook on the part of the People's Republic of China. The seeds of this
role, however, have been planted, and preliminary shoots have
sprouted. It is likely that the seventies will see the self-interest component of Chinese foreign policy take even firmer roots.

❋ 7 ❋

TAREQ Y. ISMAEL

Africa and the Middle East

Relations between the various states and empires of the Middle East and their counterparts in Africa are ancient beyond reckoning. The fall of the Western Roman Empire, and the associated disorders, diminished these connections and destroyed most of the historical records of them. Until the rise of Islam, the great barbarian invasions kept Egypt and Mediterranean Africa concerned with local affairs, and only a few Arab traders, crossing the Red Sea and sailing the coastal waters in their small vessels, maintained the Middle Eastern–African contact. Of this period little is known with any certainty. In the centuries between the Hejira and the victory of European colonialism, the Arabs held a virtual monopoly on economic and cultural exchange with sub-Saharan Africa. This well-developed trade faltered as both Islam and Sudanic empires lost their cohesion and autonomy, but it did not disappear completely even at the height of European colonial dominance.

The nature of contemporary African–Middle Eastern relations and the patterns of its interaction are the subjects of this chapter. Of the Middle Eastern countries neither Turkey nor Iran have participated in interregional or cross-regional efforts to the same extent as the Arabs. Nor do they have the historical, cultural, or geographical linkages with Africa. This chapter, therefore, concentrates primarily on the Arab world and Africa, for it is the Arabs who provide the main thrust for regional interaction. Israel, however, also devotes considerable effort to African relations. Thus, the Arab-Israeli dispute is a significant aspect of Middle Eastern–African interaction.

THE ARABS AND AFRICA

When in the middle of the twentieth century the colonial powers lost their hold on both Arab and African lands, the governments of the two regions joined the anti-colonial and anti-imperialist movement. The commonality of viewpoint extended beyond foreign policy to common problems of economic and political development. Although great diversity of opinion characterizes the politics of both regions, the Arabs and Africans have been in sufficient accord for cooperation to develop through the media of international conferences, diplomatic and trade relations, and the United Nations. In addition to cooperative efforts in matters of common interest, there have been attempts by nations of each region to gain support from nations of the other on matters of regional interest—the Arab-Israeli dispute on the part of the Arabs, for example, and the South African problem on the part of the Black African states.

Historical and Cultural Ties

The impetus given Arab expansion in the seventh century by the rise of Islam carried Arab armies into Egypt in 649 and to the rest of North Africa by the end of the century. But the spread of Islam into the Sudanic lands of Africa was a long, slow process. Islam did not replace Christianity in the Nile Valley until the thirteenth century, although converted Berbers had carried Islam across the Western Sudan by the eleventh century, and there were noted centers of Islamic civilization on the Niger at Jinna and Timbuktu by the fourteenth century. On the East African coast, trading stations became permanent settlements at various points, the largest of which—Zanzibar—became the residence of the ruler of Oman. Thus Islam was diffused from the northern and eastern coasts of Africa into the center, although the rate at which the faith was adopted by the people may have been less than appears from the tendency of the upper classes to adopt Islam as a mark of association with the highly regarded Arab culture.

The religious connection between the Arab World and Africa, even when numbers are not exaggerated, was perhaps less pervasive than mere figures of conversion might indicate. The tenets of Islam have undergone considerable modification in adaptation to an African environment. Nonetheless, Islam provided the motive for cultural exchanges such as visits of Arab travelers to the cities and universities of the Sudan, the education of Africans at al-Azhar in Cairo, the pilgrimages to Mecca by those Africans who could afford the cost, and the movements of itinerant marabouts throughout Muslim Africa. One of the major bases of cooperation between Arab and African governments is the base of understanding provided by a common religious background, however variant. It must be stated that although religion does not seem to be a controlling factor in international relations, it has often provided a tool for developing cooperation where friendship between governments already exists.

The basis of cooperation was not created by religion alone. The ancient trade routes—those down the east coast forged by the Arab traders of Yemen and Oman, those up the Nile first opened by the Pharaohs, and those across the Sahara pioneered by the Phoenicians and the Romans—all fell under the control of the Arabs of North Africa, or at least the control of their allies among converted tribesmen of the Sahara. Traffic in slaves, gold, and salt going north, and cloth and manufactured goods such as weapons going south, provided the basis for extensive trade. Again, this trade should not be overrated as a source of cooperation. Under the economic systems prevalent throughout Africa and Arabia during the period of Arab dominance, trade was necessarily limited. The economies of the day operated on a subsistence basis, and only essential primary goods and certain luxuries were exchanged—and then only by rulers and the upper classes. Furthermore, trade was controlled by various private merchants operating under various regimes. For much of this period the Arab world was divided among a variety of regimes, and the internal instability of some of these disrupted trade seriously at times.

This same shifting political situation has also had its effect upon political intervention by Arabs into Africa. Although there had been trade up the Nile and in from the east coast for centuries, and this had gradually increased in importance, it was not until the nineteenth century that Egypt, under the leadership of the Khedive Ismail and his British advisers, attempted to take advantage of the shorter distance to the interior (what is now Uganda) by the coastal route by sending an expedition. The landing on Zanzibari territory led to protests from the British government which halted the expedition. Shortly afterward, the division of African territory among the European powers prevented any further attempts to consolidate an Egyptian empire in Africa. Political relations were not always advantageous to the reputation of the Arabs in any event. The slave trade and the trade in arms had extremely damaging effects among the population of Africa. In West Africa, the spread of Islam was often accomplished with the sword rather than by peaceful conversion. In the Nile Valley, it was Arab armies, not missionaries, who took Islam up to the mountain kingdom of Ethiopia. Altogether, the African experience with the Arabs was not a happy one. However, the intervention of European powers prevented the Arabs from acquiring imperial possessions and subjected the Arabs to the experience of colonization. Under these circumstances, the Arabs, instead of being regarded as conquerors, became fellow-sufferers of imperialism. The experience of the Africans who were subjected to European rule, especially in the Belgian Congo and the Portuguese territories but to a lesser degree in the French, Spanish, and German colonies, made the misdeeds of the Arabs seem mild by comparison.

The Bases of Interaction

The common experiences of the Africans and Arabs—the subjection to colonialism, the training of nationalist politicians in Europe, the diffusion of feelings of unity over areas transcending the tribe or traditional village—gave them objective and subjective bases for common action. Until imperialism began to recede, the opportunities for communication across colonial boundaries were limited, however, so that it was not until the end of World War II that a common front could begin to form. Even then, the states of the Arab east were primarily interested in establishing their own political identities and meeting their domestic problems, and the Arab North African states were involved in a long struggle for independence. The significance of the independence of Egypt from foreign control, and of the fact that the Egyptian revolution occurred as early as 1952, should not be underrated in assessing the reasons for the role Egypt has played in Africa.

The chief basis of Arab-African interaction is ideological and subjective, but a set of problems of foreign and domestic policy is common throughout the two regions, and it is within this framework that the nationalist-neutralist ideology has been established. The problem of the relationship of former colonies to the former colonizer has been serious, especially perhaps among the former French territories. Among both African and Arab states colonized by France, the relationship to France is an important question. These states are generally more dependent upon France for economic aid and for trade than former British colonies are upon Britain. In some cases, notably that of Chad, the French have utilized military forces to enforce domestic stability; only on one occasion—in 1964 in East Africa—have the British taken a similar action, and then only briefly. The material dependence of African states upon France is not matched among the Arab states, even those of North Africa; but Tunisia's economy is based on the French connection to a significant degree, and French arms are important in the military forces of Libya. Perhaps more important on a continuous basis than material connection has been the union engendered by the French assimilationist policy. Although the policy failed to turn Africans into Frenchmen, and thus to make African territories into part of France—just as it failed in Syria, Lebanon, and Southeast Asia—nevertheless many leaders of African states were educated in France and received their first political training there. The former union of African parties in the Rassemblement Democratique Africaine was based largely upon the fact that the African territories required a unified delegation at the National Assembly in Paris, where one African leader—Felix Houphouet-Boigny— even served in several ministries. The reluctance to sever the French connection is evident from the fact that only Guinea voted "no" in the 1958 referendum, although within the next two years the other French territories chose a much looser form of association with France.

Related to the problem of the relationship to the metropolitan power has been the problem of the Cold War. For those states which had to struggle violently for their independence, foreign assistance was essential. Because the French, British, Belgians, Portuguese, and Spanish are all members of NATO, it was difficult for liberation movements to obtain any support from the states of the Western bloc. A turn to the Communist states was obvious and, in some cases, essential. After independence was obtained, the decision had to be made to continue the association with the Communists, or to return to some form of association with the metropolitan power and its allies, or some combination of the two. The need to make this decision, in a somewhat different form, also presented itself to those states whose independence was achieved without a violent revolution, but who disapproved of the methods employed by the colonial powers, and who felt a sense of fellowship for those nationalists who had turned to the East.

In addition to these problems of foreign policy, the chief problems of domestic policy were two, and in these matters there was considerable similarity between the problems of the Arabs and those of the Africans. The problem of economic development was and is crucial for these new states, and is not only common to them, but may be alleviated by common action. There have been, as some evidence for this fact, numerous attempts, some more successful than others, to establish various forms of economic unions, customs unions, common markets, and cooperative enterprises.

The problem of internal stability is not so easily susceptible to solution through common action, but it has been widely felt that some form of political union, aside from its economic advantages, could provide the basis for progress in politics and in social life. The Mali Federation of the Soudan (now Mali) and Senegal (1960–62); the United Arab Republic of Egypt and Syria (1958–61); the proposed Egypto-Iraqi-Syrian unions of 1963 and 1964; the Federation of Tanganyika, Uganda, and Kenya into an East African entity; the Conseil d'Entente of Niger, the Ivory Coast, Upper Volta, and Dahomey; and the union of Tanganyika and Zanzibar into Tanzania in 1964—all are examples of attempts to gain advantages from political unity in the fields of political stability and national development.

Aside from the possibilities of united action in international relations, at the United Nations, for example, objective circumstances do not provide as great a motive for cooperation as an ideological agreement which was, ironically, fostered by the objective conditions created by colonial rule. During the period from 1950 to 1960 there were few places in Africa which could serve as centers of African nationalist activity. One of these—the most important—was Cairo, where the Egyptian government maintained support for the offices of many African nationalist groups exiled from their homelands and provided them with facilities for radio broadcasts to the colonial territories, publishing facilities, secretarial help, and other services. This experience left many African nationalists with favorable impressions of Egypt and caused an interchange of views which no doubt created a large area of agreement between the Egyptian regime and many of the leaders of the independent states of Africa.

Nasser, more than any other Arab leader (until Ben Bella in Algeria), believed in a strong connection between the Arabs and the Africans. In his 1954 book, *Egypt's Liberation: The Philosophy of the Revolution,* Nasser devoted considerable space to Egypt's role in the African circle. He observed that Egypt, because of its location in Africa, could not "remain aloof from the terrible and sanguinary conflict going on there," and that Egypt had a responsibility in Africa that could not be given up.

The feeling of unity with Africa common to the Egyptian leadership was not shared completely by other Arab politicians, but the North Africans, whose own struggles for liberation were supported by Egypt, shared at least part of this concern. It is difficult in retrospect to discern whether anti-imperialism was a cause or a consequence of cooperation, but the two were probably interdependent. As the states cooperated in the solution of their particular problems with colonialism, they came to see imperialism as a whole as an evil they must combine to combat. The Bandung Conference of 1955, which provided an opportunity for President Nasser to meet the leaders of the anti-imperialist movement and to discover the truly global scale of its activities, added to his perceptions of the importance of African liberation the idea of a consistent framework for pursuing not only liberation, but its perpetuation.

Although there has been a significant degree of ideological agreement —especially on nonalignment, anti-colonialism, anti-imperialism, and cooperation through the United Nations and other joint endeavors of the nations of Africa, and this agreement has been linked to the domestic ideal of socialism and development—the extent of disagreement has also been significant. Again, the francophone states, which depend more heavily upon European assistance, have not been willing to go as far in cooperating with the leaders of the anti-imperialist movement as have the former British colonies. While Ghana, Kenya, Tanzania, Egypt, and Iraq have been notably anti-imperialist, only Algeria and Guinea among French-speaking African states have been active. The problem here has been one of priorities. Although some states find that the first priority is independent political and economic development, others consider that political stability and economic development are imperative, even at the expense of independent foreign policies. Much of the ideological agreement between the two regions appears in their concrete relations (to be considered later) but a survey of common ideas, some of which have been mentioned already, seems to be in order. As indicated by President Nasser's early writing, the anti-imperialist theme is important. This position has continued to be central to Egyptian policy and to the policies of such states as Algeria, Iraq, Syria, Ghana, Guinea, and Mali. In pursuit of this policy, Egypt involved herself in the Congo (nationalizing Belgian property in Egypt as an indicator of her position), and, when it was found that Egypt was over-involved, President Nasser participated in the Casablanca Conference in 1961 as a means of presenting a united front on the side of anti-imperialism. Since gaining independence from France, Algeria has also been a leading anti-imperialist state, and has perhaps been even more prepared than Egypt to support violent revolutionary actions. The two countries do not appear to have become rivals in Africa, but rather they are independently operating states.

Through a long series of international conferences, at the UN and in bilateral diplomacy, Egypt has pursued a policy of nonalignment, and in this policy she has found support among the African states. The African states, faced with the problems of economic development, have had no wish to be drawn into the competition of the Western and the Communist states unless they could benefit thereby. This has led to the position of nonalignment, the principal tenets of which are anti-imperialism, disassociation from any blocs or alliances, and the presentation of something of a united front for peace.

International Conferences

At the Bandung Conference in 1955, the first Afro-Asian People's Solidarity Conference at Cairo in 1957, and the All-African People's Conference at Accra in December 1958, the basis had been laid for three important trends. The first was the use of the international conference as a means of resolving questions among the nations of Afro-Asia and of thus providing at least the semblance of a united front. The second was the pressure by Russia and China upon the conferences and the permanent secretariats they established. The third was the inability of the Afro-Asian states to go beyond generalities to specific measures.

After Bandung, the international conference became important as a means of gathering together statesmen from Africa, Asia, and Latin America. Some of these conferences were for nonaligned nations, others for all Afro-Asians. The problems of membership became acute at times, as at the Cairo preparatory conference before the Belgrade meeting of 1961, and the Algiers meeting in 1965.

The Communist states attempted throughout the period of conference diplomacy to gain control or representation at various conferences and on various secretariats. The Afro-Asian People's Solidarity movement was a Communist effort, but was taken over by the Egyptians and the Communists failed to gain lasting control. Eventually, at Algiers, the efforts of China and Russia to oust each other from influence in Afro-Asia led to the disruption of the conference and diminished the usefulness of conferences in general.

The problem of international conferences which eventually proved insoluble was that to unity. After Bandung, it became virtually an article of faith that a high degree of agreement be reached and that no rifts appear which would provide the "imperialist" states with opportunities to divide Afro-Asia. The real divisions among Afro-Asian states on ideological grounds and for reasons of national interest, as well as the extent to which common interest in some matters was simply lacking, meant that every attempt to get beyond platitudes ended in failure. The Casablanca group of five states could maintain solidarity only for about two years; larger groups collapsed even more quickly. Any attempt to involve larger numbers of states implied some dilution of principles, and with the diversity among these states, to get agreement among all of them, it was necessary to have little or no content to the agreement.

The UAR participated in a number of conferences, and many were held in Cairo. The permanent organs of various groups were also placed in Cairo. Algiers too was the seat of several conferences. But the Arab states proved unable to sustain any African interest in condemning Israel, and aside from the Organization for African Unity (OAU), few of the organizations linking Arabs and sub-Saharan Africans proved effective. Within the framework of the OAU, however, the Arab states of Africa maintain continuing relations with African states in both the political and functional spheres.

Diplomatic Relations

The extent of bilateral diplomatic relations, including not only permanent missions but the size and apparent importance of these missions, the status of their personnel, the extent of their activities, and the success they encounter in attempting to create a climate in which trade can flourish and heads of states can meet constructively, is exceedingly important. The intermittent and occasional nature of international conferences, compounded by the limitations placed upon participants by the requirements of parliamentary diplomacy, limits their effectiveness for the long-run coordination of the policies of two states. Further, as in the United Nations, the resolutions of international conferences seldom carry any obligation for their enforcement or enactment, as the case may be, by participants, while treaties between states are ordinarily enacted into domestic law and implemented through legislative or executive action. If treaties are not enforced, there is at least an indication of a change in the relations of the states involved; while they remain in force, they provide a continuous basis for the exchange of goods and ideas.

As might be expected from Egypt's early involvement in Africa, among the Arab states the United Arab Republic has the largest diplomatic corps operating in Africa. The UAR had embassies in sixteen African countries as of 1964, and twenty-four by 1966. In 1967 Iraq had eight embassies serving ten African countries; Syria was represented in five African countries and had accepted representatives of four; Lebanon had diplomatic relations with twelve African nations; and Jordan was represented in eight. Although Algeria only became independent in 1962, by 1967 Algerian ambassadors or *charges d'affaires* were in fifteen other African countries.

Although a full discussion of all the representatives exchanged by Eastern Arab states, Arab-African states, and sub-Saharan states is beyond the scope of this chapter, some significant trends appear from the relations between the major anti-imperialist states. The UAR has relations with most African states and with the Middle Eastern states as well, and so forms something of a link between the two regions. This linkage is sometimes more than indirect, as several countries maintain embassies in the UAR accredited to other countries as well. Iraq's ambassador to the UAR is also accredited to Ethiopia and Guinea, while the ambassadors to Iraq of Ethiopia and Guinea reside in the UAR.

While Egypt has diplomatic relations with most African countries, the other Middle Eastern countries are more limited in their activities. Of the countries in which Iraq is represented, six are either completely or dominantly Arabic (Algeria, Morocco, the Sudan, the UAR, Libya, and Tunisia), and three others (Guinea, Nigeria, and Ethiopia) have large Muslim communities. Only Ghana is preponderantly non-Muslim. Syria's more limited representation includes Guinea, Somalia, the Sudan, Tunisia, and the UAR—all nations with a Muslim majority. The embassies of Algeria, Libya, Morocco, and Tunisia—all Arab-Islamic states—are in Syria. Jordan is in a similar position. Algeria's representatives reside in all of the Islamic states of Africa, but only in five or six states without large bodies of Muslims. Furthermore, seven Middle Eastern Arab states have relations with Algeria. If we consider two African states, both dominated by non-Muslims but with substantial Islamic communities, Chad has relations with Lebanon, Saudi Arabia, and Israel in the Middle East, but with Libya, Morocco, and the Sudan out of the smaller community of Arab African states. Ethiopia, which is a very active state in international affairs, has relations with Morocco, Somalia, the Sudan, and the UAR among African Arab states, as well as with Israel. Ghana and Guinea are also widely represented in the Arab states of Africa and Asia. We may conclude from this that diplomatic relations, while extensive through the area, tend to fall into patterns of affinities; with some exceptions, Asian Arab states tend to concentrate their efforts on North Africa, and African states tend to decrease their involvement east of Suez. This puts the North African states, especially the UAR and Algeria, in the position of mediators between Africa and the Arab East.

Aside from relations which may be strictly called diplomatic, in the sense of permanently established missions or embassies, there has been a considerable amount of bilateral exchanges among heads of state of the African and Arab regions. Again, Egypt has taken the lead. President Nasser received such present and former African leaders as Kwame Nkrumah, Hamani Diori, Felix Houphouet-Boigny, and Djafar Numeiry, in addition to the many gatherings of African and Arab leaders in Cairo for conferences of one sort or another. (A major exception to Egyptian initiative in conference diplomacy were the efforts of Prime Minister Ahmed Mohammed Mahgoub of the Sudan after the 1967 war with Israel when he sponsored a conference of Asian and African Arab leaders in Khartoum). Personal diplomacy has been effective in two senses. When preliminary work has been completed by professional foreign office or embassy staffs, the heads of state, or of government, as the case may be, may place the final seal of approval on the matter as a sort of ritual. When, on the other hand, the purpose is not the implementation of a policy but the creation of a mood or the plotting of a general strategy of action, then the meetings of presidents, prime ministers, and kings seem to have some effect. It may seem that a simple agreement of two states might be expressed as easily by an exchange of notes as by a meeting of the leaders of the nations. But a meeting of, for example, President Nasser and President Julius Nyerere, may have a greater impact than could be achieved by personal diplomacy. In the underdeveloped world, where charismatic leadership is almost a political necessity, simple agreements often have greater political than economic significance, and where communication between states is at best tenuous, the more traditional diplomacy of direct, especially private, meetings of heads of state and government can dissolve feelings of distrust, misunderstanding, and bias and create impressions of goodwill, commonality, and respect.

In addition to diplomatic relations, trade between Arab and African states is carried on, as it has been for centuries, but we need not deal with this at length, for in no case is the trade of any African country with any Arab country a major portion of its total trade activities. However, trade agreements provide a show of solidarity, with some minor substance. In effect, the trade agreements and loans are signs of friendship, rather than of true economic involvement, and in some cases loans granted by the UAR to African states for trade purposes have been left undrawn because the African state cannot afford the loss of foreign exchange or because there is no real market in the UAR for the goods that the African state wishes to export. Between two developing countries, trade is obviously limited by the fact that both deal largely in primary products. In the two regions, only the UAR has the manufacturing capacity to utilize imports of raw material in exchange for manufactured goods.

The United Nations

For most of the first fifteen years of the existence of the United Nations, only four African states were members—Ethiopia, Egypt, Liberia, and South Africa—and the last of these is an African state only in the geographic sense. During the early years of the United Nations, eight Middle Eastern countries were members—Turkey, Iran, and Israel (which are not the focus of this chapter), and Iraq, Saudi Arabia, Lebanon, Yemen, and Syria, which are all Eastern Arab states. Other African states became members over a period of time, and in 1960 seventeen African states joined the United Nations upon gaining their independence from various European powers. Soon after, in fact beginning before the admission of the bulk of these to the UN, the United Nations was deeply involved in operations in Africa. These African operations, undertaken at the same time that the Africans were becoming a major portion of the UN's membership, led to dissension among African states and was a test of the UN's ability to operate under new conditions.

A major source of Arab-African interaction in the United Nations is the joint membership of several states (Algeria, Libya, Morocco, the Sudan, Tunisia, and the UAR) in the African, Afro-Asian, and Arab caucusing groups. Although these groups do not bind their members to vote in a certain way, they provide a valuable opportunity for discussion of issues, and it would be strange if mutual membership did not lead to a certain amount of interchange of views. The cohesion of the African group has been relatively high as shown by Thomas Hovet, Jr., in *Africa in the United Nations:* from 1946 to 1962 the members of the group were divided on 24.5 percent of the votes, voted identically on 47.1 percent of the votes, and were voting identically or abstaining in 28.4 percent of the votes. In other words, on nearly half of all roll-call votes taken in the first sixteen sessions of the United Nations, all African states members of the organization voted yes or no, or abstained, without dissent. During this period, the numbers of members of the caucusing group grew from three (through the ninth session), to thirty-two. Identical and solidarity votes have tended to become fewer as the group has grown. From the thirteenth through the sixteenth sessions, the African members of the Arab caucusing group voted identically on 61.8 percent of the roll-calls, and divided on only 8.7 percent. The division in the Arab faction have generally been—in this period—between Libya, the Sudan, and Tunisia on the one hand, and Morocco and the UAR on the other (Algeria was not yet a member). Until the formation of the Organization for African Unity in 1963, the Casablanca group included Algeria, Ghana, Guinea, Mali, Morocco, and the UAR; these were considered the radical states in Africa. The Casablanca group voted identically on 78.6 percent of the issues between 1958 and 1962, and were divided on only 4.9 percent. They divided on only three votes on African questions during this period; in each case Guinea dissented from the choice of the other members. The African Arab states (except Algeria, which was not a member at the time Mr. Hovet conducted his study) not only formed a cohesive group, cohering with some African states; the members of this group still maintained a high degree of cohesion with the rest of the African group. In the thirteenth session (1958), Libya, Morocco, the Sudan, Tunisia, and the UAR in no cases voted in opposition to the majority of the African caucus. In the fourteenth session, the Sudan again never voted against the majority; Morocco dissented from the caucus 2.2 percent of the time; Libya on 2.3 percent of the votes; Tunisia on 2.3 percent; and the UAR, 6.4 percent. In the fifteenth session, Tunisia dissented in 4.3 percent of the votes; Sudan in 9.3 percent; Libya, 9.4 percent; the UAR, 10.2 percent; and Morocco, 15.3 percent. In the sixteenth session the degree of dissent was Libya and Morocco, 6.8 percent; Tunisia and the UAR, 8.1 percent; and the Sudan, 10.7 percent. On the positive side, from the session of 1958 through that of 1961–62, the Sudan's percentage of identical votes with the majority of the caucus ranged from 7.14 to 86.4; Morocco ranged from 69.2 to 78.6 percent; Tunisia from 68.9 to 75.8 percent; Libya from 67.5 to 88.6 percent; and the UAR from 69.8 to 79.2 percent. In the fifteenth session, Libya voted with the majority of the group more often than any other state, and in the sixteenth session, the Sudan held that honor.

We may see from the above information that the African states in general, including the Arab states in Africa, have a considerable degree of solidarity on many issues in the United Nations, and that while cohesion within the Arab group is high, its members still maintain good cooperation with other African states. For at least some purposes, there has been considerable solidarity among Arab, African, and Asian states. Taking this together we may state that in the United Nations, the African states and the Arab states had through 1962 a relationship based on considerable agreement, which was enhanced by the activity of the states common to the two groups. However, other considerations, such as the ideological agreement among the Casablanca states in face of the Congo situation, may prove more effective than agreement on general, nonvital interests.

We do not have a similar analysis of United Nations voting since 1962, but we do know that on the South Africa and Southwest African questions, there has been a high degree of agreement between Arabs and Africans since the beginning of the United Nations. On more general issues, such as peaceful coexistence, bloc voting tends to give way to individual interests, and so the agreement between the Arabs and Africans diminishes at the same time that unity within each group declines. In part, this appears to be a consequence of the fact that adherence to similar general principles does not always mean that each state foresees the same practical consequences for itself from action in line with the principles that other states do.

The 1967 Arab-Israeli war provided a test for the efforts of Arab states to gain African support for their struggle with Israel. Although many African states supported the Arab position during the war (as indicated by UN voting trends on major resolutions), one may be surprised at the lack of support, given the affinity of interests between Africa and the Arab world. Still, Israel has also been engaged in an intense diplomatic effort in Africa. Thus, the Arab role has not gone unchallenged.

ISRAEL AND AFRICA

Arab-Israeli competition, while certainly not the only factor, is perhaps the most significant aspect today of Middle East-African interaction. While the Arabs seek African support in their struggle with Israel, the thrust of Israeli policy in Africa is to counterbalance isolation from and hostility of its neighbors and Arab influence in the Third World community.

Israel's African policy is implemented through three channels: diplomatic relations, trade, and aid. Israel has conducted an intense diplomatic effort in sub-Saharan Africa to counteract the long-established ties of the Arabs with Africa. Between 1957 and 1967, Israel established diplomatic representation in twenty-nine African countries.

Israel's diplomatic effort in Africa is complemented by a small but steadily increasing volume of trade relations. Although trade with Africa accounts for less than 4 percent of Israel's total world trade, it increased some 42 percent between 1966 and 1969. Israeli exports to Africa, which in 1967 amounted to $24.44 million, reached $34.26 million in 1969. Similarly, there has been a slow but continued rise in imports: from 27.39 million in 1967 to 31.30 in 1969, according to *Le Moniteur Africain* (Dakar), July 23, 1970.

Although the volume of Israeli-African trade is not so great that Israel or the various African countries could do without it, the figures may belie its importance. Israeli-African trade relations are nascent relations between infant economies. Israel is laying the groundwork for its young industry, that, as it grows, will require increasing volumes of raw materials and markets for its products—markets that are difficult to find in industrialized nations. Israel, in fact, has made an effort to establish trade relations, however minimal, with almost all African countries south of the Sahara. Only Botswana, Burundi, Gambia, Lesotho, Mauritins, and Swaziland do not have trade with Israel, though they do have diplomatic relations. This effort is particularly striking when we note that 56 percent of all Israeli trade with Africa is concentrated in only five countries (listed in the order of importance): Republic of South Africa ($14.6 million in trade), Central African Republic ($6.6 million), Ethiopia ($6 million), Uganda ($5.1), and Gabon ($4.4). It is clear, too, that Israel's real trading partner in Africa is the Republic of South Africa. Yet no African country has stopped trading with Israel because of this—perhaps a testimonial to the adroitness of Israel's diplomacy.

In the field of foreign aid, Israel's budget is quite modest compared to those of Russia, the U.S., China, or France. In 1966, according to J. C. Froelich, in an article in *Revue Militaire Generals* (Paris, February 1968, Israel's Technical Assistance Department had a budget of $5 million, or 26 million francs, compared to the corresponding French department's budget of 1,120 million francs that year. Israeli aid, then, represents only about 0.05 percent of the total aid received by Black Africa. But figures may again distort the significance, for Israeli aid to Africa has been its most effective tool in support of its diplomatic effort. The program has created good-will for Israel throughout Black Africa. Because Israel cannot compete with the aid programs of the big powers, it concentrates its aid on small, delineated, and specifically practical projects which are immediately profitable or beneficial to the receiving country. In addition, the program is well dispersed throughout Africa; thirty of the thirty-eight countries in tropical Africa signed technical-assistance agreements with Israel between 1960 and 1966.

Israeli aid to Africa assumes three forms: the sending of experts to interested countries, the organization of internships (training programs), and the creation of mixed Israeli-African enterprises. In addition, Israel engages in a military aid program in Africa.

The importance Israel attached to Africa is clear. Out of thirty-three bilateral aid agreements concluded with the Third World, twenty were signed with African countries. Sixty percent of the Israeli experts working abroad work in Africa, while 50 percent of the foreign trainees receiving professional training in Israel are Africans. Between 1958 and 1966 some 5,000 Africans were trained in Israel. In addition, of some 4,237 itinerant on-the-job training courses provided by Israel, 3,649 were lavished on Africa.

Conclusion

In sum, there has been a considerable interchange of ideas between the Middle East and Africa. Historical, cultural, geographical, and political interplay affects both regions (although neither uniformly nor consistently). Historical and cultural ties between the Arab and the African states extend back over many centuries and were augmented in the latter half of the twentieth century with an incomplete ideology based upon anticolonialism, anti-imperialism and nonalignment. This channel of interaction was expressed through the media of international conferences, diplomatic relations, and the United Nations, in a variety of contexts. Although the early conferences created hopes that the African states could join with the Asian states to form a positive force in world politics, this hope proved illusory. In diplomatic and trade relations, as in international conferences, the extent of cooperation between African and Arab states has been limited by the degree of regional interaction. Only those Arab and African states which have been inclined to present themselves as leaders of the community have attempted to secure a large degree of coordination between the two regions. In the United Nations cooperation has been most evident, but even here it seems perhaps more likely that, while an exchange of views has been helpful, the extent of agreement is based more upon parallel action stemming from common views than on coordination of effort in an institutional sense.

The intensity of Israeli-African interaction, although limited in scope, and the dispersion of Israeli activity throughout sub-Saharan Africa, is surprising in view of Israel's small size and limited resources. Israel's initiation of an active role in African relations coincided with the emergence of a Third World force in international politics in the mid-fifties. Thus, at the same time the Africans and Arabs were initiating attempts at regional coordination, Israel was seeking diplomatic and commercial relations and offering aid and technical assistance to newly independent African states. Black African states, detached from the Arab-Israeli conflict, have not been disadvantaged by the resulting Arab-Israeli competition for friends and, for the most part, have been able to remain friendly with both sides. But for the Arabs, as indeed for the Israelis, the competition is a crucial one. Black Africa, in support of either the Arabs or the Israelis, could have a critical influence on the Middle East conflict. Where does sub-Saharan Africa stand? The test came during the Arab-Israeli war of 1967.

During the war the majority of African states opted to remain silent. Only seven states openly took sides: Guinea, Mali, Somalia, Burundi, Zambia, and Tanzania in support of the Arabs; Malawi in support of

Israel. Voting at the Fifth Emergency Special Session of the United Nations General Assembly in the aftermath of the war on major resolutions pertaining to the conflict gave a more complete picture. On the Yugoslav resolution (co-sponsored by thirteen Afro-Asian states and generally considered a compromise between Russian and American positions) sub-Saharan African voting broke down accordingly: twelve in favor, eight against, and eleven abstentions. Because the resolution was opposed by Israel and supported by the Arabs, votes in favor were generally considered to be pro-Arab, while those against were seen as pro-Israeli. The high percentage of abstentions reflects the difficulty of many African states to come to grips with the problem of taking any stance on the Arab-Israeli issue. Thus, it appears that neither the Arabs nor Israel has gained the upper hand in Africa. Rather, Arab-Israeli competition has effectively neutralized the continent. It may be that the very heat and proximity of the issue discourages African involvement. Manifestations of the Cold War both in Africa and the Arab-Israeli conflict also discourage concensus by identifying the issues of the Arab-Israeli conflict as pro-Western or pro-Soviet.

The foregoing indicates that both Israel and many Arab countries have been highly active in vying for the support of sub-Saharan countries. A cardinal Israeli aim has been to diversify her support among Third World countries. Arab efforts have been countervalent: to isolate Israel diplomatically from non-Arab Africa. During the 1960s, most of the African states withheld judgment on the central dispute, pragmatically accepting aid from both sources. From their standpoint, the net effect was additive, while to their benefactors, it was largely cancellative. This picture has changed somewhat. Although a clear-cut pattern of African support for the Arab cause has not yet emerged, recent developments suggest it has gained the initiative vis-à-vis Israel, as noted by the *Christian Science Monitor* on April 4, 1973.

Commencing in 1971, the Israelis have suffered a series of setbacks in their program of closer relations with sub-Saharan Africa. In November, several moderate African leaders visited Israel on behalf of the Organization for African unity. Headed by Senegalese President Senghor, the group, as reported by the *New York Times* on November 3, said that Israel's inflexible position on the repatriation of lost Arab lands was a "definite impediment in the growth of smooth relations with African countries!"

This setback was underscored by a more serious setback the following April, when Israel's 470-man technical team to Uganda was expelled by President Idi Amin. Israel's relations with Uganda had been very close during the 1960s under the regime of Amin's predecessor,

Milton Obote. Amin's action occurred only a few months after his meeting with Libya's President Muammar Kaddafi concerning relations between the two countries. Because the vacuum created by the Israeli departure was soon filled by Libyan aid and advisors, the connection between the two events seems very strong.

While the Ugandan realignment was the most spectacular reversal, changes also occurred in the tier of countries immediately south of the Sahara. Chad broke off relations with Israel in October, and two more governments—the Congo Republic and Niger—followed suit two months later. In both cases, Israeli assistance teams left, as well as the diplomatic contingent. The *New York Times,* December 25, 1972, reported that Egyptian and Algerian advisors have now supplanted their role in these countries.

Energetic diplomatic and propaganda efforts by Arab countries, notably Libya, have been in large measure responsible for these changes. An important direct channel of Afro-Asian contact denied to the Israelis is the OAU. At the council of ministers conference in Morocco in June 1972, African leaders passed a resolution, carried in the *New York Times* on June 27, pledging "all possible support for Egypt" in her struggle with Israel. In the same connection, Israel was condemned unanimously for her "obstructive and negative attitude" as far as preconditions for a peace settlement were concerned.

Nevertheless, African support for the Arabs was still not solidly established in terms of joint action as opposed to orientation. Although strongly worded, the Moroccan document left the nature of the "support" for Egypt indefinite. Moreover, numerous signatories, including Zaire, Kenya, and the Ivory Coast, expressed reservations about the document, fearing it would force them to choose between Arab and Israeli aid, according to the *New York Times,* June 27, 1972. The 1973 OAU Summit Conference held at Addis Ababa, however, not only condemned Israel and demanded her withdrawal from occupied Arab territory, but also passed a resolution demanding that African countries consider collective or individual, political or economic steps, against Israel if it continued to refuse to evacuate occupied Arab territories, as reported in *Le Monde,* May 30, 1973.

Israel has reacted to these changes in her relations with Africa by stepping up her assistance efforts elsewhere on the continent. The main redeployment has been in the far south: Israeli missions in Swaziland, Lesotho, and Botswana were upgraded considerably. These three states have been closely associated with the white regimes in Southern Africa since they obtained independence over the last five years. Arab countries have made no effort to build relations with Southern Africa.

Closer identification of Israel with countries unwilling to take a strong position on the South African question could further reinforce the tendency of Black African states to align with the Arabs. Indeed the similarity of the position of South Africa vis-à-vis Black African states to Israel's own situation in the Arab World gravitates toward the polarization of the continent along these lines. Israel is trying to forestall this by maintaining an active role among Black African moderates. This role was clearly becoming more and more difficult to sustain, and in 1973 became impossible. Following the Non-Aligned Nations Conference held in Algiers in September 1973, which passed a strongly worded resolution condemning continued Israeli occupation of occupied Arab lands, three more African countries broke relations with Israel.

The decisive move of Black Africans behind the Arab position occurred during the October 1973 Arab-Israeli War. By the time the ceasefire was implemented, twenty-one Black African states had broken relations with Israel. Thus, except for Malawi, Lesotho, and Swaziland, Israel has relations only with the racist regimes of South Africa and Rhodesia.

❀ 8 ❀

HARRY N. HOWARD

The United Nations and
the Middle East

THE ROLE OF THE UNITED NATIONS IN THE MIDDLE EAST

Now that the United Nations has passed its twenty-fifth birthday, it is possible to assess some of its successes, shortcomings, and failures and its limitations and achievements as an international organization designed to contribute to international peace and security. As the Charter was elaborated at the San Francisco Conference on International Organization, April–June 1945, the United Nations was established to "save succeeding generations from the scourge of war," to "reaffirm faith in fundamental human rights," to establish conditions under which justice and respect for obligations could be maintained, and to "promote social progress and better standards of life in larger freedom."

These ideals could not be achieved in such a short period of the long human story anywhere in the world, particularly not in the Middle East, because of the very complex nature of the problems involved. While the United Nations has been able to meet some basic issues, it has failed to solve others, notably in the instance of the unyielding problem of Palestine. For this reason, it has been distrusted by the Arabs and often scorned, villified, and held in open contempt by the government of Israel. Yet it should be recalled that the soldiers and diplomats of the United Nations have played a notable and vital role in the Arab-Israeli conflict and that a United Nations peacekeeping force, since 1964, has held the ring between contending Greek and Turkish ethnic elements on the island of Cyprus.

Leaving aside the role which has been played in the political field, it should not be forgotten that the United Nations has also played a significant role in the Middle East in the field of technical and economic as-

This chapter is based on the author's article, "The United Nations in the Middle East," *Current History* 60, 353 (January 1971): 7–12, 49.

sistance. Whatever the obvious structural and political weaknesses, the United Nations remains a very important instrument of international order and justice at the disposal of the peoples of the world.

BASIC MIDDLE EASTERN ISSUES IN THE UNITED NATIONS

The United Nations has been confronted with more persistent problems in the Middle East than in any other part of a very troubled world. Even at the San Francisco Conference on International Organization, which was devoted to the preparation of the UN Charter and to the establishment of the new international organization, not to the consideration or solution of substantive problems, issues bearing on the Middle East in the immediate aftermath of World War II were brought to the attention of the various delegations. Middle Eastern problems were discussed at times in committees and more often in the corridors. This was true of the question of the withdrawal of British and French troops from Lebanon and Syria and of the question of Soviet pressures on Turkey relative to territorial cessions in Eastern Anatolia and the problem of the Turkish Straits. But it was especially true of the problem of Palestine, particularly in its relationship to the new trusteeship system which was to be established under the United Nations. At one point, Secretary of State Edward R. Stettinius observed that "the Palestine question was dangerous. A combination of Palestine and the Arab League was dynamite ready to explode." Still another issue was that of the relationship of the newly formed League of Arab States (March 22, 1945) to the new international organization. Ultimately, like other regional arrangements such as the North Atlantic Treaty Organization and the Organization of American States, it was to take its place loosely within the United Nations, especially under Articles 52–54 of the United Nations Charter.

The basic issues troubling the Middle East have endured, and the United Nations has played an important role in the area in the fields of social and economic development and relief and technical assistance, as well as in the realm of international security. Some problems, as yet, have defied solution—those of Cyprus and Palestine, for example. As early as February 1946, the Lebanese and Syrian governments brought to the attention of the Security Council the problem of the continued presence of Anglo-French troops on their soil. A satisfactory solution was worked out by the parties concerned but met a Soviet veto, largely on the ground that Great Britain and France had not been sufficiently chastised in the draft proposals. Ultimately the problem was solved by the parties themselves, and the troops were withdrawn later in 1946. The discussions at the United Nations contributed constructively to the withdrawals of troops not only from Lebanon and Syria but also from Iran.

Similarly, the Iranian government complained against Soviet intervention in Iran and the Soviet failure to withdraw its troops from northern Iran. Ultimately, Soviet forces were withdrawn, and Iran assumed control in Azerbaijan in December 1946. Years later, in 1970, the United Nations played a very quiet, effective, and constructive role in facilitating the withdrawal of the long-standing Iranian claim to Bahrein, and thereby contributed to a greater degree of stability in the region of the Persian Gulf. Thanks to the good offices of the UN Secretary-General, it was amply demonstrated that the people of Bahrein desired not unity with Iran, but self-government for themselves. The UN Security Council unanimously approved the report of the Secretary-General on May 11, 1970, and on May 14, the Iranian Majlis endorsed the action of the Security Council by an overwhelming vote of 184 to 4.

The problem of Libya, involving the disposition of the former Italian colonies over which the Soviet Union at one time desired a trusteeship, first came into the deliberations of the UN General Assembly in September 1948. After long consideration of this complicated and highly charged problem, on November 21, 1949, the General Assembly recommended that Libya (Cyrenaica, Tripoli, and Fezzan) become an independent state as soon as possible and, in any event, not later than January 1, 1952. A UN commissioner and a council were appointed to assist in the processes leading toward independence, the preparation of a constitution, and the establishment of the government, and, in fact Libyan independence was declared on December 24, 1951.

The Greek Problem

The role of the United Nations in the Greek case, 1947–52, was much more significant and enduring; it involved the United Nations not merely in attempts at conciliation and political adjustment, but in the establishment of investigatory and observational machinery, with observation groups stationed along the northern frontiers of Greece with Albania, Bulgaria, and Yugoslavia, which set a very useful precedent for later United Nations activities of this nature. The actions taken had much significance not only for Greece in that very critical period immediately following World War II, when the Soviet Union appeared to be pressing forward along the Northern Tier of the Middle East, but for the Eastern Mediterranean, Turkey, and the Middle East as a whole.

Greece was in critical condition in the period immediately after World War II, with its society fragmented under Nazi-Fascist occupation and its economy all but wrecked. The problem came before the United Nations in the fall of 1946 on a complaint of the Greek government that Communist-dominated and led guerrillas were crossing and criss-crossing the northern Greek frontiers into Albania, Yugoslavia, and Bulgaria, where they found both sanctuary from battle with the Greek army and equipment and training for further combat in Greece. On December 19, 1946, the Security Council established an eleven-member Commission of Investigation Concerning Incidents Along the Northern Frontiers of Greece, representing all members of the Security Council. The commission spent some two months in Greece, heard testimony, and investigated on the ground. It duly reported in the spring of 1947 to the Security Council—UN Doc. S/360, May 23, 1947—found that the charges of the Greek government were justified, and recommended maintenance of a commission in Greece and the Balkan area to continue observation. This proposal met with five resounding Soviet vetoes when the Security Council considered the problem in the summer of 1947. The question was then remanded to the UN General Assembly which, on November 11, 1947, established a UN Special Committee on the Balkans (UNSCOB), with investigatory and observational functions. That body remained in being until November 1951, when it was replaced by a Balkan Subcommission of the Peace Observation Commission, established under the Uniting for Peace Resolution—General Assembly Resolution 377 (V)—of November 3, 1950.

It is true that the Greek army, retrained and equipped by the United States and the United Kingdom, finally crushed the Greek guerrilla effort to overthrow the Greek government and establish a "people's democracy" based on the Balkan models. But it is no less true that the United Nations commissions rendered a very constructive service in gathering evidence, pinpointing the essential facts as to the situation along the northern Greek frontiers, and highlighting the basic issues. Had Greece fallen, perhaps to become a Soviet satellite, as President Truman advised the U.S. Congress on March 12, 1947, "the effect upon its neighbor, Turkey, would be immediate and serious. Confusion and disorder might well spread throughout the entire Middle East." [1] This, at least, was the view in Western Europe and the United States at the time, and it was the possibility that these wider implications were involved that led to the elaboration of the Truman Doctrine concerning aid to Greece and Turkey. Certainly the Soviet actions in Greece, the severe pressures on Turkey, and the policies pursued relative to Iran, to say nothing of Soviet ambitions elsewhere in the Middle East and the Eastern Mediterranean, were something more than mere straws in the wind.

The Lebanese Crisis

Leaving aside the Palestine problem, which is reserved for separate and more detailed treatment, we may turn to other issues, especially to the problem of Lebanon. When revolt broke out in Lebanon during May–September 1958 against the regime of President Camille Chamoun, there were charges of massive intervention in that country on the part of the United Arab Republic. On June 11, 1958, the UN Security Council resolved to send the United Nations Observation Group in Lebanon (UNOGIL), composed of some six hundred military observers under the direction of Galo Plaza, former president of Ecuador, Rajeshwar Dayal of India, and Major General Odd Bull of Norway, to investigate and report concerning this very complex situation, and to "ensure that there" was "no illegal infiltration of personnel or supply of arms or other material across the Lebanese borders."

It is altogether probable that the presence of some fifteen thousand United States troops, who began landing on July 15 in response to the urgent appeal of the Lebanese government after the Iraqi revolt of July 14, calmed the situation and enabled the Lebanese to choose a successor to President Chamoun in accordance with Lebanon's constitutional processes. But it is also evident, despite restrictions on the movement of UNOGIL personnel and the fact that it could find little evidence of massive intervention, that UNOGIL rendered a very useful service. Its primary contribution to the settlement of the crisis no doubt lay in its moral influence and in its contribution to the establishment of conditions which tended to separate the domestic crisis in Lebanon from external complications. During the difficulties in Jordan in the same general period, the establishment of a symbolic United Nations presence had a very salutary psychological impact in that much troubled country. While the UN presence remained in Jordan for some years, United States forces left Lebanon on October 25, and British forces were withdrawn from Jordan on November 2, 1958.

Yemen

The United Nations action in Yemen, following the overthrow of the Imam in September 1962, involved somewhat similar, if more limited, operations. The problem of Yemen was serious, not only because of its proximity to Saudi Arabia and oil-rich areas, but because of its strategic location on the Red Sea. Soon after the outbreak of the revolt, both the UAR and Saudi Arabia became involved in support of the republican and royalist elements, respectively, and the UAR dispatched an estimated thirty to fifty thousand troops to Yemen. While UN Secretary-General U Thant sent Under-Secretary Ralph Bunche to Yemen as early as February 1963, and asked UNTSO Chief of Staff Major General Carl von Horn to examine the problems of UN observation, it was not until July 4, 1963, that the United Nations Observation Mission (UNYOM), composed of some two hundred officer-observers, began to function under General von Horn.

The basic and essential function in Yemen was to supervise the implementation of an agreement on the part of the UAR and Saudi Arabia, worked out by United States Ambassador Ellsworth Bunker, to withdraw assistance to the contending parties and not to attempt political settlement or peacekeeping. While the task of fact-finding was well implemented, the task of mediation and conciliation proved impossible. The mission was terminated on September 4, 1964. In evaluating the work of UNYOM, it should be kept in mind that the mission was small in numbers, that the terrain to be covered was very rugged, the physical conditions were severe, and local supplies and facilities were meager. UN personnel and equipment, moreover, were often subject to gunfire and were frequently in danger. Nevertheless, it was clear to the secretary-general that the mission had "exercised an important restraining influence on hostile activities in the area"—which was a primary reason for sending it to Yemen.

Cyprus

The United Nations did not begin to play a formal and substantive role on the island of Cyprus until 1964, although informally the problem had come before various bodies in the United Nations as early as 1950. While an independent republic of Cyprus was established in 1960, the Greek and Turkish communities on the island, to say nothing of Greece and Turkey, were unable to resolve the basic national issues relative to Cyprus. During 1963–64, there was further threat of open conflict, with all the implications which that might have for NATO, the Eastern Mediterranean, and the Middle East.

As a result of this very difficult situation and its possibilities for outright war between Greece and Turkey, on March 4, 1964, the UN Security Council unanimously resolved to establish the United Nations Force in Cyprus (UNFICYP), under the command of UNEF General P. S. Gyani. The Cyprus force was composed of some six thousand troops from the United Kingdom, Canada, Finland, Ireland, and Sweden. Attempts at mediation and conciliation, both within and outside the United Nations, were unsuccessful. While an atmosphere of "negative stability" was achieved on the island, the UN secretary-general reported in September 1970 that "no significant change" had occurred during the year, although, "by and large," "peace and quiet" had prevailed in Cyprus. The elements for a political settlement existed, and despite financial difficulties, the UNFICYP had "steadfastly continued its efforts to maintain quiet on the island and to return the life of its citizens to normality," which, however, would "not be possible until the parties find a solution to the basic issues." While no solution was found, nevertheless, the UN secretary-general reported in August 1972 that the atmosphere surrounding and underlying the problem had improved somewhat.

The Palestine Problem

Like the problem of Cyprus, the question of Palestine has involved intractable issues of contending nationalisms over the same territory. Since the submission of the problem to the United Nations by the United Kingdom, which held the mandate of the League of Nations, on April 2, 1947, the Palestine issue has proved to be the most complex and the most unyielding problem yet to confront members of the United Nations. In one form or another, the Palestine question has been before the General Assembly and the Security Council of the United Nations —to say nothing at all of other UN bodies—more consistently, more regularly, and more frequently than any other single question during the past twenty-five years, and no "solution" is even yet in sight. The origins of the problem, as we have come to know it, may be traced to the Balfour Declaration of November 2, 1917, and, more particularly, to the General Assembly's Resolution 181 (II) of November 29, 1947. That resolution recommended, by a vote of 33-13-10, the partition of Palestine into a Jewish and an Arab state, with Jerusalem and its Holy Places sacred to Christians, Jews, and Muslims as an international *corpus separatum,* and cooperation between the two constituent communities.

One result of the recommendation was the intensification of the conflict between Jews and Arabs in Palestine in the spring of 1948, a conflict which had begun essentially with the establishment of the mandate in 1920. Subsequently, President Truman, during March–April 1948, sought to backtrack into a temporary United Nations trusteeship over Palestine when he saw that the partition plan could not be implemented peacefully. The British mandate now came quickly to an end on May 15, 1948, British forces were withdrawn, the new State of Israel was proclaimed immediately, and American *de facto* recognition was extended within a few minutes. The conflict continued throughout 1948, and, basically, it has continued more or less violently (1956, 1967) ever since. Count Folke Bernadotte, as United Nations Mediator, sought unsuccessfully to conciliate the parties and bring about a peaceful adjustment. He paid with his life at the hands of Jewish terrorists in September 1948. It remained for Ralph Bunche, as Acting United Nations Mediator, to work out a series of armistice agreements during February–July 1949.

During this early period United Nations peacekeeping and peace-observation machinery was established—the United Nations Truce Supervision Organization (UNTSO)—to keep watch over violations of the truce and armistice agreements. Drawn from the military forces of a number of states—the United States, France, Canada, Sweden, Norway, Ireland, and others—and numbering at various times some seven hundred personnel, the UNTSO performed indispensable services in arranging cease-fires and presenting unbiased reports to the United Nations Security Council as a basis for resolutions which attempted to deal with the continuing conflict. The Mixed Armistice Commissions (MACs)—Israeli-Lebanese, Israeli-Syrian, Israeli-Jordanian, and Israeli-Egyptian—served, in effect, as part and parcel of the UNTSO machinery. While there has been much propaganda, often vicious, against the UNTSO, its work needs to be put into proper perspective. It may be observed that substantially after 1951, the Israeli government refused to cooperate with the Israeli-Syrian Mixed Armistice Commission, as it refused to cooperate with the Israeli-Egyptian MAC after 1956. Israel was represented on a few occasions in some emergency meetings after 1951.

Similarly, the work of the United Nations Emergency Force (UNEF), established in November 1956, in the immediate wake of the Israeli-Anglo-French attack against Egypt, needs to be put into perspective. With some five to six thousand soldiers drawn largely from "neutral" states, this body performed most effectively in the Gaza Strip and on the Sinai Peninsula in maintaining the peace along the Israeli-Egyptian armistice demarcation lines, and its success there probably contributed to easing the situation elsewhere. UNEF was withdrawn on May 18, 1967, on the demand of the United Arab Republic, immediately prior to the *Blitzkrieg* of June 5–11, 1967. But, in fact Israel had never permitted UNEF to function on Israeli-held territory, on the ground that such action would prejudice Israel's sovereignty.[2]

The Conciliation Commission for Palestine, established in January 1949 and composed of representatives of France, Turkey, and the United States, set forth comprehensive proposals for peace during 1949–51, embodying territorial adjustments, establishment of an international water authority for equitable regional development of the Jordan River system, border regulations, health cooperation, free ports (Haifa), and commercial and economic arrangements. Neither Israel nor the neighboring Arab states accepted these proposals. After 1951 the Conciliation Commission was only able to bring about the unfreezing of Arab blocked accounts in banks in Israel amounting to some $10 million, and it identified some 450,000 claims to abandoned Arab property in Israel. Despite the efforts of Dr. Joseph E. Johnson, president of the Carnegie Endowment for International Peace, who served as Special Representative of the Conciliation Commission during 1961–62, the commission was unable to do anything with regard to Arab refugee repatriation or resettlement with compensation under a free and realistic choice for the refugees, since the Israeli government rejected any substantial repatriation, which might have threatened the security of the state and the Jewish character of its society, and the Arab governments were skeptical as to resettlement. On the other hand the Arab governments did much, indeed, to assist the refugees, providing some $175 million in direct and indirect assistance, in goods, services, and cash over the years.

There are, of course, other issues, such as the problems of Jerusalem and self-determination for the Palestinians. Israel has ignored many of the more than fifty resolutions of the UN Security Council, General Assembly, and other UN bodies which have been passed since June 1967. These resolutions have declared "invalid" the Israeli "unification" (annexation) of Jerusalem; censured Israel for denials of inalienable rights under the UN Charter and The Universal Declaration of Human Rights; called upon Israel to permit the repatriation of "new refugees" displaced in 1967 and to give a realistic choice to refugees as to repatriation and/or resettlement elsewhere with compensation, according to UNGA Resolution 194 (III), December 11, 1948. But no modern Solomon has come forth with a basic, formal solution, and none appears likely to do so in the near future.

The United Nations was unable to "solve" either the political or the "humanitarian" aspects of the Palestine problem, such as those involved in the flight of some 726,000 people who became refugees. By 1973 there were more than 1,506,640 Arab refugees on the United Nations Relief and Works Agency for Palestine Refugees in the Near East (UNRWA) registration lists, with 551,612 beyond the East Bank of the Jordan and 278,255 on the West Bank, 324,567 in the Gaza Strip, 184,043 in Lebanon, and 168,163 in the Syrian Arab Republic. While there were those who felt that the problem would soon be solved through large development projects, especially in the Jordan Valley, once peace were made, it soon became increasingly clear that long-range issues were involved. While urgent, emergency measures were undertaken immediately during 1948, on May 1, 1950, UNRWA began operations in assisting these unfortunate people. The new agency, which has continued its labors since 1950, was not established to "solve" the refugee problem, much less the more general Palestine question. As defined by the resolution of the General Assembly of December 8, 1949, UNRWA's functions were and are to provide relief, medical care, and education for refugees, and to assist them to become self-supporting. The annual UNRWA budget has averaged some $45–47 million in recent years, with 48 percent going to education and training, 40 percent to relief services, and 12 percent to health services (1971–73). By January 1973, UNRWA had expended some $835,871,935 (income $837,054,445) in services to the refugees. By this time, too, it faced a probable deficit of some $3–5 million. One very noteworthy aspect of its work lay in the fact that its 510 elementary and preparatory schools, with more than 7,000 teachers, enrolled some 256,000 refugee children, while an additional 70,000 were in government and private schools, partly under UNRWA subsidy, and students in secondary schools totalled more than 21,000. Some 1,800 university graduates had been trained, and students in vocational and teacher-training centers were being turned out at the rate of some 1,500 per year. This was technical assistance of a very high order, in skills sorely needed in the Middle East, and it should be duly noted even if UNRWA could not meet the larger refugee problem or the basic political issues involved. Nevertheless, the agency continued to provide relief and health and education services to some 1,500,000 Arab refugees in the critical years after June 1967, as it might have to do until the basic issues were "solved."

The Conciliation Commission for Palestine is now substantially out of the picture, although it has maintained a formal existence in New York. Following the June War, the problem of resolving the Arab-Israeli conflict has been placed in other hands. On November 22, 1967, the UN Security Council laid down some basic guidelines for a possible general settlement, which stressed the "inadmissibility of the acquisition of territory by war and the need to work for a just and lasting peace in which every state in the area can live in security." Under the resolution, a just and lasting peace would include application of the two basic principles: (1) Withdrawal of Israeli armed forces from territories occupied in the 1967 conflict; and (2) termination of all claims or states of belligerency and acknowledgment "of the sovereignty, territorial integrity and political independence of every state in the area and their right to live in peace within secure and recognized boundaries free from threats or acts of force." The resolution also affirmed the necessity of (1) guaranteeing freedom of navigation through international waterways in the area; (2) achieving "a just settlement of the refugee problem"; and (3) guaranteeing the "territorial integrity and political independence of every state in the area through measures including the establishment of demilitarized zones."

Ambassador Gunnar V. Jarring of Sweden was chosen as the secretary-general's special representative to bring the contending parties together for peaceful adjustment of the Arab-Israeli conflict, but the road toward that desired goal proved long, difficult, and very uncertain. Discussions have taken place since the spring of 1969, mostly within the framework of the United Nations, among France, the United Kingdom, the Soviet Union, and the United States, and with the parties.

Secretary of State Rogers presented proposals for possible settlement on October 28, 1969, to which the Soviet response was negative, and on December 9, he stated the American position publicly, noting that a durable peace must meet the legitimate concerns of both sides and that the only framework for a negotiated settlement was one in accordance with the entire text of the UN Security Council Resolution of November 22, 1967. The United States, he said, supported all elements of that resolution, including the withdrawal of Israeli forces from occupied areas, and favored a "lasting peace" which required security for both Israel and the Arab States. Mr. Rogers held that any changes in the preexisting lines or boundaries between Israel and its Arab neighbors should not "reflect the weight of conquest," but should be "confined to insubstantial alterations required for mutual security." The Israeli government rejected this proposal.

As the situation grew much more dangerous and critical in the spring of 1970, on June 25, 1970, the United States revealed a new initiative, suggesting a cease-fire based on the principles of November 22, 1967. These were steps in the right direction and they were accepted by the United Arab Republic, Jordan, and Israel, if not by Syria. A ninety-day cease-fire began on August 7, 1970. The American proposals were flawed because they failed to make explicit provision for consideration of the Palestinian demand for participation in any discussions and for

self-determination. Nevertheless, by this time, American officials publicly conceded the need to consider Palestinian national aspirations to
some degree in any peace settlement. Subsequently, there were renewed
violence in Jordan during September–October 1970, and serious
charges and counter-charges of cease-fire violations were made both by
Israel and the Arab states.

There was much discussion of the troubled situation in the Middle
East during the fall 1970 session of the UN General Assembly, when
the United Arab Republic raised the problem as one which might well
erupt into further violence and threaten the peace of the world. Ultimately, on November 4, Resolution 2628 (XXV) was adopted
(57–16–39), calling for speedy implementation of the resolution of November 22, 1967, resumption of the discussions with Ambassador Jarring, and a three-month extension of the cease-fire. The discussions
were resumed and the cease-fire extended to February 7, 1971, but not
beyond that date, since the UAR insisted on some indications of concrete progress in the discussions before agreeing to a further formal extension.

Meanwhile, Dr. Jarring continued his discussions with the Israeli,
Jordanian, and Egyptian governments. During the discussions it seemed
clear that the UAR was prepared to conclude "a peace agreement" with
Israel, embodying free passage of Israeli ships through the Suez Canal
and the Straits of Tiran, assure that its territories were not used as
bases for attacks against Israel, accept demilitarized zones along its borders, and agree to some form of UN presence at Sharm el Sheikh and
other strategic points. It also seemed evident that Jordan was ready to
accept corresponding arrangements and commitments. In a memorandum of February 8, 1971, Ambassador Jarring called upon the United
Arab Republic to come to a peace agreement with Israel and he asked
Israel to withdraw from Egyptian territory. The UAR accepted the proposal; the government of Israel did not. On March 8, 1972, President
Assad declared that Syria would accept UN Security Council Resolution
242, provided that it meant recovery of all Arab territory occupied in
1967 and the "reestablishment of the rights of the Palestinian people."
Meanwhile, the Jarring discussions met another roadblock in the spring
of 1971. It seemed clear that peace could not be "imposed" by the great
powers, although they might be persuasive, or by Israel. Neither the
UAR nor Jordan was willing to come to an agreement which left large
Arab territories in Israeli hands—the Sinai Peninsula, the Gaza Strip,
East Jerusalem, and the West Bank of the Jordan River, to say nothing
of the Golan Heights in Syria.

If there is to be a settlement of the longstanding Arab-Israeli conflict, it seems elementary that fundamental justice should be rendered in the problem of the Palestinian refugees and that the principle of self-determination based on a free and realistic choice between repatriation and resettlement with compensation can no longer be ignored. With the development of a strong Palestinian sense of national self-consciousness, it may well be that this choice, based upon the oft-confirmed General Assembly Resolution 194 (III) of December 11, 1948, is now outmoded and that more radical solutions will be sought. Similarly, if there is to be a formal settlement, whatever the skepticism and the distrust, it seems clear that the United Nations will have to play a continuing role in new security arrangements, either through an enlarged and strengthened UNTSO, or a force like that of UNEF, preferably without great power participation, although such participation should not be ruled out. In any event, it is probable that a great power guarantee is essential to an equitable settlement. While some observers have proposed an additional special United States guarantee to Israel within this framework, it is possible that the Locarno formula with guarantees against an aggressor might prove less prejudicial in concept and more acceptable in practice.

CONCLUSION

From the cases examined, it would appear that the United Nations has had a limited success in dealing with the earlier Middle Eastern problems in Lebanon, Syria, and Iran in 1946. Its investigatory and observational functions were very well performed in Greece, but somewhat less so in Yemen. In the instance of Cyprus, the United Nations Force has certainly contributed to the maintenance of a degree of "negative stability" and order, even if the basic solution of fundamental problems of national and communal conflict has not been achieved. The United Nations has not succeeded in achieving peaceful adjustment of the Palestine problem, largely because of the very complicated issues, centering around the enduring, irrepressible conflict of two nationalisms over the same territory of Palestine, and the inability of the greater powers to face the issues frankly. Nevertheless, as observed above, UNTSO and UNEF have rendered very useful services in the security field, while UNRWA has served the Arab refugees in relief, health, and education. The General Assembly of the United Nations, as in the past, considered the Palestine problem—the Arab-Israeli conflict—in the fall of 1972, and it is likely further to deal with it in the future. It seemed clear to thoughtful and informed observers that, if there were yet to be hope of peaceful adjustment in this area of conflict, with all its potential for uncontrolled escalation, the United Nations would have to reassert the interest of the international community, make appropriate recommendations and decisions, and take constructive action. Although the UN is frustrated in its attempts to "solve" the Palestine problem, the UN secretary-general announced in the fall of 1972 that he had continued the effort to make progress toward a settlement and to assist the governments concerned "in avoiding clashes, escalation of tension and the proliferation of incidents through the use of observers in areas of tension and through other means." During the fall of 1973, following the outbreak of another round in the Palestine conflict, the United Nations was called upon, once more, to observe and report concerning the cease-fire, and thereby to contribute to the possibility of an enduring peace in the area.

❀ 9 ❀

TAREQ Y. ISMAEL

Domestic Sources of Middle Eastern Foreign Policy

The preceding analyses have dealt with the ongoing process of interaction between Middle Eastern countries and the dominant nations of the international arena. Authors with expertise in various fields sought to highlight the nature of this process of interaction. Out of these analyses, two pronounced features seem to emerge. First, the process of interaction between countries of the region and the "dominant" system is complex and multivaried. It is primarily the multifacetedness of the process that accounts for the variations existing in definitions and the intended empirical referents of concepts utilized by the authors. The resulting differences in analytic tools and methods of treatment, however, though they adversely affect such welcome attributes as clarity, simplicity, and uniformity, make their own contributions. They direct attention to the richness of the material being studied, pinpoint the sources of shortcomings, uncover the areas that call for more intensive study and suggest guidelines for betterment. The second feature of the preceding analyses was the interesting similarity which was revealed. Underneath the variety alluded to above, patterned regularities and common forces seem to bind members of the region as well as those of the dominant system in their interactions with the region. These regularities and forces explain the area of similarity existing in the foreign policies of Middle East countries in spite of variances in constitutions, formal organizations, levels of development or education. Hence, two tasks need yet to be undertaken: to offer definitions and concepts that seek to standardize our notions about the international relations of the Middle East, and to abstract the theoretical findings of the preceding chapters. This chapter focuses on intra-area policy sources. The final chapter introduces the concept of subordinate system and postulates rules by which the system operates. Both chapters attempt to demonstrate the unity as well as the variety of the Middle East. They seek to reveal why it is necessary to

195

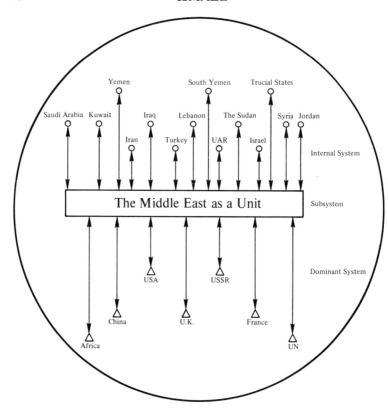

conceive of the Middle East as a subordinate system in the more expansive international system, and the limitations inherent in this conceptualization. With this done, the picutre of the international relations of the Middle East that unfolds is one of a three-level process of interaction. Each level consists of an open system of action, affected by and effecting other levels. These systems may be referred to as the "internal," "subordinate," and "dominant" systems and are illustrated by the above diagram.

THE DOMESTIC ENVIRONMENT

In the Middle East we do not find a single foreign policy but a multitude of policies, each proceeding from a separate complex of domestic circumstances, each acting in a distinct international environment. There is diversity in the history of the Middle Eastern countries; there is diversity in economic circumstances, political organization, and ideology; and there is diversity in religion and attitudes toward religion. Amidst this diversity, however, there is also regularity and predictability, even though diversity is compounded by instability in both the form and the behavior of the political systems involved. In this brief survey the full complexity of the linkages between domestic circumstance and international posture can only be indicated; only the more striking regularities and diversities can be presented, to the neglect of many subtleties and nuances which provide the full flavor of international relations. Still, we can depict the most important linkages and relate them to a systematic and coherent conception of the interrelation of domestic and foreign affairs.

Despite the diversity noted above, there are unifying factors in Middle Eastern history, culture, and society which provide the basis for the regularities of behavior we observe in comparing these states. The ancient and modern history of the region has betrayed persistent tendencies to integration. Even in the days of the pharaohs there was cultural exchange, not always friendly, between the Valley of the Nile and Mesopotamia. The two great centers of civilization in the area, in incessant competition, brought the lesser peoples of the region under their suzerainty, and the resultant cultural exchanges created lasting similarities and affinities. The Alexandrian Empire surpassed even the Persian in bringing the Near East under a single dominion; although division followed Alexander's death, a cultural unity in Hellenism persisted for centuries. The Romans, although losing the far eastern section of the region to the Parthians, brought North Africa and Spain into the great cultural area, and the Byzantines retained the eastern sections of the Roman Empire until the rise of Islam. Under Muhammad and his successors, the entire Middle East and North Africa were brought under Arab rule. Even when the Arabs were replaced by Persians and Turks as holders of political power, even when the Abbasids lost their grip on their Western domains, even as Islam lost Spain to the Christians (while conquering the Balkans), Arab-Islamic culture—art, architecture, literary forms, language, and script—give a unified basis to the entire Mediterranean basin. Especially important were the Arabic language, which provided a common means of communication, and Islam, which provide the basis for a common legal and moral system. In more recent times, all of the states of the area, with the few exceptions of Turkey, Saudi Arabia, and Yemen, experienced Western rule, although this experience was not uniform. Communications have generally been well enough maintained that major intellectual and ideological movements have been shared throughout the region.

Upon this basis of common features are overlaid the common problems of underdeveloped states seeking to make a place for themselves in the modern world. Common cultural configurations and parallel economic and political problems provide us with the basis for a generalized model of the relationship of domestic and foreign events. The major linkages will be examined here in five analytically distinct but empirically integral categories: perceptions of the outside world, religion, political trends and ideologies, traditional rivalries, and economic factors.

The interrelations of these factors will become apparent in exposition, but for clarity's sake, some will be mentioned now. It is apparent at once that religion and ideology influence one's view of the world, and that perceptions of the world furnish the reality against which ideological and religious propositions are tested, some to be discarded, others to endure. To avoid excessive redundancy, we shall here examine religion as a social institution, not as a system of belief; this means in effect that in this model we sacrifice most of the uniqueness of Islam as distinguished from other religions, except where it forces itself upon us as a component of a national world view. Economics and ideology are deeply intertwined, but here we shall set apart economic factors which may be called objective from those which are subjective—a dangerous distinction, but a necessary one—and place the latter under the heading of ideology. In this way the most troublesome areas of overlap may be minimized; they cannot be eliminated.

PERCEPTIONS OF THE OUTSIDE WORLD

Perception influences foreign policy in a variety of ways. Although goals and values more properly fall into other categories, the perceived distance from a goal or the perception of the difficulty of attaining a value condition strategies of goal-seeking. Chiefly, perception conditions the sense of the desirable through apprehensions of the possible; the rational or quasi-rational decision-making process which weighs costs against benefits, measures resources, assesses the strength of obstacles, and posits a certain ends-means (causal) relationship of factors, is limited by the perceptual resources of the decision-making body. Mistakes in policy based upon false perceptions can only be corrected through feedback, which is itself limited by perceptual skills and apparatus. Perception is conditioned by other factors: language, "reality," and emotion are chief among them. (It does not seem proper here to enter into an epistemological dispute about the relation of perception and knowledge to reality, but the author's predispositions are positivist.) In general, perception and decision-making are based upon irrational affinities to certain objects, events, and concepts; a major aspect of any perceived object is the affective response it elicits from the observer, which is logically and usually empirically prior to a rational calculation of the object's likely consequences. In the Middle East, certain categories of perceptions—more properly, affective determinants of perception— tend to form the world views of decision-makers and to cause the emergence of distinct foreign-policy patterns.

Each decision-maker's perceptual map is, of course, related to his goals for himself and for his nation; in the Middle East almost all decision-makers desire political independence and a satisfactory economic growth rate for their states, but the content of these goals must be much more clearly specified before they can be acted upon. In terms of perceptions related to these broad goal categories, by means of which the goals are specified into policy packages, perceptions of the outside world seems to vary along two dimensions: the preferability of economic and social modernization as opposed to the preservation of tradition, and the view of the outside world as generally threatening or beneficent to the perceiver. This proposition is illustrated in Table 1; a sample of cases is supplied for each category.

TABLE 1
Perceptions of the Outside World

	Beneficial World	Threatening World
Modernization Preferred	Tunisia, Morocco, Lebanon, Neo-Destorr, Wafd, Syrian Nationalist Party, Falangist	Egypt, Syria, Iraq, Ba'athists, Arab Nationalists, Palestine Liberation Movement
Tradition Preferred	Saudi Arabia, Kuwait, Gulf sheikdoms, religious reformers	Yemen (prior to 1962), Muslim Brotherhood, Sanusi movement, Mahdist movement

To those primarily interested in economic and social modernization, who see the world as a threat, memories of colonialism are still active and new encroachments on their sovereignty are an immediate threat. An additional factor is that for many of these, the threatening aspects of the world are intensified because they view the Middle East as central to world politics, and thus the most important factor in "imperialist" calculations. Those who view the outside world as a threat to tradition tend to pair modernization with Westernization, and then to reject both. Those states which do not fear the outside world, and yet wish to retain tradition, are likely to deal with the world on a functional basis, seeking to avoid diffuse contacts which lead to value-sharing. They are likely to reject revolutionary doctrines, no matter how familiar, and to accept help from distant states which seem to be interested in the maintenance of stability. States wishing to modernize, and not fearing the outside world, are likely not only to accept but to encourage and stimulate varied cultural contacts and foreign involvement in domestic institutions.

In general, the experience of Middle Eastern states has been of a gradual decline in the attachment to tradition and an increasing drive to modernization, although reactions against this trend are not uncommon. As the goals set for the state thus change, its relation to the rest of the world is also seen to change, at first tending to greater openness, then to reactions against problems arising from foreign contact; if the state is successful in modernizing, a more confident attitude emerges, allowing openness once again.

To illustrate the interaction of these variables, two cases have been chosen involving nations—Turkey and Egypt—which have passed through a number of phases. It is admitted that the examples may be loaded toward positive findings about the applicability of the model, but examination of the histories of Morocco, Algeria, Iraq, or Iran would reveal patterns equally supportive of the model. The less developed nations of the Middle East are less suitable cases for two reasons: they have experienced only slight modifications or else single revolutionary transformations in their foreign policies to date; and the information available about their foreign policies and their attitudes and perceptions is insufficient.

The perceptions of the outside world which appear reflected in Turkish foreign policy over the centuries have followed a pattern which is the product of steadily decreasing self-confidence in foreign relations, reflected in an increasing deterioration of religious faith and an increasing tendency to seek the solution to Turkey's problems in Western institutions. For the early Turkish rulers, products of a nomadic and pastoral culture, the chief pursuit of life was conquest, and the military life was the only honorable life. The world, while hostile, was believed to be inhabited by weak townsmen, and thus a place full of opportunities for the aggressive tribesmen. Although the Turks conquered the Middle East and North Africa as far as the borders of Morocco and were recognized as equals by Francis I of France, their history after the defeat at Lepanto in 1571 was marked by a steady decline of military prowess and developing weaknesses in political and administrative skills. But the Ottoman belief in their superiority persisted, except insofar as they were willing to accept finished products from the West; they were not ready to accept the processes by which these were produced. The history of the eighteenth century contains the record of the systematic humiliation of Ottoman pride in their military prowess. By the early nineteenth century, the sultan was forced to call upon his Egyptian vassal to come to his aid against ill-armed rebels in Greece. Twenty years later, only the intervention of European powers could save the Sublime Porte from subjection to the will of that same vassal, Muhammad Ali. At this point the Ottoman Empire was convinced of the threat to its structure from its neighbors, although foreign nations were regarded as threatening in inverse proportion to their distance from the boundaries of the empire.

Parallel with the development of a more fearful view of the world came the realization that, if the empire was to be preserved, it must emulate the powers of Europe in more than technique. Thus, in the mid-nineteenth century, marked by the Tanzimat of 1839, the Ottoman Empire accepted the help of states perceived as friendly to model itself after them in order to preserve it from the dangers on its borders. The impetus to modernization grew through that century, and traditions weakened among some classes as Ottoman domains were opened to foreign influence on all sides. This movement began to seem more dangerous than any threat it might serve to forestall.

The question facing Turkey at that point was whether its modernization should be purchased at the expense of its integrity. Sultan Abdulhamid II answered firmly in the negative. He revoked the constitution of 1876, which would have brought liberal institutions to Turkey, and tried to contain the influence of Europe. As it became apparent that his methods were failing, the Young Turk movement took power. Although they viewed the world as unfriendly, they were sanguine about their ability to deal with it, and they thought European knowledge could be the key to renewed greatness for Turkey. The terrible consequences of joining Germany in the First World War further disillusioned the Turks with the benefits accruing to relations with the West, and brought to power Ataturk, whose ambition was exceeded only by his desire to create a Turkey so modern that no European could find cause for faulting it. Under Ataturk we find a Turkey devoted to the modernization of society, while nearly rejecting the outside world. A combination of conviction and necessity led the Turks to renounce their possessions outside Asia Minor and to abolish the Caliphate, thus severing many of their connections with, and elements most vulnerable to, outside influence.

After the Second World War, during which Turkey remained neutral, a new political party—the Democratic Party, composed of younger members of the Republican People's Party—came to power and ended Turkey's neutrality by joining the North Atlantic Treaty Organization. Many of the goals of the government had been met, so that it was more interested in stability, while the extent of Turkey's development was sufficient to give its rulers new confidence in their ability to deal with other states. In recent years, the Turks have even cooperated to some extent with the Russians, while, at the popular level, we find expressions of the old xenophobic nationalism vented against American military personnel.

The beginnings of Egyptian modernization may be traced back to 1798 and the Napoleonic invasion which initiated Egypt's contact with Europe. This movement accelerated during the tenure of Muhammad Ali, who sent students to attend European, especially French, universities, and commissioned a number of Europeans to work in Egypt as military instructors, scientists, and engineers developing small-scale industries, or as educational modernizers. Whereas Muhammad Ali viewed the world as an open field of conquest, and focused his modernization efforts upon military development, his successors vacillated between distrust of the West as a source of unrest and a rather uncritical acceptance of the advanced technology and other modern apparatus of Europe, culminating in the financially disastrous Suez Canal. In 1879 Egypt was subjected to French and British financial control, and British political hegemony was established in 1881, after the Arabi revolt. It should be noted that one of the major causes of this revolt was the dominance of non-Egyptians in the military ranks. This was an indicator of a developing feeling that Egypt was distinct from the rest of the Turkish domains, as well as Europe, and that only exploiters came from outside.

Although attitudes encouraging modernization became more prevalent, especially through the work of such Muslim reformers as Kawakibi and 'Abduh, mistrust of the outside world as a reaction to British colonialism remained. The period of liberal dominance in Egypt was marked by ambiguous attitudes toward modernization and social change, interacting with hatred of the British and a feeling of impotence in the face of their armed force. This feeling was particularly strong after the demonstration at the 'Abdin Palace in 1942. Another manifestation of these ambiguities was the feeling that the West had led some persons into modernization and then, in the 1948 Palestine war, let them down.

The Egyptian coup d'etat of 1952 brought to power men who, while not wholly convinced of the good intentions of outside states, placed much more emphasis on modernization than had the previous regime. This led to cooperation with the outside world. Distrust was intensified by the Suez Crisis of 1956, and this led to an acceleration of the effort for modernization. Despite mistrust of the outside world, which extends even to the Soviet Union and such Arab states as Iraq and Syria, Egypt has cooperated with the outside world in order to gain its modernization objectives. It should be noted that the primary goal of modernization is the removal of the need for Egypt to depend upon any outside powers, and if this were accomplished, it might be possible for the Egyptians, like the Turks, to take a more open and confident attitude toward the international scene.

These case studies could be expanded to book length, but even in this simplified form they indicate several things. First, the evaluation of modernization and tradition and the perception of the character of external actors provide us with variables which seem to explain many of the differences in Middle Eastern foreign policies. We thus find this model useful as an organizing principle for the comparative analysis of foreign policy. Also, we note that changes in reality, however evident to an external observer, are often not translated into policy until decision-makers have internalized an intellectual structure capable of accounting for the changes. Finally, we find it necessary to turn to historical and other factors to account for the development of particular perceptual maps characteristic of the various national elites.

RELIGION

The role of traditional Islam in shaping the foreign policy of Middle Eastern states underwent three main periods of development. In the period extending from the seventh to the sixteenth century, Muslim jurists viewed non-Muslim states as falling within the "abode of war" waiting to be incorporated into the "abode of submission," Islam. A Muslim state had the duty to spread the faith whether by violent or by peaceful means, and especially to ensure that Islamic law and justice were made supreme.

The first clear departure from this concept of foreign relations occurred in 1535 when Suleiman the Magnificent, in a treaty with Francis I, agreed to a "valid and sure peace," and each guranteed the subjects of the other the protection of certain rights within his territory. This event signaled the advent of the second period. Wheras the first was marked by competition and warfare, the second was one of coexistence and moderation. Majid Khadduri enumerates three principles as having developed during this second stage. These were "the separation of religious doctrine from the conduct of foreign relations," the principle of "peaceful relations among states," and "the principle of the territoriality of the law." [1] (It should be noted that this period coincided with the rise of secularism and the decline of the crusading spirit in Western Europe). With the dismemberment of the Ottoman Empire following the First World War and with the later rise of separate Middle Eastern countries to independence, Muslims had become completely reconciled to the Western secular system of foreign relations.

Islam's role in shaping foreign policy entered upon its third and present stage during the first few decades of the twentieth century. Proper understanding of this role requires that one look at it in the context of the wider social revolution which is now taking place in the Middle East. Islam as a way of life embracing all of man's social relations is being challenged by secular nationalism and other new doctrines. The confrontation is of a peculiar nature because Islam is identified with a set of institutions as well as a set of ideas; to attack either is frequently held to attack both. A second and perhaps more important effect of the social revolution is that Islam is felt to be in retreat, even (or perhaps especially) by leading Muslim intellectuals. While the struggle against Western colonialism was led by nationalists influenced by Western secular liberalism, the religious leaders remained occupied with a static tradition. The stagnation lay in the set of their minds, rather than in any lack of effort at reform, for they were unable to use the spirit of the Islamic past to revitalize and reform institutions, but rather sought to restore institutions which were totally obsolete. The failure of Islamic thinkers to separate institutions and ideas entailed the undermining of the ideas and authority of the faith when the institutions were rejected. In recent years Islam has so declined in authority and vitality that it has become a mere instrument of state policy, although it is still active as a folk religion, and the Islamic tradition lends a unique cast of thought even to the most secularized of those nurtured in it. In Middle Eastern international relations, it must be conceded that the foreign policies of the various states are not based upon religious considerations, and that religion is far more an instrument of, than an influence upon, foreign policy.

Religion may be regarded as a factor retarding desired development, as it was by Ataturk; or as a useful integrating force, as by the Egyptian oligarchy; or as the source of national identity and governmental authority, as by the Saudi royalty. Or, as in Lebanon, religion may be a divisive force because the population is divided between two faiths, and each religious community views the other as a threat. On an international plane, Islam is generally a unifying force, but the different sects and the manner in which Islam has been adapted to local conditions mitigate its integrative value. Religion is primarily influential in those states where it is central to the identity of the state. Iran, for example, is the major center of Shi'ism in the Middle East, and this tends to reinforce its separate identity, which was, however, established by centuries of existence as an independent empire. Likewise, Judaism is a key identifying characteristic of Israel, although "Israeliness" rather than "Jewishness" appears to be the most salient feature of national identity. The Muslim-Jewish distinction does reinforce the Arab-Israeli conflict, but this is based at least as much upon territorial and political factors as upon religion. We see for example the case of Pakistan, a state founded upon its Islamic character, but which was forced to abandon a "Muslim" foreign policy when other Muslim states supported India. In short, religion appears effective in states where its influence coincides with that of other major cultural forces, but religion is not the primary cultural element in any Middle Eastern state. Only through cultural traits of which it is the distant progenitor is religion any longer effective.

POLITICAL TRENDS AND IDEOLOGICAL ORIENTATIONS

One criterion used for delineating the Middle East as a subordinate international system is the ideological context of its politics. This context is a necessary element in any explanation of the foreign policies of member states and the international relations of the region. Political trends and ideologies significant to the formation of foreign policy and international relations of the area include nationalism, anti-imperialism, nonalignment, and socialism. A survey of basic symbols of sentiment and identification embodied in these ideologies is necessary to clarify the attitudes and behavior of ideologically motivated political movements and political leadership.

Nationalism

A common generative principle underlies Arab, Iranian, and Turkish nationalism. Its early manifestations appear in the work of Al-Afghani, 'Abduh, Rida, the Young Ottomans, the Arab delegates to the Ottoman Assembly, and the first Syrian nationalists. The speeches, writings, and other political activities of these people and their colleagues initiated a movement of protest and a demand for reform that spread through the entire area in the late nineteenth and early twentieth century. This movement, motivated by resentment of foreign encroachments and a desire to equal the West, played a slowly developing counterpoint to the increasing involvement of Europeans in the area. It is perhaps indicative of this relationship that Arab nationalism first became a major popular force at the time of the partition of the area—a division that the Arabs have yet to reverse—and that Turkish nationalism was given concrete form in a successful war for Anatolia after all of the Ottoman Empire was lost. The capacity of regional leaders to generate powerful cooperative forces was limited to the purely local level, a limit not entirely due to foreign intervention.

While the latter may be envisaged as a form of direct spark to nationalism in the area, it by no means covers the more or less indirect foreign (mainly Western) contribution to the then rising Middle Eastern tide of nationalism. The Western missionaries, philanthropic organizations, and educational instutitons on the one hand, and the impact left on the indigenous students who pursued their education in the West on the other, have constituted additional exogenous promoters of the nascent nationalist sentiments and feelings in the area.

The intellectual basis of Arab and all Muslim nationalisms except the Turkish lies in a questioning of the traditional Islamic system. As mentioned above, this questioning has not always been productive of a solid new basis for the melding of culture and society, but has often led to the distingegration of the social order. Nationalist ideas burgeoned in this atmosphere, and since World War II, nationalism has become the most popular ideology in the area of the Middle East. However, nationalism is often an incomplete ideology trying to perform the function of the Islam of old. This is particularly the case in the eastern Arab lands, less so in North Africa and Iran, and hardly relevant to Turkey. In Israel much less ambiguity pertains than in any former or present Muslim land.

The principles common to nationalist movements in the Middle East (with the possible exception of Turkey, but not excepting Israel) are an emphasis on the role of human will, the necessity for freedom or self-determination, the superiority of the body politic to any of its parts, and the duty of national groups to nurture their distinctive characteristics. It is thus similar to the romantic or integral forms of European nationalism, rather than to the liberal form. Middle Eastern nationalisms owe more to Fichte than to Mill. This intensifies the personal and social conflict consequent upon ambiguities in loyalties. Arab forms of nationalism, in particular, seek to provide a complete guide to conduct through a mystical devotion to the nation. But ambiguity results from the lack of an authoritative and legitimate identification of the nation.

Arab nationalism, considered as the belief in the national identity of the Arab people and the wish to see them brought into a single polity, is the source of the Arab unity movement in the Middle East. It has had an immense impact on Arab politics even with the most traditional leadership paying homage to its ideals. More significant, however, is the association of the movement with structural reforms. Nasser's assumption of the leadership of the Arab nationalist movement allowed a closer and increased identification of that movement with socio-economic changes undertaken in Egypt. Arab nationalism has thus been viewed as opposed to feudalist social structures, capitalist exploitation, and the persistence of privileged classes. This recent development presents a basic contrast to the Arab nationalist movement sponsored by the Hashemites in the second decade of the twentieth century. That movement was dynastic, not popular, and its basis was the belief in the legitimacy of the Hashemite claim to govern all Arabs. In the interwar period, much pan-Arab thought was based upon capitalist assumptions and a desire to place the Arab world on an equal plane with Europe by placing Arab capitalists on an equal footing with European capitalists. It is in part the failure of those earlier movements which has stimulated the emergence of the more radical form of Arab nationalism since World War II.

Nationalism has also been a force dividing the Arabs. Even pan-Arabism was divisive when it threatened the privileged classes which had vested interests in the perpetuation of each of the autonomous states. More fundamentally, strong provincial feelings exist in individual Arab countries on the levels of both the people and the elites. Having led a separate existence for two or three decades, these states have become the normal point of reference for their citizens. It has proven difficult to utilize feelings of a broader unity to stimulate effective action. As a result, Arab unity can only be accomplished if each participant state gains in terms of its local interests. The failure to meet this difficult requirement was the major cause of the collapse of the union of Syria and Egypt in 1961. Even in Egypt, there are indications that the problem of divided or ambiguous loyalties has been resolved in favor of a strong identification with the Egyptian state as it is.

Nationalism has affected Arab foreign policy and international relations in various ways. First, the policy of each country is dichotomous. It is affected by the perceived interest of both its own community and pan-Arabism. Second, because of the size of Egypt's population, its economic development, its status as the leading center of Arab culture, and the popularity of Nasser's leadership (which Sadat is attempting to transfer to himself), Arab foreign policy has often been identified with that of Egypt. It would seem that any future union opposed by Egypt is

bound to fail. Third, both fear of Egyptian predominance enhanced by
the foreign-supported forces of provincialism in the area as well as fear
of the more progressive "Nasserist" policies by obsolete and/or less
progressive governments suggest that only a loose confederate system
predicated on this basis would work. This partly explains why the
Egyptian-Syrian union was dissolved and why there exists at present a
search for a more decentralized political structure by the leaders of
Egypt, the Sudan, Libya, and Syria. Fourth, unlike Turkish and Iranian
nationalism, Arab nationalism is still a frustrated movement. Because
of the failure either to demolish the boundaries separating Arab countries or to make the people content within their own countries, to reju-
venate Arab society or to make the Arabs masters of their fate, Arab
nationalism will increasingly tend to exhibit radical contours.

Zionism (i.e., Jewish nationalism), like Arab nationalism, projects itself into a glorious past. While the Arabs recall the days of the Prophet,
the Ummayads, and the Abbasids, the Israelis refer back to the united
kingdom of Saul, David, and Solomon. And just as the Arabs minimize
the importance of the period since 1258, the Israelis shade over the
Diaspora.

Zionism developed primarily as a Jewish response to antisemitism in
Europe in the nineteenth century. The World Zionist Organization, established in 1897, was dedicated "to create for the Jewish people a
home in Palestine secured by public law." Through British support, the
World Zionist Organization was able to facilitate the immigration to
Palestine of hundreds of thousands of European Jewry. And in 1917
Britain gave official approval to the establishment of a Jewish "homeland" in Palestine. But Zionist efforts to secure a homeland for Europe's Jewry met with growing opposition from the indigenous population of Palestine. The peoples of Palestine viewed the growing tide of
Jewish immigration from Europe with alarm and feared that their rights
would be compromised to accommodate Zionist plans. Hostility between the Arab and Jewish communities in Palestine was thus ear-
marked by growing violence during the interwar period. Britain, who
had made conflicting promises to both the Arabs and Zionists over Palestine during the First World War,* turned the matter of Palestine over
to the United Nations after the Second World War. Against strong
Arab objections, but with American and British support, and with Eu-

* In the Hussein-McMahon correspondence of 1916 Britain promised the
Arabs an independent Arab state that included Palestine; a year later, it issued
the Balfour Declaration promising the Jews a homeland. There is also the Sykes-
Picot Agreement in which Britain and France parcelled the Middle East between
themselves.

ropean and American public opinion roused strongly in favor of Zionist goals by the disclosure of the Nazi holocaust against the Jews, the United Nations voted to partition Palestine into an Arab and Jewish state. The World Zionist Organization immediately proclaimed the State of Israel, and the Arabs mobilized in opposition to the new state.

The subsequent Arab-Israeli war consolidated the position of the new Jewish state at the expense of dispossessing and uprooting around one million Palestinian Arabs who have since then been dispersed in the area as refugees. These developments commenced the now chronic hostilities between Israel and the Arab governments and, more than ever, exposed the area to protracted international rivalry. From 1948 (particularly since 1955–56), the Middle East has become one of the most sensitive regions where the interests of the post-1945 superpowers (the U.S. and the USSR) have been in keen competition. The Cold War has thus manifested itself in the Middle East, and Middle East issues can no longer be separated from Cold War issues.

Among at least some Israelis, territorial ambitions are generated by a desire to see the past greatness of Israel physically restored; for others, the ingathering of all Jews would provide satisfactory evidence of the success of Zionism. For those who see Israel's greatness in spiritual rather than material terms, there may be less emphasis on growth, but perhaps more stress on the uniqueness of the community and a sense of superiority to its neighbors. Among others, of a Kiplingesque bent, the role of Israel in the Middle East is defined by its modern and Western character; this is precisely the element of Israeli society most infuriating to the Arabs.

Israeli nationalism is past-oriented and romantic; it is illiberal in that it is based on a doctrine of social exclusiveness, and yet it is egalitarian within the community. It is socialist and communalist, but perhaps more individualist than any other nationalism in the area. Its military forces are at once the symbol of its unity and the shield of its liberty, but so far the army has not monopolized the loyalty of the people. Perhaps its greatest source of strength is that almost all Israelis participate in Zionism. This strength affects foreign policy, too. While the government is thus provided great resources to draw upon, it is forced to satisfy the nationalist goals of the people.

Turkish and Iranian nationalisms are both confined largely to the urban, modern, middle, and upper classes in the respective states. Both recall the glories of the past, as is typical for nationalism in the area, although the Turks have used this process to justify the permanent cession of their imperial domains as well as to bolster their pride. The Turks are the more self-confident, as the only defeated power of World

War I to win a secondary war and force a peace treaty upon the Allies (Lausanne, 1923). Iran, on the other hand, was partitioned in one form or another between the Russians and British until 1946, and was only narrowly able to escape that fate. In foreign policy, the chief effect of Iranian nationalism has been a not too successful attempt at neutralism, exercised through a formal commitment to the U.S., and an attempt to gain national control of oil production. The latter is motivated also by economic principles. The Turks have focused their nationalism upon certain essential objects; it is probably the least romantic of the area in that respect. A major affect upon Turkish foreign policy of their type of nationalism is that they, unlike any other state of the area, feel able to negotiate with European states on equal terms; elsewhere one sees the false assertiveness of the Israelis or the Syrians and the withdrawal of Lebanon or Morocco (Egypt and Algeria may be in the marginal areas of overcoming this problem).

Neutralism and Nonalignment

The policy of neutralism is followed by most of the Arab states, albeit in varying degrees. The non-Arab states—Turkey, Israel, and Iran —are all associated with Britain and the United States. The first state to adopt a policy of nonalignment in the Middle East was Egypt, and its peculiar circumstances had a lasting effect upon its brand of neutralism.

Until 1954, the Egyptian leadership had evolved no ideology, although Egypt remained oriented toward the West on Cold War issues. Domestic reforms, the defense of the revolution from internal dangers, and the removal of the vestiges of British colonialism were their main concerns. The absence of any concept of neutralism is evidenced by the lack of any reference to it in Nasser's *The Philosophy of the Revolution,* published in Arabic in 1954 and in English the next year.

The Anglo-Egyptian treaty of 1954, leading to the evacuation of British troops, increased the Egyptian government's area of maneuverability. Commercial agreements were then made with socialist-bloc countries, but some indicators suggest that this was done in order to pressure Western countries into giving Egypt increased aid. Although some financial assistance was forthcoming, the major issue that led to the deterioration of relations was the refusal of the West to provide Egypt with urgently needed military equipment. (Israeli raids on Egyptian positions in Gaza in early 1955 had demonstrated the vulnerability of Egyptian defenses and the need to update the army's military equipment).

Nasser responded by purchasing arms from the Communist bloc—Czechoslovakia in particular. He also succeeded, after launching an early crusade against the Western-initiated Baghdad Pact, in founding an Arab Command, consisting of Egypt, Syria, and Yemen. Secretary of State John Foster Dulles, in a move calculated to force Egypt back into the Western sphere of influence, made the American offer to finance the High Dam at Aswan. In no time, however, Egypt's uninterrupted campaign against Western imperialism and military pacts resulted in the withdrawal of the American loan offer (as well as other offers previously made by Britain and the World Bank). Nasser retaliated by nationalizing the International Maritime Suez Canal Company on July 26, 1956. The failure of the subsequent British-French-Israeli tripartite invasion of Egypt to achieve its objective of toppling Nasser and replacing his regime with one more amenable to Western influence was the decisive point in establishing Egypt's independence of the West. Henceforth, animated by fear of Western domination and cautious identification with the Eastern bloc, Nasser prepared a policy of neutralism.

The abovementioned forces which contributed to the emergence of Egypt's policy of neutralism were mainly the product of Western policy; other forces, however, were also operative. Growing disillusioned with Western policies in the Middle East but still distrustful of the Eastern bloc, Egypt's leadership turned to the Asian world for allies and guidance. The repeated visits of Prime Minister Jawaharlal Nehru of India to Cairo, and the 1955 Bandung Conference, afforded them the opportunity to become acquainted with neutralism through its principal exponent and to observe its strength. On his return from Bandung, Nasser conferred with Nehru in New Delhi. Of this visit he later said: "My visit to India was the turning point in my political understanding. I learned and recognized that the only wise policy for us consisted in adopting positive neutralism and nonalignment. On my return home, the reception that greeted this policy convinced me that it was the sole possible policy that could attract the broadest support of the Arab people." [2]

Egyptian neutralism passed through passive and negative stages before it became (in 1956) a genuinely positive concept. It is probable that without the support mentioned above the reaction of Egypt to Suez would have been entirely different. During the past decade this policy has even shown elements of messianic neutralism. Despite these transformations Egyptian neutralism exhibits two distinctive features which afford permanence and continuity to foreign policy through all the shifts. The more obvious is the close association of neutralism with nationalist sentiments and aspirations. Rather than being a mere product and reflection of the Cold War situation, Egyptian neutralism (like that of the other Arab states) is a nationalistic assertion. Each of the four stages in Egypt's neutralism has been prompted by the desire to preserve or increase the country's independence from the Western powers. The position of Egypt at the outset of the Cold War was one of complete indifference and a concern with the problems of British occupation and Palestine. The rejection of the Western-sponsored Allied Middle East Command Organization and, therefore, of Cold War alliance systems came in 1951. The crucial years 1955–56, in which a policy of neutralism was consciously developed, witnessed Egypt's assertion of its right as an independent country to deal with outside powers regardless of their position in the Cold War. By the end of the fifties and into the early sixties, Egypt felt its immediate needs satisfied and was sufficiently stable and self-confident to embark upon an articulation of its ideological program. Henceforth, the Egyptian leadership came to involve themselves in Cold War issues. In this period Egypt was seeking to establish itself internationally.

The second distinctive feature of Egyptian neutralism is its pragmatic character. Since it is conceived as a policy that serves Egypt's national interests, it has exhibited signs of great flexibility and a rejection of doctrinaire approaches to international issues. Not surprisingly, Nasser was attacked by both East and West, and he was willing to condemn either when their policy conflicted with Egypt's political objectives. The present situation, including the lesser appeal of Anwar as-Sadat to the people, makes this even-handedness more difficult.

Of the fourteen Arab League members, only Jordan has been continuously opposed openly to neutralism. The other thirteen reveal a great diversity in their form of neutralism, with corresponding differences in their degrees of sympathy for one of the two blocs. Syria began to define its neutralism almost at the same time as Egypt. The writings of Michel Aflaq and Salahuddin Bitar, founders and leading theoreticians of the Ba'ath (Arab Renaissance Socialist) Party, attest to the early awareness of the problem. However, Syria's official policy remained one which rejected alliances that, in its view, infringed upon its sovereignty. By 1956–57, Syria had become opposed to any Cold War alliance in any form. This development signified the shift from merely protesting the either/or formula of the Dulles era to an emphatic assertion of neither/nor. Between 1958 and 1961, Syria was merged with Egypt in the United Arab Republic, with the two countries having a unified foreign policy. The governments that have succeeded the 1961 secession have all held to a foreign policy of non-alignment, although they have also been more sympathetic to the East than to the West.

Iraq's foreign policy was one of unreserved alignment with the West until the revolution of July 1958. During General Abdul Karim Kassim's regime, a policy more favorable to the Eastern bloc was pursued. Since the fall of Kassim at the hands of another military coup d'etat in 1963, Iraq's brand of neutralism has been similar to that of the UAR. Following independence, Lebanon followed a pro-Western policy. It accepted Western assistance without reservations and consented to the 1957 Eisenhower Doctrine. Popular opposition to this policy, among other domestic and regional factors, culminated in the 1958 civil war and the election of General Fuad Shihab to the presidency of the republic. Since then, a more open-minded and seemingly even-handed policy (which is still essentially pro-Western but for all purposes more discreetly stated and implemented) has been observed in Lebanon's foreign policy.

With respect to the countries of the Arabian Peninsula, Kuwait declared its policy of neutrality through its first elected national assembly in 1963. Saudi Arabia has, on the whole, been less of a neutral and has allowed the construction of U.S. air bases on its territory. Although it participated in the 1961 Belgrade Conference, Saudi Arabia retains these bases. Still, its commitment to the West is based on internal interests—financial and social stability—and is not profound. As to Yemen and Southern Yemen, the former adopted a policy of neutralism since its close alliance with Egypt in the mid-fifties and has adhered to that policy following the overthrow of the imamate in 1962. Since achieving independence from Britain in 1968, Southern Yemen has declared its attachment to neutralism.

With respect to the Arab countries of North Africa, the Sudan chose neutralism following General Ibrahim Abboud's coup of November 1958. Libya remained tied to Western policy through various treaties with the U.S. and Britain until its coup in 1969. The new military leadership of Libya succeeded in securing the evacuation of foreign troops and have moved toward a close alignment with Egypt. Tunisia's foreign policy is based upon cooperation with the West, a near necessity in economic terms, although it has been less pro-Western since the 1961 Bizerte clashes with French troops. Algeria's Provisional Government opted for neutralism and its post-independence governments have not forgotten that it was France's ties to NATO that allowed the war to persist for so long, at the cost of many Algerian lives. Thus, Algeria is anti-Western, although it has not allowed the Eastern bloc to monopolize foreign trade or aid relations. Finally, Morocco has oscillated between neutralism and alignment with the West depending on the government in office. Officially, neutralism remains its avowed policy.

The pursuit of a neutralist foreign policy has allowed a relatively small and weak country—the UAR—to play an active role in international affairs. It has also triggered the movement toward neutralism among the other Arab countries. Once more, Nasserism asserted itself as the pioneer movement to which other elements of the Middle East system would react, whether positively or negatively.

Anti-imperialism

The concept of anti-imperialism is inextricably linked to nationalism. In the Middle East imperialism is almost synonymous with Western influence, although Turks and Iranians would not find the idea of Soviet imperialism strange. Anti-imperialist feelings underlie relations to the outside world along three dimensions. First, an emphatic rejection of the colonial relationship takes place, and the colonizer's claim to moral and political superiority is denied. As we asserted above, this reaction varies with the extent to which colonialism affected the state in question and the personal reactions of elites to the experience. Second, the right to self-rule and independence is asserted. This right legitimates the sacrifice of material benefits in favor of autonomy; such legitimation is essential to avoid internal division. Third, the culture of the former metropole is reduced to a position of mere quality with the indigenous culture. Feelings in this realm are often ambiguous, as, on the one hand, equality or even superiority is claimed for the native culture while, on the other hand, cultural borrowing continues or is accelerated. Such concepts as neocolonialism, nonalignment, reactionism, and revolutionism should be understood not only as indicators of the degree of attachment to the sovereign entity, but also as repudiations of previous humiliation and subservience.

In an article in the *Middle East Journal* 19, 4 (1965), Hisham Sharabi finds the changes in the political and economic systems of the Arab world to represent "an ideological rebellion against Europe and Western social and political values." He notes that anti-Western feelings have existed since 1875, the beginning of the movement of social change. Sharabi, like other area scholars, sees with the beginnings of cultural and political contact with the West the emergence of a dual attitude in the Middle East: an attitude of both acceptance and rejection. Such a dichotomy has been presented in terms admitting only of a resolution in favor of one or the other position; Dankwart Rustow, however, in Richard Nolte's *The Modern Middle East,* sees it resolved in a constant synthesis of tradition and westernization. Both positions are artificial: some degree of synthesis is certainly occurring, and the total rejection of one or the other is impossible. Yet at various levels of society and for various individuals clear choices must often be made between modes of action or thought, and this dichotomous situation for the individual creates a perception of a total division of the two cultures.

In the case of Turkey, the incessant efforts of post–World War I political leaders seem to have decided the outcome in favor of total identification with the cultural and political values of the West. Yet the Turks have always denied that they borrowed from the West, and so they have created a pride in change just as if each artifact were indigenous to Turkey. The resolution of the matter is not complete in Turkey, for as values are diffused they will be diluted with the folk beliefs and traditions of the people and thus become less Western; as democracy progresses, the process of value diffusion may reverse itself, and Turkify the Westernized elites.

With the exception of a few coastline communal minorities, the Arab intellectual elite has adopted, after a long process of transformation, the other position. It has turned away from the Western model and looked inward to its history and inherited value system, to mold its own future. Though offering a diverse panorama, the ideologies of Nasserites, Ba'athists, Arab Nationalists, Muslim Brethren, and Syrian Nationalists are all manifestations of such a transformation and radically negate Bourguibism and notions similar to it, which are derided and looked upon as outmoded. This sort of cultural nationalism creates an artificial history necessary for emotional stability but which has the danger of forcing the Arab intellectuals to lose contact with reality as they forget the origins of some of their ideas. By insisting upon their uniqueness, they condemn themselves to commit the mistakes of others.

An attitude of anti-imperialism affects the conduct of foreign policy in two distinct manners. First, it shrouds relations with Western powers with a spirit of suspicion. Foreign acts construed as hostile to the interests of the Middle Eastern country by its policy-makers are interpreted as preliminaries for neocolonialist ventures. Second, such an attitude elicits commitments in the realm of foreign policy that would set the country on a path conflicting with that of the Western powers. Material or moral assistance to Algerian, South Arabian, Lebanese, Somali, Angolan, or South African rebels has frequently strained relations between Egypt, for instance, and some Western powers. Denial of the right to such activities has limited the possibilities of enduring cordial relations with Western powers. The Arab-Israeli conflict remains the most illustrative case. Perceived as an outpost of Western imperialism and as a

European colony on Arab soil, Israel remains the most thorny problem between the Arab world and the West.

Socialism

Multiple theses have been advanced to explain the adoption of socialist ideologies and programs by an increasing number of Middle Eastern countries in the last two decades. Socialism may be viewed as a rationalization of the assumption by the state of the control and direction of the economy, and, as such, is synonymous with "etatism." Others have argued that socialism is the nationalist's emotional response to problems his society faces in its movement from traditionalism. Loss of the attributes of community is compensated by the adoption of an ideology that connotes harmony and mutual responsibility in society—hence, Nasser's rejection of the concept of class warfare. Geopolitical considerations and the relative strengths of the national bourgeois classes have also been advanced as reasons that explain the differences between countries that move toward increased government ownership and those less amenable to such a program. Yet another thesis presents socialism as a necessary development of the process of change. All of these interpretations may be said to share an awareness of certain common attributes of Middle Eastern socialist countries. The basis of socialism in the Middle East is only partially economic; it is primarily political and moral, and it is this which determines the character of its manifestations.

Most Middle Eastern countries were under some form of foreign dominion until the 1930s, and their economies displayed the disabilities characteristic of underdeveloped colonial and semicolonial states. The result was a structural disfigurement of the economy and a stifling of the development of a dynamic, indigenous entrepreneurial class. The enforced orientation of the economy to meet the needs of a foreign state resulted in a disjointed economic system. Some portions of the economy were oriented to the village, some to a market-town, some to a capital city, and some were related most intimately to a class of entrepreneurs and capitalists representing, and often operating in, a distant nation. This left little room for entrepreneurship at the local level, and thus the land ethic which tied up local capital in relatively unproductive status symbols was not decisively opposed. Upon independence, it became evident that the disarticulation of the economy demanded one of two policies: continued dependence upon the metropolis or another foreign state, or creation for the resources of the indigenous society of the missing sectors of its economy. The choice between these alternatives has profound consequences, not the least in foreign policy, but it is not an economic choice.

This fundamental choice—between an independent economy and one based upon an adjunct or tributary relationship to a foreign economy —is of course based upon the attitudes and feelings of the decision-makers and stands in a relationship of reciprocal complementarity to these other orientations. The basis of the choice may be seen as a need to establish a boundary between the "evil" external to the territory and the "good" within, or the lack of such a need. We are interested here chiefly in the manifestations and consequences of that choice, rather than its psychic and historical bases. It should be noted, however, that the complex of attitudes consistent with the pursuit of economic independence is similar to that usually identified with nationalism.

In the popular Middle Eastern mind, encouraged by nationalist rhetoric, the distinction has long been clearly defined. Those states which choose an independent economy, usually expressed in terms of independence from the West, were identified as members of the "progressive camp," while those which maintained close ties with the West in economics as in other matters were placed in the "conservative camp." When, in the 1930s and 1940s, a choice became possible in both economics and foreign policy, we find a linkage between the two which is general throughout the Middle East.

While the conservatives have not been articulate in expressing their economic policies, the progressive camp has sought to justify its position and to stimulate the spread of nationalist economic policies in a large body of statements. We may summarize the progressive position in the following principles: (1) the colonial powers are responsible for the economic backwardness of the region; (2) maintaining economic cooperation with the West entails the retention of an underdeveloped economy; and (3) the rejection of economic dependence upon the West implies rejecting the traditional capitalist pattern of growth and development.

It is worthwhile to examine these principles at greater length, remembering their essentially emotional and political, rather than economic, nature. That is, these principles are prior to, rather than consequent upon, economic analysis, for the decision-makers of these polities. Although they relate to nonalignment, anti-imperialism, and nationalism, their economic content makes them particularly important for an examination of the effects of socialism upon foreign policy (although, in part, socialism and foreign policy are thus both consequences of a single cause—nationalism).

The responsibility of colonial powers for poverty and backwardness has been at times mitigated by an attribution of responsibility to the local elite, especially if, as in Egypt, that elite was of foreign origin. This placement of guilt at the door of the metropole is expressive of several attitudes, including a belief in the virtue of the nation, a wish to escape responsibility, and an evasion of the hard choices of development. It provides a justification for internal reform—the expunging of institutions foreign in their origins or preserved through foreign intervention. It also expresses the belief that the colonial powers are not concerned with justice or popular welfare, but are motivated by greed, racism, and a will to power. Past actions indicate evil intentions which justify avoidance of future contact.

The profit motive of Western capitalists, as demonstrated by past actions, and reinforced by the economic institutions those actions have produced, is held to preclude Western private investment in projects useful for the independent development of the former colonial state. Risk capital is not available for infrastructure development or the modernization of agriculture. On the other hand, Western public investment is also suspect, as the governments are held to value only the welfare of their own capitalists, or are motivated by security needs irrelevant to the Middle East. Thus, all collaboration is seen as thralldom, again expressing a view of relations with the West which postulates an essential inequality and inevitable exploitation.

The nature of the rejection of Western connections may be seen from the principle that an independent policy requires non-Western, or non-capitalist, forms of economic organization. This is justified on a number of grounds, but chiefly on the two that capitalism is essentially exploitative, and that the colonial experience had destroyed the possibility that the conditions necessary for indigenous capitalism will arise. Here again there is an emotional as well as an objective basis for the argument, chiefly stemming from the need to reject Western institutions through which colonialism operated and to assert the quality of local culture. These three principles, taken together, form a decision-making matrix in which the adoption of socialism, anti-Westernism, and association with noncapitalist states become virtual necessities.

The more conservative states differ from this pattern in various respects; for one reason or another, each of them rejects one of these principles. The Saudi Arabians, for example, have not been subjected to colonialism, have been able to maintain a feeling of equal status with Western states, and have not viewed their erstwhile poverty as a consequence of foreign intervention, but rather as a product of natural circumstance or the will of God. Never having been called upon to accept Western institutions by force, Saudi Arabia has no need to forcefully reject them. The Saudis are conservative because they see no need for radical change, and they maintain contact with the West because they perceive little threat from that quarter.

In contrast, Tunisia, another member of the conservative camp, sees the source of its difficulties in its traditional culture and seeks the solution to its problems in the West, to which the Tunisian leaders are acclimated. Whereas the Saudis have had no colonial experience, the Tunisians were successfully colonized in the sense that, while France failed to maintain a permanent hegemony in Tunis, the Tunisians were Europeanized by the experience and passed their crisis of identity before independence.

In summary of the above points, one could say that the conservatives have no overwhelming need to reject the West and thus tend to accept it as the lesser of two evils, if not as a positive good, while the progressives are vehemently against the Western political and economic formulae and are thus forced to seek solutions to their problems in some other fashion. Furthermore, the ideology of socialism imparts to the governments of the progressive states considerable powers in engineering the process of social change, and has been instrumental as a justification of foreign-policy orientations which may have had other sources.

As may be observed, socialist and nonsocialist Middle Eastern countries are, as a result, unable or unwilling to conduct enduring and stable cooperative relations, for even minor differences easily lend themselves to absorption in the wider ideological issues. Outside the Middle Eastern circle, the division has influenced the conduct of each country's foreign policy in the ways indicated above. Socialist countries have refused to recognize the rules of behavior set by the Cold War and have moved increasingly toward cooperation with the Eastern bloc in terms of trade, technical assistance, and cultural agreements. A similar but opposing tendency has developed among nonsocialist Middle Eastern countries. Close alliances have been worked out between Jordan, Saudi Arabia, Tunis, and Morocco, on the one hand, and either the United States or the United Kingdom on the other. In various instances, the cleavage between socialists and nonsocialists has determined the position adopted by the country in international crisis situations. The Indo-Pakistani and Greco-Turkish disputes over the status of Kashmir and Cyprus, respectively, as well as the Vietnamese war, are cases in which support extended to either of the contesting sides correlates with the social ideology of the country extending support.

Economic Factors

Under the heading of socialism a number of factors related to economics have been considered, but some of a more objective nature remain to be briefly discussed and related to foreign policy. The major economic factors are development, oil, and foreign aid. The foreign aid question has been alluded to with relation to anti-imperialism and the orientations underlying socialist ideology. The need for aid, which conflicts, or is seen to conflict, with the need to maintain an independent position in international relations, places a strain on foreign-policy decision-making. While some freedom of action must be yielded to gain aid, too great subordination of national independence to foreign interests may make relations with other states difficult and may arouse nationalist reaction within one's own country. Balanced aid is one means of dealing with this problem, as used by Egypt, Algeria, and, more recently, Iran and Turkey. Another solution, which appears to be unstable, is to accept aid, and the necessary dependence, while denying publicly that the dependent relationship exists; either the public or the aid donor usually prevents the long continuation of this approach. It is probable that the only long-term solution is multilateral aid.

The need of Middle Eastern countries to develop is great, and while they may cooperate on some enterprises, they are often dealing in similar products for similar and limited markets, and so they are competitive. The need of each to improve manufacturing and to find markets tends to lead to attempts to penetrate the economies of the other states of the region or to cut them out of markets abroad. Indirectly, the underdeveloped state of these economies affects foreign policy by increasing the difficulty of maintaining a high level of military and diplomatic activity.

Oil is a similar factor in the area. It is divisive because some states have a great deal of it, and others have very little. Those who possess the oil feel that they should use it, at least primarily, for their own people, and those who do not have it feel that it might better be turned to more generally beneficial projects. Kuwait, a very small and militarily weak state with great oil wealth, has provided funds for an Arab Development Bank, and Libya and Saudi Arabia have contributed to Arab defense, but most oil money has been spent in the country of its production or in non-Arab trade centers. The oil-producing states, while they have attempted to coordinate marketing (with some success in the winter of 1970–71), are placed in a competitive position because of limitation on markets. Because production is arranged through foreign companies, and because greater production means greater revenues, it is difficult to limit production, and price controls are therefore somewhat limited in their effect.

TRADITIONAL RIVALRIES

Inter-Arab Rivalries

Discernible in Arab politics are two rivalries which have persisted for relatively long periods of time. The older is that between Egypt and Mesopotamia, two ancient seats of hydraulic civilizations whose rivalry is derived mainly from geopolitical considerations. Since they became centers of organized polities, both Egypt and the "land between the rivers" have been great prizes when weak, and great regional powers when strong. They have seldom been unified—most recently in the early days of Muslim expansion. They have been separate and significant centers of power who have had to take account of one another's actions and to be wary of each other. At many periods of history they have contested for dominance of Syria and the trade routes of the Eastern Mediterranean. To this natural rivalry have been added, at most times, various issues which, for reasons peculiar to each country, have divided their leaders.

In the modern history of the Middle East, the ancient rivalry between these two competitive civilizations has continued in the rivalry between King Farouk of Egypt and the Hashemite kings of Iraq and Jordan, and to the bitter disputes between President Nasser and General Kassim. This competition was focused on the control of lands lying between them and, after the Second World War, particularly upon Syria and Palestine.

Throughout the era of Abd al-Illah and Nuri es-Said, the Iraqi objective was either to federate Syria with Iraq or to set up a close alliance. Egypt, on the other hand, had the limited objective of ensuring a neutral or pro-Egyptian Syria. The contest was decided for a time in 1958 in Egypt's favor with the proclamation of the United Arab Republic. With the increased monopolization of power in Kassim's hands following the 1958 Iraqi coup, the dispute with Egypt was rekindled. Ideological similarities were not sufficient to bring the two countries closer.

For a five-year period (1963–68) following the overthrow of Kassim, relations between the two countries were friendly, only to return to their normal state of diplomatic and propaganda warfare. At present, Egyptian-Iraqi disputes manifest themselves in their conflicting Palestine policy.

Another traditional rivalry, but one which has not been very active since 1958, has been the quarrel between the Hashemites and the House of Saud. Personal feuds underlie the hostilities between the two. The revival of Wahhabism at the turn of the twentieth century under the leadership of King Ibn Saud and its expansion in the Arabian Peninsula brought the movement in direct confrontation with the Hashemite rulers of Mecca and Medina. Control of the two holy cities fell to Ibn Saud when he finally defeated the Hashemites at Mecca in 1924. By this time, the British had set Prince Faisal and Prince Abdullah, the sons of the Sharif Hussein al-Hashimi of Mecca, upon the thrones of Iraq and Transjordan, respectively. Although Ibn Saud acknowledged their position in the 1927 Jedda Treaty with Britain, the rivalry was not settled. The direct British protection which was extended to the Hashemites deterred the Saudis from attacking them. The differing religious practices were also to nourish personal feuds. Wahhabism is a puritanical movement that calls for a return to the early teachings and practices of Islam and rejects all later additions, viewing all other Muslims as "backsliders in the Faith." The latter, in turn, accuse them of being "primitive reactionaries." The 1958 Iraqi revolution, reducing as it did the Hashemite realm to the tiny state of Jordan, allowed the Saudis to cease regarding the Hashemites as threatening, and to regard Hussein of Jordan as a ruler with similar interests against the radical states of Egypt, Syria, and Iraq.

The Arab-Israeli Conflict

Although a conflict of such recent origins should not perhaps be spoken of as traditional, its importance to the decision-makers of the area is as pervasive as if it had persisted for centuries. A full exposition of the conflict would, with supporting documents, occupy several volumes, but here we may approach it as part of the decision-making matrix for Middle Eastern elites, and use it to elucidate some of the points brought out above.

The close interweaving of various historical and ideological trends is nowhere better illustrated than in the case of the conflict between Israel, on the one hand, and the various Arab states on the other (now widened to include the Palestinian guerrillas, who are, moreover, sometimes involved in conflict with Israel, sometimes with Jordan or Lebanon). It seems a matter of almost pure chance that the rise of Zionism should coincide with the growing national awareness among the Arabs, stemming, as these two nationalisms did, from almost entirely separate origins. The complexity of the situation is at least partially a result of the ambiguity of the position of the British, induced, in turn, by a complex of forces arising in the United Kingdom, Europe, the Middle East, and elsewhere. No process was able to work itself out in isolation; each reacted against the others, modifying them and being modified in turn.

It is probable that the origins of Israel would have led to allegations of colonialism in any case, the juxtaposition of Jewish immigration with imperialist inroads in the area made such an identification almost inevitable. It is probable that conflict would have resulted from the presence of such a foreign entity in the area in any case, but its creation at a time when the Arabs felt the need to assert their strength as an answer to imperialist humiliations left little room for peaceful solutions. It is possible that the matter might have been settled peacefully after 1948, but it is difficult to see how this could have been accomplished unless one assumes basic changes in the nature of each of the regimes involved.

Here some of the domestic factors make themselves known. Both Arab and Israeli nationalism are founded upon persecution and division and are romantic and exclusivist—both are based upon some concept of the chosen people. The kinds of sensitivities and brutalities—often corollaries of each other—resulting from this sort of feeling can be observed in the history of German and Italian nationalism, as well as in the Middle East. Again, both Arab and Israeli ideologies are socialist oriented, and the identities involved here make the sort of cynical elite diplomacy of nineteenth-century Europe impossible; this concession is a betrayal of Israeli hopes, that compromise a betrayal of the Egyptian people, and so forth. Both are anti-imperialist, in a very real sense, and each appears imperialistic, or expansionist, to the other, not wholly without grounds, and thus each can feel trespassed against, each draws moral security from knowing that the other is the aggressor, and each feels threatened and on the defensive. Other factors enter in— perceptual, religious, economic—but they come down to a situation of mutual positive feedback for hostility. Each side predicates its acts upon an assumption of hostility on the part of the other, and thus its acts appear hostile to the other.

Other domestic factors in the conflict may be quickly reviewed. No government in the region is so secure that it can afford to alienate a large section of effective public opinion. Israel and Lebanon have perhaps the largest proportions of active citizens in the area, but at least the army, and usually other groups as well, must be satisfied in every nation. The Israeli government is sharply divided, and apparently the political alignments in Israel are at the point of undergoing radical change. This has been forestalled by the perceived need for national unity in the face of military threat and by the government's ability to utilize Egyptian intransigence to avoid decisions about the conflict itself. The recent developments, beginning with the initiatives of U.S. Secretary of State Rogers in 1969, have forced Israel's government to continually narrow its base of support as it is forced to make more and more decisions of substance. Faced with the choice of war or a fall from power, the Israeli cabinet may let its decision be forced upon it by vacillating. With the other states of the area the choice is equally troublesome; one may risk a coup if one is not militant enough for the armed forces, disastrous defeat if one pushes one's opponent too far, and domestic discontent if too much of one's limited resources are devoted to military needs rather than to economic development.

Conclusion

The fact that the states of the area are diverse in their internal politics has meant that their needs and interests, as well as their capabilities, have been equally diverse. In all states, domestic policy is primary, and foreign policy is often used as an instrument to further national integration, mobilization, development, and support for the elite. Despite the diversity of Middle East political systems, unifying factors exist that structure both intraregional and inter-regional relations. They impart to the foreign policy of member countries a degree of regularity in behavior and, thus, allow some predictability. The factors include the foreign-policy decision-makers' mode of perception of the outside world, religion, political trends and ideologies, economics and traditional rivalries. With regard to perceptions, they seem to vary along two dimensions: modernization versus tradition, on the one hand, and the viewing of the outside world as beneficiary versus threatening, on the other. Each state falls within any of the four categories, and its position seems to influence its dealings with outside powers and the degree of diffuseness of such relations. Concerning religion, it gives a semblance of unity to Middle East countries on the international plane but its integrative value is compromised by the existence within its fold of multiple and hostile sects. Religion, as a factor conditioning foreign policy, seems to be most pronounced where it is central to the identity of the state, such as is the case with Iran, Pakistan, Saudi Arabia, and Israel. As to political trends and ideological orientations, the most significant of these in the formulation of foreign policy include nationalism, anti-imperialism, nonalignment, and socialism. These factors contribute significantly to some of the cleavages existing among countries of the region and conditions the interaction between Middle East countries and members of the dominant international system. Within the Arab world, they led to the emergence of two camps, the progressive and the conservative. While facilitating the cooperation of the former with the Eastern bloc, they led the latter to maintain stronger relations with the Western block. Economic factors, which include development, oil, and foreign aid, seem to perpetuate divisiveness in the area and strain relations with world powers. Finally, traditional rivalries offset ideological bonds and perpetuate division in the area. Though the above generalizations may seem too broad at the first instance, their utility is impressive when employed to understand the interaction of the subsystem with the dominant system in particular cases, as evidenced in previous chapters.

❀ 10 ❀

TAREQ Y. ISMAEL

Oil: The New Diplomacy

In 1971 President Muammar Kaddafi of Libya nationalized the British Petroleum Company in retaliation for Britain's support of Iran's sequestration of three Arab Gulf islands. It was the first time in the Middle East that oil property was nationalized as an overt act of political retaliation. And it signaled the transition of Middle East oil from the economic to the political arena, indicating that the decade of the seventies would be an era of oil diplomacy in the international relations of the Middle East. While the new diplomacy has yet to take shape, oil portends to be not only a key issue in the international relations of the area but also a powerful factor in the dynamics of the international system. President Kaddafi's action did not in itself catapult oil into this role of international political lubricant. It merely marked the coincidence of a set of circumstances that made the consideration of oil as a key political issue not only feasible from the point of view of the Middle East, but indeed essential from the point of view of the Western world.

THE MISCIBILITY OF OIL AND POLITICS

In fact, oil and politics are an old mixture in the international relations of the Middle East. The history of the concessions is not merely an account of the enterprise, skill, and daring of Western entrepreneurs; it is also a record of international intrigue and political maneuvering on an imperial scale. From the time the British navy began switching to oil in order to fuel its ships around the turn of the century, secure sources of oil became an increasingly important concern of the British government. In 1914 it purchased a 51 percent share of the Anglo-Persian Oil Company stock. Anglo-Persian held an oil concession over virtually the whole of Persia (except for five northern provinces). Thereafter, the Persian government found itself dealing not with a private commercial

226

enterprise but with a sovereign nation that controlled a vast concession over Persia's most valuable resource.

In Iraq, too, Britain acquired 75 percent control of the Turkish Petroleum Company, which held a concession over Mesopotamian oil granted by the Ottoman government in Istanbul. But with the dismemberment of the Ottoman Empire as a result of World War I, the fate of the concession came into question. Britain, as mandatory power in Iraq following the war, wielded broad powers and circumvented legal procedures to have the concession reaffirmed. Even before an autonomous Iraqi government was formed, and before the treaty defining Iraq's obligations under the mandate was ratified, the British High Commissioner in Iraq in effect forced the newly installed king and his cabinet to ratify the concession. And while the British Foreign Office was moving to secure Mesopotamian oil for the British navy, the American State Department intervened to see that American business interests were not closed out.

The consolidation of concessions throughout the Middle East followed complex patterns of commercial and diplomatic maneuvering that culminated in an international combine with virtually total control of Middle East oil. By the Second World War, control of Middle East oil was concentrated in seven fully integrated companies. These companies were not only joint owners in the various producing companies operating in the Middle East but also through complicated contractual and partnership arrangements mutually controlled every aspect of the exploration, exploitation, production, refinement, and marketing of Middle East oil. Thus, the oil industry that operated in the Middle East represented an international cartel embracing American, British, and some European interests who in essence had usurped sovereignty over the Middle East's most important economic resource.

THE QUESTION OF SOVEREIGNTY

The question of sovereignty over oil resources was an inherent controversy of the concessions. The original concessions were secured from despotic rulers of traditional societies who bartered away a national resource the value of which they did not comprehend, under broad terms whose significance they did not understand, to enterprises whose power they did not anticipate. Unfamiliar with Western techniques, values, and skills, and alien to the principles of free enterprise and corporate law that motivated and molded the oil industry, these rulers unwittingly exchanged their nation's sovereignty over its natural resources for generations to come for immediate and short-term rewards. The Iran and Saudi concessions were each to last for sixty-five years; the Iraq and Kuwait concessions for seventy-five. Virtually the whole territories of these countries were conceded to the concessionaires with exclusive rights to exploration and exploitation of the resources, without any controls as to the rate of development of the concession or the rate of production of the resources, under fixed terms and revenues that did not take changing circumstances into account. The governments even forsook their rights to tax the concessions for the duration of the agreements. These and other provisions of the concessions alienated the countries from their oil resources and placed the countries' economic posterity under foreign corporate control.

While many benefits accrued to the Middle Eastern countries from the oil industry's exploitation of their oil resources, it soon became apparent that the oil revenues which Middle Eastern governments were receiving were not commensurate with the value of the resource. In fact, foreign governments were receiving more in tax payments from the industries than were the producing countries from oil revenues. For example, in 1949 Aramco, operating in Saudi Arabia, paid the United States government $43,000,000 in taxes on its net earnings, while it paid the Saudi government $5,000,000 less in oil revenues on which those earnings were based. In 1950 the Anglo-Iranian Oil Company (AIOC), operating in Iran, paid Iran £16,000,000 in oil revenues, had an after-tax net profit of £33,103,000, and made tax payments to the British government of £50,707,000. And while AIOC's profits increased tenfold between 1944 and 1950, Iranian oil revenues increased only fourfold. Such inequities served to heighten a growing tension between the oil companies and the producing countries.

With the rapid influx of Western concepts, techniques, and skills that accompanied the intrusion of two world wars and the burgeoning oil industries, the ranks of an articulate, educated middle class in the Middle East rapidly expanded. This class—impatient of the slow pace of change in their tradition-bound societies and intolerant of foreign domination—increasingly questioned the terms of the concessions, indeed, the very nature of the concessions. Following World War II their main struggle centered around getting better terms from the concessionaires. Endless rounds of negotiations between the various governments of the producing countries and the oil companies had by the mid-fifties achieved better revenue terms for the producing countries. Nevertheless, sovereignty over oil resources still remained under foreign control. While the economies of the Middle Eastern countries depended upon oil revenues, they had no voice in the rate of exploration, exploitation, and production of the resources—factors upon which their revenues depended. Nor did they have a voice in the determination of posted prices. Posted prices, used as the basis for calculating revenues, reflected more the cost of oil production than its actual market value. All these factors were under the firm control of the concessionaires who based their calculations on the profit motive rather than on the economic needs of the countries. This was the essence of the sovereignty issue. As summarized by a former Iraqi Minister of Economics, Dr. Nadim Pachachi, "Our whole economic development is geared to the revenues from the flow . . . of oil. Our whole political stability depends on the flow . . . of oil. It is not just a private matter involving a private company's profits. It is a matter that affects the whole state of Iraq." [1]

The strength of foreign corporate control over Middle East oil resources was amply demonstrated in Iran following World War II. Iranian nationalist unrest against foreign interference in Iranian affairs had been exacerbated by World War II, which brought Russian and British troops into Iran. Following the war, the Tudeh Party spearheaded the struggle to regain Iranian sovereignty. Foreign control over oil resources, Iran's main source of revenue, was naturally a primary issue. In 1948, Iran opened negotiations with AIOC to recapture its sovereignty over oil resources. Negotiations failed, and in 1951, under the leadership of the ardent Iranian nationalist, Dr. Mohammad Mossadegh, the Iranian government nationalized its oil resources. Explaining the nationalization before the UN General Assembly, the Iranian representative, Nasrollah Entezam, stated, "As you know, oil is the main source of our national wealth. It is therefore proper that we can countenance its exploitation only as a way of ensuring the general welfare of our people." [2]

With the support of their governments, the oil companies brought economic, diplomatic, business, and military pressures on Iran. Iranian oil was excluded from the world markets, and the oil companies were able to fill the gap simply by increasing oil production from other areas. With Iran unable to market its oil, the country was thrown into economic chaos. In 1953, a coup popularly attributed to the United States Central Intelligence Agency threw Dr. Mossadegh out of office. Thereafter, the oil companies reopened negotiations and in the settlement regained sovereignty over Iran's oil.

The Iranian experience had a profound effect throughout the Middle East, where nationalist unrest against the oil companies was boiling. The episode effectively demonstrated the power of the oil companies and their vast control over the world's oil industry. It would not be until the decade of the seventies that Middle Eastern governments would again challenge the power of the companies.

THE CHANGING OIL MARKET

During the decade of the fifties, and running into the decade of the sixties, the supply of oil greatly outpaced consumption. In order not to glut the market and upset stable prices, the oil companies maintained below maximum-capacity levels on producing wells, held some wells in reserve, and left many proven fields undeveloped. Hence, when they wished to exclude Iran from the oil market, they merely increased production from other wells to compensate for the loss of Iranian oil. In short, it was a consumer's market, under the firm control of several fully integrated oil industries who formed a cartel to maintain their mutual interests.

By the decade of the seventies, the picture had changed considerably. Not only had the power of the international oil cartel been challenged by the emergence of a plethora of small, independent, and highly competitive companies anxious to break into the international oil industry, but a rapidly increasing rate of oil consumption, particularly in the industrialized nations, made oil a dearer commodity. Not only has the world's consumption of energy been increasing at exponential rates— from 1950 growing at the rate of approximately 5 percent a year, with consumption thus doubling every fifteen years—but oil and natural gas have become increasingly more important energy sources. Their consumption has grown at the higher average rate of 7.8 percent a year since 1950—i.e., doubling every decade—and has risen from just over one-third of total energy consumption in 1950 to nearly two-thirds of the much larger total in 1970. Over the same period petroleum has constituted virtually all of the massive expansion of world trade in primary fuels. And while in 1968 ten industrialized countries accounted for 75 percent of world energy consumption, the demands of the developing countries are rapidly increasing and are expected to represent a large increase in world consumption by the end of the century.

With these increasing demands on a depletable resource, oil has become a supplier's market. During the sixties exploration raised hopes for the discovery of vast oil reserves in the North Sea and other offshore areas. However, these hopes have been dampened by the difficulties of exploiting such reserves. And geologists now generally agree that there is no chance of finding oil in such reserves as has been found in the Middle East. The Middle East contains 60 percent of the world's proven oil reserves and is the largest center of world oil production. With supply no longer outpacing demand, and indeed, the prospect that demand will shortly overcome supply, the Middle East has moved into a very favorable market position.

The magnitude of the demand on Middle Eastern oil is pinpointed by projections of future needs. The area produced 41.3 percent of the world's crude oil in 1972. The major portion of Middle East oil has been going to Europe (which receives 80 percent of its oil from the area) and Japan (which receives 85 percent of its oil from the Middle East). On the basis of present growth trends in energy consumption, however, *The Economist,* July 7, 1973, predicted that by 1980 Western Europe and Britain will alone require about 1.2 billion tons of oil per year, compared to 800 million tons consumed in 1973. Also by 1980, Japan, which will be 90 percent dependent upon Middle East oil, will require 210 million tons a year compared to the 150 million tons consumed in 1970, according to the *Middle East Economic Digest,* January 19, 1973.

With both Europe and Japan heavily dependent on ever-increasing quantities of Middle East oil, the competition is compounded by predictions that the United States will be requiring large-scale imports of oil. Up until the decade of the seventies, the United States had been a net exporter of oil, importing only about 3 percent of its oil needs from the Middle East. Its present needs are some 16 million barrels of oil a day, but by 1985 the U.S. will require 25 million barrels a day. In early 1972, however, U.S. oil fields began producing at maximum capacity, indicating that future expanding needs would have to be met by importation. Because it appears that other sources will be unable to take up the slack in American production, it is estimated that by 1985 America will require 35 percent of its oil from the Middle East.

To sum up these projections, based on present estimates, the U.S., Europe, and Japan will consume 71 million barrels of oil a day by 1980, compared with 38 million at present. But these countries and other suppliers outside the Middle East will produce just 35 million barrels a day. The shortfall can be filled only by the Middle East. The region has both the capacity and potential of pumping 61 million barrels daily by 1980, compared to its present production of approximately 22 million barrels daily. But whether or not the area will increase its production to meet these growing needs is both an economic and political issue.

Not only has the pattern of oil production and consumption radically changed, but so, too, has the nature of the Middle East oil industry. The greedy despots and untutored sheiks who signed the original concessions have been supplanted by a growing corps of skilled technocrats and dedicated public servants who over the decades marking the growth of the Middle East's oil industry learned to bargain with the oil companies with increasing shrewdness. Through successive battles at the bargaining tables, they won for their countries better terms under the concessions. And with the creation of the Organization of Oil Producing and Exporting Countries (OPEC) in 1960, through collective bargaining the producing countries greatly increased their power vis-à-vis the oil companies and won back some of the sovereignty over oil resources usurped by the oil companies.

The turning point in the relationship between producing countries and oil companies occurred in 1970 when President Muammar Kaddafi of Libya rejected prevailing royalty rates, demanding higher prices and higher taxes of his concessionaires. The companies refused, and Libya, falling back on $2 billion in currency reserves, immediately slashed production from 3.3 million barrels per day to 2.5 million. After a ten-month stand-off the oil companies were unable to hold out longer against European need for Libyan oil and their own financial dependence on it. Thus they agreed to increase Libya's oil royalties by 120 percent within two years—from about $1 per barrel in 1969 to about $2.20 per barrel in 1971—and to continue to increase the royalties by 10 percent a year until 1975. Within a few months the other Middle East producers received similar price increases.

The incident effectively demonstrated the changes that had occurred in consumption and market circumstances. The check that had been put on fomenting nationalist aspirations by the Iranian nationalization experience was removed, and by mid-1972, Iraq, Libya, and Algeria had nationalized all or major parts of their oil industries; Saudi Arabia, Kuwait, Abu Dhabi, and Qatar signed participation agreements with the companies operating in their territories whereby they acquired an initial share in the equity and operations of the companies of 25 percent, rising five years later by 5 percent a year to reach 51 percent by 1982; and Iran was negotiating an arrangement that would bring it benefits comparable to the participation agreements.

Libya's ability to economically sustain the oil cutbacks indicated another fundamental change. Most of the Middle Eastern oil-producing countries have built up huge monetary reserves. In spite of ambitious social and economic programs instituted in these countries to raise the standard of living and education of the populations, most of them are in the enviable position of having more money flowing in from oil revenues than their economies can absorb. *Time* magazine reported on

April 2, 1973, that Middle East oil income, about $4.4 billion a year just five years ago, had soared to $10 billion a year by 1973, and by 1980 may reach $40 billion. It has been estimated that the Middle East and North African oil producers have about $7 billion of reserves in Eurodollars, and another $10 billion in gold reserves. By the end of this decade, according to Horace C. Bailey, senior vice-president of Chemical Bank, Middle East governments will have as much as $175 billion in their treasuries, representing what is likely to be the largest hoard of foreign-held money ever accumulated, as noted in the *International Herald-Tribune,* March 21, 1973.

Such huge reserves are subject to the shifts in the international monetary market. In the monetary crisis of March 1973, *Newsweek,* July 23, 1973, estimated that the Arab oil-producing states lost as much as $600 million. Thus, many Arab countries are considering the costs of producing more revenue than their economies can absorb. With oil prices rising, and the value of monetary reserves unpredictable, the concept of "banking the oil"—i.e., leaving it in the ground where its value is sure to increase—rather than over-producing above revenue needs is beginning to take hold. Kuwait has already put a three-million-barrel a day ceiling on its production. With continuing runs on the dollar, explained Abdul Wahab Mohammed, the under-secretary of Kuwait's Foreign Ministry for Finance and Oil, in the *International Herald-Tribune,* April 7, 1973, "a barrel in the ground is worth much more to us than a barrel on the market now." And according to a Saudi cabinet minister, as reported in the *Middle East Economic Survey,* July 13, 1973: "We have found that the maximum revenues we can usefully absorb is brought in by production of seven million barrels a day. Anything we produce over that harms our own interests, by keeping prices down and by disturbing our economic balance."

Thus, the situation has changed considerably from the 1950s and 1960s when Middle Eastern governments were literally begging the oil companies to increase production in order that they might have increased revenues at their disposal. At a time when oil is becoming more important to the countries that consume it, the revenues are becoming less useful to the Middle Eastern states that produce it. Furthermore, oil is a wasting resource whose depletion will leave many of the Middle Eastern countries without an economic base. As a measure against the time when their resources are depleted, then, they are seeking to industrialize their nations and build diversified economic infrastructures with oil revenues rather than building up huge monetary reserves, and are linking oil production to development projects. Also, in countries such as Saudi Arabia, where oil is the only natural resource, the governments are tying oil supplies to joint-venture projects on their soil in an attempt to attract the kinds of energy-intensive industries that make use of their only resource.

One of the immediate effects of the changes in the oil market is that the industrialized world is paying more for its energy. Until the decade of the seventies, oil was one of the cheapest forms of energy. From the $1 per barrel that Libya received for its crude in 1969, the price had skyrocketed by 1973 to as high as $4.90 per barrel, as reported in the *Middle East Economic Digest,* August 17, 1973. Although because of its low sulphur content the cost of Libyan crude is higher than other Middle Eastern crudes, similar increases comparable in scale have occurred throughout the Middle East, and there is every indication that prices will continue to rise as Western European countries, Japan, and the United States compete for supplies of Middle Eastern oil.

OIL AND POLITICS

The intensity of consumer competition is heightened by threatened oil shortages. Oil has been described as the jugular vein of the industrialized world, and the increasing competition for limited supplies of such a vital commodity raises the specter of fear that in a wild scramble for oil, prices will soar even more rapidly and political maneuvering to secure supplies will affect the whole system of Western alliances. With the prospect of the U.S. becoming a major oil importer, Western Europe and Japan fear that America will attempt to seek privileged access to supplies through bilateral arrangements. In fact, Western European countries, particularly France, and Japan are seeking to improve their relations in the Middle East to secure their own access to supplies.

One solution to the competition that has been considered in both the United States and Europe is an organization of oil-importing countries which could deal with international allocation of available oil if chronic shortages occur and thus avoid an international price war in which importing nations would bid up prices. However, on May 4, 1973, the *Middle East Economic Digest* reported that OPEC gave warning that such a move would have "negative effects on the present energy situation." The plan was also rejected by John K. Jamieson, chairman of the world's biggest oil company, Exxon. Jamieson said in the same journal that such a move could "create a hostile atmosphere and harden the opposition between the two camps rather than open up lines of mutual accommodation. . . . It could lead to a series of reprisals and counter-reprisals that would rule out the possibility of rational compromise in future negotiations." Japan has also rejected the idea, with the government expressing its view that the establishment of friendly bilateral relations between consuming and producing countries is the best way to deal with the energy crisis and other problems between them, rather than a policy of confrontation which would hurt the consumers before the producers, as the *Middle East Economic Survey* stated on May 4 and July 20, 1973.

One major obstacle to an organization of consuming nations is that some of the consumers are unwilling to share the burden of American policy in the Middle East. The Arabs have long simmered at America's partisan support—economic, military, and diplomatic—for Israel in the Arab-Israeli conflict. Without such support, they maintain, Israel would have been forced to pull out of the Arab territories it occupied in the June 1967 War. Because of American support, Israel is not only able to retain occupation of the territories, but is attempting to Israelize large sections of them in the effort to establish a "greater" Israel. Now that the producing countries have control over their oil industries and are no longer in need of increased revenues, the question of increased production has taken on heavy political overtones. In a political consideration of production, America will be at a great disadvantage due to its partisan role in the Arab-Israeli conflict. Therefore, some consumers see the security of supplies as a matter of friendly bilateral relations and neutrality in the Arab-Israeli conflict, and are hesitant to link the future of their supplies with those of America's. Japan, in particular, is seeking to build such relations. Following a three-day conference of Japanese diplomats to the Middle East held in Tokyo in July 1973, a call was made for closer economic cooperation with the oil-producing countries and a search for new ways to increase and stabilize the supply of crude oil to Japan. As a political measure to stabilize supplies, the diplomats recommended that Japan retain its neutral position and continue its support of United Nations Security Council Resolution 242 of November 1967 which calls for Israel to withdraw from the occupied Arab territories. And in the October 1973 Arab-Israeli War, Western European countries who have strong pro-Israel biases—such as Britain and West Germany—made an effort to establish at least an aura of neutrality by banning arms shipments to the Middle East combatants. When America undertook to supply Israel with large amounts of arms, Britain did not allow American transport planes to stop on British territory, and West Germany put in a protest over America's shipment of arms from its bases there, *The Economist* reported on November 3, 1973. Thus, America was left alone in its full-scale support of Israel, and there is little doubt that Western Europe's heavy dependence on Middle

East oil played an important part in the decisions to remain uninvolved.

Would the Arabs—indeed, could the Arabs—bring oil into the battle against Israel? Clearly under current market and economic conditions the Arabs could cut back production or freeze it at its present level without harming their own interests. And with the rising demand for oil, even a freeze would precipitate severe shortages in Western Europe, and to a lesser extent, in the United States. In 1972 Arab leaders made fifteen public threats to use oil as a political weapon against the United States to force a more even-handed American position in the Middle East. But these threats originated from such radical regimes as the Ba'ath of Iraq and Kaddafi of Libya. The consuming world had learned to live with such firebrands as these radical Arab nationalists, for the real wealth of oil lies in the Arab Gulf states and Saudi Arabia. This entire area is under the control of conservative monarchial regimes who have strong relations with the West and are in ideological conflict with the radical Arab nationalist regimes.

Saudi Arabia in particular, which holds 24 percent of the world's proven oil reserves, is the swing producer in the Middle East. By 1972, plans were already under way to increase Saudi production from the current 7 million barrels per day to 20 million per day by 1980 to meet the increasing energy needs of Western Europe and the United States. In spite of the fact that beyond a certain level of production it becomes an economic sacrifice of the nation's dwindling asset, Saudi Arabia planned to increase production because, as expressed by official circles in the *Middle East Economic Survey,* June 15, 1973, it felt a moral obligation to provide the United States and the world with crude oil. In fact, Saudi Arabia's friendship with the United States has been so strong, and its antagonisms with Arab nationalist regimes so deep, that American policy-makers tended to scoff at the idea of oil as a political weapon. Saudi Arabia and the Arab Gulf sheikhdoms, which generally follow the Saudi pattern in foreign relations, appeared secure sources of increasing quantities of oil irrespective of the pattern of American policy in the Middle East.

However, Saudi Arabia too became disgusted with American policy in the Middle East and took under serious consideration the imposition of restraints on its oil production. By the end of the summer 1973 it was apparent that Saudi Arabia and most of the Arab Gulf sheikhdoms were prepared to use their key positions as major world suppliers of crude oil to bring pressure on the U.S. government to moderate its pro-Israeli policy. Ahmad Zaki Yamani, Saudi Minister of Petroleum and Mineral Resources, first conveyed the Saudi decision to the U.S. government during a visit to Washington in April 1973. In June, Saudi

Minister of State for Foreign Affairs Omar Saqqaf reaffirmed the Saudi position in press statements. Finally, the *Christian Science Monitor* reported on July 6, 1973, that King Faisal himself publicly endorsed the warning issued by his two ministers when he stated in a press interview that Saudi Arabia will find it "difficult to continue cooperation with the United States in the petroleum field unless Washington moves toward a more balanced policy in the Middle East."

Saudi officials made it clear, however, that Saudi Arabia would not be stampeded into an emotional and premature use of oil as a weapon. "The Saudi preference," according to *Middle East Economic Survey,* August 31, 1973, "is clearly for a graduated use of the oil lever which would take the form of progressively increasing curbs on rates of production growth." The purpose of this approach is evidently to provide the United States with both a political incentive and sufficient time to review its Middle East policy. In the words of Prince Saud, "the employment of such a weapon must be linked to a specific aim which would convey to your enemy precisely what you are after, and what he ought to do if he wishes to spare himself the harm of an economic boycott." Furthermore, Saudi officials emphasized that the oil weapon would be used discriminately, as far as possible, with a clear differentiation between the United States, Israel's principal patron, and Europe and Japan, who are more sympathetic to the Arab cause. A series of statements by leaders of the Arab Gulf sheikhdoms over the summer months of 1973 indicated that most of them were prepared to follow a similar course.

The Saudi and Arab Gulf decisions to use oil for political leverage against the United States confirmed the threat to American supplies. Although American officials, including President Nixon, denied that oil would influence American policy in the Middle East, in fact the strategic and economic danger of large-scale and long-term oil shortages became a major policy concern in Washington. Senator J. William Fulbright, chairman of the Senate Foreign Relations Committee, in a speech to the Senate on May 21 carried in the *Middle East Economic Survey* on May 25, expressed concern over the future of U.S. interests in the Middle East. He warned that present American policy could result in an oil embargo against the U.S., and that the resulting energy crisis might cause the U.S. to contemplate military intervention in the area via its "military potent surrogates," Iran and Israel. He further added that the U.S. was damaging its own interests in the Middle East by its emotional commitment to Israel and that "to the Arabs, the United States seems not only hostile, but gratuitously and irrationally so. In terms of our own national interest, I am bound to agree."

Although the U.S. Department of State dissociated itself from Senator Fulbright's comments, stating "the idea of using force which was mentioned in the speech does not reflect in any way any thought within this administration," nevertheless, in the summer of 1973, it was reported in *The Daily Star* (Beirut), September 5, 1973, that the U.S. military undertook desert maneuvers for the first time in forty years. Middle East observers were quick to make a connection between this and U.S. energy needs. President Houari Boumediene of Algeria warned in the same edition of *The Star* that such "big military maneuvers in California in conditions similar to the Middle East were a political-psychological preparation for such intervention." Indeed, in its September 10, 1973, issue, *Newsweek* reported that the Pentagon held a secret seminar on energy at the joint-chiefs-of-staff level.

THE OCTOBER 1973 WAR AND THE OIL WEAPON

Although the Saudi position hoped to offer America time and incentive to respond to Arab pressures for a more even-handed American policy in the Middle East, the October 1973 Arab-Israeli War brought the matter to a head. United States support to Israel remained unwavering, confirmed by its large-scale arms shipments to Israel during the fighting. The Arab states imposed immediate embargoes on oil shipments to the U.S. and Holland (which also staunchly supported Israel), and instituted immediate reductions in oil production, to be followed by monthly cutbacks "until such time as total evacuation of Israeli forces from all Arab territory occupied during the June 1967 war is completed, and the legitimate rights of the Palestinian people are restored." Iraq went even further, nationalizing all U.S. interests operating there and Dutch interests in the Basrah Petroleum Company.

At the time of this writing it is still too early to tell the political and economic effects of the embargoes and cutbacks. But whatever response —political, economic and/or military—the oil weapon elicits, it is clear that oil will be a primary issue in the international relations of the Middle East until oil is replaced as a principal energy source. For the consuming states, access to and security of oil supplies will be primarily a political matter on which rests the very foundation of industrialized society. For the producing states, oil will be the principal tool in the implementation of their political, economic, and social aspirations. Oil and politics, as we pointed out in the beginning of this chapter, are an old mixture in the international relations of the Middle East. Whereas the consuming nations have guided the politics and economics of oil, and indeed, of the producing nations themselves, since the initiation of the oil industry, today the producing nations have wrested control of their resources and will use them in the determination of their own destinies.

❉ 11 ❉

TAREQ Y. ISMAEL

The Middle East: A Subordinate System in Global Politics

We tend to visualize the Middle East as a geographic, historic, and cultural unit. However, the area's role in international politics is generally viewed through the prism of Cold War politics and theories of bipolarity. Regional interaction has been examined primarily from the viewpoint of comparative politics as a manifestation of national political processes. Is the term "Middle East" simply a geographic designation for a group of states buffeted in international politics by the big powers? Or can we characterize the area as a political unit in international affairs? In systems theory we do in fact have an analytic tool to answer this question.

The concept of an international political system is a theoretical construct of international political behavior. To bring meaning and order to the vast array of information generated by the interaction of states, to identify regularities in behavior and to recognize deviations from regularity, we visualize international politics as an adaptive, self-regulating, and self-transforming system of action with characteristics of structure and process. Systems theorists often use the analogy of the human organism to render the concept of system less abstract. We may conceive of the human organism as a physiological system composed of subsystems—nervous system, digestive system, circulatory system, and so on—which themselves can be successively broken down into systems to focus with ever-increasing precision on details. We can pass from the gross view of the human organism to the micro-view of the cellular system without losing perspective. Our construct of an international political system is similar. The international system is the total view of all the action and interaction taking place at all levels—from the micro-national components of foreign policy processes to the supranational character of the United Nations. The concept of descending levels of systems keeps the relationships ordered. Systems theory requires much refinement, however, for the variables distinguishing and relating different levels of the system are not yet fully understood.

For our purposes we may consider that there are three arenas of political action—the globe, the region, and the nation-state—that correspond to three subsystems—in the global arena, the dominant system is seen in the confrontation of the most powerful of nations; in the region, the subordinate system is the total interaction of relations within that region; and in the nation-state, the internal system is the totality of relations of the organizations composing its domestic politics. Of these three subsystems, we know a great deal about the dominant and internal systems but little about subordinate systems and the linkages they provide between the nation-state and the global arena. In an article in the March 1970 issue of *American Political Science Review,* Michael Haas considers subordinate systems adequately defined as "a relatively self-contained network of political interactions" between members of a region of limited scope! However, since the subordinate system is ideally defined in terms of interaction, regionality alone is an insufficient indicator, for it neither defines the scope nor the nature of interaction. Because international transactions do correspond somewhat to regional divisions, it may seem natural to seek a subordinate system in the region bounded by the Mediterranean, the Sahara, the Black Sea, the Indian Ocean, or some less precise physical limits, just as we might seek one on the continent of North America. Yet geographic criteria do not define the subordinate system. Rather, we define it as a system of action which, according to Morton Kaplan in *System and Process in International Politics,* is "a set of variables so related, in contradistinction to its environment, that describable behavioral regularities characterize the internal relationships of the variables to each other and the external relationships of the set of individual variables to combinations of external variables."

In describing the Middle East as a subordinate system, we are seeking to identify consistent patterns of interaction that give a characteristic structure to the internal and external relations of the area. What variables describe the Middle East? Leonard Binder (who defined the Middle East as the area from Libya to Iran, fringed by Afghanistan, Pakistan, and the Maghrib), noted in *World Politics* X(1958) that common membership in the Ottoman Empire, which left traces of similar institutions, was descriptive of the Arab states and Turkey. He also noted the criteria of Islamic culture, Pan-Arabism, common language, and ease of communication as related to the systemic quality of the Middle East, although these criteria are not relevant for every state in the system equally. Do different criteria indicate different groupings of states?

Bruce M. Russett, in *International Regions and International System,* posited four variables, in addition to geographic proximity, for operationally defining "region": social and cultural homogeneity, similarity of political attitudes and behavior, political interdependence, and economic interdependence. He utilized factor analysis and related modes of data manipulation for each of his five criteria to allow high correlations on certain factors to form clusters of nations. On socio-cultural measures, all of the states previously designated by Binder—the area from Libya to Iran, fringed by Afghanistan, Pakistan, and the Maghrib—fell into a common region—Afro-Asia—with the exception of Israel. United Nations voting patterns did not reveal a very homogeneous grouping. Turkey and Iran voted with the Western community; Israel and Pakistan with the Latin American group; Afghanistan, Egypt, Syria, Algeria, Iraq, Tunisia, the Sudan, Morocco, and Yemen voted among the Afro-Asians; Lebanon, Jordan, Libya, and Kuwait formed a group called Conservative Arabs by Russett; and Saudi Arabia fell into no group at all. A more cohesive appearance results from the analysis of international organization membership data from 1962. Pakistan falls in Russett's Asian group; Turkey is West European by organizational membership, as indicated by its presence in NATO; Yemen and Afghanistan were unclassifiable. Syria, Egypt, Morocco, Libya, Lebanon, Tunisia, Iraq, the Sudan, Israel, Algeria, Jordan, Saudi Arabia, Kuwait, and Iran comprised a single group, although Israel and Egypt also ranked in the Western European groupings. Russett's analysis of trade-pattern data from 1963 also turned up an Arab category, although its members were not all Arab states, nor were all of the Arab states in the grouping. It was indicated that Lebanon, Saudi Arabia, Syria, Jordan, Kuwait, Iraq, the Sudan, Egypt, and Libya were closely related by trade. A definite relationship appeared when these states were placed on an index of geographic proximity. Pakistan, Afghanistan, the Sudan, and Yemen were marginal on this dimension, with Algeria, Tunisia, and Turkey also somewhat apart from the main group. In terms of proximity to Africa, Asia, and Europe, the other states mentioned by Binder are very similar.

Russett concluded that the Middle East is a distinct, if not highly integrated region. His results support Binder's estimate, although the boundaries of the region are still vague. The scope of any possible regional grouping which could be called the Middle East is limited to North Africa and Southwest Asia. A certain group of Eastern Arab states is well established as the core of the region.

Louis J. Cantori and Steven L. Spiegel, in *The International Politics of Regions: A Comparative Approach,* have advanced a framework for analysis of subordinate systems which incorporates and synthesizes many of the most useful ideas so far posited. They place the patterns of interaction which characterize subordinate systems in comparative perspective by going beyond the idea of regional cohesion to other pattern variables which structure the analysis of the features and regularities of regional international relations. These are the nature of communications, power relationships, and the structure of relations. Cantori and Spiegel further suggest that we employ the concepts of core, periphery, and intrusive sectors of the system, along with the pattern variables, in order to determine the membership of a system and its structure. These concepts may be summarized as follows: the core may be considered the political center of gravity and is generally marked by a high level of cohesion and intense interaction. The peripheral sector includes those states "which are alienated from the core sector in some degree by social, political, economic, or organizational factors, but which nevertheless play a role in the politics of the subordinate system." The intrusive sector is composed of external-power participation in the affairs of the subordinate system. States operating in the intrusive sector are normally members of other subordinate systems, while peripheral states are not, although they may be marginal participants in two systems.

Utilizing their four pattern variables, Cantori and Spiegel define the core of the Middle East subordinate system to include relations among the United Arab Republic, Yemen, Saudi Arabia, Kuwait, Iraq, Lebanon, the Sudan, Jordan, Syria, South Yemen, and the Persian Gulf states. Social and organizational cohesion, reflecting a common history and intense diplomatic activity, provide the criteria for the delineation of the core. (It is largely on grounds of social difference that Israel is excluded from the core). Although the North African Arab states share many of the elements constituting social cohesion, the pattern is more diffuse—a result of distinctive experiences during the colonial period and the struggle for independence—and these states only nominally participate in the diplomatic relations of the core. In fact, Cantori and Spiegel consider them a separate subordinate system. The Maghrib has at most a tenuous place in the Middle Eastern periphery.

In terms of real or potential complementarity of economic resources, one measure of economic cohesion, Cantori and Spiegel draw no conclusions for the Middle East. But they did find a definite relationship when trade, measured in import-export totals, was examined. Little political cohesion could be demonstrated for the Middle East by the criterion of similarity of regime. The states in the Middle East are divisible into three categories: mobilization systems, military oligarchies, and modernizing autocracies, while Europe, for example, is dominated by reconciliation systems. Organizational cohesion—which is possibly a promoter of regional consciousness—is expressed through the Arab League, the Council of Arab Economic Unity (CAEU), and the Arab Common Market (ACM). While all three organizations are linguistically exclusive, Cantori and Spiegel think it significant that only the Arab League is a trans-core grouping, while the CAEU and the ACM are restricted to members of the core. The cohesive elements in the Middle East core sector may be ranked in the following order of strength: social, economic, organizational, and political.

Certain critical comments are in order on the schema of Cantori and Spiegel: their choice of indicators may not be particularly appropriate to the Middle East. For example, their measure of political cohesion relies upon similarity of internal structure, a view perhaps conditioned by the importance of ideology in the postwar relations of the United States and the USSR. This measure should be balanced with some attention to the foreign-policy goals of the regimes in the area. The criteria of organizational unity equate the ACM and CAEU and the Arab League, and use the result as one means of distinguishing the core from the periphery. In fact, the former two organizations are mere paper agencies and reflect, if anything, the lack of cohesion in the system.

Communication in the Middle East core reinforces social cohesion. Radio, television, and printed media, together with interchange among the elite for education, tend to reinforce regional consciousness and promote political interaction. This is not to say that increasing communication necessarily or always indicates increasingly friendly relations between two states. The core is particularly notable for the profound disjuncture of power between the UAR and the remaining states in the sector. As measured by its capacity (in terms of population, GNP, consumption of energy, and total armed forces), Egypt is the most powerful nation in the core.

Both Russett and Cantori and Spiegel were concerned with developing criteria broad enough to be generally applicable. While the methods of Cantori and Spiegel certainly provide useful criteria for the definition and description of subordinate systems in general terms, they require modification in dealing extensively with specific areas. Russett's criteria, although they do not go far enough into political interaction for our purposes, are more rigorously defined and provide reliable corroboration where applicable. We see that Binder's conclusions, based upon his intimate knowledge of the Middle East and presented in 1958, are largely substantiated by the more theoretical approach. Thus, in Binder's article, in the system of Cantori and Spiegel, and in at least three of Russett's categories appear Iraq, Jordan, Saudi Arabia, Yemen, the United Arab Republic, the Sudan, Lebanon, Kuwait, the Persian Gulf Shiekhdoms, Syria, Turkey, Iran, and Israel. The Maghrib and Afghanistan are at best tenuously associated. Libya, on the other hand, is tending to form closer relations with members of the system on a number of political and organizational dimensions.

We have established the separate identity of the Middle East, but we must place it in the context of international politics as a whole. At a later point, we will discuss the linkages and the influences between the system and extra-systemic powers; first, we shall clarify the concept of subordinate system as it relates to global politics. Binder's term "subordinate international system" appears to have two meanings: first, that the system is of lesser scope than the total global system; and, second, that less power resides there than in the dominant subsystem of the globe—the U.S.–USSR subsystem. This is not to say, and Binder makes this very clear, that the subsystem is dominated by the bipolar global system. Relations within the subordinate system are not wholly a product of great-power relations, although influence flows more readily from the great powers into the Middle East than in the opposite direction.

The position of the Middle East in the global system is indicated by the power ranking of its members, which will be examined in more detail with reference to intra-systemic relations. Cantori and Spiegel have assessed state power on a composite measure of material and motivational indices and have constructed a seven-level scale descending from primary powers (U.S., USSR), to colonies. The three peripheral states of the Middle Eastern system (Turkey, Iran, and Israel) are minor powers, that is, powers of the fourth rank. Of core states, only the UAR ranks as a minor power, while seven states fall in the category of regional states and two are micro-states—the fifth and sixth ranks, respectively. (Jordan would move downward from regional to micro-state status if the loss of the West Bank were to prove permanent). By way of comparison, we may note that there are two secondary powers in the West European core, along with three middle powers and one micro-state. Cantori and Spiegel rank the Middle East below both West Europe and Latin America in aggregate power.

This power ranking indicates something of the ability of the region to resist outside penetration, but this ability is diminished by the divisions within the system. The "intrusive system" is a significant element in regional politics, but it is not the controlling factor. Disparities of power do not constitute the full measure of influence, as the relations of the U.S. with Israel on the one hand, and with Egypt on the other, illustrate. This situation has remained more or less constant since the beginnings of Middle Eastern resurgence (about 1940) coincided with the decline of Western power, and the development of regional autonomy resulted. Despite the growing influence of the Soviet Union in the area, the basic autonomy of the system, and thus its continued existence as a system, does not seem to be threatened by this trend.

THE DISTRIBUTION OF POWER

The distribution of power in the Middle East, considered on a state-by-state basis, has been relatively stable since World War II. The stability in the distribution of power can be seen in the balance that has existed among Arab countries of the region, as well as between Arab countries and non-Arab countries in the region. For instance, since its establishment in 1948, Israel has maintained a continuous superiority of power in relation to the combined powers of neighboring Arab countries. Also, among Arab countries, Egypt has continued to rank as the first Arab power, with Iraq and Syria trailing behind it. Finally, Turkey and Iran, though they have not been locked in battle with each other or with other regional countries since the Second World War, have maintained relatively large military establishments and strong alliances that qualify them to rank as first-rate regional powers. But this stability is contradicted by the frequent shifts which have taken place in coalitions and the objects toward which they are directed, sources of power, and the power needs of the various members of the system. In addition, although the material factors of power have remained fairly stable in their distribution among the states, the motivational factors have varied due to the internal instability of several states in the system. In the first place, new governments are usually more cautious than material power necessitates, and, secondly, domestic upheavals sometimes result in major shifts in the goals of the state in the system and in its alliance partners.

In relation to individual states, the power distribution, as indicated above, varies widely from what Cantori and Spiegel call minor powers to the micro-states. The four most powerful states in the region, according to their findings, are Iran, Turkey, Israel, and the UAR, from East to West. They class Saudi Arabia, Kuwait, Iraq, Lebanon, the Sudan, Jordan, and Syria as regional states, and Yemen and South Yemen as micro-states. Binder considered the most powerful states of the region to be Turkey, Israel, Egypt, Iran, Iraq, Syria, and Jordan, in that order, with Egypt and Iran on a basis of approximate equality. He considered that most of the other countries in the system were on a plane with Syria and Iraq, or somewhat less powerful. The ordering among the states in both sectors, according to Cantori and Spiegel, by size of military establishment, is Turkey (482,000), Iran (180,000), the UAR (166,000), Iraq (82,000), Israel (71,000), Syria (60,500), Saudi Arabia (36,000), Jordan (31,800), Yemen (23,000), the Sudan (18,400), and Lebanon (10,800). Figures for Kuwait and South Yemen were not available. Although other factors, including those used by Cantori and Spiegel, modify the ranking gained from these figures, the disjunctures are of some importance: one would have to place Turkey in a class by itself; Iran with the UAR; Iraq, Israel, and Syria together; and break again after either Jordan or Yemen. Israel's equipment, technology, and militia system—as well as the evidence of her 1967 victory—would place her in a higher class than size of standing forces would indicate. Still, despite the foreign aid and military clashes which have taken place since 1957, it is notable that the order of states in power possession has remained stable throughout this period.

This apparent stability is belied by the shifting alliance structure of the area. There have been numerous alliances and blocs formed and dissolved in the Middle Eastern system. At any one time, the capabilities of at least some states are theoretically open to collective use. Although these alliances have changed frequently, and many of them never came into effect, certain features frequently appear. These include anti-Israeli alliances appearing in times of tension, blocs constructed to counter a growth in the power of a single state, a tendency for alliances to form among states of similar ideological character, and the tendency for either Egypt or Iraq to serve as the focus of alliances.

The balance of power between Israel and the neighboring Arab states has been constantly in favor of the former. Arab-Israeli relations, however, are not posited upon the continuation of a tense and unstable balance, but upon the resolution of conflict in favor of one party. The Israelis desire an area in which they can complete the realization of their doctrinal objectives. Permanent quasi-war may be a useful mechanism for obtaining aid and integrating a multinational society, but the strain on the economic, social, and political structure of the state is recognized to be intolerable in the long run. On the other hand, the Arabs desire the removal of the threat of Israeli expansion, which may be achieved in a number of ways, ranging from voluntary de-Zionization to military defeat. Again, the developing Arab countries find the strain of military preparedness difficult to sustain in light of the economic and political needs of their people. In this situation, most of the Arab states take advantage of periods of lowered tension to attend to other matters, but in periods of increased likelihood of war, the focus of policy shifts to Israel, and some coordination of military policy can be found to take place. Thus, prior to the war of 1967, a defense coordination system was formed among Egypt, Jordan, and Syria. It should be noted that this organization broke down as soon as the war was over.

Among the Arab states there is a tendency to restrict the ability of any state to develop hegemonial power. After the union with Syria yielded a major increase in Egyptian power, the other states of the region tended to follow parallel policies of opposition, thus substantially isolating the new UAR in the area. Even the revolution in Iraq, which brought to power a regime much more compatible with Nasser's than the monarchy, did not create a reversal in this trend, as General Kassim moved to secure a place as an independent center of power. When, in 1961, the British announced the imminent end on the protectorate in Kuwait, Iraq announced its intention to annex the small, oil-rich state. In reaction, other Arab states, both conservative and radical, joined in creating a military force which garrisoned Kuwait to forestall the Iraqi program.

The Arab Cold War thesis, while not denying a polarization along other lines as well, states that the conservative states (e.g., Saudi Arabia, Libya until 1969, and Jordan) and the reforming or radical states (e.g., Egypt and Syria) have few interests in common and many opposing interests, especially given the influence events in one Arab country can have upon events in another. Although one could find a bipolar system developing out of this division, the possibility of divisions in each camp (for example, Saudi-Hashemite or Egyptian-Iraqi) is great enough that a multipolar system is perhaps more likely. The balance of power thus tends to follow ideological lines.

Another discontinuity in the power distribution in the Middle East is the tendency of blocs to form around Egypt and Iraq, but seldom to include both states. There is a definite historical basis for a rivalry between Egypt and Iraq for power in the region, and Robert MacDonald, in *The League of Arab States,* has persuasively argued its existence as a major factor in the creation of blocs within the Arab world. Possibly for reasons of historical rivalry, possibly as a consequence of the anti-hegemonial bias of the system, and possibly as a consequence of a variety of historical accidents, it has seemed to be difficult to secure cooperation between Egypt and Iraq, and the two states have seldom joined in a common bloc. The rivalry of Farouk and Nuri al-Said in the 1940s, and of Nuri and Nasser in the fifties, and then of Nasser and Kassim in the early sixties, seem to indicate that changes of regime do not prevent the persistence of the rivalry, and the failure of union negotiations in 1963 and 1964 provides further evidence that even when the leaders of both states desire an alliance, matters of national interest seem to prevent close cooperation.

The shifts and changes along these cleavages are facilitated by the existence of a large number of neutral states. That is, most of the time there are only a few states closely associated with any one pole of a conflict. This may mean a shifting of alignments at short intervals, but the resultant appearance of instability may be illusory, because no state is allowed to develop the kind of secure hegemony that could encourage aggression, and unbalanced situations are quickly brought into equilibrium. In terms of polarity, the system may be termed either a very loose bipolar system, or a loose multipolar system.

In the matter of the distribution of power, two other subject areas should be mentioned. First, recent talks of a confederation among the UAR, Libya, and Syria or Libya and Tunisia could lead to a new configuration of power altogether. The Egyptian power base is hindered in its conversion into substantial usable power by the poor ratio of land to people, but is advanced by the number of skilled and highly trained people available in Egypt and Syria. The capital available in Libya, together with the population and skill pool of Egypt and Syria, could form a power base greater by far than the sum of the power of the three states as presently organized. Thus we must recognize the potential here for basic change in the system.

We must also have regard to the role of Iran and Turkey in the power configurations of the system. Clearly, the system is dominated by Arab politics, but Iran is becoming more engaged in Arab politics than at any time in recent memory. Iran's efforts to make common cause with Persian Gulf oil producers in the winter of 1970–71 are a reflection of the increasing interest of Iran in taking advantage of British withdrawal from Arabian Gulf states. Considering Iran's long record of conflict with Iraq over various boundary questions, this increasing interest could heighten the possibility of clashes in the area. On the other hand, Iran recently settled amicably a boundary dispute over the maritime boundary of the sea-bed oil exploration areas in the Gulf with Saudi Arabia. The power position of Iran makes its participation in alliances and alignments within the system likely to greatly modify the power configurations in the area.

How significant have these shifts and changes in alliances and alignments been? As noted they are limited in various ways, and many of them have been transitory; on the other hand, they have involved the fall of governments, the risk of world war, and many headlines. It is something of an important question to set some sort of limit to the importance of these variations in the political behavior of the members of the system. At one extreme would be the conversion of the Middle East into a new system, but this kind of event is difficult to establish beyond question, and the standards of observers vary widely. We shall here briefly examine the experience of the Middle East in light of one such set of standards.

In the March 1970 issue of the *American Political Science Review* Michael Haas has established certain rules of criteria for determining the transformation of a system. Since some of his rules depend upon the membership of a major power in the system, we can only utilize those which appear appropriate for the Middle Eastern system. On the other hand some of his rules require a change in a major power to qualify a change as transforming only because he presumes the presence of another great power in the system; thus, the absence of major powers in the Middle East allows for a more flexible situation. Adapting Haas, we may postulate the beginning of a new system whenever there is a change in either the polarity of the system or the power distribution. For example, the formation of the Baghdad Pact in 1954–55 brought at least a formal decline in the number of neutral states in the area and associated a number of states in a single power center. By Haas's criteria this was a transformation of the system. In a second case, in 1961, the Iraqi policy toward Kuwait mentioned above created a tight bipolar system with Iraq as one pole and the other Arab states at the other (Israel and Turkey did not participate). Again this transformed the system by Haas's criteria.

However, by the criteria set forth by A. L. Burns in *Of Powers and their Politics,* the Middle East has not been transformed from one kind of system to another since World War II, or before. The point of disagreement seems to lie in Burns's concentration upon global and long-term political action, and Haas's focus upon small regional systems in limited periods of time. More specifically, in the long view taken by Burns it is less reasonable to assert that a continual series of transformations has taken place than that "variations in the structures and processes within a system may usefully be interpreted as constructive or positive alternative efforts by members of a system to regulate or cope with stress flowing from environmental as well as internal sources." As an alternative to viewing the system as frequently changing to other varieties of system, and then returning to its previous form, we may consider these changes as the operation of a system which reacts flexibly to changing circumstances and persists through change. Perhaps this distinction is of less than great importance, but it seems that for the analysis of a particular region over continuous time periods, it is more practical to reserve the concept of transformation for truly cataclysmic changes.

The Middle Eastern subordinate political system appears, therefore, to have certain features which are constant enough to allow of definition: its membership, its boundaries, the distribution of power within the system, the power position of the system vis-à-vis the global system, and, by a convention of convenience, a single, flexible set of operating rules.

The Rules of Systemic Interaction

As it appears that we may conveniently regard the system as persistent since 1945 without a transforming change, it should be possible to discover a set of interaction rules which may serve as a shorthand means of describing the system. It may be that such a set of rules already exists, corresponding to one of the various typical systems devised by earlier writers; on the other hand, it may be necessary for us to devise a set of rules, more or less approximating one of the earlier systems, in order to maintain a degree of correspondence to the Middle Eastern reality sufficient for our purposes. Before proceeding, the term "rule" should be elucidated. We do not mean thereby a regulation enforceable by a superior force, or a "natural law," or international legal restrictions on the behavior of states. We mean two things: first, a definition of a type of behavior characteristic of a system such that variance from this behavior is not possible within the analytic system; second, descriptions of normal behavior such that deviance from the norm is likely to induce a profound change in the empirical system.

Establishing such a set of rules is easiest in a system with a highly developed set of consciously adopted rules, a long history of fairly stable interaction, and a set of intellectual constructs of international politics common to the statesmen and the analysts. Western Europe is the prime example of this sort of system. Rules may be found there because states have attempted to establish and follow explicit rules; in the Middle East we have a somewhat different situation. Therefore, before attempting to describe the system in terms of rules and regularities, we should discuss some of the obstacles to doing so.

First, the system is not highly integrated, so that members are not continuously active over time, but participate in an intermittent fashion.

The difficulty thus created is analogous to the problems created for the International Court of Justice by its lack of judicial business as compared with the ordinary municipal court: in a small sample of events, regularities are difficult to discover.

Another difficulty arises from the lack of a conscious commitment of the members of the system to a clear set of rules. In part, this difficulty arises from the recent origin of many states in their present form; regular patterns of behavior have simply not been worked out yet. Another source of this lack of commitment to a set of rules is the failure of existing rules—boundaries, jurisdictions, the rules for the conduct of diplomatic relations—to command respect as legitimate, due to their origin in a colonial system believed to be illegitimate. Associated with this problem is that created by the existence of a strong movement toward pan-Arabism; the present states lack legitimacy because they are believed to lack permanence.

Also, rules often appear to be specific to national roles; that is, a given rule may not apply equally to all states. For example, the rule, to be enunciated fully later, that coalitions depend for their formation and strength upon the ideological similarity of the states involved does not seem to apply with as great regularity to the very small states of the system. Ideological considerations seem to be of less importance in coalition formation for Kuwait and Yemen than for the UAR and Syria.

The failure of some states to develop consistent foreign policies, due, at least in part, to their domestic instability, also inhibits rule formation. A major factor in the creation of a system of rules in Western Europe was the consistent foreign policy of Britain in the nineteenth century. In the Middle East, only Turkey can be said to have held to a consistent foreign policy for the period since World War II. Domestic instability also inhibits rule formation through the creation of law by treaty and undermines the stability of alliances—both elements of the regularization of European politics.

A further feature of the Middle Eastern system which militates against rule formation is the position of Israel. Rules which apply among the Arab states, or between the Arab states and Turkey or Iran, do not apply as between the Arab states and Israel. Only in the case of Israel has an attempt been made through direct armed action to change the form of government of a regional state. In the Arab-Israeli conflict, there has been a commitment by the antagonists to change each others' form of government through armed action. While this objective is publicly avowed by the Arab side, it is equally but more subtly held by Israel. The May 1967, September 1970, and April 1973 Israeli official statements threatening armed intervention and the modification of governments in Syria, Jordan, and Lebanon, respectively, are illustrative. The major difference in Arab-Israeli, as opposed to Arab-Arab relations, is the attitude toward the influence of outside powers; because the conflict is of overriding importance, the possibility of excessive outside influence is regarded of lesser importance.

In addition to warnings about the perils of rule-making, we should also have some standards by which to judge the rules we may construct. First, these are neither to be natural laws, in the sense of good or just behavior, or in the Hobbesian sense of rational conduct, nor absolute behavioral laws according to which we may always expect men and states to act. These are rules in the sense of regularities within a limited framework; principles with which the behavior of the actors may be expected to coincide, unless the system changes. We should note that changes in the system may be induced from outside, thus causing changes in the rules, or that members, by contravening the rules, may themselves change the system. We may also find transformation rules, that is, rules which define the type of system which may be expected to result from a particular set of changes in other rules. The rules are a form of shorthand; a blueprint, as it were, which makes it possible for us to more easily conceptualize the working of the system.*

First, we require a rule which defines the system as system—a rule on boundaries which may be related to empirical tests. We may express such a rule in communications terms as follows: As a system, the Middle East has relatively greater communications internally than externally. Because of this, communications into the system may be readily viewed as restricted to channels, while communications within the system form such a multiplicity of channels as to be more easily viewed as a seamless process.

The second rule defines the primary motive of states in the system: actors will attempt to increase capabilities. On the one hand, this rule gives us a guide to action, an analogy to empirically observable behavior. We should note, however, that any system in which actors no longer seek to increase capabilities will be radically modified. The third rule should note a major limitation on this principle: actors will prefer non-

* Morton Kaplan has created a number of analytic systems, at least some of which he feels to be analogous to empirical systems. Each of these analytic systems has a set of rules, internally consistent and exhaustive, which create the sort of blueprint we are looking for here. However, none of Kaplan's systems is sufficiently analogous to the Middle Eastern system to be utilized here in its entirety. His constructs have, however, been very useful in stimulating the present author's thinking about regularities in the Middle Eastern system, and the similarity of some of the rules will be evident to anyone familiar with Kaplan's work.

military means to military means of increasing capabilities. (This does not mean that war will be avoided at all cost).

It seems appropriate to introduce the notion of risk, of rational calculation, into the model, as actors neither blindly pursue power nor reject every enterprise with any risk of war. The fourth rule is that present capabilities will not be sacrificed to potential gains of capabilities where probabilities of success are low or uncertainty is high. This rule may be obviated if the actor perceives that there is no choice, and yet this falls within the rule, for the removal of all choice indicates that the actor suffers no uncertainty.

Coalition formation seems to be adequately subsumed under the second rule, but some limits upon that strategy should also be set forth. Coalitions depend for their formation and strength upon the degree of ideological compatibility of the states involved. This fifth rule is obviously situational; it is easier for similar than for unlike states to form a coalition, and there is less chance of coalitions enduring between or among unlike than among like states. Another, sixth, rule concerning coalition formation is that actors will tend to oppose an attempt by a single actor or a coalition to establish a dominant position. Thus, there is a limitation on coalition size and a tendency for counter-coalitions to form.

As a means to increase capabilities, actors will support supranational organization, but support will lessen if one state tends to dominate the organization, and the organization will be weakened if the states are unlike ideologically. Thus, the seventh rule is limited by the fifth and sixth. The eighth rule does not concern the internal working of the system, but rather its linkages to outside actors, and we will devote a separate section to it.

EXTERNAL LINKAGES

The linkages of the Middle Eastern system to the remainder of the global system are seen here as a consequence of the politics of the Middle East and of world politics, rather than a product of the latter alone. While the nuclear capabilities of the U.S. and the USSR make it possible for them to influence the system irrespective of the wishes of its members, in practice a coincidence or conjunction of circumstances external and internal to the system is required for that influence to be durable and effective. The consequences of influence depend upon the system influenced as well as upon the nature of the influence itself.

First, external involvement in Middle Eastern affairs is typically limited to certain spheres of activity—chiefly economic and military. Economic development and military preparedness are legitimate values, although among the Arab states military force is justified in terms of anti-imperialism (e.g., anti-Israel), even though force is in fact used among the Arab states, as in the case of Yemen. All military forces are "defensive" in the justificatory rhetoric. Obviously, where the need is greatest, the greatest involvement is permitted. Thus, in the period after the June 1967 War, Soviet influence in Egypt reached a peak. The danger for the autonomy of the system is that in an extended period of severe crisis, external influence might become pervasive and permanent.

Second, external connections are channeled. Diplomatic personnel are permitted, their activities constrained by the formulae of international law and practice, as are executives of oil companies, who are limited by the nature of their purposes, and trade and military missions, who are also performing well-defined functions of narrow scope. Tourists have perhaps the broadest scope of contact (students are placed in a contact situation in which influence flows primarily from host country to student, and again, students are constrained in their activities), but tourists are normally resident for only short periods of time, and their contacts with a nation are notoriously shallow. Access to mass media is normally limited, although there are a few exceptions (Voice of America, Radio Moscow), and foreign citizens are generally prevented from participation in the broad social life of a Middle Eastern country. Communications which originate outside the Middle East are thus channeled and cannot pervade the atmosphere.

Finally, external parties deal with the system through the official state structure of the members. Again, we must stress, the system is composed of the interactions of members, and with very few exceptions these members are states, and the interactions at any one time are directed by elites undivided in any one state. Thus, the influence of outside powers is limited. For example, the Soviet Union has had more influence in Egypt than in Jordan, but, even if Soviet influence had been absent, Egyptian policy was likely to be more favorable to Soviet interests than was Jordanian policy. The Egyptian actions which may be attributed to Soviet influence are quite limited.

CONCLUSION

The Middle East is sometimes pictured as a highly unstable group of nations, continually buffeted by the struggles of the great powers and bereft of continuity and identity. Yet, we have shown, the Middle East has identifiable boundaries and a definite membership that has remained essentially consistent over a considerable period of time. The power of the Middle East with regard to the global system has not varied since World War II, and the power distribution within the Middle East has also been quite stable. It is further possible to find sufficient stability in the Middle Eastern system to define an analogous analytic system with definite rules. The most evident form of instability in the area is the constantly changing configuration of coalitions and alliances, and yet these shifts are reactions to internal and external pressures and appear to increase the stability of the system over the long run. The system possesses enough continuity that we are led to doubt that external influences determine the events within it, and it appears that such influences are indeed channeled and limited. The Middle East is a subordinate system—it is not the focus of international politics, nor is it the power center of the globe—but it is an autonomous system, with its own internal mechanisms, and its own characteristic features. These characteristic features are conditioned by domestic influences on foreign policy to link the foreign policies of the individual states into a systematic pattern of international behavior.

Notes to the Chapters

2—BRITAIN AND THE MIDDLE EAST

1. A. P. Thornton, *The Imperial Idea and Its Enemies: A Study in British Power* (Garden City, N.Y.: Doubleday, 1959), p. 400. The reference is to Balfour's statement that he had not much love for wooden guns.

2. Lord Salisbury to Edward Malet, October 16, 1879, Great Britain, Public Record Office, F.O. 78/2297, in J. C. Hurewitz, *Diplomacy in the Near and Middle East: A Documentary Record* (Princeton, N.J.: Van Nostrand, 1956), 1:191–94.

3. MacDonald to Allenby, October 7, 1924, *Parliamentary Papers, 1924,* Egypt No. 1, Cmd. 2269, in ibid., 2:128–31.

4. Stephen Hemsley Longrigg, *Oil in the Middle East: Its Discovery and Development* (London: Oxford University Press, 1954), p. 277.

5. Great Britain, *Parliamentary Papers, 1931,* Treaty Series No. 15, Cd. 3797.

6. British and Foreign State Papers, 109:436–39, in Hurewitz, *Diplomacy,* 2:4–7.

7. For information on the foundation of Hashemite rule in Transjordan, see Arnold J. Toynbee, *Survey of International Affairs, 1925* (London: Oxford University Press, 1926), and *Supplement, 1925;* Hurewitz, *Diplomacy,* 2; and Howard M. Sachar, *The Emergence of the Middle East, 1914–1924* (New York: Knopf, 1969). Article 25 of the Mandate for Palestine read: "In the territories lying between the Jordan and the eastern boundary of Palestine as ultimately determined, the Mandatory shall be entitled, with the consent of the Council of the League of Nations, to postpone or withhold application of existing local conditions, and to make such provision for the administration of the territories as he may consider suitable to those conditions."

8. Mandate for Palestine, Article 2, Cd. 1785 of 1922, in Arnold J. Toynbee, *Survey of International Affairs, 1930* (London: Oxford University Press, 1931), pp. 228–29. Balfour hoped the Jews would found a Jewish state. See Carroll Quigley, "Lord Balfour's Personal Position on the Balfour Declaration," *Middle East Journal,* Summer 1968.

9. Great Britain, *Parliamentary Papers,* Cd. 1700 of 1922, 3692 of 1930, 6019 of 1939. MacDonald's letter to Weizmann is in Walter Z. Laqueur, ed., *The Israel-Arab Reader: A Documentary History of the Middle East Conflict* (New York: Bantam, 1970), pp. 50–56.

10. Lloyd George favored the creation of a Jewish state in Palestine: "There could be no doubt," he wrote of the Balfour Declaration, "as to what the Cabinet then had in their minds. It was not their idea that a Jewish State should be set up immediately by the Peace Treaty without reference to the wishes of the majority of the inhabitants. On the other hand, it was contemplated that when the time arrived for according representative institutions to Palestine, if the Jews had meanwhile responded to the opportunity afforded them by the idea of a National Home and had become a majority of the inhabitants, then Palestine would thus

become a Jewish Commonwealth. The notion that Jewish immigration would have to be artificially restricted in order to ensure that the Jews should be a permanent minority never entered into the heads of anyone engaged in framing the policy. That would have been regarded as unjust and as a fraud on the people to whom we were appealing [for support in World War I]." Lloyd George, *Memoirs of the Peace Conference* (New Haven, Conn.: Yale University Press, 1939), 2:736–37.

11. Winston S. Churchill, *The Second World War*, Vol. II, *Their Finest Hour* (New York: Bantam, 1962), pp. 368, 382. Churchill commented on the gravity of the decision: "It is odd that while at the time everyone concerned was quite calm and cheerful, writing about it afterwards makes one shiver" (p. 358).

12. George Kirk, *Survey of International Affairs, 1939–1946: The Middle East in the War* (London: Oxford University Press, 1952), pp. 21–22. For the attitude of the Free French government in exile, see Charles de Gaulle, *War Memoirs*, 3 vols. (New York: Simon and Schuster, 1967).

13. Dean Acheson, *Present at the Creation: My Years in the State Department* (New York: Norton, 1969), p. 171. The British effort included the establishment of an Anglo-American Committee of Inquiry and intensive negotiations with the United States. Both are discussed in Harry S. Truman, *Memoirs* (Garden City, N.Y.: Doubleday, 1955), 2:167ff, and Acheson, *Present at the Creation*, pp. 171ff.

14. Truman, *Memoirs*, 2:184. Truman believed his investigator, Earl G. Harrison, for example, who assured him that the White Paper of 1939 could be changed so as to increase Jewish immigration "without too serious obligations." As the British well knew, the White Paper represented in 1945 as in 1939 the maximum level of Jewish immigration allowable without precipitating civil war. See ibid., pp. 163–65.

15. Ibid., p. 163.

16. On February 7, the British offered to continue their role for five years. Jewish immigration would be raised to four thousand a month for two years, and authorities in the Arab and Jewish areas would be granted significant powers, including control over land transfers in their areas. After four years an elected constituent assembly would be asked to establish an independent state. If this failed, the UN Trusteeship Council would advise on future procedure. Both sides rejected the offer. Kirk, *Survey of International Affairs*, pp. 236–37.

17. Acheson, *Present at the Creation*, p. 396. Acheson added: "Within a month the United States was locked in the desperate Korean battle; in a few months more all three governments were both deeply concerned and divided over the defense of Europe. . . . In the autumn of 1956, when one of the states mentioned in the Declaration of May, 1950, did violate frontier and armistice lines, the three governments were even more deeply divided. . . . Again, when two years later Lebanon complained ineffectively to the United Nations for protection against threats of foreign (Egyptian) intervention and then to the United States, American forces landed alone in July, 1958. The Tripartite Declaration of May, 1950, was dead, if it had ever lived."

18. The Conservatives also tried to involve the United States in saving the British position in Egypt. See Acheson's account of Churchill's request before a joint session of Congress and the refusal of the American government to send troops in *Present at the Creation*, p. 565. Acheson defined American "concerns" in the region as: "Egyptian aspirations, the security of the Suez Canal, the British position in the Middle East, and the need for stability where the old order was

passing and new xenophobic ferment, fanned from Moscow, grew daily" (p. 566). The Truman administration tried through diplomacy to "damp down" the Anglo-Egyptian crisis, but they would send no troops. They acted as mediators trying to bring the disputants together, before and after the July coup d'état. The British were stubborn and the Egyptians tried to use an American lever on the British. The Americans wanted a settlement and saw no reason for the British not to begin withdrawal and to concede Egyptian sovereignty over the Sudan. The Sudan touched East Africa and the Red Sea, and the British insisted the Sudanese must be free to choose their own future and, implicitly, an independence from Egypt that would serve British imperial interests. In particular, they were reluctant to abandon Suez when no other base seemed to exist. See Anthony Eden, *Full Circle* (Boston: Houghton Mifflin, 1960), p. 259.

19. "Base" hardly conveys the size of the British Training Area on the Suez Canal with three principal air bases, general headquarters, and stores and munitions for 80,000 men. A rough calculation based on the map in Peter Calvocoressi, *Survey of International Affairs, 1951* (London: Oxford University Press, 1954), p. 283, shows the "base" to have covered 3,000 square miles, its western edge reaching to less than thirty miles from Cairo.

20. Acheson, *Present at the Creation*, pp. 562, 564.

21. Dulles mentioned a security pact for the Northern Tier on June 1, 1953. See Hurewitz, *Documents*, 2:342. Eden stated unequivocally in *Full Circle* that the United States "played a leading part to inspire the project" (p. 375). This is corroborated by Eisenhower's statement in his memoirs that "the British, with our support and encouragement, were in the process of completing negotiations for what came to be known as the Baghdad Pact. . . . I hoped that this arrangement might quickly be approved by all the nations involved," *The White House Years: Waging Peace, 1956–1961* (Garden City, N.Y.: Doubleday, 1965), p. 26. When the pact proved highly unpopular in the Arab world, the United States officially treated the arrangement coolly, sending observers and money but abstaining from membership. At least one observer, Kenneth Love, was fooled by the official chill. Love observed, for example, that "Dulles was taken as much by surprise as Nasser was," in *Suez: The Twice-Fought War* (New York: McGraw-Hill, 1969), p. 199.

22. An agreement was signed on October 29, 1952, between the Egyptian government and delegations from the northern Sudanese parties. The agreement surpassed the recommendations in the Sudanese government's draft statute for self-government in every important area, including extent of direct elections, reduction of safeguards for the non-Moslem south, limitation of the discretionary powers of the governor-general, and rapidity of progress toward full sovereignty. Kirk, in Peter Calvocoressi, *Survey of International Affairs, 1952* (London: Oxford University Press, 1955), pp. 205–207, 220–27.

23. *Full Circle*, p. 271. The opening words of Eden's rejection of the Egyptian denunciation are interesting in light of Eden's subsequent response to nationalization of the Suez Canal: "The Anglo-Egyptian Treaty of friendship and alliance of 1936 contains no provision for unilateral denunciation at any time. If the principle were accepted that one party to such a treaty were entitled to denounce that treaty unilaterally, no reliance could be placed on any international agreement, and the whole basis and structure of international relations would cease to exist," ibid., p. 251.

24. Ibid., pp. 270, 288–89. In 1955, nearly 15,000 ships passed through the

Suez Canal. Two-thirds carried oil, three-quarters belonged to NATO countries, one-third belonged to Britain. Wilfred Knapp, *A History of War and Peace, 1939–1965* (London: Oxford University Press, 1967), p. 404.

25. Eden, *Full Circle*, p. 245.

26. Ibid., pp. 393–94.

27. *United States Interests in the Middle East* (Washington, D.C.: American Enterprise Institute, 1968), p. 66. The stoppage of exploration has made Iraq the only major oil producer not to achieve a significant increase in production, while the dispute with the IPC prevented the opening of revenue negotiations and caused Iraq a relative loss in per-barrel revenue.

28. Acheson, *Present at the Creation*, p. 505.

29. *World Trade Annual, 1968*, Statistical Office of the United Nations (New York: Walker, 1969), pp. 11–17.

30. James B. Akins, "The Oil Crisis: This Time the Wolf is Here," *Foreign Affairs*, April 1973: 463. *The Middle East and North Africa*, 15th ed. (London: Europa Publications, 1968), pp. 38–48. In 1968, total production for the Middle East was 575 million tons; for the USA, 512 million tons; for Soviet and Eastern Europe, 337 million tons.

31. See Gaitskell's speech in the Commons, August 2, 1956, quoted in Hugh Thomas, *Suez* (New York: Harper and Row, 1966), pp. 179–80. See also Anthony Nutting's account of the warm reception given by the Conservative Party Conference in Llandudno on October 11, to a belligerent speech he delivered on behalf of Lord Salisbury. The speech threatened Nasser with the use of force if negotiations at the UN failed to satisfy Britain's demands. *No End of a Lesson*, p. 87.

32. *Full Circle*, p. 478.

33. Text is in ibid., p. 562. Nutting, at least, believed Eden purposely disregarded the progress represented by the six principles in order to justify the decision to use force against Egypt. Eden said of the principles: "They just flapped in the air" (p. 563). Love agreed, citing one of Eden's "senior cabinet colleagues": "Eden regarded this as too near a solution for comfort; he was determined on war from the beginning," *Suez*, p. 466.

34. Nutting believed the dismissal was a result of friction between a young king and his older, experienced, British subordinate. Glubb himself told of the friction between them in his *A Soldier with the Arabs* (London: Hodder and Stoughton, 1957), pp. 366–67, 421–22.

35. The Cabinet strongly favored the use of force against Nasser, but may not have explicitly approved the plan for cooperation with Israel. Some members of the Cabinet may not have wanted to be told too much. See Macmillan, the *Times* (London), November 2, 1970.

36. For an example of the Labor Party's intention in 1964 to withdraw from Aden and Singapore, see P. C. Gordon Walker, "The Labor Party's Defense and Foreign Policy," *Foreign Affairs*, April 1964, p. 396. For a helpful discussion of Britain's economic plight during the middle and late 1960s, when the decisions to withdraw altogether from the Middle East were made, see Robert V. Roosa, "Where Is Britain Heading?" *Foreign Affairs*, April 1968:503–18. As Roosa made clear: "Britain's root problem is that she has been attempting for too long to do more than her own capabilities, as currently mobilized and motivated, could support or afford." The private sector was actually in surplus for twelve of fifteen years from 1952 to 1966, but the surplus was small and was swallowed by rising government deficits from overseas spending that grew to £525–550 mil-

lion in 1964–66. In 1966 alone, the British government stationed 55,000 British troops east of Suez, recruited locally 20,000 more, and spent altogether there £317 million. The same year the British military presence in Aden and the Persian Gulf cost £66 million, according to Michael Howard, "Britain's Strategic Problem East of Suez," *International Affairs*, April 1966:179–83.

37. The British government continues to send British officers and men on secondment to Muscat where they aid the royal government in combatting the rebellion in Dhofar. See "Statement on Defense, 1973," Cmnd. 5231, February 1973.

38. *The Military Balance, 1972–1973* (London: International Institute for Strategic Studies, 1972), pp. 30–35. Turkey, another regional power, possesses a gross national product and a population slightly larger than Iran's. At around 450,000 the Turkish armed forces are more than twice the size of the Iranian.

39. D. C. Watt, "The Arabian Peninsula in British Strategy," *Military Review*, February 1961, cited in his *Survey of International Affairs, 1961*, p. 532, n. 2.

40. "Supplementary Statement on Defense Policy 1970," Cmnd. 4521. The other three powers are Britain, Australia, and New Zealand.

3—FRANCE AND THE MIDDLE EAST

1. Anthony Moncrieff, ed., *Suez Ten Years After* (New York: Pantheon, 1966), p. 60.

2. *Official Statements*, No. 208 (New York: French Embassy, Press and Information Service, July 1964): hereafter referred to as *Official Statements* with appropriate number and date.

3. André Fontaine, "What is French Policy?" *Foreign Affairs* 45 (October 1966):73.

4. *Official Statements*, No. 207, January 10, 1968.

5. The French position was expressed by General de Gaulle in an address honoring Dr. Yusuf Zuáyan, prime minister of Syria, *Official Statements*, No. 177, January 1968, and again expressed in an address by de Gaulle honoring President Abdul Rahman Arif of Iraq, ibid., No. 183, February 9, 1968.

6. *France and the United Nations* (New York: French Embassy, Press and Information Service, n.d.).

7. *Official Statements*, No. 183, February 9, 1968, emphasis added.

8. Ibid., No. 185, February 12, 1968, emphasis added.

9. *Background Information on the Relationship Between Algeria and the French Oil Companies* (Algiers: Presumably published by the Algerian government, 1971), p. 13.

10. *French Foreign Policy: Official Statements, Speeches, and Communiqués*, July–December 1970, p. 36; hereafter cited as *FFP*.

11. *UN Monthly Chronicle* 9, 3 (March 1972):70.

12. *FFP*, July–December 1970, p. 127.

13. "First visit to France by Leonid Brezhnev, Secretary-General of the C.P. in the USSR (October 25–30, 1971)" (New York: French Embassy, Press and Information Service, 1971).

14. *Official Statements*, No 1270, July 10, 1969.

15. *FFP*, July–December 1970, pp. 89–90.

16. Ibid., p. 4.

17. Ibid., p. 37.

18. *Official Statements,* No. 1270, July 10, 1969.

19. *FFP,* January–June 1970, p. 11.

20. Ibid., July–December 1970, p. 126, emphasis added. The General Assembly, on December 10, 1964, had recognized the Palestinians as a "people" with the right to self-determination.

21. *Official Statements,* No. 73 / 120.

22. *FFP,* July–December 1970, p. 126.

23. Ibid., p. 127.

24. *Official Statements,* No. 73 / 120.

4—THE SOVIET UNION AND THE MIDDLE EAST

1. Walter Laqueur, *The Struggle for the Middle East* (London: Macmillan, 1969), p. 181.

2. *President Gamal Abdel Nasser's Speeches and Press Interviews, 1960* (April–June) (Cairo: UAR Information Department, 1961), p. 98.

3. Charles D. Cremeans, *The Arabs and the World: Nasser's Arab Nationalist Policy* (New York: Praeger, 1963), p. 286.

4. Ibid., p. 280.

5. John S. Badeau, *The American Approach to the Arab World* (New York: Harper and Row, 1968), pp. 158–59.

6. Laqueur, *The Struggle for the Middle East,* p. 23.

7. Ibid., pp. 16–17.

8. Franklyn D. Holzman, "Soviet Trade and Aid Policies," in J. C. Hurewitz, ed., *Soviet-American Rivalry in the Middle East* (New York: Praeger, 1969), p. 108.

9. Badeau, *The American Approach to the Arab World,* p. 165.

10. Geoffrey Kemp, "Strategy and Arms Levels, 1945–1967," in J. C. Hurewitz, ed., *Soviet-American Rivalry in the Middle East* (New York: Praeger, 1969), pp. 21–22.

11. V. Israelyan, et al., *Soviet Foreign Policy: A Brief Review, 1955–1965,* trans. Vic Schneierson (Moscow: Progress Publishers, 1967), p. 141.

12. Badeau, *The American Approach to the Arab World,* p. 160.

13. John C. Campbell, "American Search for Partners," in J. C. Hurewitz, ed., *Soviet-American Rivalry in the Middle East* (New York: Praeger, 1969), pp. 199–200.

14. Harry N. Howard, "The Middle East in World Affairs," in Tareq Y. Ismael, *Governments and Politics of the Contemporary Middle East* (Homewood, Ill.: The Dorsey Press, 1970), p. 471.

15. J. C. Hurewitz, "Origins of the Rivalry," in J. C. Hurewitz, ed., *Soviet-American Rivalry in the Middle East* (New York: Praeger, 1969), p. 3.

5—THE UNITED STATES AND THE MIDDLE EAST

1. United States Department of State, *The Foreign Relations of the United States: Diplomatic Papers* (Washington, D.C.: U.S. Government Printing Office), *1941,* III:928–29; *1942,* IV:289; *1944,* V:1–2; cited hereafter as *USFR.*

2. Ibid., *Conferences at Washington, 1941–1942, and Casablanca, 1943*, pp. 487–89.

3. Ibid., *1944*, V:885–87.

4. Ibid., *1946*, VII:801–923; Dean G. Acheson, *Present at the Creation* (New York: Norton, 1969), chapter 22; Harry N. Howard, "The Turkish Straits After World War II: Problems and Prospects," *Balkan Studies* 2, 1 (1970):35–60.

5. See *Aid to Greece and Turkey: A Collection of State Papers*, in United States Department of State, *Bulletin*, Supplement, 16, 409A (May 4, 1947):827–909; Joseph M. Jones, *The Fifteen Weeks* (New York: Viking, 1955).

6. See especially *USFR, 1942*, IV:548, and, for background, *USFR, 1938*, II:953–55.

7. Acheson, *Present at the Creation*, p. 169. For background, see also *USFR, 1945*, VIII:678–844; *USFR, 1946*, 576–77; United States Department of State, *Anglo-American Committee of Inquiry* (Washington, D.C.: U.S. Government Printing Office, 1946).

8. J. C. Hurewitz, *Diplomacy in the Near and Middle East: A Documentary Record, 1535–1914* (Princeton, N.J.: Van Nostrand, 1956), II:308–11; United States Department of State, *American Foreign Policy: Basic Documents, 1950–1955* (Washington, D.C.: U.S. Government Printing Office, 1957), II:2237; cited hereafter as *AFP*.

9. *AFP, 1950–1955*, II:2168–75, 2176–80, for the Dulles pronouncements of June 1, 1953, and August 26, 1955.

10. For relevant documentation, see *AFP, 1957*, pp. 783–857.

11. *AFP, 1962*, p. 783.

12. United States Senate, Committee on Foreign Relations, 91st Congress, 1st Session, *Hearings, United States Commitments to Foreign Powers* (Washington, D.C.: U.S. Government Printing Office), pp. 66–67.

13. *AFP, 1963*, pp. 580–81.

14. *AFP, 1964*, pp. 703–704; Richard P. Stebbins, *Documents on American Foreign Relations 1966* (New York: Harper and Row, 1967), pp. 172 ff.

15. United States Senate, Committee on Foreign Relations, 91st Congress, 1st Session, *Hearings, United States Commitments to Foreign Powers*, pp. 50–51.

16. Report of the Committee on Foreign Relations, United States Senate, 91st Congress, 1st Session, Report 91–129, *National Commitments* (Washington, D.C.: U.S. Government Printing Office, 1969), pp. 26–27.

17. See his press conference of January 27, 1969, in United States Senate, Committee on Foreign Relations, 91st Congress, 1st Session, *A Select Chronology and Background Documents Relating to the Middle East*, 1st rev. ed. (Washington, D.C.: U.S. Government Printing Office, 1969), pp. 274–76.

18. Arthur Lall, *The UN and the Middle East Crisis, 1967* (New York: Columbia University Press, 1968).

19. For text of December 9, 1969, speech, see *United States Foreign Policy, 1969–1970: A Report of the Secretary of State* (Washington, D.C.: U.S. Government Printing Office, 1971), pp. 409–12. See also the *New York Times*, November 6–9, 20, 27, December 15, 24, 1969, for the ups and downs of the discussions. The formulations of the address embody substantially the proposals of October 28, 1969.

20. See *The Near East Conflict*, hearings before the Subcommittee on the Near East of the Committee on Foreign Affairs, House of Representatives, 91st Congress, 1st Session, July 21–23, 28–30, 1970 (Washington, D.C.: U.S. Government Printing Office, 1970), pp. 295–96. *New York Times*, July 24, 27, August 5, 8,

1970; *United States Foreign Policy, 1969–1970*, p. 458; Israeli Embassy, *Policy Background: Israel's Acceptance of the U.S. Peace Initiative* (Washington, D.C., August 13, 1970).

21. See UN Documents A/8401/Add.1: *Introduction to the Report of the Secretary-General on the Work of the Organization*, September 1971, pp. 78–82; A/8541/S/10403: *The Situation in the Middle East*, November 30, 1971.

22. For text see *United States Foreign Policy 1971: A Report of the Secretary of State* (Washington, D.C.: U.S. Government Printing Office, 1972), pp. 461–68; *U.S. Foreign Policy for the 1970's: The Emerging Structure of Peace: A Report to the Congress by Richard Nixon, President of the United States, February 9, 1972* (Washington, D.C.: U.S. Government Printing Office, 1972), pp. 133–40; United States Department of State, *GIST*, 1 (rev. 3, March 1972). See also the *New York Times* and the *Washington Post,* October 5–6, 1971, for the possibility that the United States was offering Israel arms, economic assistance, and a guarantee for an agreement to the American program.

6—THE PEOPLE'S REPUBLIC OF CHINA
AND THE MIDDLE EAST

1. American Consulate General, *Survey of China Mainland Press,* Hong Kong, 1404 (November 5, 1956):33.

2. Muhammed Anis, *Al-Mutamar al-Asyawi al Ifriqie* [The Afro-Asian Conference], We Choose for You Series, No. 44 (Cairo: We Choose for Your Committee, n.d.), pp. 204–205.

3. W. A. C. Adie, "Chinese Policy Towards Africa," in Sven Hamrell and Carl Gosta Widstrand, eds., *The Soviet Bloc, China, and Africa* (Uppsala: Almqvist and Wiksells, for the Scandinavian Institute of African Studies, 1964), p. 46.

4. Richard Lowenthal, "The Sino-Soviet Split and its Repercussions in Africa," in Sven Hamrell and Carl Gosta Widstrand, eds., *The Soviet Bloc, China, and Africa* (Uppsala: Almqvist and Wiksells, for the Scandinavian Institute for African Studies, 1964), pp. 131–45.

5. Ahmad Shuqairy, *Min Alqumah ila Alhazimah: Ma'a Almulok Wa Alrosaa* [From the Summit to the Defeat with Presidents and Kings] (Beirut: Dar Alawden, 1971), p. 219.

6. Ibid., pp. 229–32.

7. General Secretariat of the Afro-Asian Journalists' Organization, *Tayyed Hasim Li Nidhal Alsh'ab al-Filistini* [A Decisive Support for the Struggle of the Palestinian Nation] (Peking, 1967), p. 7.

8. American Consulate General, Hong Kong, *Survey of China Mainland Press,* 5037–40 (December 20–23, 1971):32–33.

8—THE UNITED NATIONS AND THE MIDDLE EAST

1. See *Congressional Record* 99:1999; *Aid to Greece and Turkey: A Collection of State Papers,* United States Department of State *Bulletin,* Supplement, 16, 409 A (May 4, 1947):827–909. The president was authorized to withdraw assistance not only when requested by the two governments, or if he thought the purposes

had been substantially achieved, but also if the Security Council or the General Assembly found that further assistance was unnecessary or undesirable.

2. For statement of Prime Minister David Ben-Gurion in the Israeli Knesset, November 7, 1956, see United States Department of State, *United States Policy in the Middle East, September 1956–June 1957. Documents* (Washington, D.C.: U.S. Government Printing Office, 1957), pp. 199–204. Mr. Ben-Gurion declared that Israel would "not consent, under any circumstances, that a foreign force— called whatever it may—take up positions whether on Israeli soil or in any area held by Israel." Israel maintained that position in 1967 and afterward. See also David P. Forsythe, *United Nations Peacemaking: The Conciliation Commission for Palestine* (Baltimore, Md.: The Johns Hopkins Press, 1972).

9—DOMESTIC SOURCES OF MIDDLE EASTERN FOREIGN POLICY

1. In Richard Nolte, ed., *The Modern Middle East* (New York: Atherton Press, 1963), p. 153.

2. R. K. Karanjia, *Arab Dawn* (Bombay: Asia Publishing House, 1958), p. 187.

10—OIL: THE NEW DIPLOMACY

1. As quoted in George W. Stocking, *Middle East Oil: A Study in Political and Economic Controversy* (Kingsport, Tenn.: Vanderbilt University Press, 1970), p. 141.

2. U.N. General Assembly, Sixth Session, *Official Record,* November 14, 1951, 128; A/PV, 344.

Background Readings

1—HISTORICAL BACKGROUNDS

Actes de la Conférence de Montreux concernant le régime des Détroits. 22 juin–20 juillet 1936. Compterendu des séances pleniéres et de procés-verbal des débats du comité technique. Liege, Belgium, 1936.

Anderson, M. S. *The Eastern Question.* New York: St. Martin's Press, 1966.

Anderson, M. S., ed. *The Great Powers and the Near East, 1774–1923: Documents of Modern History.* New York: St. Martin's, 1971.

Antonius, George. *The Arab Awakening: The Story of the Arab National Movement.* Philadelphia: Lippincott, 1939.

Ben-Gurion, David. "On the Road to the State." *Jewish Observer and Middle East Review* 13, 16 (April 26, 1964); 19 (May 5, 1964); 20 (May 22, 1964).

Earle, Edward Mead. *Turkey, the Great Powers, and the Baghdad Railway.* New York: Macmillan, 1923.

Erkin, Feridun Cemal. *Les Relations Turco-Soviétiques et la Question des Détroits.* Ankara: Basnur Matbaasi, 1968.

Fisher, Alan. *The Russian Annexation of the Crimea, 1772–1783.* Cambridge: At the University Press, 1970.

Foreign Relations of the United States. Diplomatic Papers, The Conferences at Cairo and Teheran 1943. Washington, D.C.: U.S. Government Printing Office, 1964.

Gafencu, Gregoire. *Preliminaries de la Guerre á l'Est.* Paris: Egloff, 1944.

Gidney, James B. *A Mandate for Armenia.* Kent, Ohio: Kent State University Press, 1967.

Goodrich, Leland M., ed. *Documents on American Foreign Relations.* Vol. IV, *1941–1942.* Boston: World Peace Foundation, 1942.

Hourani, Albert H. *Arabic Thought in the Liberal Age, 1798–1939.* New York: Oxford University Press, 1962.

——. "The Decline of the West in the Middle East." *International Affairs* (January 1963).

——. *Syria and Lebanon: A Political Essay.* London: Oxford University Press, 1946.

Howard, Harry N. "The Entry of Turkey into World War II." *Belleten* 31, 122 (April 1967):221–75.

——. *The King-Crane Commission: An American Inquiry in the Middle East.* Beirut: Khayats, 1963.

——. *The Partition of Turkey, 1913–1923.* Norman: University of Oklahoma Press, 1931.

——. *The Problem of the Turkish Straits.* Washington, D.C.: U.S. Government Printing Office, 1947.

——. "The Turkish Straits After World War II: Problems and Prospects," *Balkan Studies* 2 (1970).

267

Hurewitz, J. C. *Diplomacy in the Near and Middle East: A Documentary Record, 1535–1914.* Princeton, N.J.: Van Nostrand, 1956.

Jelavich, Barbara. *The Ottoman Empire, the Great Powers, and the Straits Question, 1870–1887.* Bloomington, Ind.: Indiana University Press, 1973.

Kerner, Robert J., and Howard, Harry N. *The Balkan Conferences and the Balkan Entente, 1930–1936: A Study in the Recent History of the Balkan and Near Eastern Peoples.* Berkeley: University of California Press, 1936.

Kerner, Robert J. "The Mission of Liman von Sanders." *Slavonic Review* 6 (1927–28).

Khalil, Muhammad, ed. *The Arab States and the Arab League: A Documentary Record.* Beirut: Khayats, 1962.

Kirk, George. *Survey of International Affairs. The Middle East in the War, 1939–1946; The Middle East, 1945–1950.* London: Oxford University Press, 1953, 1954.

Klieman, Aaron S. *Foundations of British Policy in the Arab World: The Cairo Conference of 1921.* Baltimore, Md.: The Johns Hopkins Press, 1970.

Laqueur, Walter Z., ed. *The Israel-Arab Reader: A Documentary History of the Middle East Conflict.* New York: Bantam, 1970.

———. *The Struggle for the Middle East: The Soviet Union in the Mediterranean, 1958–1968.* New York: Macmillan, 1969.

Lenczowski, George. *Russia and the West in Iran, 1918–1948: A Study in Big Power Rivalry.* Ithaca, N.Y.: Cornell University Press, 1949.

MacDonald, Robert W. *The League of Arab States: A Study of the Dynamics of Regional Organization.* Princeton, N.J.: Princeton University Press, 1965.

Marx, Karl, and Engels, Friedrich. *The Russian Menace to Europe.* Edited by Paul W. Blackstock and Bert F. Hoselitz. Glencoe, Ill.: The Free Press, 1952.

Moorehead, Alan. *The March on Tunis: The North African War, 1940–1943.* New York: Dell, 1968; originally published 1941, 1943.

Nolte, Richard H., ed. *The Modern Middle East.* New York: Atherton, 1963.

Palestine Partition Commission Report. October 1938. Cmd. 5854.

Palestine Royal Commission Report. July 1937. Cmd. 5479.

Papadopoulos, George. *England and the Near East, 1896–1898.* Salonika: Institute for Balkan Studies, 1969.

Ramazani, Rouhollah K. *The Persian Gulf: Iran's Role.* Charlottesville, Va.: University Press of Virginia, 1972.

Sachar, Howard M. *Europe Leaves the Middle East, 1936–1954.* New York: Knopf, 1972.

Sontag, Raymond J., and Beddie, James Stuart, eds. *Nazi-Soviet Relations 1939–1941. Documents from the Archives of the German Foreign Office.* Department of State Publication 3023. Washington, D.C.: U.S. Government Printing Office, 1948.

Sousa, Nasim. *The Capitulatory Regime of Turkey: Its History, Origin, and Nature.* Baltimore, Md.: The Johns Hopkins Press, 1933.

Toynbee, Arnold J. *Survey of International Affairs, 1925.* Vol. I, *The Islamic World.* London: Oxford University Press, 1927.

Trumpener, Ulrich. *Germany and the Ottoman Empire, 1914–1918.* Princeton, N.J.: Princeton University Press, 1968.

Weber, Frank G. *Eagles on the Crescent: Germany, Austria, and the Diplomacy of the Turkish Alliance, 1914–1918.* Ithaca, N.Y.: Cornell University Press, 1970.

Weisband, Edward. *Turkish Foreign Policy, 1943–1944: Small State Diplomacy and Great Powers.* Princeton, N.J.: Princeton University Press, 1973.

Zayid, Mahmud Y. *Egypt's Struggle for Independence.* Beirut: Khayats, 1965.

2—BRITAIN AND THE MIDDLE EAST

Acheson, Dean. *Present at the Creation: My Years in the State Department.* New York: Norton, 1969.

Adelman, M. A. "Is the Oil Shortage Real? Oil Companies as OPEC Tax Collectors." *Foreign Policy,* Winter 1972–73.

Akins, James E. "The Oil Crisis: This Time the Wolf is Here." *Foreign Affairs,* April 1973.

American Enterprise Institute. *United States Interests in the Middle East.* Washington, D.C., 1968.

Anthony, John Duke. "The Union of Arab Amirates." *The Middle East Journal.* Summer 1972.

Antonius, George. *The Arab Awakening: The Story of the Arab National Movement.* Philadelphia: Lippincott, 1939.

Barraclough, Geoffrey. *Survey of International Affairs, 1955–1956.* London: Oxford University Press, 1960.

Barraclough, Geoffrey, and Wall, Rachel. *Survey of International Affairs, 1956–1958.* London: Oxford University Press, 1962.

Beaufre, André. *The Suez Expedition, 1956.* New York: Praeger, 1969.

Bell, Coral. *Survey of International Affairs, 1954.* London: Oxford University Press, 1957.

Benians, E. A., Butler, James, and Carrington, C. E., eds. *The Cambridge History of the British Empire.* Cambridge: At the University Press, 1959.

Bullard, Reader. *Britain and the Middle East from the Earliest Times to 1963.* 3rd rev. ed. London: Hutchinson University Library, 1964.

Busch, Briton C. *Britain and the Persian Gulf, 1894–1914.* Berkeley, Calif.: University of California Press, 1967.

———. *Britain, India, and the Arabs, 1914–1921.* Berkeley, Calif.: University of California Press, 1971.

Calvocoressi, Peter. *Survey of International Affairs, 1951.* London: Oxford University Press, 1954.

Churchill, Winston S. *The Second World War.* Vol. II, *Their Finest Hour.* New York: Bantam, 1962.

Cross, Colin. *The Fall of the British Empire.* New York: Coward-McCann, 1969.

Eden, Anthony. *Full Circle.* Boston: Houghton Mifflin, 1960.

Eisenhower, Dwight D. *The White House Years: Waging Peace, 1956–1961.* Garden City, N.Y.: Doubleday, 1965.

Finer, Herman. *Dulles Over Suez.* Chicago: Quadrangle, 1964.

De Gaulle, Charles. *War Memoirs.* 3 vols. New York: Simon and Schuster, 1967.

Gordon Walker, P. C. "The Labor Party's Defense and Foreign Policy." *Foreign Affairs,* April 1964.

Great Britain. *Parliamentary Papers.*

Hammond, Paul Y., and Alexander, Sidney S., eds. *Political Dynamics in the Middle East.* New York: American Elsevier, 1972.

Holden, David. "The Persian Gulf: After the British Raj." *Foreign Affairs,* July 1971.

Howard, Michael. "Britain's Strategic Problem East of Suez." *International Affairs,* April 1966.

Hughes, Emmet John. *The Ordeal of Power: A Political Memoir of the Eisenhower Years.* New York: Atheneum, 1963.

Hurewitz, J. C. *Diplomacy in the Near and Middle East: A Documentary Record, 1535–1914.* Princeton, N.J.: Van Nostrand, 1956.

——, ed. *Soviet-American Rivalry in the Middle East.* New York: Praeger, 1969.

Kelley, J. B. *Britain and the Persian Gulf, 1795–1880.* Oxford: The Clarendon Press, 1968.

Kerr, Malcolm. *The Arab Cold War, 1958–1970.* London: Oxford University Press, 1971.

——. " 'Coming to Terms with Nasser': Attempts and Failures." *International Affairs,* January 1967.

Khadduri, Majid. *Independent Iraq 1932–1958: A Study in Iraqi Politics Since the Revolution of 1958.* New York: Oxford University Press, 1969.

——. *Political Trends in the Arab World.* Baltimore, Md.: The Johns Hopkins Press, 1970.

King, Gillian. *Imperial Outpost—Aden: Its Place in British Strategic Policy.* London: Oxford University Press, 1964.

Kirk, George. *Survey of International Affairs, 1939–1946: The Middle East in the War.* London: Oxford University Press, 1952.

Klieman, Aaron S. *Foundations of British Policy in the Arab World: The Cairo Conference of 1921.* Baltimore, Md.: The Johns Hopkins Press, 1970.

Knapp, Wilfrid. *A History of War and Peace, 1939–1965.* London: Oxford University Press, 1967.

Langer, W. L. *The Diplomacy of Imperialism, 1890–1902.* New York: Knopf, 1935.

——. *European Alliances and Alignments, 1871–1890.* 2nd ed. New York: Knopf, 1950.

Laqueur, Walter Z., ed. *The Israel-Arab Reader: A Documentary History of the Middle East Conflict.* New York: Bantam, 1970.

Lenczowski, George. *The Middle East in World Affairs.* 3rd ed. Ithaca, N.Y.: Cornell University Press, 1962.

——. *Oil and State in the Middle East.* Ithaca, N.Y.: Cornell University Press, 1960.

Lloyd George, David. *Memoirs of the Peace Conference.* New Haven, Conn.: Yale University Press, 1939.

Longrigg, Stephen Hemsley. *Oil in the Middle East: Its Discovery and Development.* London: Oxford University Press, 1954.

Love, Kenneth. *Suez: The Twice-Fought War.* New York: McGraw-Hill, 1969.

Macmillan, Harold. *Tides of Fortune, 1945–1955.* New York: Harper and Row, 1969.

Marlowe, John. *A History of Modern Egypt and Anglo-Egyptian Relations, 1800–1953.* 2nd ed. Hamden, Conn.: Anchor, 1965.

Monroe, Elizabeth. *Britain's Moment in the Middle East, 1914–1956.* Baltimore, Md.: The Johns Hopkins Press, 1963.

——. "British Bases in the Middle East—Assets or Liabilities?" *International Affairs,* January 1966.

———. "Kuwayt and Aden: A Contrast in British Policies." *Middle East Journal,* Winter 1964.

Nutting, Anthony. *No End of a Lesson: The Story of Suez.* New York: Potter, 1967.

O'Ballance, Edgar. *The War in the Yemen.* Hamden, Conn.: Anchor, 1971.

Paget, Julian. *Last Post: Aden 1964–1967.* London: Faber and Faber, 1969.

Quigley, Carroll. "Lord Balfour's Personal Position in the Balfour Declaration." *Middle East Journal,* Summer 1968.

Robertson, Terence. *Crisis: The Inside Story of the Suez Conspiracy.* London: Hutchinson, 1964.

Roosa, Robert V. "Where is Britain Heading?" *Foreign Affairs,* April 1968.

Rouhani, Fuad. *A History of the Organization of Petroleum Exporting Countries.* New York: Praeger, 1972.

Sachar, Howard M. *The Emergence of the Middle East, 1914–1921.* New York: Knopf, 1969.

Schurr, Sam H., et al. *Middle Eastern Oil and the Western World: Prospects and Problems.* New York: American Elsevier, 1971.

Schwadran, Benjamin. *The Middle East, Oil, and the Great Powers.* New York: Praeger, 1955.

Sharabi, Hisham. *Arab Intellectuals and the West: The Formative Years, 1875–1914.* Baltimore, Md.: The Johns Hopkins Press, 1970.

———. *Nationalism and Revolution in the Arab World.* Princeton, N.J.: Van Nostrand, 1966.

Taylor, A. J. P. *The Struggle for Mastery in Europe, 1848–1918.* Oxford: The Clarendon Press, 1954.

Thornton, A. P. *The Imperial Idea and Its Enemies: A Study in British Power.* Garden City, N.Y.: Doubleday-Anchor, 1959.

Tibawi, A. L. *A Modern History of Syria: Including Lebanon and Palestine.* New York: St. Martin's Press, 1970.

Toynbee, Arnold J. *Survey of International Affairs, 1925, 1930.* London: Oxford University Press, 1926, 1931.

Vatikiotis, P. J., ed. *Egypt Since the Revolution.* New York: Praeger, 1968.

Ward, A. W., and Gooch, G. P., eds. *The Cambridge History of British Foreign Policy, 1783–1919.* New York: Macmillan, 1923.

Watt, D. C. *Survey of International Affairs, 1961.* London: Oxford University Press, 1965.

Webster, C. K. *The Foreign Policy of Palmerston.* 2 vols. London: G. Bell and Sons, 1971.

Wise, David, and Ross, Thomas B. *The Invisible Government.* New York: Random House, 1964.

Woodward, E. L., and Butler, R., eds. *Documents on British Foreign Policy, 1919–1939.* London: HMSO, 1952.

3—FRANCE AND THE MIDDLE EAST

Abouchid, Eugene Ebe. *Thirty Years of Lebanon and Syria.* Beirut: Sader Rihani, 1948.

Anderson, M. S. *The Eastern Question, 1774–1923.* New York: St. Martin's Press, 1966.

Antonius, George. *The Arab Awakening: The Story of the Arab National Movement.* Philadelphia: Lippincott, 1939.

Background Information on the Relationship Between Algeria and the French Oil Companies. Algiers: Presumably published by the Algerian government, 1971.

Bar-Zohar, Michel. *Suez Ultra Secret.* Paris: Fayard, 1964.

Bromberger, Merry and Serge. *Les Secrets de l'Expedition d'Egypte.* Paris: Editions des Quatre Fils Aymon, 1957.

———. *Secrets of Suez.* Translated by James Cameron. London: Pan Books, 1957.

Childers, Erskine B. *The Road to Suez: A Study of Western-Arab Relations.* London: McGibbon & Kee, 1962.

Clark, D. M. *Suez Touchdown: A Soldier's Tale.* London: Peter Davies, 1964.

Collins, R., and Tignor, R. *Egypt and the Sudan.* Englewood Cliffs, N.J.: Prentice-Hall, 1967.

Connell, John. *The Most Important Country: The True Story of the Suez Crises and the Events Leading to It.* London: Cassell, 1957.

Cummings, Henry H. *Franco-British Rivalry in the Post-War Near East.* London: Oxford University Press, 1938.

David, Philippe. *Un Gouvernment Arabe a Damas: Le Congres Syrien.* Paris: Marcel Girard, 1923.

Dayan, Moshe. *Diary of the Sinai Campaign.* New York: Harper and Row, 1966.

Eden, Anthony. *Full Circle: The Memoirs of Anthony Eden.* Boston: Houghton Mifflin, 1960.

Eytan, Walter. *The First Ten Years: A Diplomatic History of Israel.* New York: Simon and Schuster, 1958.

Fontaine, André. "What is French Policy?" *Foreign Affairs* 45 (October 1966).

French Foreign Policy: Official Statements, Speeches, and Communiques. New York: Ambassade De France, Service de Presse et d'Information (semi-Annual since 1966).

Frye, Richard N., ed. *The Near East and the Great Powers.* Cambridge, Mass.: Harvard University Press, 1951.

Ginay, E. "DeGaulle and Israel." *New Outlook* 2, 1 (January 1968).

Hall, H. Duncan. *Mandates, Dependencies and Trusteeship.* Washington, D.C.: Carnegie Endowment for International Peace, 1948.

Hitti, Philip K. *History of Syria.* New York: Macmillan, 1951.

Hourani, Albert H. *Minorities in the Arab World.* New York: Oxford University Press, 1947.

———. *Syria and Lebanon: A Political Essay.* London: Oxford University Press, 1946.

Howard, Harry N. *The Partition of Turkey: A Diplomatic History, 1913–1923.* New York: H. Fertig, 1966.

Hurewitz, J. C. *Diplomacy in the Near and Middle East: A Documentary Record, 1535–1914.* Princeton, N.J.: Van Nostrand, 1956.

Kirk, George. *The Middle East in the War. Survey of International Affairs, 1939–46.* Edited by Arnold Toynbee. London: Oxford University Press, 1952.

Lall, Arthur. *The United Nations and the Middle East Crisis, 1967.* New York: Columbia University Press, 1968.

Lenczowski, George. *The Middle East in World Affairs.* 3rd ed. Ithaca, N.Y.: Cornell University Press, 1962.

Lloyd George, David. *The Truth About the Peace Treaties*. 2 vols. London: Gollancz, 1938.

Loder, John DeVere. *The Truth About Mesopotamia, Palestine and Syria*. London: George Allen and Unwin, 1923.

Longrigg, Stephen. *Syria and Lebanon under French Mandate*. London: Oxford University Press, 1958.

Love, Kenneth. *Suez: The Twice-Fought War*. New York: McGraw-Hill, 1969.

MacCallum, Elizabeth P. *The Nationalist Crusade in Syria*. New York: Foreign Policy Association, 1928.

Miller, David Hunter. *My Diary at the Conference of Paris, with Documents*. 21 vols. New York: Appeal, 1924.

Morgan Jones, John. *La Fin du Mandat Francais en Syrie et en Liban*. Paris: Pedone, 1938.

Nutting, Anthony. *No End of a Lesson: The Story of Suez*. New York: Potter, 1967.

O'zoux, Raymond. *Les Etats du Levant sous Mandat Francais*. Paris: Larousse, 1931.

Peretz, Don. *The Middle East Today*. 2nd ed. New York: Holt, Rinehart, 1971.

Puryear, Vernon J. *France and the Levant*. Berkeley, Calif.: University of California Press, 1941.

Robertson, Terence. *Crisis: The Inside Story of the Suez Conspiracy*. London: Hutchinson, 1964.

Rouleau, Eric. "French Policy in the Middle East." *World Today* 24, 5 (May 1969):209–18.

Sharabi, Hisham. *Governments and Politics of the Middle East in the Twentieth Century*. Princeton, N.J.: Van Nostrand, 1966.

Suez Ten Years After: Broadcasts from the B.B.C., Third Programme. Peter Calvocoressi, et al. Edited by Anthony Moncrieff. London: British Broadcasting Co., 1967. Reprinted New York: Pantheon, 1967.

Tibawi, A. L. *A Modern History of Syria Including Lebanon and Palestine*. New York: St. Martin's Press, 1969.

Thomas, Hugh. *The Suez Affair*. New York: Harper and Row, 1967.

Williams, Ann. *Britain and France in the Middle East and North Africa, 1914–1967*. London: Macmillan, 1968.

Wright, Quincy. *Mandates Under the League of Nations*. Chicago: University of Chicago Press, 1930.

Ziadeh, Nicola. *Syria and Lebanon*. London: Benn, 1957.

Zeine, Z. N. *The Struggle for Arab Independence: Western Diplomacy and the Rise and Fall of Feisal's Kingdom in Syria*. Beirut: Khayats, 1960.

4—THE SOVIET UNION AND THE MIDDLE EAST

Hopwood, Derek. *The Russian Presence in Syria and Palestine, 1843–1923: Church and Politics in the Near East*. London: Oxford University Press, 1969.

Hurewitz, J. C., ed. *Soviet-American Rivalry in the Middle East*. New York: Praeger, 1969.

Ismael, Tareq Y. *Governments and Politics of the Contemporary Middle East*. Homewood, Ill.: The Dorsey Press, 1970.

[Kennan, George F.] "X." "The Sources of Soviet Conduct." *Foreign Affairs* 25, 4 (July 1947):566–82.

Laqueur, Walter Z., ed. *The Israel-Arab Reader: A Documentary History of the Middle East Conflict.* New York: Bantam, 1970.

——. *The Soviet Union and the Middle East.* New York: Praeger, 1969.

——. *The Struggle for the Middle East.* London, Macmillan, 1969.

Lee, Christopher D. "The Soviet Contribution to Iran's Fourth Development Plan." *Mizan* 11, 5 (September–October 1969).

Lenczowski, George. *Russia and the West in Iran, 1918–1948: A Study in Big Power Rivalry.* Ithaca, N.Y.: Cornell University Press, 1949.

——. *Soviet Advances in the Middle East.* Washington, D.C.: American Enterprise Institute, 1971.

Morrison, David. "The Middle East: The Soviet Entanglement." *Mizan* 11, 3 (May–June 1969):165–73.

——. "Soviet Involvement in the Middle East: The New State." *Mizan* 11, 5 (September–October 1969):258–64.

Proctor, Jesse Harris. *Islam and International Relations.* New York: Praeger, 1965.

Spector, Ivan. *The Soviet Union and the Muslim World.* Seattle: University of Washington Press, 1959.

Stavrou, Theofanic George. *Russia: Interests in Palestine, 1882–1914: A Study of Religious and Educational Enterprises.* Salonika: Institute for Balkan Studies, 1963.

5—THE UNITED STATES AND THE MIDDLE EAST

Acheson, Dean G. *Present at the Creation: My Years in the State Department.* New York: Norton, 1969.

American Friends Service Committee, et al. *Search for Peace in the Middle East.* Philadelphia: American Friends Service Committee, 1970.

Anderson, M. S. *The Eastern Question, 1774–1923.* New York: Macmillan, 1966.

Baker, R. S., and Dodd, W. E. *The Public Papers of Woodrow Wilson.* New York: Harper, 1927.

Daniel, Robert L. *American Philanthropy in the Near East, 1820–1960.* Athens, Ohio: Ohio State University Press, 1970.

De Novo, John A. *American Intersts and Policies in the Middle East, 1900–1939.* Minneapolis: University of Minnesota Press, 1963.

Evans, Laurence. *United States Policy and the Partition of Turkey, 1914–1924.* Baltimore, Md.: The Johns Hopkins Press, 1965.

Field, James A. *America and the Mediterranean World, 1776–1882.* Princeton, N.J.: Princeton University Press, 1969.

Finnie, David H. *Pioneers East: The Early American Experience in the Middle East.* Cambridge, Mass.: Harvard University Press, 1967.

Fisher, Sydney N. "Two Centuries of American Interest in Turkey." In *Festschrift for Frederick B. Artz.* Durham, N.C.: Duke University Press, 1964.

Francher, Michael. *The United States and the Palestinian People.* Beirut: Institute for Palestine Studies, 1970.

Gordon, Leland J. *American Relations with Turkey, 1830–1930: An Economic Interpretation.* Philadelphia: University of Pennsylvania Press, 1932.

Grabill, Joseph L. *Protestant Diplomacy and the Near East: Missionary Influence on American Policy, 1810–1927.* Minneapolis: University of Minnesota Press, 1971.

Harris, George. *Troubled Alliance: Turkish-American Problems in Historical Perspective, 1945–1971.* Stanford, Calif.: The Hoover Institution, 1972.

Hesseltine, William H., and Wolf, Hazel C. *The Blue and the Gray on the Nile.* Chicago: University of Chicago Press, 1961.

Howard, Harry N. "The Entry of Turkey into World War II." *Belleten* 31, 131 (April 1967):221–75.

———. *The King-Crane Commission: An American Inquiry in the Middle East.* Beirut: Khayats, 1963.

———. "The Regional Pacts and the Eisenhower Doctrine." *The Annals* 401 (May 1972):85–94.

———. "The Turkish Straits After World War I: Problems and Prospects." *Balkan Studies* 2, 1 (1970):35–60.

———. "The United States and the Problem of the Turkish Straits: The Foundations of American Policy (1830–1914)." *Balkan Studies* 3 (1962):1–28.

Hurewitz, J. C. *Diplomacy in the Near and Middle East: A Documentary Record, 1535–1914.* Princeton, N.J.: Van Nostrand, 1956.

Israeli Embassy. *Policy Background: An Analysis of the U.S. Mideast Peace Plan.* Washington, D.C., December 24, 1969.

———. *Policy Background: Israel's Acceptance of the U.S. Peace Initiative.* Washington, D.C., August 13, 1970.

———. *Policy Background: The U.S. Response to Israel's Aircraft Needs—An Assessment.* Washington, D.C., March 26, 1970.

Jones, Joseph M. *The Fifteen Weeks.* New York: Viking, 1955.

Khadduri, Majid. *Major Middle Eastern Problems in International Law.* Washington, D.C.: American Enterprise Institute, 1972.

Lall, Arthur. *The UN and the Middle East Crisis, 1967.* New York: Columbia University Press, 1968.

Lenczowski, George. *Russia and the West in Iran, 1914–1918.* Ithaca, N.Y.: Cornell University Press, 1949.

———. *Soviet Advances in the Middle East.* Washington, D.C.: American Enterprise Institute, 1972.

Letters of President Johnson and Prime Minister Inonu, June 5, 13, 1964. *Middle East Journal* 20, 3 (Summer 1966).

Love, Kenneth. "Election Fever and the Rogers Mission." *Middle East International* 1, 4 (July 1971).

———. *Suez: The Twice-Fought War.* New York: McGraw-Hill, 1969.

Mosher, Lawrence. "Zionist Role in the U.S. Raises Concern." *The National Observer,* May 18, 1970.

Murphy, Robert. *Diplomat Among Warriors.* New York: Pyramid, 1965.

Negotiation of the Treaty of 1830. House Document No. 250, 22nd Congress, 1st Session.

Nutting, Anthony. *No End of a Lesson: The Story of Suez.* New York: Potter, 1967.

Reddaway, John. "Strategy for a Long Haul." *Middle East International* 6 (September 1971).

Stebbins, Richard P. *Documents on American Foreign Relations 1966.* New York: Harper and Row, 1967.

Thomas, Hugh. *The Suez Affair*. New York: Harper and Row, 1967.

Tibawi, A. L. *American Interests in Syria, 1800–1901: A Study of Educational, Literary, and Religious Work*. London: Oxford University Press, 1966.

Trumpener, Ulrich. *Germany and the Ottoman Empire, 1914–1918*. Princeton, N.J.: Princeton University Press, 1968.

UN Document S/10070: "Report by the Secretary-General on the Activities of the Special Representative to the Middle East." January 4, 1971.

United States Senate Committee on Foreign Relations, 91st Congress, 1st Session. *A Select Chronology and Background Documents Relating to the Middle East*. 1st rev. ed. Washington, D.C.: U.S. Government Printing Office, 1969.

United States Department of State. *Anglo-American Committee of Inquiry: Report to the United States Government and His Majesty's Government in the United Kingdom*. Lausanne, Switzerland, April 20, 1946. Washington, D.C.: U.S. Government Printing Office, 1946.

———. *Mandate for Palestine*. Near Eastern Series, 1. Prepared in the Division of Near Eastern Affairs. Washington, D.C.: U.S. Government Printing Office, 1931.

———. Memorandum of October 14, 1938. *The Foreign Relations of the United States: Diplomatic Papers*. Washington, D.C.: U.S. Government Printing Office, 1938.

———. *The Suez Canal Problem, July 26–September 22, 1956: A Documentary Publication*. Washington, D.C.: U.S. Government Printing Office, 1957.

———. *United States Policy in the Middle East, September 1956–June 1957*. Washington, D.C.: U.S. Government Printing Office, 1957.

United States Foreign Policy, 1969–1970: A Report of the Secretary of State. Washington, D.C.: U.S. Government Printing Office, 1971.

U.S. Foreign Policy for the 1970's, a New Strategy for Peace. A Report to the Congress by Richard Nixon, President of the United States. February 18, 1970. Washington, D.C.: U.S. Government Printing Office, 1970.

Vali, Ferenc A. *Bridge Across the Bosphorus: The Foreign Policy of Turkey*. Baltimore, Md.: The Johns Hopkins Press, 1971.

Wainhouse, David, et al. *International Peace Observation: A History and Forecast*. Baltimore, Md.: The Johns Hopkins Press, 1966.

Weber, Frank. G. *Eagles Over the Crescent: Germany, Austria, and the Diplomacy of the Turkish Alliance, 1914–1918*. Ithaca, N.Y.: Cornell University Press, 1970.

Weisband, Edward. *Turkish Foreign Policy, 1943–1945: Small State Diplomacy and Great Power Politics*. Princeton, N.J.: Princeton University Press, 1973.

Yost, Charles. "Last Chance for Peace in the Middle East." *Life* 70, 13 (April 9, 1971).

Zinner, Paul E. *Documents on American Foreign Relations 1958*. New York: Harper, 1959.

6—THE PEOPLE'S REPUBLIC OF CHINA
AND THE MIDDLE EAST

Brzezinsky, Zbigniew, ed. *Africa and the Communist World*. Stanford: Stanford University Press, 1963.

Documents on International Affairs. The Bandung Conference. London: Oxford University Press, 1955.

General Secretariat of the Afro-Asian Journalists' Organization. *Tayyed Hasim Li Nidhal Alsh'ab al-Filistini* [A Decisive Support for the Struggle of the Palestinian Nation]. Peking, 1967.

Hamrell, Sven, and Widstrand, Carl Gosta, eds. *The Soviet Bloc, China, and Africa.* Uppsala: Almqvist and Wiksells, 1964.

Jansen, G. H. *Non-alignment and the Afro-Asian States.* New York: Praeger, 1966.

Khalili, Joseph E. *Communist China's Interaction with the Arab Nationalists Since the Bandung Conference.* New York: Exposition Press, 1970.

Shuqairy, Ahmad. *Min Alqumah ila Alhazimah: Ma'a Almulok Wa Alrosaa* [From the Summit to the Defeat with Presidents and Kings]. Beirut: Dar Alawden, 1971.

7—AFRICA AND THE MIDDLE EAST

Ajami, Fouad, and Sours, Martin H. "Israel and Sub-Saharan Africa: A Study of Interaction." *African Studies Review* 13, 3 (December 1970).

Baulin, Jacques. *The Arab Role in Africa.* Baltimore, Md.: Penguin, 1962.

Hovet, Thomas Jr. *Africa in the United Nations.* London: Faber and Faber, 1963.

Ismael, Tareq Y. *The U.A.R. in Africa: Egypt's Policy Under Nasser.* Evanston, Ill.: Northwestern University Press, 1971.

——. "The United Arab Republic in Africa." *The Canadian Journal of African Studies* (Autumn 1968): 181–83.

Jansen, G. H. *Nonalignment and the Afro-Asian States.* New York: Praeger, 1966.

Nasser, Gamal Abdel. *Egypt's Liberation: The Philosophy of the Revolution.* Washington, D.C.: Public Affairs Press, 1955.

8—THE UNITED NATIONS AND THE MIDDLE EAST

American Friends Service Committee, et al. *Search for Peace in the Middle East.* Philadelphia: American Friends Service Committee, 1970.

Badeau, John S. *The American Approach to the Arab World.* New York: Harper and Row, 1968.

Buehrig, Edward H. *The UN and the Palestinian Refugees: A Study in Nonterritorial Administration.* Bloomington, Ind.: Indiana University Press, 1971.

Building for Peace: A Report to the Congress by Richard Nixon, President of the United States. February 18, 1970. Washington, D.C.: U.S. Government Printing Office, 1970.

Burns, Lieutenant General E. L. M. *Between Arab and Israeli.* New York: Obolensky, 1962.

Campbell, John C. "The Arab-Israeli Conflict: An American Policy." *Foreign Affairs* 49, 1 (October 1970):51–69.

Cattan, Henry. *Palestine and International Law.* London: Longmans, 1973.

——. *Palestine, the Arabs and Israel: The Search for Justice.* London: Longmans, 1969.

Chamoun, Camille. *Crise au Moyen-Orient.* Paris: Gallimard, 1963.

Council on Foreign Relations. *Documents on American Foreign Relations.* New York: Simon and Schuster, 1969.

Foreign Area Studies, American University. *Area Handbook for Iran.* Washington, D.C.: U.S. Government Printing Office, 1971.

Forsythe, David P. *United Nations Peacemaking: The Conciliation Commission for Palestine.* Baltimore, Md.: The Johns Hopkins Press, 1972.

Fulbright, Senator J. William. "Old Myths and New Realities—II. The Middle East." *Congressional Record* 116, 147 (August 24, 1970).

Goldmann, Nahum. "The Future of Israel." *Foreign Affairs* 48, 3 (April 1970):443–59.

Hatfield, Senator Mark. "Search for Peace in the Middle East." *Congressional Record* 116, 99 (June 17, 1970):S9021–39.

Higgins, Rosalyn. *United Nations Peacekeeping: Documents and Commentary: The Middle East.* New York: Oxford University Press, 1969.

Howard, Harry N. "Greece and Its Balkan Neighbors (1948–1949): The United Nations Attempts at Conciliation." *Balkan Studies* 7 (1966):1–26.

——. *The United Nations and the Problem of Greece.* Washington, D.C.: U.S. Government Printing Office, 1947.

——. "United States Policy Toward Greece in the United Nations, 1946–1950." *Balkan Studies* 8 (1967):263–96.

Israeli Embassy. *Policy Background: An Analysis of the U.S. Mideast Peace Plan.* Washington, D.C., December 24, 1969.

——. *Policy Background: The Components of a Secure Peace.* Washington, D.C., March 10, 1971.

——. *Policy Background: The U.S. Response to Israel's Aircraft Needs—An Assessment.* Washington, D.C., March 25, 1970.

Khalidi, Walid, ed. *From Haven to Conquest.* Beirut: Institute for Palestine Studies, 1971.

Khalil, Muhammad. *The Arab States and the Arab League.* Beirut: Khayats, 1962.

Khouri, Fred J. *The Arab-Israeli Dilemma.* Syracuse, N.Y.: Syracuse University Press, 1968.

Lall, Arthur. *The UN and the Middle East Crisis, 1967.* New York: Columbia University Press, 1968.

Liqueur, Walter L., ed. *The Israel-Arab Reader: A Documentary History of the Middle East Conflict.* New York: Bantam, 1970.

Lenczowski, George. *Russian and the West in Iran, 1918–1948.* Ithaca, N.Y.: Cornell University Press, 1950.

Meir, Golda. "Israel in Search of Lasting Peace." *Foreign Affairs* 51, 3 (April 1973):447–61.

Murphy, Robert. *Diplomat Among Warriors.* New York: Pyramid, 1965.

Pelt, Adrian. *Libyan Independence and the United Nations: A Case of Planned Decolonization.* New Haven, Conn.: Yale University Press, 1970.

Peretz, Don, Wilson, Evan M., and Ward, Richard J. *A Palestine Entity?* Washington, D.C.: Middle East Institute, 1970.

Qubain, Fahim. *Crisis in Lebanon.* Washington, D.C.: Middle East Institute, 1961.

Ramazani, Rouhollah K. *The Persian Gulf: Iran's Role.* Charlottesville, Va.: University Press of Virginia, 1972.

Roots, John McCook. "An Interview with David Ben-Gurion." *Saturday Review* 54, 14 (April 3, 1971):14–16.

Safran, Nadav. *From War to War: The Arab-Israeli Confrontation.* New York: Pegasus, 1969.

Truman, Harry S. *Memoirs.* Vol. II, *Years of Trial and Hope.* Garden City, N.Y.: Doubleday, 1956.

UN Doc. S/10929. 18 May 1973. Report of the Secretary-General under Security Council Resolution 331 (1973) of 20 April 1973.

UN Doc. TD/B/C.4/104. 26 January 1973. Report of the Economic Effects of the Closure of the Suez Canal. Study by the UNCTAD Secretariat.

UNRWA-UNESCO, Department of Education. *Statistical Yearbook, 1969–70.* No. 6. Beirut, 1970.

———. *UNRWA-UNESCO Education Services for Palestine Refugees.* Beirut, 1970.

United States Department of State. *American Foreign Policy: Current Documents 1958.* Washington, D.C.: U.S. Government Printing Office, 1962.

———. *American Foreign Policy: Current Documents 1967.* Washington, D.C.: U.S. Government Printing Office, 1969.

———. *United States Policy in the Middle East, September 1956–June 1957. Documents.* Washington, D.C.: U.S. Government Printing Office, 1957.

———. Historical Office. *Foreign Relations of the United States. Diplomatic Papers 1945.* Vol. I, *General: The United Nations.* Washington, D.C.: U.S. Government Printing Office, 1967.

United States Foreign Policy, 1969–1970: A Report of the Secretary of State. Washington, D.C.: U.S. Government Printing Office, 1971.

U.S. Foreign Policy for the 1970's. A New Strategy for Peace. A Report to the Congress by Richard Nixon, President of the United States, February 18, 1970. Washington, D.C.: U.S. Government Printing Office, 1970.

Von Horn, Major General Carl. *Soldiering for Peace.* New York: McKay, 1967.

Wainhouse, David, et al. *International Peace Observation: A History and Forecast.* Baltimore, Md.: The Johns Hopkins Press, 1966.

Wenner, Manfred W. *Modern Yemen, 1918–1966.* Baltimore, Md.: The Johns Hopkins Press, 1967.

World Peace Foundation. *Documents on American Foreign Relations, 1945–1946.* Princeton, N.J.: Princeton University Press, 1948.

———. *Documents on American Foreign Relations 1948.* Princeton, N.J.: Princeton University Press, 1950.

Yost, Charles. "Last Chance for Peace in the Middle East." *Life,* 70, 13 (April 9, 1971).

9—DOMESTIC SOURCES OF MIDDLE EASTERN FOREIGN POLICY

Abdel-Malek, Anouar. *Egypt: Military Society, the Army Regime, the Left, and Social Change under Nasser.* Translated by Charles Lamm Markmann. New York: Random House, 1968.

Aflaq, Michel. *Fi Sabael Al Ba'ath.* Beirut: Dar al-Tal'ia, 1963.

Bell, Wendell, et al. *The Democratic Revolution in the West Indies.* Cambridge, Mass.: Schenkman, 1967.

Binder, Leonard. *Factors Influencing Iran's International Role.* Santa Monica, Calif.: The Rand Corp., 1969.

——. *The Ideological Revolution in the Middle East.* New York: John Wiley, 1964.

Cottam, Richard W. *Nationalism in Iran.* Pittsburgh: University of Pittsburgh Press, 1964.

Cremeans, Charles D. *The Arabs and the World: Nasser's Arab Nationalist Policy.* New York: Praeger, 1963.

Deutsch, Carl. *Nationalism and Social Communication.* Cambridge, Mass.: MIT Press, 1953.

Fein, Leonard J. *Politics in Israel.* Boston: Little, Brown, 1967.

Halpern, Manfred. *The Politics of Social Change in the Middle East and North Africa.* Princeton, N.J.: Princeton University Press, 1963.

Halstead, John P. *Rebirth of a Nation: The Origins and Rise of Moroccan Nationalism, 1912–1944.* Cambridge, Mass.: Harvard University Press, 1967.

Hayes, Carlton J. H. *Essays on Nationalism.* New York: Macmillan, 1926.

——. *The Historical Evolution of Modern Nationalism.* New York: Richard R. Smith, 1931.

Kedourie, Elie. *Nationalism.* Praeger, 1961.

Kerr, Malcolm. *The Arab Cold War, 1958–1967.* New York: Oxford University Press, 1967.

Kohn, Hans. *The Idea of Nationalism.* New York: Collier, 1967.

Martin, Laurence W., ed. *Neutralism and Nonalignment: The New States in World Affairs.* New York: Praeger, 1962.

The Middle East and North Africa (1967–1968). London: Europa Publications, 1967.

Nolte, Richard, ed. *The Modern Middle East.* New York: Atherton Press, 1963.

Pye, Lucian, and Verba, Sidney, eds. *Political Culture and Political Development.* Princeton, N.J.: Princeton University Press, 1965.

Sayegh, Fayez A., ed. *The Dynamics of Neutralism in the Arab World: A Symposium.* San Francisco: Chandler, 1964.

Shafer, Boyd. *Nationalism: Myth and Reality.* New York: Harcourt, Brace, 1955.

Sharabi, Hisham. "The Transformation of Ideology in the Arab World." *Middle East Journal* 19, 4 (1965).

Smith, Wilfred Cantwell. *Islam in Modern History.* New York: Mentor Books, 1957.

Thompson, Jack H., and Reischauer, Robert D., ed. *Modernization of the Arab World.* Princeton, N.J.: Van Nostrand, 1966.

Zonis, Marvin. *Political Elites and Political Insecurity in Iran.* Princeton, N.J.: Princeton University Press, 1971.

10—OIL: THE NEW DIPLOMACY

Frank, Helmut J. *Crude Oil Prices in the Middle East: A Study in Oligopolistic Price Behavior.* New York: Praeger, 1966.

Issawi, Charles, and Yeganeh, Mohammed. *The Economics of Middle Eastern Oil.* New York: Praeger, 1962.

Lenczowski, George. *Oil and State in the Middle East*. Ithaca, N.Y.: Cornell University Press, 1960.

Longrigg, Stephen Hemsley. *Oil in the Middle East: Its Discovery and Development*. 3rd ed. London: Oxford University Press, 1972.

Mughraby, Muhamad A. *Permanent Sovereignty Over Oil Resources: A Study of Middle East Oil Concessions and Legal Concessions*. Beirut: Middle East Research and Publishing Center, 1966.

Sayegh, Kamal S. *Oil and Arab Regional Development*. New York: Praeger, 1968.

Toriguian, Shavarsh. *Legal Aspects of Oil Concessions in the Middle East*. Beruit: Hamaskaine Press, 1972.

11—THE MIDDLE EAST: A SUBORDINATE SYSTEM IN GLOBAL POLITICS

Binder, Leonard. "The Middle East as a Subordinate International System." *World Politics* X (1958).

Brecher, Michael. *The Foreign Policy System of Israel: Setting, Images, Process*. Oxford: The Clarendon Press, 1972.

Burns, A. L. *Of Powers and their Politics*. Englewood Cliffs, N.J.: Prentice-Hall, 1968.

Cantori, Louis J., and Spiegel, Steven L. *The International Politics of Regions: A Comparative Approach*. Englewood Cliffs, N.J.: Prentice-Hall, 1970

Haas, Michael. "International Subsystems: Stability and Polarity." *American Political Science Review* 64 (March 1970).

Kaplan, Morton A. *System and Process in International Politics*. New York: John Wiley, 1957.

MacDonald, Robert W. *The League of Arab States: A Study of the Dynamics of Regional Organization*. Princeton, N.J.: Princeton University Press, 1965.

Russett, Bruce M. *International Regions and International System*. Chicago: Rand McNally, 1967.

Index

283